# Emotional Problems
# of Development
# in Children

# Emotional Problems of Development in Children

Martin Herbert
*School of Social Work,*
*University of Leicester, England*

1974

## Academic Press
### London   New York

*A subsidiary of Harcourt Brace Jovanovich,* **Publishers**

ACADEMIC PRESS INC. (LONDON) LTD.
24/28 Oval Road,
London NW1

*United States Edition published by*
ACADEMIC PRESS INC.
111 Fifth Avenue
New York, New York 10003

Library of Congress Catalog Card Number: 0-74-970
ISBN Casebound edition: 0-12-341450-4
ISBN Paperback edition: 0-12-341456-3

PRINTED AND BOUND IN ENGLAND BY
HAZELL WATSON AND VINEY LTD
AYLESBURY, BUCKS

# Preface

Having been involved for several years in teaching developmental and clinical courses to undergraduate and postgraduate professional students, I am very conscious of how little cross-fertilization there is between the developmental and abnormal branches of psychology. Such mutual exclusiveness is particularly unfortunate when it comes to the assessment, understanding and modification of emotional (i.e. psychological) problems of childhood. A view put forward in this book is that so-called "abnormal" behaviour in children is not very different from "normal" behaviour in its development, persistence and susceptibility to change. It seems to me to be more fruitful to ask how a child develops behaviour in general, rather than to limit the question to how he acquires abnormal behaviour as such. For this reason I have attempted to describe problem behaviour and its evolution in the context of the crucial events—social, emotional, cognitive and physical—taking place at different stages of development. Many deviant emotions and behaviours can be conceptualized as the consequences of the child's failure to learn successful ways of coping with developmental tasks, or as resulting from his learning inappropriate strategies for dealing with life. This viewpoint means that the practitioner seeking to formulate causes and devise therapeutic programmes to alleviate the child's problems, can draw on experimental and developmental psychology for basic principles of learning and development to aid his task.

This book is an attempt to achieve a tentative synthesis of these disciplines for those students and practitioners who have the responsibility of giving advice about problem children, or who are directly concerned with the care and treatment of such youngsters. It is my hope to provide a useful guide to some of the theoretical issues and empirical studies and information which are relevant to child psychopathology. The subject-matter is such a vast one that I have been forced to select which topics to discuss and which ones to treat at some length. The same considerations have caused me to terminate the discussion rather abruptly at the beginning of adolescence. To make up for these shortcomings a detailed bibliography is provided; this should allow the reader to explore particular problem areas more fully.

*January 1974*                                                             Martin Herbert

# Contents

## Part III. Infancy (From birth to approximately eighteen months)

## Part VI. Middle Childhood: The School-age (From about five to eleven or twelve years of age)

# Acknowledgements

It is impossible to acknowledge by name all those to whom I am indebted for ideas and research findings which appear in this book. However, I would like to express my appreciation for the stimulating influence of two distinguished psychologists and teachers, Professor Ronald Albino and Professor Kurt Danziger, and of a friend and colleague Derek Wright. My gratitude also goes to the Maudsley Hospital and Institute of Psychiatry for the opportunity to work with, and thus learn about clinical practice from, Drs. Denis Leigh, Michael Rutter, Peter Scott and Monte Shapiro. I owe a special debt to Gaynor for her encouragement and invaluable assistance in the production of this text.

The author wishes to acknowledge the cooperation of the following publishers and journals in giving permission to reproduce data, tables and figures: Basic Books Inc., Grune and Stratton Inc., Macmillan Publishing Co. Inc., Methuen & Co., Penguin Books Ltd., Pergamon Press Ltd., Peter Davies Ltd., Prentice-Hall Inc., Russell Sage Foundation, Society for Research in Child Development at the University of Chicago Press, Teachers College Press, The Avenue Publishing Co., The Commonwealth Fund, University of California Press, University of London Press, W. B. Saunders Co., Journal of Abnormal Social Psychology, Journal of Child Psychology and Psychiatry, American Journal of Orthopsychiatry and the International Journal of Social Psychiatry, Routledge and Kegan Paul Ltd.

*For my parents, Sydney and Kathleen*

# Part I

# Basic Concepts: Emotional Problems of Development

# Introduction

"DEVELOPMENT" is typically defined as a progressive series of orderly, coherent changes leading toward the goal of maturity. This may be the grand design, but as many long-suffering parents know to their cost, their children's progress through life is often disorderly and incoherent, and the changes (when change is not being resisted) are not always in the direction of maturity. When this happens, such reactions are quite likely to be labelled as emotional problems and thought of as abnormal.

The term "emotional problems" as it refers to particular aspects of development, is nothing more than a convenient bit of shorthand—a quick way of referring to the difficulties of a variety of troubled and troublesome children. It is as uninformative in its over-inclusiveness as those other labels—"abnormal", "maladjusted" and "psychiatrically ill"—which are applied to children who create problems for themselves, their parents, and their teachers, as they grow up. These terms are used so frequently in clinical circles that the uninitiated might be excused for thinking that they refer to neat and tidy clinical categories, or to certain kinds of children diagnosed as problematical because they display special attributes—precisely and objectively defined symptoms.

In reality, the generic term "emotional problems" (chosen for this book because it is so widely used and because of the absence of any precise alternative) applies to a heterogeneous collection of childhood manifestations ranging from withdrawn behaviour, dependency, fears and bed-wetting, to stealing, aggressive behaviour, truancy and poor achievement. These are the kinds of "disturbance" which are sometimes thought to indicate (if the case-loads of Child Guidance Clinics are any guide) emotional problems requiring professional attention. The trouble is that most children, at one time or another, have suffered from problems such as these. Lapouse and Monk (1958, 1959) studied emotional problems among a non-psychiatric sample of 482 children using structured interviews given to their mothers. The youngsters were between the ages of 6 and 12 and were assigned to the experimental group so as to constitute a representative sample of the child population of Buffalo, USA. The findings (see Table I below) demonstrate the surprisingly high prevalence among "run-of-the-mill" school-going children of problems which are widely regarded as symptomatic of emotional disorder in children.

TABLE I. The frequency of selected behaviour characteristics in a weighted representative sample of 482 children aged 6 to 12, as reported by mothers. (From: Lapouse and Monk, 1959.)

| Behaviour | Per cent of children |
| --- | --- |
| Fears and worries, 7 or more present | 43 |
| Wetting bed within the past year | |
|     All frequencies | 17 |
|     Once a month or more | 8 |
| Nightmares | 28 |
| Temper loss | |
|     Once a month or more | 80 |
|     Twice a week or more | 48 |
|     Once a day or more | 11 |
| Stuttering | 4 |
| Unusual movements, twitching or jerking (tics) | 12 |
| Biting nails | |
|     All intensities | 27 |
|     Nails bitten down (more severe) | 17 |
| Grinding teeth | 14 |
| Sucking thumb or fingers | |
|     All frequencies | 10 |
|     "Almost all the time" | 2 |
| Biting, sucking or chewing clothing or other objects | 16 |
| Picking nose | 26 |
| Picking sores | 16 |
| Chewing or sucking lips or tongue or biting inside of mouth | 11 |

Unfortunately, a search through the clinical literature for the defining attributes of the "problem child" proves to be fruitless. There are no unambiguous diagnostic criteria of emotional problems to be found there. The reason is that (with few exceptions) ". . . disorders of emotions and behaviour in childhood do not constitute 'diseases' or 'illnesses' which are *qualitatively* different from the normal". (Rutter *et al.*, 1970.)

The concept of developmental "stages" provides one means of structuring the book. Emotional problems associated with particular phases of development might form the basis of the discussion. Unfortunately, developmental theorists have not always agreed on what constitute the most meaningful and fruitful developmental dimensions for a division of childhood into stages. Some (e.g., Gesell *et al.*, 1940) have chosen chronological or age-related stages as a framework for research; others (e.g., Piaget, 1954) have emphasized cognitive stages. Psychoanalysts (e.g.,

Freud, 1939) postulate the crucial importance for personality development of psychosexual stages in which different erogenous zones and associated needs predominate; others again (e.g., Sullivan, 1953) conceptualize stages in the child's capacity to understand the interpersonal environment he inhabits.

Erikson (1965) regards early personality development as stages in the development of patterns of reciprocity between the self and others. At each stage a conflict between opposite poles of this relationship has to be resolved. There is a series of crises to which Erikson gave the names of "trust–mistrust", "confidence–doubt" and "initiative–guilt". Danziger (1971) sees a connection between these bi-polar pairs and Piaget's ideas concerning assimilation and accommodation. Assimilation occurs when the child alters the environment to meet his own needs. Accommodation occurs when the child modifies his own behaviour in response to the demands of his milieu. "Play" and "imitation" are examples of cognitive behaviour marked by a lack of balance, in one direction or the other, between assimilatory and accommodatory processes. Danziger states that it is possible to understand Erikson's bi-polar pairs as involving a similar lack of balance or conflict in the development of social reciprocity. This conflict assumes qualitatively different forms at different stages of development; Erikson provides intuitively meaningful terms to describe what is happening to the child. Danziger maintains that "over 'conceptual bridges' like these it is possible for there to be a creative dialogue between clinicians and experimentalists without the virtues of either approach being lost in the process".

Some theorists (Whiting and Child, 1953; Sears et al., 1957) have by-passed the concept of stages and focus attention on critical and universal socialization tasks such as feeding and weaning, elimination-, sex-, aggression and dependency-training and so on. Danziger (1971) observes that the practical problems of life have always suggested the choice of behavioural categories for study. He points to the situation where studies on the need for achievement outnumber studies on all other conceivable human needs put together and questions whether this preoccupation is related to the ideology of entrepreneurship and concern about economic under-development. As he puts it:

The social worker, psychiatrist or clinical psychologist, acting as the agent of society, is understandably worried about individual aggressiveness or pathological forms of dependency. Almost without exception, the categories of human behaviour for which antecedents have been sought in childhood are categories that define current social problems ... it is our definition of social problems like delinquency and helplessness in psychological terms like aggressiveness and dependency that makes such categories interesting for the potential research worker (Danziger, 1971).

The author will follow this tradition and consider the problems associated with various important socialization tasks. Wherever possible, they will be considered in the light of developmental events and schemata described by some of the theorists mentioned above. The chronological ages quoted as guidelines in connection with stages of development are undoubtedly arbitrary, because the rates of maturation and development vary from child to child. Each stage of development corresponds to a particular social demand and, again, there are individual differences in the timing of demands made by parents and their children. Particular emotional problems tend to be associated with these stages and with the mastery of specific socialization (or developmental) tasks, although by no means exclusively so. Havighurst (1953) defines a developmental task as one "which arises at or about a certain period in the life of an individual, successful achievement of which leads to his happiness and to success with later tasks, while failure leads to unhappiness in the individual, disapproval by society and difficulty with later tasks". In our analysis of emotional problems of development, we shall be concerned with the difficulties associated with such tasks as learning to talk and to control elimination, restraining aggressive and sexual inclinations, developing moral attitudes and social skills, adjusting to school-life and mastering academic competencies, becoming self-directed and self-confident. The child who does not display some degree of maladjustment at one time or another, in one or other of these areas of development, is rare. This raises the question of when it is no longer good sense for parents to "soldier on" alone, when faced with what they perceive as a child with emotional problems. Under what conditions does the manifestation of "disturbed behaviour" become too serious to be treated philosophically as the emotional equivalent of growing pains? When is it no longer sufficient to give sympathetic understanding and moral support to what are conceived as temporary aberrations associated with developmental crises? An attempt will be made to specify, in the pages that follow, some of the judgements involved in deciding whether a child is in need of professional guidance for these problems.

# 1. Identifying Emotional Problems in Children

ALL SORTS OF terms (or euphemisms) have been used to refer to psychological disorders in the growing child. There is the popular and ubiquitous expression "problem child", and other designations such as "nervous", "highly strung", "emotionally disturbed", "difficult", to mention but a few. Parents and teachers, as well as many clinicians, tend to use the phrase "emotional problems" simply as a synonym for the term "psychological difficulties" so as to distinguish a category of problems from those which are primarily somatic ones. This usage will be adopted by the author. Although rather vague, it is probably as good as any other, as long as it is remembered that it also applies to those difficulties which are referred to by some theorists as "behaviour" problems. It also refers to those disabilities of thinking, intellect and achievement (the so-called "cognitive" problems) which may be involved in any overall psychological disturbance. After all, those categories into which we isolate and reify psychological processes, are no more than arbitrary, if conceptually convenient heuristic devices.

There is much disagreement about the precise definition of psychological disorder or mental illness in childhood. A popular, if dubious way of identifying pathology in the clinical literature, has been to accept the "fact" that it is present in a person if he has been referred to a clinic and is attending for treatment (see: Scott, 1958 b and c). This is implicit in research studies which compare "abnormal" groups (selected on the basis of their registration with the clinic) with "normal" control groups. This procedure, apart from being unhelpful for the assessment of the individual child, is misleading. In the first place, diagnostic judgements of psychiatrists have proved to be rather unreliable in the case of adult problems (Ash, 1949; Mehlman, 1952) where the psychiatric taxonomies are, if anything, less confused than they are in the case of children (see: Zubin, 1967; Kanner, 1960). Referral rates in a particular area are affected by such factors as teachers' and doctors' attitudes, the quality and quantity of the school psychological services available, and the socio-economic status of the area concerned. Researchers (Wolff, 1967a; Shepherd *et al.*, 1971) compared the problems of clinic attenders with those of selected non-clinic-attending children, and found it difficult to distinguish between them. There were differences but in degree only.

The word "problem" is closely bound up with the concept of a deviation from some norm. The word "norm" from its Latin root means a standard, rule or pattern. When a behaviour is designated as "abnormal", it generally implies (with its prefix "ab" meaning "away from") a deviation from a standard. Terms like "normal" and "abnormal" are commonly applied to children as if they are mutually exclusive concepts like black and white. They are also used in a global manner to characterize certain children. Thus the label "abnormal" attached to a particular child seems to suggest that he is deviant in some absolute and generalized sense. This is misleading; the most that can be said of any child is that certain of his actions or attributes are more or less abnormal.

Williams (1956) illustrates the fallacy of dividing people into two categories, the normal and the abnormal. Implicit in the use of the concept "normal" is a reference to some region of a statistical distribution (more often than not 95%) which arbitrarily signifies a region of normality. Anyone who has a trait which puts him outside that region is labelled deviate. But as Williams observes:

If we consider . . . that among the numerous attributes that human beings possess there may be many which are not mathematically correlated, we are confronted with an idea which is opposed to the basic dichotomy of normal and abnormal mentioned above. If 95% of the population is normal with respect to one measureable item, only 90·2% $(0·95^2)$ would be normal with respect to two measureable items, and 60% $(0·95^{10})$ and 59/100 of 1% $(0·95^{100})$, respectively, would be normal with regard to 10 and 100 uncorrelated items.

The existence in every human being of a vast array of attributes which are potentially measureable, and often uncorrelated mathematically, makes quite tenable the hypothesis that *practically every human being is a deviate in some respect* (Williams, 1956).

It may be useful to know that a child is abnormally aggressive or has an abnormally high IQ; it tells the clinician something about the child's personality or intellectual status in relation to the distribution of traits found in the general population. This use of the term abnormal is neutral—it simply provides a statistical or quantitative judgement about an individual. The psychologist measures, say, IQ and finds that the child's score is nearly three standard deviations above the mean. That child is abnormal ("away from the norm") in a quite objective sense—his score is deviant, rare or unusual. The whole point of this way of looking at problem behaviour is that normality is viewed as merging almost imperceptibly into abnormality; the abnormal is thought of here as an exaggeration of the normal. If normality and abnormality are seen as the extremes of a continuum, then any child can be more or less normal or abnormal—but only with regard to particular characteristics.

Having selected important and measurable dimensions for individual analysis, and having estimated their statistical deviance (where norms are available) the clinician must still shift away from this relatively "secure" ground of quantitative analysis. To take an obvious example, a high IQ is generally thought to have favourable consequences for the individual, while a low IQ has unfavourable implications. And it is some sort of prediction about the individual's ability to cope with various life situations that the clinician is concerned about. At this point he is required to make subjective assessments about the quality of attributes and acts or, to put it another way, the advantages and disadvantages of their consequences. It is these value judgements about the implications of behaviour which are particularly susceptible to bias and error as they apply to individual cases. Even if the psychologist possesses empirical evidence of a relationship between an attribute and a criterion variable (say, IQ and academic success), his data is based on the study of groups and he is dealing with an individual prediction. Even his IQ measure is a global one which masks the speed, persistence and accuracy of the child's intellectual functioning (see: Furneaux, 1965), any of which may have important implications in the judgement being made about the child's future performance.

A major source of error is the tendency to ascribe to the child properties which over-emphasize the generality and invariance of personality traits and behaviour. The child's personality, in actuality, consists of a mosaic of attributes of varying generality and situational-specificity. As it is, the global effect of these varied characteristics, as they interact within the individual child, has to be evaluated. A particular trait which is relatively innocuous within one combination of attributes or in the context of a particular social situation, may be highly disruptive in another. Feelings of hostility may be a relatively harmless characteristic in a child with good impulse control, but potentially dangerous where the child has poor self-control and where external controls are minimal (e.g., out of school). This kind of evaluation, in order to have a basis in reality, must be related to the child's transactions with his environment. The clinician, encapsulated in his consulting room, gets a picture of a very limited sampling of these transactions—and then, usually, at second-hand.

It seems fairly clear from the evidence that there is no absolute distinction between the characteristics of those who come to be labelled "problem children" and other unselected children (Kanner, 1960; Wolff, 1967a;

Shepherd *et al.*, 1971).* The differences are relative, a matter of degree. Emotional problems, signs of psychological abnormality are, by and large, exaggerations, deficits, or handicapping combinations of behaviour patterns common to all children (see Table II below). Expressions of emotional and behavioural acts have certain allowable *intensity levels*. Very "high" intensities—emotional responses of excessive magnitude—which have unpleasant consequences for other people, are likely to be regarded as signs of an emotional disorder. If aggressive children become destructive, sadistic or harmful, their hostile emotions tend to be labelled as pathological. There is an opposite extreme. A child may suffer not only because he is over-aggressive or over-anxious, but because he is under-aggressive and not anxious enough; or indeed, because certain appropriate emotional responses are entirely absent from his repertoire. These problems are called emotional (or behavioural) deficits, and are frequently interpreted as symptoms of emotional disturbance. A *high rate of emission* of certain behaviours may also be taken as a criterion of the seriousness to be attached to such activities and therefore the appropriateness of the label "problem". The rare incident of stealing, bullying or bed-wetting may be overlooked; however, frequent acts of this sort are likely to be categorized as "deviant".

Different cultures (Benedict, 1934; Whiting, 1963), different strata of society (Bronfenbrenner, 1958; Newson and Newson, 1970), and various professions (Wickman, 1928; Tolor *et al.*, 1967) tend to have differing standards concerning these matters; they do not always agree about what is normal, appropriate or desirable behaviour. At the individual level, subjective biases such as autistic perceptions and needs, ethnocentric prejudices and preferences (Vernon, 1964), also guarantee wide variations in person perception and hence a diversity of standards in defining normality (Valentine, 1956).

Another feature of problem behaviour in childhood is its transitoriness. So mercurial are some of the changes of behaviour in response to the rapid growth and the successive challenges of childhood, that it is difficult to pinpoint the beginning of serious problems. A long-term study (MacFarlane *et al.*, 1954) of the development of 126 American infants showed the incidence and shifts in their problem behaviours as manifested at different ages between 21 months and 14 years. These children constituted the control group for another "guidance" group (N = 126) in the California Growth Study initiated in 1929. Every third child born in Berkeley during an 18-month period was selected for investigation. Problems were

---

* This generalization seems to apply even in the case of minimally brain-damaged children (see page 48). The gross cases of physical and/or mental handicap seen in autistic and severely brain-damaged children do not come into this category.

investigated by means of open-ended interviews with the mothers. Of the 126 infants selected at birth, 86 were still available for assessment at adolescence. This shrinkage produced a bias toward upper-middle-class socio-economic membership in the sample, and thereby a constraint on any over-confident generalizing from the results. Nevertheless, they are of interest. There were 46 problems selected for analysis. Table II below indicates high frequency problems for different ages.

TABLE II. Behaviour problems shown by one-third or more of normal boys and girls, aged 1¾–14 years at each age level. (Adapted from MacFarlane et al., 1954).

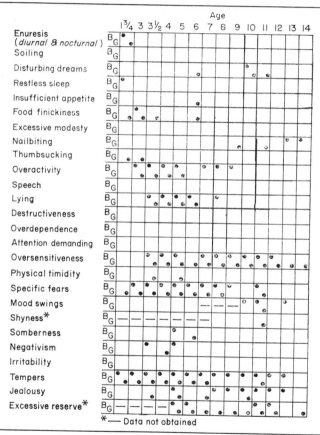

Table III below, provides figures from an English epidemiological study* of children aged 5 to 15.

For most children in the MacFarlane and Shepherd studies, problems

* This study by Shepherd et al., is described in detail on page 230.

TABLE III. Percentages of children recorded as showing "extreme" types of behaviour at each age from five to fifteen. (From: Shepherd *et al.*, 1971.)

| GIRLS | 5 years | 6 years | 7 years | 8 years | 9 years | 10 years | 11 years | 12 years | 13 years | 14 years | 15 years |
|---|---|---|---|---|---|---|---|---|---|---|---|
| Very destructive | 2 | — | 1 | — | * | * | — | * | — | 1 | — |
| Fear of animals | 5 | 5 | 3 | 3 | 3 | 1 | 2 | 2 | 1 | 1 | 7 |
| Fear of strangers | 1 | * | 2 | 2 | * | 2 | 1 | 1 | 1 | 2 | — |
| Fear of the dark | 11 | 5 | 8 | 7 | 8 | 8 | 6 | 5 | 4 | 5 | 4 |
| Lying | 2 | 2 | 1 | 1 | 3 | 1 | 3 | 1 | 1 | 3 | 2 |
| Dislike of school | 1 | 3 | 2 | 4 | 3 | 2 | 3 | 3 | 5 | 7 | 4 |
| Stealing | 1 | — | — | — | * | — | — | * | — | 1 | — |
| Irritability | 10 | 9 | 9 | 10 | 12 | 10 | 12 | 10 | 11 | 16 | 11 |
| Food fads | 20 | 19 | 20 | 22 | 21 | 23 | 17 | 17 | 15 | 17 | 9 |
| Fear of other children | — | * | 1 | 1 | * | 1 | * | 1 | * | 1 | — |
| Always hungry | 5 | 6 | 6 | 10 | 9 | 10 | 10 | 13 | 15 | 11 | 16 |
| Small appetite | 21 | 17 | 21 | 18 | 13 | 12 | 12 | 8 | 7 | 8 | 5 |
| Worrying | 5 | 7 | 4 | 4 | 6 | 4 | 7 | 5 | 1 | 4 | 5 |
| Whining | 7 | 5 | 5 | 3 | 6 | 2 | 5 | 4 | 3 | 5 | — |
| Restlessness | 20 | 16 | 20 | 16 | 13 | 13 | 13 | 11 | 11 | 10 | 4 |
| Underactivity | — | 2 | 1 | 1 | 2 | 3 | 3 | 4 | 7 | 7 | 5 |
| Jealousy | 8 | 4 | 5 | 5 | 6 | 3 | 4 | 3 | 3 | 6 | 4 |
| Wandering | * | * | — | 1 | 1 | * | 1 | 2 | 1 | 2 | 4 |
| Withdrawn | 2 | 1 | 2 | 2 | 3 | 2 | 2 | 3 | 2 | 3 | 7 |
| ⎰ Disobedient | 10 | 10 | 8 | 8 | 11 | 7 | 10 | 10 | 12 | 14 | 14 |
| ⎱ Always obeys | 8 | 7 | 7 | 9 | 9 | 8 | 14 | 11 | 12 | 10 | 12 |
| Truanting—at all | * | 1 | 1 | * | 1 | * | * | 1 | 1 | 3 | 4 |
| Tics | 1 | — | 1 | 1 | 1 | * | — | * | — | 1 | — |
| Mood change | 5 | 2 | 4 | 3 | 5 | 3 | 5 | 5 | 7 | 7 | 14 |
| Reading difficulty | 5 | 7 | 14 | 14 | 10 | 13 | 10 | 11 | 5 | 7 | 4 |

| BOYS | 5 years | 6 years | 7 years | 8 years | 9 years | 10 years | 11 years | 12 years | 13 years | 14 years | 15 years |
|---|---|---|---|---|---|---|---|---|---|---|---|
| Very destructive | 3 | 2 | 2 | — | 2 | 1 | 1 | 1 | 2 | 1 | 2 |
| Fear of animals | 3 | 3 | 2 | 1 | 1 | 2 | 2 | 1 | 1 | 1 | — |
| Fear of strangers | 2 | 1 | 1 | 1 | — | * | * | 1 | 2 | * | 4 |
| Fear of the dark | 9 | 6 | 8 | 8 | 10 | 7 | 6 | 5 | 2 | 2 | 2 |
| Lying | 5 | 3 | 5 | 2 | 3 | 3 | 3 | 5 | 4 | 2 | 2 |
| Dislike of school | 4 | 5 | 5 | 3 | 5 | 5 | 5 | 6 | 7 | 10 | 4 |
| Stealing | — | 1 | 1 | 1 | 1 | * | 1 | 1 | 2 | 1 | — |
| Irritability | 10 | 7 | 13 | 11 | 12 | 14 | 11 | 14 | 11 | 9 | 16 |
| Food fads | 19 | 20 | 22 | 22 | 22 | 18 | 23 | 19 | 17 | 17 | 16 |
| Fear of other children | 1 | * | — | — | * | 1 | 1 | 1 | 1 | * | — |
| Always hungry | 11 | 10 | 10 | 14 | 16 | 13 | 16 | 19 | 15 | 23 | 39 |
| Small appetite | 11 | 13 | 17 | 14 | 11 | 10 | 13 | 9 | 7 | 5 | — |
| Worrying | 4 | 5 | 5 | 7 | 6 | 5 | 3 | 3 | 5 | 4 | 5 |
| Complaining | 7 | 6 | 8 | 5 | 4 | 3 | 4 | 4 | 3 | 2 | 2 |
| Restlessness | 23 | 19 | 25 | 21 | 22 | 19 | 20 | 18 | 15 | 17 | 20 |
| Underactivity | 1 | 2 | 1 | 1 | 1 | 2 | 2 | 4 | 3 | 6 | 2 |
| Jealousy | 6 | 2 | 4 | 4 | 4 | 5 | 3 | 4 | 2 | 3 | 2 |
| Wandering | 3 | 1 | 2 | 3 | 3 | 3 | 3 | 4 | 4 | 8 | 2 |
| Withdrawn | 2 | 2 | 4 | 3 | 3 | 3 | 2 | 3 | 3 | 2 | 7 |
| ⎰ Disobedient | 17 | 11 | 14 | 12 | 12 | 13 | 13 | 14 | 11 | 12 | 9 |
| ⎱ Always obeys | 8 | 7 | 7 | 8 | 7 | 6 | 7 | 7 | 9 | 9 | 16 |
| Truanting—at all | 1 | — | 1 | — | * | 2 | — | 2 | 1 | 2 | 16 |
| Tics | * | 1 | 1 | 2 | 1 | 2 | 1 | 2 | 2 | 1 | 2 |
| Mood changes | 4 | 3 | 3 | 2 | 5 | 3 | 4 | 4 | 2 | 2 | 2 |
| Reading difficulty | 7 | 18 | 21 | 27 | 25 | 17 | 21 | 22 | 13 | 13 | 9 |

*Note:* * = less than 0·5 per cent.

manifested themselves briefly at certain periods, and then became minimal, or disappeared completely. Problems such as moodiness, overdependence, sombreness, and irritability showed the greatest persistence; among the problems which declined in frequency with age were elimination (toilet training) problems, speech problems, fears, thumbsucking (MacFarlane *et al.*, 1954). Many mothers are fully aware of this transitoriness of emotional problems. Where one mother might regard her two-year-old infant's violent tantrums as abnormal, and rush off to the doctor for assistance, another might say philosophically: "Well, he's going through a difficult phase—it's those 'terrible two's'!" Her "diagnosis" recognizes that problem behaviour is sometimes a normal reaction to a difficult phase of life and that he will grow out of it—something the clinician calls "spontaneous remission". Of course, he may grow into another problem as he moves into another phase of development with its particular demands and typical problems. The point is that what is normal at one age may not be so at another.

Nearly two-thirds of the clinic attenders in the Buckinghamshire sample (Shepherd *et al.*, 1971) improved markedly and, significantly, this was unrelated to treatment but was linked to environmental factors. Information collected over a period of time indicated that patterns of behaviour commonly thought of as pathognomonic of "emotional disorder" in children, tend to recede spontaneously in response to developmental changes or life circumstances. Because the persistence of such indices appears to be the exception rather than the rule, the *duration* of disturbance must be taken into account when any behavioural item is being judged as symptomatic of a serious condition. It is a useful rule of thumb to discover whether a problem has endured so long that the mother perceives her relationship with the child to be, on balance, more tense and unhappy than relaxed and enjoyable.

*Intensity, high rate,* and *duration* of problems then are all dimensions to be taken into account in judging the seriousness of a child's problems. The *number* of deviant behaviours coexisting in the same child is also an indication of maladjustment (Rutter *et al.*, 1970; Shepherd *et al.*, 1971). The more "symptoms" reported as such by the mother, the greater is the likelihood that the child will be found to be disturbed on clinical examination.

Kanner (1953) has pointed out that the tendency to exaggerate the clinical significance of isolated "symptoms" is due to the biased picture obtained from studying such problems in selected clinical groups, rather than in the wider population of children. The same bias besets the analysis of causes in psychopathology. In clinic-based studies the researcher only sees children who are allegedly maladjusted and who also may have had certain "unfavourable" life experiences. Causal significance is attributed to these events. The problem, *inter alia*, is his ignorance of the number of children in the wider population who have endured these life experiences but who have not become "maladjusted".

Theorists like Freud, Erikson and Ausubel have recognized that "crises" may be associated with different phases of development—that there are developmental tasks which put a heavy burden on the adjustive capacities of the child. Ausubel and Sullivan (1970) state that "one of the chief types of developmental discontinuity is brought about by significant and relatively rapid shifts in the individual's biosocial status. The periods in which qualitatively new and discontinuous (inter-stage) changes in personality organization are being formulated may be designated as transitional phases or developmental crises. During these transitional periods the individual is in the marginal position of having lost an established and accustomed status and of not yet having acquired the new status toward which the factors impelling developmental change are driving him." What are these factors? Ausubel and Sullivan postulate two major categories of precipitant:

(1) An urgent need within the culture for a fundamental modification of the social and personality adjustment of an entire group of children who are in a given stage of developmental equilibrium;
(2) The occurrence of marked changes within the individual such as developments in physical attributes, basic drives, competencies and perceptual abilities, which are so crucial that the present status or mode of adjustment are incompatible with his present appearance. A classical example is the so-called "crisis of ego-devaluation" separating infancy from childhood. A degree of self-help is made possible by the development of motor, perceptual and social skills. The parents are motivated to rear the child in the traditions of their culture utilizing the child's dependent relationship to ensure conformity. They now withdraw much of the attentive and uncritical deference they previously allowed the child because of his helpless status as a baby; furthermore they begin to make fairly exacting demands of the child's self-control.

It is no accident that one of the most common synonyms for childhood abnormality is "maladjustment". When people use the word abnormal in everyday conversation—that is without pretensions to precision or objectivity—it is generally used to describe a particular way of thinking, of speaking and of behaving; in other words, acting in a manner, and to a standard, that is socially unacceptable. To many members of society, behaviour is abnormal if it fails to conform to the behaviour of others. Used in this way to evaluate childhood abnormality, the adult is asking whether the child refuses or is unable to adjust his behaviour to the expectations his society has for children of his age—whether, in fact, he behaves very differently from his peers.

The family and the school are the most important representatives of society during the child's formative years. They have the task, among others, of translating a totally dependent, primitive, and hedonistic infant, into a more or less self-sufficient, sophisticated and responsible member of the community—the process called socialization. Parents and teachers perceive themselves as having certain obligations to the immature child and to the society for which he is being fitted. They have a set of expectations with which the child's progress and present behaviour are compared. He becomes a problem when he fails to conform to these guidelines of intellectual, social and moral behaviour. These guidelines which he is being asked to adjust to in the name of social life are, of course, the norms which give rise to the designation abnormal. If the child cannot, or will not, adjust to the norms, he is likely to be labelled maladjusted.

It would at least be helpful if there were fairly precise indices of optimal psychological functioning, of positive mental health. These would provide a baseline for comparisons; the recognition of malfunctioning or problematic behaviour could be based upon significant deviations from these standards. Unfortunately the task of defining mental health or ideal normality proves more formidable than the specification of abnormality. It is a particularly obscure concept in the case of children. Surveys of the concepts to be found in general use (Jahoda, 1958; Scott, 1958c; Nunnally, 1961) demonstrate that there is little agreement over what values are most significant for mental health. Indeed, it seems unlikely that there are any constants that will serve as universal criteria of assessing psychological well-being. As Wolberg (1967) observes:

It is much easier to evaluate the subtleties and nuances of the behaviour of a specific individual in terms of his total life situation than to draw up a fixed set of more or less abstract criteria that can be arbitrarily and indiscriminately applied to everyone. Multiplied manyfold the situation is comparable to that of judging the merits of a particular painting as contrasted with formulating a set of explicit and universally applicable criteria for differentiating all "bad" paintings.

Nevertheless, debates continue as to whether there are universal criteria for mental health which are valid for the human race as such, and according to which the state of health of an individual in any society, and, indeed, of society itself, can be judged (Fromm, 1956). As healthy adjustment in the opinion of the author, cannot be discussed meaningfully as an abstract quality of abstract children, we shall be concerned with the particular strategies developed by individual children to meet the specific needs and problems of *their* life situations. A view also put forward in this book is that abnormal behaviour in children does not differ, by and large, from normal behaviour in its development, its persistence and the way in which it can be modified. It seems more profitable to ask how a child develops behaviour in general rather than to restrict the question to how he develops problem behaviour *per se*. Following from this, the diagnostic task is to assess the implications and consequences of a child's general life-style and the stratagems he has adopted in order to cope with the demands of growing towards maturity. This analysis is made in the light of the child's individual circumstances.

In the pages that follow, problem behaviours are so-called because they have unfavourable consequences. They also tend (although not in every case*) to deviate widely from accepted social standards. It is tempting to add "reasonable" standards. Of course, problem behaviours may be "normal" or appropriate reactions to highly "abnormal" or pathological home influences. They are still labelled problematical because, although wholly understandable and proportionate to their cause, they have disabling consequences for the child in the broader context of life and society (e.g., school). "Emotional problems", when they do not represent deficit problems (a failure to learn adaptive responses), are conceptualized as strategies of adjustment which the child has learned to his own disadvantage (and often to the disadvantage of others) in the attempt to cope with the demands of life. They are therefore referred to as maladaptive strategies; they are inappropriate for dealing with the stresses and strains of growing up. The development of maladaptive responses (or the failure to acquire adaptive skills) may be due to neurological defects or other inherited or acquired impairments. The latter may be a result of faulty training and example, or other environmental deficiences. This means that in trying to remedy a child's problems, the clinician can draw on psychology (and in particular, developmental psychology) for basic principles of maturation, development and learning. Developmental psychology is concerned with the description and explanation of changes in behaviour that are a consequence of maturational influences and life-experiences.

The evaluation of normality and abnormality within a developmental framework requires a familiarity with *general principles* of development with particular reference to personality. It necessitates a comprehensive knowledge of children—how (in general terms) they look, think and talk, their skills and limitations at various ages, their typical repertoires of behaviour and the life-tasks and crises that they confront. Such a comparative or normative approach needs to be complemented by an idiographic analysis which takes into account biographical and other intrinsic influences which give him his *unique* quality.

Allport (1937) defines personality as the dynamic organization within the

---

* A child may manifest behaviour which is acceptable in the wider social context but is "problematic" because it offends his particular caretakers; likewise he may display behaviour (say shoplifting) which is "normal" in the eyes of his delinquent parents but "abnormal" in the view of the community.

individual of those psychophysical systems that determine his unique adjustments to his environment. This definition emphasizes the psychological and physical bases of the attitudes, habits, values, emotions, beliefs, motives and sentiments, which determine the unique and dynamic adjustments each child will make to the situation (family, school, community) he finds himself in. They in turn are shaped by the environment; so there is a continuing transaction and interaction between the child and his milieu.

We tend to judge the child by the effect he has on us. This outward aspect—the "persona" or mask—is, of course, only part of the story; we also need to discover the subjective or interior organization of his acts. The child's personality can be analysed in terms of traits which might consist of outgoing, sociable, extravert or inward-looking, and withdrawn, introvert tendencies. It may present dispositions to aggressive or peaceful behaviour, attitudes of passive dependency or fierce independence, idiosyncratic ways of meeting problems or frustrations and so on, and these and many other qualities are integrated and organized into a whole. The nucleus, core or "centre of gravity" of this personality-structure is the concept of self; it lies at the heart of the child's individuality. Self-attitudes —as the most central and organizing aspects of personality—provide one of the crucial gauges of the child's adaptation or adjustment to his life-situation. The quality of this self-image is the key to a child's healthy psychological adjustment to life, because it involves his meaning for others, how he wants to be seen by others, and also what he wishes to be like. Positive self-attitudes are the basic ingredients of positive mental health, and negative self-concepts among the critical predispositions to maladjustment (Coopersmith, 1967).

The term adjustment as it applies to personality and self, has multiple meanings. The notion of integration is one of these. We speak of a well-integrated personality when the many facets of personality—different attitudes, opinions and beliefs which make for a harmonious self-concept— are organized into a smoothly functioning and congruent whole; that is, when internal conflicts and contradictions are at a minimum, and the person enjoys a unifying outlook on life (see: Allport, 1937).

Autonomy is another criterion of adjustment and refers to the extent the individual is capable of independent or self-directed behaviour. Obviously this notion of self-containment can only be applied in a relative sense to children, as they are all dependent to a large extent on adults at this pre- and primary-school stage. Nevertheless, excessively dependent, clinging behaviour is a particular manifestation of maladjustment.

Growing up consists largely of learning to do things for oneself and having confidence in one's ability and competence. And doing things for oneself does not only include skills like dressing oneself, going to school alone, mastering mathematics and coping with stresses of life, but also social skills such as making friends, being able to talk to the opposite sex in a relaxed manner, making pleasant contacts with people. Unfortunately, for a number of complex reasons, many youngsters never learn to have real confidence in themselves and they evaluate themselves in a negative manner (feeling inferior and inadequate) which in itself is likely to increase the likelihood of future failure.

## Learning Theory and the Development of Problem Behaviour

The concept of learning has already cropped up several times in our discussion. This raises another issue concerning the emphasis of this book. There has been a fairly radical change in the last twenty years or so, in the way theorists and clinicians have conceptualized the development of problem behaviours in childhood. As Gelfand (1969) puts it:

In the past, children's problem behaviours were thought to stem from under-lying mental-conflict states such as insecurity, unresolved Oedipal conflicts, or repressed hostility. It was believed that such unrecognized thoughts and feelings could result in a wide variety of specific behavioural deviancies. Therapy was the province of trained psychotherapists, who often treated both the parents and the child for supposed mental disturbances. Actually, parents and teachers played a very minor role in the child's therapy. While they were sometimes advised to be more warm, loving, or understanding, they were often left to their own devices to translate such instructions into action. As a result, many did not know speci-fically how they should change their handling of the child . . . Now many social scientists no longer interpret abnormal behaviour exclusively in terms of hypothesized mental conflicts but, instead, view both socially desirable and inappropriate behaviour as products of social learning experiences. This concept of problem behaviour as a learned response has led to a new method of treatment, behaviour therapy, which is based on the assumption that behaviour that has been learned can be unlearned or modified directly and often in brief periods of treatment.

Learning is usually defined as any enduring change in behaviour which results from instruction or experience. All parents and teachers attempt to control the behaviour of the children in their care. Informal theories of learning, assumptions about the effects of punishments and rewards, or the threat of them, underlie their training and child-rearing practices. The punishments and rewards they use may be symbolic rather than actual. Few parents would deny that it is possible to modify behaviour consider-ably in many ways. Psychologists have made it their business to study the processes of learning, of social influence and attitude formation which make it possible to control and modify, not only "normal" reactions but also "abnormal" reactions, behaviours and attitudes. They have also enlisted parents, teachers and social workers on a more systematic basis, to

apply social learning principles to the modification of emotional problems (Patterson, 1971; Jehu, 1970).

Gelfand and Hartmann (1968) point out that children (as compared with adults) are particularly responsive to behaviour-orientated therapeutic interventions. They are frequently referred to clinics for help with circumscribed problems such as enuresis, phobias, temper-tantrums and the like. These are the types of problem which are most amenable to behaviour therapy (Marks and Gelder, 1965; Rachman, 1971). These therapeutic techniques require careful control over the client's environment, something more easily achieved in the home and classroom with youngsters than for adults.

It is not difficult for critics of learning theory approaches to therapy (see: Breger and McGaugh, 1965) to point out the limitations of concepts such as conditioning and reinforcement; they are hardly likely to account for all the complexities of human behaviour. As they make clear, learning theory has had to cope with the subtleties of human behaviour by emphasizing the importance of internal and unobserved mental events, hence the necessity for concepts such as "thinking", "insight", "planning", "reasoning", "strategies" and the like. Punishment and reward are *not* the only contingencies controlling behaviour. And so we could go on.

Bannister (1966) observes that all psychological theories seem to imply some sort of model man, some notion of what man essentially is. In satirical mood, he caricatures "psychoanalytic man" as a battlefield, a dark cellar in which a maiden aunt and a sex-crazed monkey are locked in mortal combat, the affair being refereed by a rather nervous bank clerk. He suggests, no less irreverently, that learning theory (S-R) man seems to be a pingpong ball with a memory. However, George Kelly (1961) is in deadly earnest when he deprecates the tendency of social scientists—particularly, psychologists—to patronize the human beings they study by using explanatory models which imply that their behaviour in relation to each other is less sophisticated than that of psychologists themselves. As he puts it:

Abstraction and generalization of human activity are not the exclusive prerogative of professional psychologists. What they do any person may do. Indeed, every person does! Each individual the psychologists study abstracts and generalizes on his own, for he is even more vitally interested than they can ever be in the task of understanding himself and his relationship to other persons and values. Thus the psychology of personality is not simply a matter of distinterested psychologists assessing a disinterested organism but of psychologists, who happen to be professionally and casually interested in their chosen subject matter, assessing a non-professional psychologist, who, on his part, is intimately and urgently involved with the job of making sense out of the life upon which his existence depends (Kelly, 1961).

Kelly uses the metaphor, "man the scientist". Like the scientist, the individual is trying to understand and predict (i.e., anticipate) events in his world. Gwynne Jones (1968) gives a balanced summing-up of the present status of the learning or behaviourally-orientated approach as follows:

It would seem fair to claim that behaviour therapy has established its right to be taken seriously, but offers no panacea. It is a developing, open system of theory and practice closely linked with the rapidly expanding field of experimental psychology, and sharing the concepts and language of that field. It has already made a contribution to psychiatry by focusing attention on the undoubtedly important learning processes involved in the aetiology of neurosis and in its treatment. It has also drawn attention to the importance of the role which overt behaviour may have in these processes. At the same time, an apparent neglect of the equally or more important roles of verbal and interpersonal factors is a temporary consequence of its present stage of development and is being rectified.

The fact is, of course, that no one theory can accommodate the complex and many-sided behaviours—adaptive and maladaptive—which are manifested by human beings. Because the subject matter of this book is so vast, it is not always possible to provide a critical analysis of the admittedly controversial role of learning in the evolution and treatment of emotional problems. There are many unresolved difficulties in the extension of theory to this applied field. To mitigate somewhat a largely descriptive and therefore somewhat bland account of the learning/behavioural model, the reader's attention is drawn to a selection of papers for more detailed and critical accounts: Beech, 1963, 1966, 1969; Kanfer, 1961, 1965; Meyer and Crisp, 1966; Lovibond, 1966; Marks and Gelder, 1966; Kiesler, 1966; Bijou, 1965, 1968; Katahn and Koplin, 1968; Durfee, 1969; Yates, 1970; Pawlicki, 1970; Careera and Adams, 1970; Friedman, 1970; Eysenck, 1960a, 1970; Graziano, 1971; Agras, 1972; Blom, 1972.

Three basic concepts will be kept very much in mind in this analysis of children's problems (see: Cameron, 1955): (i) the child is a maturing, developing organism; (ii) this maturation and development is taking place in relation to an internal and external environment, to which the child is reacting and adapting (adjusting), some of these reactions and adaptations becoming established in the child; (iii) the child is a unique individual pursuing his own aims and purposes.

Ultimately, as was argued above, the professional judgement of a child's mental well-being or its opposite, must be made in individual terms, taking into account the child's unique personality, his particular circumstances and all the opportunities, disappointments and stresses associated with them. According to Cameron (1955), it is the task of the clinician to ascertain where a child stands on the developmental scale, whether his progress and status—mental and physical—are appropriate to his age, retarded or advanced. In the light of this background information the psychologist or psychiatrist has to decide whether or not the child requires help. He may do this by applying several criteria of judgement to the facts he has gleaned about the child and his circumstances. This involves asking a series of questions:

1. Is the child's adjustive behaviour appropriate to his age, intelligence and social situation?
   There are two supplementary questions to the one above:
   (a) Is the environment making reasonable demands of the child?
   (b) Is the environment satisfying the crucial needs of the child—that is to say, the needs that are vital at his particular stage of development?

2. Finally, the clinician needs to ask the question: what are the consequences—favourable or unfavourable—of the child's pattern of traits and ways of behaving? Does his style of life in general, or his problems in particular, prevent him from leading a happy life in which he is able to grow and to enjoy social relationships, and work and play effectively?

Generally speaking, there is an association between intense and prolonged feelings of unhappiness and other evidence of mental disorder. It is a characteristic of certain mental disorders in adults and problem behaviours in children, that the person feels a loss of his sense of well-being or contentment. Specifically, then, the clinician will ask whether the child's adjustments are such as to make him unhappy and depressed or excessively anxious, morbidly guilty, inflexible in the face of failure, unable to establish affectionate, loving and lasting relationships. These are some of the questions asked; is the child in touch with reality? Is he relatively efficient (given demands that are reasonable ones for his age and ability) at coping with developmental tasks—learning to read and count, think abstractly, make friends with other children, cope with teachers, etc? Is he overly anxious or timid in novel or difficult situations? Is he too lacking in anxiety so that he fails to learn from disciplinary situations and fails to understand the consequences of his actions? The child with emotional problems often has a low threshold of "frustration-tolerance"; the blocking of his goals leads easily to disruptive patterns of behaviour which in turn lead to punishment or rejection and thus further frustration. The well-adjusted, resilient child seems to be able to rise above his frustrations, accepting them philosophically and looking for substitute outlets. The point about these questions is that *multiple criteria* determine the diagnosis of emotional problems and whether they require treatment.

A specific approach to the assessment of psychopathology in children has been called "target behaviour assessment" (see: O'Leary, 1972). The term usually refers to the process of observation of not only the child's undesirable behavioural strategies and his weaknesses, but also a comprehensive review of his appropriate behaviours and strengths, and the kind of background environmental details we have already referred to. Target assessment has evolved with and is generally based on the same assumptions as the "behaviour therapy" or "behaviour modification" approach to treatment. As O'Leary puts it:

One of the important features of target assessment is that it provides information that has direct implications for treatment. The distinction between assessment and treatment is often necessarily vague, and the two procedures are integrally related. The diagnostician's job is (1) to identify the target behaviours to be increased or decreased in frequency or changed in topography, (2) to identify the environmental factors that elicit, cue, or reinforce the target behaviours, and (3) to identify what environmental factors can be manipulated to alter the child's behaviour.

This form of assessment involves some important assumptions about behavioural attributes. Behaviourally orientated psychologists tend to view behaviours with, say, aggressive or anxiety attributes, as instances or *samples* of response classes rather than as outward and visible *signs* of internal or underlying dispositions. As Wiggins (1973) observes, the language of personality, to the extent that it is used by social behaviourists, is employed *descriptively* rather than inferentially. Conventional trait attributions are thought to represent nothing more than giving two names to the same class of behaviour (see: Bijou and Peterson, 1971). Thus, if a child is seen to hit another child, there is no reason to infer that the child who does the striking is not only aggressive but also has a "need for aggression". Behaviours with aggressive attributes would be classified in terms of their frequency, intensity and duration. Diverse attributes would be considered to be members of the same response class if it could be shown that such attributes enter into the same functional relationships with antecedent, concurrent and consequent stimulus conditions, rather than because they co-exist or co-vary in a group of persons. Wiggins, (op. cit.) notes that:

. . . the issues of *stability* and *generality* become empirical questions rather than assumptions. Given a change in stimulating conditions, particularly conditions of reinforcement, the frequency, intensity, or duration of the response class of interest should be predictable from a knowledge of the functional relationships between these attributes and the stimulus conditions which control them. Under these circumstances, it is more important to determine whether or not an individual is capable of performing a response, rather than trying to estimate the typical or characteristic level at which he responds.

All of this means that there are some important differences between traditional diagnostic procedures (using play, projective techniques and the like) and target behaviour assessment. To quote O'Leary again

Diagnosis using projective techniques is generally conducted in a clinical office or playroom. The diagnosticians using a dimensional approach rely heavily on the observations provided by others, e.g. teachers and parents. In a target assessment approach the diagnostician focuses on direct observation of the child in the situation in which the problem behaviour occurs wherever possible. Diagnosis *in situ* increases the probability that the important controlling variables in the child's environment will be considered in the development of a treatment procedure. In addition to parent and teacher reports target assessments will often involve observing the parent–child or teacher–child interactions in the home or classroom.

We stated earlier that the child is always observed from a developmental perspective. Hutt and Gibby (1959) describe childhood emotional difficulties within a developmental framework, and in terms of four main categories of adjustment problem.

The first category is called *transient adaptive problems*, and includes the temporary disturbances which result from growing up, from coping with physical illness, exceptional circumstances such as changes of environment or culture. The child may present "symptoms" but they are appropriate to the stresses and strains being experienced. Once the stressful situation is changed for the better or the child has had the time to work through the new problems, the symptoms subside—a sign that a new adjustment has been made. Any anxiety or impairment of the self-concept is temporary and relatively mild.

The second category is called *persistent non-adaptive problems* (or persistent maladjustment). The behaviours in this category are those brought about by the more or less permanent incapacity of the child's ego to tolerate anxiety and to deal with conflict in an effective manner. These children use inappropriate adjustive strategies and experience anxiety which is disproportionate to the objective situation which elicits it. Their personal and social relationships are impaired. The youngsters show excessive inhibition, shyness, quarrelsomeness and so on. They manifest other symptoms such as regressive behaviour, compulsions, anxiety states, psychosomatic syndromes, marked aggressiveness and excessive dependency. These children are unable to work up to their full potentiality at school.

Isabella Maclean (1966) in her monograph "Child Guidance and the School", states that it is sometimes forgotten that the greatest number of children who come to child guidance clinics are essentially "normal" albeit with developmental difficulties. Burt and Howard (1952) estimated that 90% of the type of problems of maladjustment seen in the schools are social and psychological in origin, and not due to medical pathology.

The third category is called *extreme persistent non-adaptive problems* and here anxiety is so severe and conflict so great that the ego loses its capacity for harmonious and integrated action. In this category, children show bizarre and inexplicable changes in mood; their ideation or thinking is out of key with their feelings, and delusions and hallucinations may be present. This is "psychotic" symptomatology. In common language, such children "have lost touch with reality".

The fourth category of problems is called *constitutional* problems, and this includes behaviours that are primarily due to physical factors present at birth, or occurring after birth. Brain diseases or other damage, for example, affect the integrated functioning of the nervous system and produce mild or severe emotional problems.

Hereditary and physical (i.e., biological) factors are thought to play a significant part in the causation of many of the problems in the third and fourth categories and these are the factors we shall look at in the next chapter. All the adjustive systems—physical capabilities, social and psychological skills and strategies—acquired by the child, and all the developmental changes that occur as he grows up, result from two basic processes: maturation and learning. Since these two complex processes always interact, it is not always possible to disentangle their effects or to isolate the relative contribution of each to a child's development.

McCandless (1969) defines maturation as those developments in the organism which are a function of time or age; it refers to neurophysiological and biochemical changes from conception to death. These changes are in the direction of greater complexity and are qualitative shifts which allow a structure to begin functioning or to function at progressively higher levels. We shall begin by examining the influence of some of these maturational factors on problem behaviour. This requires an account of the biological foundations of behaviour and development. As a bio-social organism the child's development can be impaired by social *and* by inherent or acquired biological defects. We shall deal first with prenatal and genetic factors. Not all the developmental abnormalities used to illustrate genetic and prenatal influences, are directly relevant to the childhood problems we are concerned with. Nevertheless they are important to know about.

# Part II

# Biological Foundations of Emotional Problems

# Introduction

EVERY individual sets out in life as a barely visible particle of matter—no more than a single fertilized cell or zygote. Development begins forty weeks before birth when the spermatozoon, or male germ cell, from the father, enters and fuses with the ovum produced by the mother. From the moment of conception, the individual carries forward into life, in his cells, the information which determines the genetic aspects of his development. Everything that is manifested in the estimated 25 million million body cells which make up the newborn infant was precisely blueprinted in that first germ cell. The genes (which can be described as minute chemical factories) produce substances which influence the behaviour and development of the entire cell. They are capable of modifying their activity in keeping with the environment in which they find themselves. From conception, the environment in which the child finds himself and all the inherited capacities he possesses (the genes in that original cell turn up in all the cells that eventually constitute the adult) interact to produce a complete and unique human being. The first environment will, of course, be the maternal uterus. How successful the individual will be in meeting the challenges of life will depend, to a large extent, upon the integrity of the adjustive systems—neuro-muscular, physiological and psychological—with which he emerges at birth.

Corner (1944) describes the hazards of the human embryo as follows:

Accepting the shelter of the uterus, it also takes the risks of maternal disease or malnutrition, and of biochemical, immunological and hormonal maladjustment. Even before it sinks its roots in the living tissues of the endometrium (lining of the uterus) it has a week's journey to make, as long as a submarine takes to pass beneath the polar ice cap ... it has to carry most of its supplies with it on its trip down the oviduct and uterine lumen, and to add to its difficulties is surrounded by a far more variable and chemically active medium than ice cold seawater.

It is important to remember that the unborn baby is never actually a part of the mother's body despite its tenancy of her womb. Courts of law have given recognition to the fact that the foetus, developing and growing inside the mother, is always a *distinct* individual. It has its own unique pattern of genes, and possesses its own nervous system and blood stream. There is no direct nerve connection between the mother and infant. Their bloodstreams are separated by a semipermeable barrier—the placenta. As Scheinfeld (1967) states, "... the mother's blood, which carries the nourishment, stops on one side of the wall and the blood elements are broken down and strained through it. There is therefore no more *direct blood tie* between a mother and child than between a father and child." Nevertheless, there is an interchange of certain substances between the circulatory systems of mother and child by way of the placenta; they include vitamins, hormones, antigens, antibodies, blood proteins, oxygen, amino acids, drugs and viruses. Obviously, the well-being of the host mother can influence the development of the essentially "parasitical" foetus.

The nine months between conception and birth present more risks to the developing individual than any similar span up to the ninth decade. It is, of course, a period of rapid growth and development. The child-to-be faces trials which begin with fertilization and implantation; they continue with the development of the organs of the body and the establishment of the mechanisms required for the regulation of the internal environment; they come to an end with the birth process. The time scale for each physiological transition is finely prescribed, and failure to make the change at the correct time and in the correct manner is dangerous and can result in death or permanent damage to the organism (see: Corner, 1961). It should be emphasized that despite the potential hazards, the vast majority of babies emerge into the world as reasonably intact beings. The total incidence of fairly serious malformations—abnormalities of structure—due to faulty intrauterine development, is variously estimated at between one-half and two per cent of all births.

# 2. Genetic and Prenatal Influences on Emotional Problems

WE SAID EARLIER that the human being is unique. This is basically what developmental psychology is all about—the emergence of individual differences. This individualism begins with the "lottery" whereby we receive our genetic ingredients.

## Heredity: Beginnings of Individual Differences

The actual genetic constitution of the individual—the "genotype"—is the total set of genes which is present in every cell of the body. The genes—responsible for inherited traits—are strung together on compact but minute threads of material called chromosomes. Each parent has 23 *pairs* of chromosomes. However, the father's germ cell (the fertilizing sperm) contributes only 23 *single* chromosomes to the new being; and the mother's contribution is only 23 *single* chromosomes. In either parent's case, which chromosomes of any pair go into which sperms (or ova) is a matter of chance. The net result is that half of a child's heredity comes from his father and half from his mother; and the person-to-be starts life with a complement of 23 *pairs* of chromosomes (i.e., 46). This set consists of 22 matched pairs—the non-sex *autosomes*—and one pair of sex chromosomes. In the male the sex chromosome pair consists of an X and Y chromosome; in the female there are two X chromosomes. No two children (except monozygotic twins) receive the same assortment of genes. The fertilized zygote brings together various combinations of parental chromosomes and in this way different genes are given to each child of the same parents. Montagu (1963) estimates that in a single mating the possible combinations between the 23 chromosomes of the female and those of the male respectively, are 8,388,608 and the chance of any one such combination being repeated more than once is 1 in approximately 70 million million (i.e., $2^{23} \times 2^{23}$). There can be wide variations within a family group—theoretically, the hereditary varieties a couple could produce number seventy million million; nevertheless a child is somewhat more similar to his blood relations than to anyone else. As Scheinfeld (1967) observes: ". . . about half the chromosomes—or a few more or a few less—of any two children of a family would be the same. Nor would the *unlike* chromosomes necessarily be different in all their genes".

Genes inherited at conception normally remain unaltered throughout life, and are transmitted to the individual's children in the same form. They may change (mutate) in exceptional circumstances as in the case of exposure to excessive radiation. The total number of human genes is not known definitively as they are of ultramicroscopic size. The estimates vary from approximately 40,000 to 120,000 or more genes in the 23 pairs of human chromosomes. The genes on the chromosomes in the sex cells are the ones which get transmitted to successive generations. They always work in pairs, each gene being paired with a gene on the corresponding chromosome. Thus one member of the gene-pair comes from the father, the other from the mother. Genes are sometimes identical in a pair (homozygous), sometimes different (heterozygous). Those which are "dominant" (e.g., for brown eyes) determine which characteristic will show up when paired with another "recessive" gene (e.g., blue eyes). Genes may show their effects late in life (e.g., there is evidence for a genetic contribution to the psychoses of later life—the pre-senile and senile dementias). They may produce their effect early on in development (e.g., sex differences).

Genes have two basic functions: they must be able to replicate themselves and they must be able to determine the architecture of protein molecules. Protein and enzyme synthesis is controlled by genes. One gene is responsible for the synthesis of one enzyme. Some characteristics (for example a form of mental subnormality called "phenylketonuria") are controlled by a *single* abnormal gene. In phenylketonuria an enzyme necessary for normal development is not produced. This enzyme is required to convert phenylalanine into tyrosine, and its absence means that phenylalanine accumulates in body tissues. This results in the interference with cerebral development and functioning. The unconverted phenylalanine is secreted in the urine as phenylpyruvic acid and the condition can be identified by a simple chemical test now carried out as a matter of routine in the first few weeks of life. If it is identified the infant is put on a diet which is free from phenylalanine, and this prevents subnormality occurring. This disorder is of interest because it reveals a mechanism whereby genetic events are translated into behaviour. It also illustrates how an environmental intervention (dietary control) can mitigate an inherited defect.

A large number of degenerative conditions of the central nervous system are hereditary (e.g., certain types of ataxia) as are various degenerations of

2. GENETIC AND PRENATAL INFLUENCES ON EMOTIONAL PROBLEMS

the neuromuscular system. These disorders are determined by a variety of single genes—dominant and recessive, autosomal (non-sex) and sex-linked.

Many characteristics in which there is quantitative variation, particularly complex ones like intelligence, temperament, stature, longevity and athletic ability, depend on the action of many genes (called "polygenic" inheritance). Polygenic mechanisms are believed to produce attributes which are continuous and approximately normally distributed, e.g., height, weight, blood pressure and intelligence. Hereditary theories of natural selection usually posit that a large contribution to evolutionary advance is produced by the accumulation of physiological genes which cause minor differences in such biologically crucial variables as fertility, intelligence, stature and longevity.

The term "phenotype" is used to describe all the observable features or characteristics of an individual at any given point in time. Personality is an example of a phenotype. It is the end product of an interaction between all that the individual has inherited and all the environmental influences which have moulded him. The same sort of interaction—but on a more restricted basis—is thought to occur in the evolution of the so-called "personality problems" (see: page 74). Specific problems acquired by individuals cannot be *inherited* by their offspring. The chromosomes in their germ cells are not affected by what they learn with their brain cells. Thus, the father cannot transmit his fear of confined spaces (claustrophobia) to his child through genetic mechanisms. What the individual inherits is the potential for behaving in certain ways. In the present example he might inherit a predisposition (in the form of a labile nervous system) to acquire neurotic fears (see Chapter 15). There is a well-established genetic component in the predisposition to depressive illness (Rainer 1966a) and schizophrenia (Rainer 1966b). Polygenic inheritance is the preferred hypothesis for accounting for variation in the predisposition to neurotic reactions (Slater and Cowie, 1971) and schizophrenia (Kay, 1963).

In the psychiatric field then, what is inherited is usually a susceptibility to develop a particular problem. Whether or not this disorder is manifested depends to some extent on the experiences a person has during his life. In an adverse environment he may break down, in a benign one he may remain reasonably "well-adjusted". There are rare exceptions to this generalization. Certain genotypes will manifest themselves without regard to the nature of the environmental experience. The abnormal gene producing Huntington's Chorea is an example of this exception. A single dominant gene is the necessary and sufficient cause of this psychosis.

The relationship between phenotype and genotype is complex. The same phenotype can be produced by different genotypes. For example, a type of blindness—retinitis pigmentosa—can be caused by at least five different genotypes. What appears phenotypically to be the same mental illness—schizophrenia—may have several different genotypes. Conversely, the same genotype may produce different phenotypes. The same gene may produce different effects due to the influence of other genes (modifiers) and of differing environmental influences. This variation is termed the "penetrance" of the gene. Penetrance is a statistical concept and refers to the frequency with which phenotype corresponds to genotype. Epiloia (tuberous sclerosis), a form of subnormality accompanied by epilepsy, is caused by a single abnormal gene. Because of variation in the penetrance of this gene, patients may be:

   (i) subnormal but not epileptic,
  (ii) epileptic but not subnormal,
 (iii) neither subnormal nor epileptic but showing other signs of the condition such as tumours and rashes.

To summarize, what appears to be the same effect may be produced by different genes, and the same gene may produce different effects due to the influence of other genes and of environmental experiences. Environmental influences can determine whether an individual achieves all his genetic potential. Thus a child who has the genetic possibility to be tall may remain stunted if he suffers from chronic malnutrition. Similarly, a youngster who is well endowed genetically with intellectual potential, will fail to achieve it if he is deprived of opportunities to learn. The opposite is also true: an unusually strong environment may lend assistance to limited genetic potential. A normal set of genes and an appropriate environment are each needed for satisfactory development and behaviour.

## Transmission of Hereditary Information

The information which shapes the individual's development is borne by the genes which are made of DNA (deoxyribonucleic acid), a chemical constructed like a twisting ladder—the well-publicized double helix (Watson and Crick, 1953). The regular structure of the chemical enables the genes to be accurately interpreted and reproduced.

The work of molecular biologists has shown that the body's "information" is stored in coded form in the large molecules of DNA (of which there are thousands in each chromosome); they act like blueprints. From these, ribonucleic acid (RNA) copies are made, like prints from a negative and these in turn specify the enzymes which carry out all the cell's operations, including the manufacture of more RNA copies. Each gene—with its code—is responsible for giving information for one specific part of the body, or one substance needed in the body's chemical system. There is a particular gene—to take one example—which is responsible for the selection and assembly of the correct sequence of amino acids (out of the 20 kinds available) that will provide a crucial protein ingredient of haemoglobin. If a mistake occurs in the selection of a single acid, the correct one being replaced by an incorrect one, the wrong information will be delivered to the haemoglobin and a deficiency, such as sickle-cell anaemia, will ensue.

## Genetic Accidents

The mechanism of heredity is remarkably reliable, and the vast majority of infants born are within the normal range of variation. The basic chemical structure of the chromosomes appears to be particularly stable. Genetic errors do sometimes occur and they take many different forms. The cause of abnormalities in the inherited material may be a defect of the genes or of the chromosomes as a whole.

(i) Any deviation from the norm in genetic information is called a mutation. The DNA structure of the gene may be wrongly copied, so that the message of that part of the genetic code is lost or changed. A mutation in the genetic matrix (DNA) of the chromosome is not visible under today's microscopes but is recognized by its effects. They are inferred from features in the individual and family pedigree. Gene changes occur in exceptional circumstances such as excessive radiation from X-rays or nuclear bombing. They can occur spontaneously but this is rare—about once in 50,000 generations for any particular gene. A mutant gene can be passed on from one generation to the next in exactly the same way as a normal gene. It becomes a permanent characteristic. This is the basis of evolutionary change—for better or worse. According to Darwinian theory (Darwin, 1859) certain mutations are advantageous for survival and those individuals who inherit them will tend to be preserved by the process of natural selection. On the whole the effects of mutation are deleterious. The resultant pathological condition is often self-limiting owing to its severity and the inability of the affected individual to reproduce. Although deleterious genes arise by mutations or changes in the chemical structure at specific points on chromosomes, these changes cannot be conceptualized in the same way as gross morphological changes in chromosomes. This brings us to the second type of genetic error.

(ii) In this case the abnormality is in the structure or number of chromosomes due to translocations and deletions. Errors may occur in the processes of forming sex cells and fertilization, which cause chromosomal anomalies with important consequences for development and behaviour. Mutations or abnormalities at the chromosome level can usually be seen directly, because changes in chromosome structure or number are visible under the most powerful microscopes. Chromosome abnormalities are found in approximately one in every 200 live births. Most, though, are found in spontaneous abortions (miscarriages).

Any of the 46 chromosomes in the human complement can undergo changes that make them abnormal in size, morphology or number. Chromosomal anomalies which involve a numerical over-representation (trisomy) show themselves (*inter alia*) in several distinct clinical syndromes. Three of these conditions are:

(a) autosomal trisomy G (Down's syndrome or mongolism);
(b) trisomy E (Edward's syndrome); and
(c) trisomy D (Patau's syndrome).

In these trisomic syndromes, the trisomic chromosome usually exists as a separate extra chromosome, so that the total number of chromosomes in the cell is 47. They are associated with defects in the central nervous system and produce severe mental impairment. Mongolism—a condition in which the individual has an extra *autosome*—is the commonest type of chromosome abnormality in the living baby, occurring in one in every 600 or 700 infants. An extra *sex chromosome* rarely leads to abortion and has a much less severe effect on development. Males and females endowed in this way may appear quite normal though some are mentally retarded. Of the syndromes involving sex chromosome anomalies which are associated with deviations in development and behaviour, the best known are:

(a) Turner's syndrome (XO), in which patients lack one sex chromosome. They appear to be female but have no ovaries. These people are usually small and show infantile development of the mammary glands.
(b) Klinefelter's syndrome (XXY), in which patients have an excessive number of sex chromosomes. They appear to be males, but have a defective hormonal balance and undeveloped testes, which usually lack mature sperm.
(c) The XYY syndrome. There is some evidence for an association between the presence of an extra Y chromosome in males and antisocial conduct (Ward 1968). However the status of the evidence is a highly controversial matter (see: Owen, 1972).

The effect of an extra chromosome varies according to which one is in excess. Generally it can be stated that the smaller the extra chromosome, the less severe is the effect on development.

## Prenatal Influences

The first trimester of pregnancy is the most crucial in the child's development. The major organs and basic tissues are being laid down and developed during the first eight weeks after conception and these are therefore the ones during which disturbances in the child's first environment—the uterus—can produce major effects on its growth and development. After this phase it is difficult if not impossible, to affect the morphology of the organism in any fundamental manner; the embryo has all the important external and internal features of a human being.

Ashley Montagu (1964) puts it in this way:

During this critical period, the development of the human body exhibits the most perfect timing and the most elaborate correlation that we ever display in our entire lives. The building and launching of a satellite, involving thousands of people and hundreds of electronic devices, is not nearly so complex an operation as the building and launching of a human being. His development proceeds in an orderly manner and at a regular rate, with specific changes occurring at specific times. Every organ and every tissue—in fact, every cell—has its own timetable for coming into existence, for developing, for taking its place in the machinery of the body, and for beginning to carry out its functions. And every small timetable is meshed with every other timetable. The whole process is so orderly, in fact, that embryologists have been able to draw up a schedule that accounts for all parts of the human body and shows how each part fits into the whole: a countdown, in effect, that starts with the instant of conception and goes on until birth.

During its critical period in the timetable, a particular organ system is both highly sensitive to growth enhancing agents and vulnerable to deleterious influences. If the organ system does not develop normally during its critical period, it does not have another chance to get things right.

## Physical and Psychological Factors in Pregnancy

There are several physical and psychological factors which, by disturbing the mother, can have a disruptive effect on the embryo or foetus. The stressors include maternal disease, malnutrition, fatigue, and emotion, tissue damage and extreme environmental conditions. The most likely route for the effects of maternal stress on the foetus, is via neuro-endocrinal changes in the mother, with concomitant effects in the chemical composition of her blood. Active substances are transmitted to the foetus by transplacental transfer and these may be capable of affecting its neural, endocrinal or other structures (Montagu, 1962, Sontag, 1966). This neurohumoral bond between mother and unborn infant is the medium whereby maternal activity, fatigue, emotionality and personality are postulated to influence the activity level, irritability and autonomic functioning of the foetus (Sontag, 1944, 1960; Montagu, 1962; Pasamanick et al., 1956; Pasamanick and Knobloch, 1961). Those physical agents which are capable of altering the design or morphology of the organism have their most deleterious effect during the germinal period (first two weeks) and the embryonic phase (2–8 weeks) when the organ systems are first emerging. From about the beginning of the third month to birth (the foetal stage) various illnesses and toxins can produce permanent damage, but they no longer change the basic structural design of the organism. Among the potentially malign agents are:

### X-ray treatment

Heavy dosages of radiation during early pregnancy can produce disorders of the central nervous system including deformation, blindness or microcephaly (Murphy, 1947).

### Drugs

There is evidence that serious damage can be inflicted on the unborn child by the mother's ingestion of certain drugs during critical periods of gestation. The best known examples are barbiturates (Montagu, 1963) and thalidomide (Taussig, 1962). Various narcotics can pass the placental barrier and an infant may be born with an addiction (Nyswander, 1956).

### Disease

Infectious diseases like rubella (German measles), poliomyelitis and gonorrhoea, contracted by the mother, during the first trimester of pregnancy, are among the hazards (Montagu, 1962; 1964), which can lead to changes in the physical and mental status of the unborn child. They may cause stillbirths, miscarriages, blindness, deafness, microcephaly and mental subnormality. The microorganisms producing syphilis can pass through the placental barrier infecting and damaging the unborn child in a devastating manner.

### Malnutrition

Mothers who are well nourished during pregnancy suffer less from illness and miscarry less often than mothers on a poor diet. The children of mothers who are on good diets during pregnancy also have better health records during the first six months of life (Ebbs et al., 1942; Sontag, 1950, 1960; Montagu, 1962; Pasamanick et al., 1966). Serious maternal malnutrition can lead to mental subnormality or to physical abnormalities such as rickets, epilepsy, cerebral palsy, general physical disability and emotional instability in the child (Hepner, 1958).

### Blood Type Incompatibility

A mother whose blood type is incompatible with her infant (where she is rhesus negative and the unborn child rhesus positive) may lose her child or have one which is brain-damaged—unless remedial steps are taken by the doctor (Pasamanick and Knobloch, 1959, 1960; Pasamanick et al., 1966).

## Maternal Stress

Can a child, before he is born, be influenced in any way by his mother's emotions? In the folklore of all human societies there has existed the persistent belief that the emotional experiences, attitudes and behaviour of the pregnant mother may affect the child she carries, thereby interfering with the otherwise normal processes of pregnancy. Ferreira (1965) has reviewed some of the scientific evidence which has given increasing respectability to at least some of the beliefs about the influence of maternal "impressions" during pregnancy and the effects of mothers' reactions to their coming maternal role (Wallin and Riley, 1950; Gebhard *et al.*, 1958). Admittedly, this evidence is extremely difficult to evaluate (see: Joffe, 1968). It tends to be based more on retrospective correlational evidence than evidence arising from the direct experimental manipulation of variables. And it is notoriously difficult to infer cause–effect relationships from *post facto* measures of association. The reasons for the bias towards correlational studies are obvious in the case of human subjects—ethical consideration precludes direct experimentation. Unfortunately, observations concerning the effects of prenatal influences on postnatal developments in the child are contaminated by the mother's handling of her baby after birth, and by genetic factors which cannot be controlled. Nevertheless, the work of people like Lester Sontag and Hudson Jost at the Fels Institute, and findings by investigators like Ferreira, demand serious attention from the student of child behaviour.

Ferreira (1960) produced evidence in a double-blind study, of a connection between the mother's emotional status during pregnancy and "upset" behaviour in the offspring. During the last four weeks of pregnancy, 163 women answered a questionnaire that had been designed to discover whether they disliked being pregnant or were in any way unhappy about their expected babies. The babies of all the women were then carefully observed and their behaviour was judged in each case to be either "upset", or normal. There were 28 children classified as "upset", and 135 normal. A significant correlation was found between the women who had been unhappy about pregnancy and the babies who were upset.

Turner (1956) observed a syndrome in infants—restlessness, excessive crying, irritability, vomiting, and frequent stools—and she noticed that this group of symptoms was particularly marked among illegitimate babies. She concluded that the mothers of these children are likely to be under considerable stress during their pregnancies, and that this stress produces these symptoms.

At the Fels Institute it has been demonstrated that the women who show the highest autonomic activity (i.e., fast heart beat and respiration rate and high skin conductivity) tend to have the most active foetuses. Sontag's findings (Sontag, 1962) indicate that foetuses that are highly active during the last two months of pregnancy are very likely to be labelled "socially apprehensive" at the age of two-and-a-half years. Sontag (1966) investigated women who were undergoing emotional stress during pregnancy. During the periods when mothers were disturbed, the body movements of the foetuses increased by several hundred per cent. The increased activity of the foetus would continue for several hours even when the maternal disturbance lasted only a short time. When the stress endured for several weeks, the activity of the foetus over the entire time was greatly increased. One result of increased activity such as this is to lower the birth weight of the children. A typical consequence of severe emotional stress during the mother's pregnancy, is, according to Sontag, the infant who, from the beginning, is hyperactive, irritable, squirming and who cries for his feeding every two or three hours. Because his irritability involves the control of his gastro-intestinal tract, he empties his bowels at unusually frequent intervals, spits up half his feedings and generally makes a nuisance of himself. He is to all intents and purposes a neurotic infant when he is born—the result (allegedly) of an unsatisfactory foetal environment.

The mechanism whereby a pregnant woman's emotional distress may influence the foetus is a matter of speculation. Emotional conflicts and their physiological concomitants mediated by the endocrine system and the hypothalamus may exert an influence upon the contractility of the uterus, vascularization and oxygenation (see: Israel, 1962; Fessel, 1962). Ferreira (1965) outlines several channels through which the pregnant woman can let her developing child "know" of her distress and negative attitudes. Montagu (1962) suggests that under the influence of the psychosomatic state of the mother the foetus may become "sensitized" to postnatal stress; it develops abnormal patterns of response that carry the potential for being translated into postnatal "neurotic" behaviour. He speculates that if a foetus is exposed, during the critical period for the development of his hypothalamic structures, to a high level of adrenergic substances (resulting from maternal psychosomatic response to stress) he will adapt to this changed biochemical environment as if it were the normal state of affairs. Foetuses which are exposed to lower level of adrenergic substances during the critical period will adjust to these levels. This may lead to the creation of permanent adaptation levels; these affect the individual after birth in the sense that he will require higher (or lower) production of adrenergic substances regardless of environmental conditions.

As we cautioned before, much of the work on the relationship between maternal attitudes and emotions and the long-term consequences for the child-to-be is beset by grave methodological problems which make it difficult to arrive at confident generalizations.

## Obstetric Factors and Types of Behaviour Disorder

Theorists often stress the importance of an adequate physical constitution as a prerequisite for sound psychological adjustment. This applies particularly to the physical integrity of the central nervous system. We have seen that during the first nine months of life the embryo and then the foetus must overcome a succession of hurdles. The final hurdle—the process of birth—is in many ways the most dramatic. Certainly a child who has developed normally during the nine prenatal months can be seriously harmed by some accident during the process of birth. Injuries can be caused by exceptionally long labour, abnormal positioning of the baby, by direct trauma to the brain or as a result of damaging haemorrhages.

The ancient Chinese were well aware of the psychological *sequelae* of birth complications. Modern empirical studies bear out their aphorism: "difficult birth, difficult child". According to Rogers *et al.* (1955), Pasamanick and Knobloch (1960, 1961) there is convincing evidence of correlations between complications of pregnancy and birth and behaviour disorders in children; the latter constitute part of what they call a "continuum of reproductive casualty".

Prematurity and other complications of pregnancy and birth are associated with a high risk of foetal and neonatal death, usually due to the damage sustained by the central nervous system. These theorists postulate a remaining proportion of infants who are brain-injured but to an extent that is not fatal. These sublethal effects, depending on the degree or extent of damage, produce one or more of a graded series of neuropsychiatric disorders, ranging from cerebral palsy, epilepsy and mental subnormality to childhood behaviour disorders and reading difficulties. They suggest that many behaviours which are considered pathological, are mistakenly attributed to deleterious early experiences (such as "maternal deprivation") rather than to the more basic injury to the central nervous system itself. While they are aware that many influences besides abnormalities of pregnancy and childbirth produce behaviour disturbances, they report that an analysis of the medical histories of children with emotional problems reveals more complications of pregnancy and a greater incidence of prematurity than occurs in a control group of matched subjects. Such complications are especially evident in confused, hyperactive and disorganized children. They also occur in youngsters suffering from hearing defects, strabismus, infantile autism and symptoms of a delinquent nature.

The type of impairment produced by injury to the brain depends (*inter alia*) upon the regions damaged. During birth the most exposed parts of the brain are the cerebral hemispheres. Immature or dividing cells are more susceptible to alteration than mature cells, and in the nervous system nearly all cell division takes place during embryonic life. This, then, is the time when it is most vulnerable to ionizing radiation, teratogenic drugs and infections. Birth, however, is a time when the organism is particularly susceptible to mechanical and (some would say) psychological insults.

## Psychological Trauma of Birth

Much has been made of the translation of the neonate from the tranquillity of the womb to the "buzzing" and "blooming" world outside this sheltered environment. There is insufficient evidence to prove or disprove the theories (Rank, 1929; Greenacre, 1945), that birth is a *psychological* trauma for the newborn infant. Indeed, the formulation of a theory about the traumatizing influence of birth and its role as the prototype for later anxiety attacks is probably not susceptible to scientific testing. On the other hand there is no doubt that birth can, in certain circumstances, be the source of such physical shock to the neonate that damage is caused to the central nervous system. The effects vary according to the duration and difficulty of birth.

## Physical Trauma of Birth

### ANOXIA

The development and normal functioning of the brain depends upon large supplies of oxygen conveyed to it by the blood. A reduction in this blood supply results in a shortage of the oxygen necessary to the maintenence of brain metabolism. Perinatal anoxia (lack of or deficiency of oxygen) can be caused by many factors. Brief, intermittent periods of severe anoxia may be associated with the rhythmic uterine contractions of labour. Anoxia may be mild but prolonged in the case of partial, premature separation of the placenta. It can also be relatively brief in duration but exceptionally severe in the case of complete placental separation, massive loss of blood by the mother, or other complications of labour and delivery. Anoxia resulting from different causes may have varying consequences. The hippocampus (important in establishing a continuous record of memories) is one of the most sensitive areas of the brain; it is frequently damaged by anoxia. If damage to the brain is widespread and affects the integrity of the temporal lobes, mental impairment is highly probable.

There is evidence (Layman, 1959; Shirley, 1939) that babies born precipitately after a short, sharp labour, or born after their mothers have endured difficult pregnancies (such as full or partial placenta praevia) tend to be irritable, hyperactive and difficult as babies and as older children. Precipitate labour—labour of less than two hours' duration—has potentially detrimental effects on later intellectual development because it introduces the infant to oxygen too suddenly with the result that he may suffer from anoxia (Yacorzynski and Tucker, 1960).

Studies (Montagu, 1962; Ucko, 1965) suggest a correlation between asphyxia at birth and the incidence of neurological abnormalities between one and five years from birth. In extreme cases there is no doubt that human babies do suffer gross and sometimes fatal brain damage from birth asphyxia and resultant oxygen deprivation. But the extent to which this lack of oxygen contributes to the much more common minor degrees of neurological impairment, mental subnormality or behaviour problems, remains to be established. Correlations have been reported between anoxia and perceptual and psychomotor deficits (Corah et al., 1965), overexcitability (Honzik et al., 1965; Ucko, 1965) and low developmental quotient scores in the first two years of life (Stechler, 1964). Ucko (1965) suggests that asphyxia at birth may result in quite specific temperamental attributes in later life, notably unusual sensitivity, over-reactivity to stimuli, and a tendency to become upset when customary routines are upset (cf: the "difficult child" described on page 98). Fraser and Wilks (1959) in Aberdeen, compared the later development of a group of asphyxi-ated infants and a control group of matched normal subjects. Many more asphyxiated children than controls had minor impairments of motor ability, perception and impulse control.

PREMATURITY

Prematurely born infants are particularly susceptible to brain injury during birth. The skull of the premature infant does not provide as effective a protection to brain-tissue as is provided in the case of an infant born at full term. Serious nervous system injuries may occur. Pressure during birth may cause the fracture of bones. Should this happen in the vicinity of nerve centres, there may be temporary or permanent injury to some of them, or to the sense organs, particularly the ears and eyes (Pratt, 1954). Babies who are of low birth weight for their gestational age (more than two standard deviations below the mean) are found to have more abnormalities of the nervous system than the normal population. Pre-maturity at birth is correlated with various later complications such as excessive distractibility, hyperactivity, hyper-irritability, impaired intel-lectual capacity, hypersensitivity to sound, personality disturbance and reading difficulties (Shirley, 1938, 1939; Hirschi et al., 1948; Cutler et al., 1965; Braine et al., 1966; Knoblock et al., 1959; Knoblock and Pasa-manick, 1966).

Drillien (1964a) studied (longitudinally) the *sequelae* of premature births in over one thousand mothers. Using the Bristol Social Adjustment Guide, he tested the school-going children at ages $6\frac{1}{2}$ and $7\frac{1}{2}$. He found that the proportion of youngsters considered maladjusted or unsettled, increased as birth weight decreased. Obstetric difficulties—severe complications of pregnancy and/or birth—were associated with an increased risk of disturbed behaviour in the offspring. An intensive investigation of 112 babies whose birth-weight was three pounds or less, revealed defects of vision in 37% of those who were of school-going age. Eight per cent had some degree of congenital defect. Other defects included cerebral diplegia (18%), epilepsy (7%) and speech defects (8%). At five years or more, one-third of this subgroup were below the fifth percentile for mature controls in weight; nearly one-half were behind in height and over one-quarter in both weight and height. Over one-third were likely to be ineducable in ordinary schools for reasons of physical or mental defect or both. Only 30% of the school-age children could be described as manifesting no behaviour disturbance. Drillien (1964b) found that the most common behaviour problems associated with very severe prematurity (birth weight of 3 lb. or less) were hyperactivity and restlessness. These problems, and distractibility, are probably the only types of behaviour disorder of childhood which can be associated (with any degree of confidence as to causality) with perinatal factors (see: Pasamanick *et al.*, 1956; Stott, 1965; Ucko, 1965). However, as Wolff (1967b) points out, it would not be surprising if other behaviour disorders of a reactive nature (e.g., delinquency) followed on the educational and social failures invariably experienced by hyperactive, restless and distractible children (see Chapter 3).

The National Child Development Study—a longitudinal study of a national cohort of some 16,000 children born in 1958—included an extensive and detailed survey (Butler and Bonham, 1963) of English, Scottish and Welsh neonates. The cohort was traced in 1965 and assessed on various educational, behavioural, health and environmental factors. Davie *et al.* (1972) report that there is evidence—as yet tentative—of a relationship between the period of gestation and subsequent adjustment. Early results suggest that after allowance is made for social class, those children born at term (39–41 weeks) are the most stable; those born pre-term and post-term manifest most evidence of poor adjustment. A similar relationship has been shown between gestational maturity and tested reading performance.

Wolff (1967b) studied the frequency of obstetric complications in the prenatal histories of 100 primary school children referred to a psychiatric department and in a matched control group of non-referred children. Like Brandon (1960) (who compared a group of maladjusted children from Newcastle with a group of controls), Wolff found no significant differences in the obstetric histories.

Wolff maintains that her results do not contradict the findings of others that prematurity and obstetric damage can predispose children to develop behaviour disorders in later life. She states that:

It is not surprising that, when special risk groups of children are examined, relationships between specific hazards and subsequent behaviour disturbances are found which disappear when they are looked for in a more general childhood population. This merely means that the hazardous events are rare and cannot account for the majority of behaviour disorders found in children. When large populations are studied, as in the Baltimore studies, statistically significant relationships may be found between behaviour disorders and traumatic antecedent events, when in fact such events are causally operative in only a minority of disturbed children (Wolff, 1967b).

The complexity of disentangling causes and effects from the masses of correlations in the literature, is illustrated by the problems associated with prematurity. They include primiparity, maternal age, malnutrition, multiple births, pyelonephritis, vaginal bleeding, prolonged rupture of membranes, habitual abortion, previous history of infertility, acute infections, and toxaemia during pregnancy. If we consider only the last of the factors —toxaemia—we find that behaviour problem cases show a greater incidence of this complication of pregnancy in their antenatal histories than control cases. Toxaemia can produce anoxia which, in turn, can engender a variety of cerebral dysfunctions ranging from mild behavioural-control problems to cerebral palsy. The causal relationship between brain-injury and psychological disturbances is complex enough, as we shall see; the known correlation between prematurity and (say) nervousness is just as difficult to specify in meaningful cause-effect terms. The point is that an interlacing network of prenatal influences robs umbrella concepts like "prematurity" of their explanatory value, unless the links in the causal chain are elaborated.

The abnormalities of pregnancy and birth which seem to be important in the large scale, retrospective studies made by the Baltimore (Pasamanick) group of researchers involve infection, malnutrition and other forms of stress which in turn are related to low socio-economic status. Mothers from the low socio-economic stratum of society also tend to receive less intensive medical care during pregnancy and delivery.

Stott (1959, 1966, 1962) argues that *some* emotional disturbances in children result from a particular susceptibility to stress due to a congenital impairment of temperament—an impairment of the brain occurring at or before birth. His investigations demonstrate that if a child suffers from one form of physical or neurological impairment, there is a greater chance that he will be affected by a second; if he suffers from two, there is a still greater chance of a third, and so on. He refers to this as the law of "multiple congenital impairment". He has found that, in general, maladjusted children show a greater incidence of physical illness and organic defects than do non-maladjusted children.

Neurological dysfunctions, in Stotts' view, predispose the child as he gets older to adopt maladaptive patterns of behaviour in times of stress. The postulated impairment of temperament is thought to lead to faulty motivation; it affects the child's general style of responding to situations. Stott (1966) has described what he believes to be a clearly defined childhood problem—"unforthcomingness". The unforthcoming child has an impairment of natural assertiveness or "go". This kind of child is content with a modest level of effectiveness. He does not feel the challenge to solve problems, to keep abreast of other children in their play, work, or other achievements. In the face of any difficulty he lacks confidence to the extent that he—as the teacher puts it—"retreats into his shell". Stott describes the general manner of such unforthcoming children as "mousy". Because they are unventuresome and timid, they are very dependent upon their mothers. This has led some psychologists to suppose (wrongly according to Stott) that their overdependence has been brought about by anxious, over-solicitous mothers, who have always done everything for their children, thus robbing them of their initiative.

Stott, on the other hand, found a relationship between this type of personality problem and a history of illness or other stresses suffered by by the mother during pregnancy. It was particularly associated with disturbance experienced during the later phase of her pregnancy. Stott believes that it is at this stage that the fine mechanisms that control behaviour develop. Unforthcomingness is particularly prevalent among children who are academically retarded and unhealthy within an intellectually normal population.

What is the outlook for such children? Stott claims that, whether the impairment of temperament is due to tissue damage or to delayed maturation, there is a definite tendency to spontaneous correction. This occurs at a slow but steady rate during childhood, and often with dramatic speed following puberty. Such a tendency to grow out of congenital temperamental weakness has its counterpart in many physical problems such as bronchitis, asthma and clumsiness.

# 3. Physical Adjustive Systems: The Brain and Nervous System

THE BRAIN CAN be compared with an incredibly intricate machine. Like a machine, it can go wrong; but unlike most machines, its standards of reliability are remarkably high. It is relatively rare for the brain to be seriously impaired. Rutter (1967) estimates, on the basis of his epidemiological studies of children on the Isle of Wight, that 5% of the population of children is brain damaged in some way. The integrity of the brain and nervous system are crucial determinants of a child's success in adapting to his internal and external environment. This complex control system must always be on the alert, attending selectively to what is crucial in the individual's ever-changing surroundings, processing information and regulating countless adjustments required in his interaction with the environment. Functioning like a computer of a homeostat, the brain maintains the life-preserving physiological equilibrium in the body. It stores and integrates vast amounts of information, and exercises choice over how and when to react to particular situations. Each and every second of waking life, more than a hundred million electrical impulses flow into the brain. Even during sleep, more than fifty million neuronal "messages" are being relayed, every second, to and from the brain and different parts of the body. All this requires a staggering level of dependability and delicacy of analysis—in times of calm and crisis, health and disease, and around the clock for years on end.

## The Reliability of the Brain

A formidable problem of automation is the fact that no man-made device is yet able to maintain itself so as to provide precise and dependable standards of performance over really prolonged periods of time. Despite its advantages over the human brain, the modern computer is generally cumbersome and requires regular maintenance. It is unreliable to the extent that a malfunction in one of its numerous working parts can lead to the shutdown of the entire system. Compare this vulnerability with the performance of the brain, a computer—to use a popular analogy—small enough to carry about in one's skull.

There are several properties of the brain that promote this reliability and efficiency. Specialization and flexibility are combined in the organization of the nerve cells in such a way that speed and accuracy are assured, and an additional bonus of compensatory capacity which allows it to circumvent emergencies, sometimes including even disease or damage to brain tissue. The superfluous number of functional units in its construction provides a latent reserve so that certain brain centres can undergo a dynamic readjustment of their function and take over from other damaged structures. Information seems to be stored in multiple form, in different tissues of the brain, so that much of it survives the destruction of neural structures which are necessary to its recording. This is a vital safety factor in a creature as complex as man. Asratian, a Soviet neurophysiologist, points out (Asratian, 1965) that nature has solved the problem of unreliability brilliantly, in the working of inhibition in the brain. The basic elements of the nervous system—the billions of nerve cells designed to sense, store and transmit information—function as minute live "relays" for scores of years. When these are in a state of inhibition they are cut off from external activities—they cease to respond to stimuli and do not conduct impulses of excitation.

Before the discovery of inhibition, the old concept of the nervous system was one of a purely excitatory system. The main property of the cell consists of the capacity to generate impulses—that is—to be excited. Excitation is an active process involving expenditure of energy. The excitation of nerve cells increases the activity of the organs with which these cells are linked. Obviously there cannot be an exact correspondence between stimulating events—the inputs of the system—and the responses or outputs of the nervous system. If the entire brain was an excitatory system, every stimulus of sufficient intensity would automatically and immediately produce a reaction. If there was no "screening" process at work, any intense or varied stimulation would cause an over-loading of the nervous system, resulting in the disintegration of behaviour.

Based on contemporary research in his laboratories at the Institute of Higher Nervous Activity and Neurophysiology in Moscow, Asratian contends that all forms of inhibition in the normally functioning nervous system have protective/restorative properties. Every transition of nerve cells into a state of inhibition is used for their "preventive maintenance". He believes that even brief inhibition enables nature to carry out running repairs, restoring the capacity to work and normalizing the physico-chemical composition of the cells. Biochemists have shown that periods of excitation of nerve cells produce decrements in the content of those chemical substances such as adenosine triphosphoric acid, which are postulated to be sources of energy. The use of radioisotope methods has shown that during excitation there is a gradual suppression of the metabolism of the nucleic acids which contribute to the process of protein synthesis, the process whereby the cells' chemical composition is renewed. Simultaneously there is a build-up of metabolic waste products such as ammonia, lactic acid and inorganic phosphorus. In the view of the Soviet scientists inhibition constitutes, above all, rest, recuperation and protection for the highly reactive nerve structures. A typical example of restorative inhibition is provided by nightly natural sleep, during which inhibition spreads to a great mass of the structures of the brain. Furthermore, protective inhibition develops very quickly in animals debilitated by disease or run down by excessive nervous stress.

Even an instrument as sturdy as the brain (as we saw in Chapter 2) can be impaired. Its functions may be adversely affected by injuries (such as a blow, a fall or some penetrating wound), oxygen deprivation (for example, asphyxia at birth), infections, tumours, degenerative diseases, mechanical trauma (brought about by difficulties during birth), toxic influences on the embryo *in utero*, and genetic aberrations.

The effects of brain malfunctioning do not always show themselves in the obviously handicapping problems like mental subnormality, cerebral palsy, blindness or deafness. The original injury may be so "minimal" that there are not always clear-cut neurological signs to assist in diagnosis. And yet the insidious and cumulative effects of the cerebral dysfunction itself, plus the fact that it so often goes undetected, make the child vulnerable to stress.

Minimal brain-damage (or minimal cerebral dysfunction), as it is called, can have effects on the motor and sensory abilities of the child and on the functions with which he interprets the messages from his environment and coordinates his reactions to such information. A list of the dysfunctions commonly associated with brain damage (Herbert, 1964) illustrates the potentially serious implications for the child:

1. Motor incoordination, overactivity (hyperactivity).
2. Perceptual anomalies.
3. Learning and memory deficits.
4. Distractibility (difficulties of attention).
5. Language and other communication difficulties.
6. Problems of concept formation.
7. Intellectual disabilities.

Apart from the influence of brain injury itself on emotional tone and control, any one of these functional difficulties listed above may lead to emotional problems in the child. Some of these are dealt with later.

## Minimal Cerebral Dysfunction

Some theorists postulate the existence of a *general* condition of "minimal cerebral dysfunction" referring to it as if it is a unitary syndrome. They also talk about "the brain-damaged child" although the former term is gaining ground because of the difficulty of establishing definitive evidence of actual brain injury. The cluster of symptoms which is supposed to describe the "brain-damaged child" includes over-activity, motor inco-ordination, distractibility, impulsiveness and perceptual disturbance. This notion of brain damage as a unitary problem has been criticized as not being consistent with the facts (Meyer, 1957; Herbert, 1964). The symptoms resulting from different types of brain injury are (not surprisingly) extremely varied (Piercy, 1964), and the popular stereotype applies to only a very small proportion of the cases of brain-damage in the general population. In short, it is misleading to talk of the brain-damaged child as if there were only one type; there is a variety of brain-injured children with many quite different problems, each of which calls for intensive individual analysis and treatment of a kind that some of the current generalizations about the brain-injured child do not provide.

Parents and teachers are often told by psychiatrists that a particular child's difficulties at home and at school are "a result of brain-damage", suffered perhaps prenatally or at birth. This is no more helpful a diagnosis than a general practitioner telling a mother her child is "physically ill" when she consults him for a diagnosis of a bodily malaise. Certainly no programme of rehabilitation—remedial teaching or behaviour modification—could be planned on the basis of such an over-inclusive diagnosis. What is needed, in describing a child, is not a meaningless label but precise psychometric information about his specific physical and intellectual strengths and weaknesses, and also about any emotional difficulties which have a bearing on his ability to learn.

So many children with school learning problems fail to show any positive evidence of neurological damage or dysfunction, that a new diagnostic term has begun to make headway in the clinical world. It reflects educational criteria rather than medical criteria and is called *"learning disability"*. The child with a learning disability exhibits a disorder in one or more of the basic psychological processes involved in understanding or using spoken or written language: listening, thinking, talking, reading, writing, spelling or arithmetic. Such disorders include conditions which have been referred to in the past as perceptual handicap, brain injury, minimal brain dysfunction, dyslexia, and developmental dysphasia.

## Motor Incoordination

The problem of motor incoordination is one facet of neurological impairment which is worth looking at straight away, as it is one of those predisposing influences to maladjustment which is often overlooked.

Poor motor coordination—a discrepancy between the mind's intention and the body's execution—is commonly found in the child with minimal brain-damage. It is evident in his awkwardness of movement, his clumsiness at sport and his difficulties with the fine muscular control demanded by writing. Such a child—so often called "ham-fisted"—may suffer a great deal as a result of rebukes for his clumsiness from parents and teachers, and as a consequence of teasing and mocking from his playmates. His handicap may be accepted as being within the normal range (albeit the lower end) of motor skills displayed by children at large. Because there are no obvious or dramatic neurological signs and symptoms of his underlying central dysfunction, the condition often goes undetected.

Annell (1953) describes the picture presented by children with difficulties in fine motor function. She reports that it was not uncommon for their difficulties to remain unremarked or misunderstood at home. Direct inquiries disclosed that these children had been able to sit up and walk at the usual age but had been late in learning to dress themselves—in many cases they were unable to do so independently when they started school. Their table manners were frequently bad; they spilt liquids and ate clumsily. Articulatory difficulties of speech were often present as were writing difficulties. At school, hand-writing and drawing were particularly troublesome. Many of these children were enuretic and encopretic. It is difficult to determine whether these symptoms are due primarily to lack of sphincter control associated with general difficulties in fine motor functions, or whether they are part of a secondary psychogenic reaction. As a rule these two influences were thought to be jointly responsible.

Annell is concerned that disturbances in fine motor function may be overlooked or misinterpreted. When a child was unable to dress himself at the normal age it was often assumed that he had been spoiled by his mother. Attempts were made to make the child dress himself or eat properly by means of scolding or punishment. The general consequence was that the child felt misunderstood and unfairly treated and lost his feeling of trust in his mother and his surroundings and "reacted with secondary nervous symptoms of various kinds".

A pilot validation study (Stott et al., 1966a) conducted in Glasgow schools and using the Gollnitz Revision of the Oseretzky Test of Motor Ability, revealed that youths with a record of anti-social behaviour had, as a group, poorer motor coordination than non-delinquents. Stott's studies (1966) of troublesome children produced repeated evidence of neurological problems which were associated with a variety of motor and other disabilities. The physical defects which were found to be common, were squints, defective hearing, poor muscular coordination and speech defects.

The Plowden Report (1966) stresses the need for the development of diagnostic tests for use by teachers. Plowden believes that "early and accurate identification of handicapped children is essential however slight their disability". Some children who avoid activities because of some minor physical handicap may not develop vital skills. Their problems need to be recognized early so that every effort can be made to involve them in situations likely to remedy their deficiencies. Stott et al. (1966b) and Moyes (1969) have devised a test of motor development which helps to identify clumsy children early on in life. The early identification of physical difficulties might help to stop the drift by some youngsters towards socially unacceptable behaviour of a serious kind. The Plowden Report states that "teachers need to be alert to detect and bring forward for expert examination without delay any child who fails to make satisfactory progress or seems to have sensorimotor,* social or emotional difficulties".

## Hyperkinesis

Another problem commonly associated with the diagnosis of brain-injury is hyperkinetic behaviour. Rutter (1967) has made a study of hyperkinetic children, and has this to say:

These children are the despair of the school teacher. They are usually of below-average intelligence and may show any of the other developmental abnormalities already described—delay in speech, clumsiness, difficulty in learning to read, poor perception and understanding of shape relationships and difficulties in differentiating right from left. Often, too, the children have fits. In middle and later childhood this over-active pattern of behaviour is often gradually replaced by an inert under-activity in which the children seem to lack drive and initiative, poor relations with other children continue and anti-social behaviour may develop.

## Specific Reading Backwardness

This problem is much commoner than the clumsiness syndrome, and is usually found in boys. In the Isle of Wight survey (Rutter et al., 1966, 1970) 4% of the children were found to be reading at least 28 months below the level expected on the basis of their age and intelligence. They were all children of normal intelligence. Many backward readers were found to be clumsy and delayed in their speech. The backward readers showed difficulties in telling right from left. They also suffered from what is called "motor impersistence" (that is to say they couldn't hold any movement, such as shutting their eyes, for very long) and they had general

---

* Some of the techniques which have been used to detect these deficits are described in the following pages.

difficulties in concentrating. Reading backwardness often goes hand in hand with difficulties in arithmetic and spelling, and it is not uncommon for there to be a family history of reading difficulties. Emotional problems are frequently associated with backwardness in reading—a third of the children with severe reading backwardness also exhibited marked anti-social behaviour.

## Perceptual Deficits

It is reported that brain-injured children suffer from perceptual disturbances (such as a tendency to be attracted to the details of a stimulus), and consequently have an inability to conceptualize and respond to the gestalt. Perceptual anomalies in which the subject confuses, reverses or fails to discriminate figure and background have also been reported (Werner and Strauss, 1941; Cruickshank et al., 1961).

These distortions have been studied by means of the Marble Board Test (Strauss and Lehtinen, 1947). On this test, the subject is required to copy designs set out by the examiner on a marble board. An incoherent, disconnected or disorganized type of copying procedure is said to be characteristic of brain-damaged children. Studies using the Marble Board Test (Dolphin and Cruickshank, 1951; Shaw and Cruickshank, 1956) have demonstrated mean differences between the performance of brain-damaged and control groups. But it is not clear to what extent the variance is due to cerebral pathology or whether the considerable overlap in the distribution of scores contra-indicates the use of the test for the diagnosis of individual cases.

Gallagher (1957) found no significant difference in the number of correctly reproduced designs on an adaptation of the test, between a group of brain-injured (exogenous) and non-brain-injured (familial) mentally retarded children. He concludes that if the particular brain-injury does not relate to perceptual processes, the individual may perform quite adequately on perceptual tasks in relation to his own general mental development. Strauss and Lehtinen (1947) make it clear that whereas the presence of a severe visuo-motor disturbance is strongly indicative of brain-injury, the fact of brain-injury does not necessarily imply a visuo-motor defect.

A perceptual test like the Marble Board Test can be misleading. It is possible that the test's ability to detect brain-damage is an artefact of, or inflated by, criterion contamination. Criterion contamination occurs when the type of information which is central to the test being validated, is used in the selection of the criterion groups against which the test will be validated. In constructing a diagnostic test it is essential to have an adequate independent criterion of brain-injury. However, there is no discussion of the proportion of brain-damaged children in the standardization sample who were diagnosed as such according to an independent criterion of injury. The validity of the test is also called into question by the experiments of O'Connor (1958). In a study of two feeble-minded groups matched in intelligence, the correlation between intelligence level and M.B.T., irrespective of known brain-injury, was found to be about 0·7. A group of imbeciles and normal children were matched for mental age (M.A.). They naturally differed in chronological age (C.A.). It was found that there was no difference in "jumping scores" between brain-injured and normal subjects; that differences in "jumping scores" were due to intelligence level rather than brain-injury; and that differences in error scores were related to M.A. rather than brain-injury; and that differences in error scores were related to M.A.

The Bender Visual-motor Gestalt Test (B.G.) (Bender, 1938) and variants of this test (e.g., The Minnesota Percepto-diagnostic Test: Fuller and Laird, 1963) have been used to diagnose brain-damage. These tests provide an analysis of visuo-motor performance as revealed by a subject's ability to copy designs. Several research workers (Bensberg, 1952; Graham et al., 1960; Koppitz, 1962; Fuller, 1963) using the B.G. or adaptations of it, reported significant differences between the performance of brain-injured children (drawn largely from subnormal populations) and non-brain-injured controls.

Despite such differences between groups, from the clinical point of view, the overlap of scores is usually so great that the correct prediction of an individual's group membership is little better than chance. An example of this is Feldman's investigation (1953) in which the optimal cut-off point correctly identified 57% of the exogenous group, and incorrectly classified 18% of the endogenous subjects as brain-injured. A variety of "organic signs" derived from the B.G. have been described as crucial for diagnostic purposes, although there is little agreement as to which they are. Some of these signs have been found in the records of normal preschool children, and in neurotic and psychotic patients. In the studies of the B.G. mentioned above, the most frequently reported neurological indices are: rotations, reversals, use of lines for dots, perseveration and distortion. What agreement does exist, concerns the postulated sensitivity of the rotations index to brain-damage.

The assumption underlying the use of the B.G. is that the group differences are associated with the neurological diagnosis. However, rotations may result from factors other than internal perceptual distortions due to cerebral pathology. There is evidence of a negative correlation between IQ and rotation of designs (O'Connor, 1958; Silverstein and Mohan, 1962). External stimulus variables such as orientational cues from the test environment may be pertinent to the phenomenon (Freed, 1964).

A major criticism of B.G. and other perceptual studies is the failure to control such factors as visual field defects. The demonstration by Shapiro *et al.* (1962) that rotation of Kohs Blocks is dependent to some extent on the presence of visual field defects, emphasizes this weakness.

## Attention Problems

Hutt *et al.* (1963) devised an objective measure of attention span (and other variables such as mobility) and found that brain-damaged children performed at an inferior level to controls. The question of distractibility is important for as Gallagher (1957) says, "It is conceivable that the child's perceptual abilities, as measured in the perceptual organization studies, could be markedly improved by merely removing, or developing a tolerance for distracting stimuli. Under these circumstances, it is well to reflect on the possibility that poor performance of brain-injured children on these perceptual tasks may be as much due to poor attention as to inadequate central perceptual skills." The rationale for the special educational procedures of Strauss and Lehtinen (1947) and Cruickshank *et al.* (1961) with brain-injured and hyperactive children has been based partly on such considerations.

## Learning and Memory Deficits

Pond (1961) concludes from his study of brain-damaged children that they are handicapped in those functions which are concerned with memory and learning. He states that in older subjects the term dementia is usually applied, and this implies most typically a loss of recent memory and the capacity to learn new material.

Tests have been designed on the basis of postulated deficits in these functions.

### VISUAL MODALITY

The Visual Retention Test (Benton, 1955) involves visuo-motor performance as well as learning and immediate memory. Benton reports a correlation of 0·7 between test scores and intelligence. Performance on the test shows a progressive rise from the age of 8 years until a plateau is reached at about 14 years of age. Clinical interpretation is made on the basis of the patient's C.A. and an "expected" score, which is equivalent to his assumed premorbid intelligence. The assessment of his "original" intelligence is derived from a consideration of his educational and socio-economic background, and possibly his performance on other tests—a subjective and highly unreliable procedure. Benton's scoring system is based upon the number of designs correctly reproduced and error categories of response, viz., rotations, size distortions, etc. Wahler (1956) in a study of "error" scores, compared normal and brain-damaged subjects. There were no significant differences in the incidence of different types of error between the two groups, although several types of error seemed to suggest the need for further research.

Benton (1955) reports that 4% of normal children with average intelligence made defective scores on the test. About 15% made scores classified as either borderline or defective. Of the brain-injured children (also of average intelligence) about 20% showed a defective performance while approximately 55% made scores classified as borderline or defective. He concludes, "It is seen that not quite as sharp a discrimination is achieved in the application of the Visual Retention Test to children as is the case in its application to adults. Nevertheless, a significant discrimination of considerable clinical value is attained." Diagnostic statements are made on the basis of the number of points scored below an "expected" score by a patient of a certain level of intelligence.

Hanawalt (1959) gave the test to 22 delinquent youths (median age 12·5 years) and found that the scoring indicated two questionable cases, three suggestive of brain-injury, and ten strongly suggestive of brain-injury. He points out that the group might have had a higher incidence of brain-damage than the normal population, but it was a sample of the usual type of delinquent and not a sample of neurological cases. Benton claims that the test is relatively insensitive to emotional influences, but Rowley and Baer (1961) demonstrated that an excessively high number (36%) of emotionally disturbed children made borderline (but not grossly defective) performances on the Visual Retention Test.

Graham and Kendall (1960) developed a Memory-for-Designs Test (M.F.D.) similar to that of Benton: an immediate memory test using a series of line drawings of geometric figures. The test was standardized on both adult and child normative groups. The criterion group of brain-damaged subjects was chosen on the basis of the "organic syndrome", i.e., impaired intellectual functions (recent memory defect, disorientation, etc.) plus positive evidence from at least one of the following sources of information: neurological examination, case history and physical tests (e.g., X-ray, E.E.G. etc.). Therefore, if the test is one of poor memory, then criterion contamination is involved. However, this is difficult to determine. The test can hardly be called a memory test since forgotten or incomplete reproductions are not penalized.

The authors conclude that "while there is considerable overlap in the score distributions of these two groups, the overlap is largely due to failure to detect disorder rather than to misclassification of normal subjects. That is, with a poor performance, there is a high probability of brain disorder; but a good performance does not indicate an intact brain".

It is presumably the insensitivity of this type of test which accounts for the negative results of Richie and Butler (1964) and Gallagher (1957).

## THE AUDITORY MODALITY

White (1959) studied the applicability of the Walton-Black Modified Word Learning Test to children. He studied a group of 40 normal, 18 psychiatric, 8 defective and 17 brain-damaged children. The majority of the latter group suffered from cerebral palsy.

It was found that the brain-damaged children as a group could learn as well as their non-brain-damaged controls. The learning task was impossible for children below the age of six. There was a relationship between vocabulary level and learning test score, low vocabulary being associated with a poor learning score. Age and IQ had no effect on learning scores in the normal and neurotic children. Spastics as a group could learn as well as normal children. However, a large proportion of the children who had suffered from meningitis could not learn. White (op. cit.) states that different results may be obtained with other brain-damaged children; and indeed, with such small numbers, the above results cannot be regarded as conclusive.

## Problems of Concept Formation

A frequently reported characteristic of the brain-injured child is the abnormal "concreteness" of his thinking. This is generally measured by sorting tests such as the Goldstein-Scheerer Color-Form Sorting Test (Goldstein and Scheerer, 1941) and the Wisconsin Card Sorting Test (Berg, 1948). Concreteness is defined as the inability to form abstract concepts and an inability to "shift" from one stimulus or idea to another (also termed rigidity or perseveration).

Several studies (Cotton 1941; Werner, 1946; McMurray, 1954a; Clawson, 1962; Ernhart et al., 1963; Weiss, 1964) have reported on aspects of concept formation which differentiate brain-damaged children from non-brain-damaged controls, the general finding being that the former are more "concrete" in their thinking than the controls. Weatherwax and Benoit (1958) as a result of their experiment urge caution in denying that brain-injured children are capable of abstract thought.

There has been much opposition in the literature to the dichotomy of "abstract" and "concrete" abilities, and doubts about the validity and usefulness of such separate categories. It has not been conclusively established that the ability to abstract is anything more than general intelligence.

Whatever the merits of the theory, the tests of conceptual thinking have been inadequately standardized for diagnostic purposes. Piaget's (1950) studies of concept formation have shown that developmental factors are important determinants of concreteness of thinking in children. These findings demonstrate the need for caution before attributing concrete responses to cerebral pathology.

## Intellectual Deficits

There are serious difficulties in drawing conclusions from standard intelligence tests given to brain-injured children, many of whom are mentally retarded or physically handicapped. Gallagher *et al.* (1956) contend that there is room for doubt that relationships derived from normal standardization populations will hold true for such an atypical group.

IQ level in itself is of little diagnostic value in detecting cerebral pathology, as the entire range of intelligence will be found in a large sample of brain-damaged children (Cotton, 1941; Meyer and Simmel, 1947; French, 1948). Some of these children produce superior performance. However, there is an overall negative correlation between IQ and brain-injury (Beck and Lam, 1955; Pond, 1961).

Psychologists have studied the patterns of successes and failures obtained by brain-injured children on tests of general intelligence. This approach is based upon the hypothesis that brain-injured children often show selective impairment of intellectual functioning. For example, it is postulated that verbal items are more resistant to deterioration than performance items. This has been the basis of the popular "verbal minus performance" index of brain-damage. The Wechsler Intelligence Scale for Children (W.I.S.C.) is particularly suited to this type of analysis as it is possible to estimate the statistical significance of an abnormal discrepancy between verbal and performance scales. Unfortunately, the interpretation of this index is complicated by the possibility that a spuriously high or low verbal score may be the partial result of home background factors. In addition, large discrepancies have been obtained from patients with no brain-damage, and an absence of discrepancies found in children with demonstrable brain-damage. Field (1960) has provided tables whereby the significance of any given verbal-performance discrepancy may be calculated according to its frequency in the general population. Among children aged $10\frac{1}{2}$ years, 25% have discrepancies of 13·8 or greater and 10% obtain discrepancies of 19·7 or more.

Neither Norris (1960) nor Rowley (1961) could confirm the validity of this index. The explanation given for the allegedly poor performance ability of brain-damaged children is that they suffer from a visuo-spatial defect. Norris used Maxwell's (1959) W.I.S.C. "factor scores", on the assumption that a "purer" visuo-spatial measure should give better discrimination. An analysis of the records of 198 children referred to a psychiatric hospital demonstrated that the "verbal minus performance" index did not differentiate brain-damaged from non-brain-damaged patients.

Heller (1963) studied the broader diagnostic implications of abnormal discrepancies by an analysis of the Wechsler Scale records of 1268 patients (564 adults, 704 children) at the same hospital. He tested the hypothesis that among a population with putative mental illness, individuals who have a wide variation in their intellectual abilities would be found in a greater proportion than occurs in the general population. The incidence of discrepancies of any given size was found to be very similar to that which is found in the normal population. The correlation between verbal and performance IQ's in the sample of "psychiatric" children was not significantly different from that of the normal population. Had there been any substance to the hypothesis, the correlation would have been lower than normally occurs.

By an analysis of the pattern or scatter of subtest scores on tests like the Stanford-Binet Test (Hoakley and Frazeur, 1945); the Cattell Infant Intelligence Scale (Kralovich, 1959) and W.I.S.C., it is thought to be possible to discern a typical profile of subtest scores, diagnostic signs which are pathognomonic of brain-damage.

An extensive literature (e.g., Beck and Lam, 1955; Rowley, 1961) has demonstrated, theoretically and empirically, the difficulties inherent in the diagnostic use of subtests. Their reliability coefficients (where published) are seldom high enough to bear the weight of diagnosis. The factorial composition of subtests is often not fully understood, or its implications for diagnosis, viz., the changing factorial composition of subtests for different age groups not appreciated. A complicating factor in assessing the significance of subtest deviations in brain-damaged subjects, is the demonstration of greater dispersions of test scores in neurotic children than in normal controls (Maxwell, 1961) and the apparent sensitivity of certain subtests said to be pathognomonic of brain damage (e.g., block designs) to psychopathology (Caputo et al., 1962; Frost, 1960).

McFie (1961) after reviewing the literature on the relationship between lateralization of brain-injury and test results, also comes to the conclusion that there is no support for the "verbal minus performance" formula of brain-damage. He states that in children, there is evidence of a striking difference between the intellectual effects of localized cerebral lesions sustained in the first year of life and those sustained later. In cases of unilateral injury after one year of age, the impairment appears to approximate to the conventional adult pattern—of verbal deficit with left, and performance deficit with right, hemisphere lesions.

Annett et al. (1961) also found patterns of impairment in brain-injured children which were similar to those found in studies of adults with unilateral lesions and EEG foci. The children with unilateral EEG foci contralateral to the preferred hand, were poor on tests involving language. Their ability to define words was particularly weak, but they were not notably impaired on non-language tests. The children with foci ipsilateral to the preferred hand showed severe deficits on a number of tasks which involve the reordering of visually perceived material in new spatial relationships (e.g., Picture Arrangement, Block Design, Object Assembly and Coding). Their arithmetic was also poor; but vocabulary was similar to that of the control group. Wedell (1960) showed that visual perceptual disability is more common in cerebral palsied children with left than with right hemiplegia.

McFie (1961) was impressed by the trend (a statistically significant level was not reached) of subtest scores obtained by brain-damaged children in his study. They parallel, in general, the pattern found in adults, viz., Digit Span and Similarities subtest deficits associated with left hemisphere involvement; Picture Arrangement and Block Design deficits associated with right hemisphere involvement. There were no mean deficits on Picture Completion with lesions in either hemisphere. The considerable mean deficit on the Vocabulary test with lesions in either hemisphere is altogether different from McFie's (1960) findings in adults, which showed no mean deficit on this test with lesions in any location. The failure of vocabulary to "hold up" in this and other studies, should induce caution in assessing the validity of applying the Hunt-Minnesota Test for Organic Brain-Damage (Hunt, 1943) to children between the ages of ten and sixteen, as is done by Avakian (1961).

In recent years two tests of language ability have been developed on the basis of Osgood's theory of linguistic behaviour: The Illinois Test of Psycholinguistic Abilities (I.T.P.A.) (Kirk and McCarthy, 1962) and the Differential Language Facility Test (D.L.F.T.) (Sievers, 1959).

Sievers (1959) found differences in performance on the D.L.F.T. between non-brain-damaged retarded children, brain-damaged retarded children and normals. The normals tended to be superior to the brain-injured group in overall language ability, and this appeared to increase with mental age. They were also more successful than the other groups on subtests requiring expression without semantic meaning. The non-brain-injured children performed better than the brain-injured children on subtests involving the making of semantic connections between visual objects. Furthermore, differences in performance were found within a brain-damaged sample when it was subdivided into groups according to E.E.G. tracings (Sievers and Rosenberg, 1961). The authors state that this finding adds to the evidence that brain-injured children are not a homogeneous group.

The authors of the I.T.P.A. (Kirk and McCarthy, 1962) make it explicit that their test (consisting of nine subtests which were standardized on 700 children between the ages of $2\frac{1}{2}$ and 9) is not presented as an instrument of classification, i.e., for the purpose of labelling a child as belonging to a particular group, type, or category, but as an instrument which assesses a child in such a way that an educational or remedial programme can be initiated. The test describes deficits in various psycholinguistic functions found particularly among cerebral palsied, brain-injured and some emotionally disturbed children.

## Theoretical Criticisms

It is common practice to use the diagnostic tests to make a dichotomous classification of "brain-damaged" versus "non-brain-damaged" children. Assuming that there was in existence a test which could do this reliably, how much would it contribute to the task of making a diagnosis? The value of diagnosis lies in its descriptive functions, and its implications for aetiology, treatment and prognosis. A label without implications would be pointless.

Meyer (1957) demonstrates however, in his review of the literature, that the concept of brain-damage as the sole factor in differentiating brain-injured from non-brain-injured groups is meaningless from both the practical and theoretical point of view. It does not elucidate particular signs and symptoms, but implies the homogeneity of patients who present a variety of cerebral pathologies which differ in type and localization, aetiology and prognosis, and result in a variety of neurological and psychological signs. He concludes that if brain pathology *per se* is not a qualitatively differentiating factor, then there is no point in attempting to measure its presence or absence alone. He says, "Although the discovery of a lesion and its locus has important bearings on prognostic and diagnostic implications, in itself it does not make progress towards explaining the appearance of symptoms or the neurological mechanisms responsible for such behaviour . . . Instead one should aim at measuring its amount and correlate it with other factors which may contribute to the appearance of symptoms."

Meyer deals mainly with the problems of applying the concept of brain-damage to adults. If anything, the picture is more obscure in the case of brain function in children, complicated as it is by developmental factors. There is evidence that the less differentiated structure of the child's brain results in a more diffuse impairment of intellect than is usual in brain-damaged adults. Despite this relative plasticity of the child's brain, there is also evidence that psychological deficits have some relationships to the locus of the injury. Extreme "field" or "localization" theories of brain function are unwarranted. So is the assumption that any demonstrable brain lesion necessarily results in discoverable clinical symptoms. When factors such as age, previous personality, environmental background, locus and type of injury, are known to be important determinants of the effects of cerebral insults, the common emphasis on brain pathology as the sole independent variable producing symptoms is seen to be unacceptable.

Thus it is not surprising that investigations of variously defined samples of "brain-damaged" or "exogenous" children should report contradictory findings. Yates (1954) points out that when random groups of brain-damaged patients are given a test, the results nearly always fall into an abnormal, skewed distribution. Many of the brain-injured group respond like normal or psychiatric controls, while others obtain abnormal scores. This may account for the significant differences between groups reported in some studies.

It would seem then that the unqualified use of the term "brain-damage" in a diagnostic psychological report on a child is a gross over-simplification. The difficulty of establishing criteria for brain-injury in children is not confined to psychology. In medicine, it is complicated by the subjective nature of neurological examination, and by problems of reliability and validity in E.E.G. interpretation. Pond (1961) states that on the basis of his findings there are no absolutely unequivocal clinical signs, physiological tests, or psychological tests that can prove a relationship between brain-damage and any particular aspect of disturbed behaviour. Most of the psychological tests are derived empirically on the basis of criterion brain-damaged groups, diagnosed as such by the neurologist. Thus the validity of these tests cannot be higher than the independent neurological validity— itself imperfect. A review of the available tests makes it clear that there is no satisfactorily valid and reliable psychological diagnostic test of child-hood brain-injury. A study by Schulman et al. (1965) establishes this fairly conclusively. Their study set out to answer three central problems: (1) to what extent do eight so-called indices of brain-injury (derived from the Draw-A-Person Test, the B.G. Test, the Wechsler Intelligence Scale for Children, E.E.G. records, and a neurological examination) co-vary? (2) To what extent do the behavioural measures (hyperactivity, distractibility, inconsistency, and emotional liability) included in the "brain-damage behaviour syndrome" co-vary? (3) To what extent do the diagnostic measures, singly or in groups, predict the presence of these behavioural variables? The analysis was based upon results of all these tests obtained from a group of 35 undifferentiated, retarded boys—relatively homo-geneous in terms of age and educability. Criticisms of the design of the experiment arise mainly from the restricted and homogeneous nature of the sample, a fact likely to reduce the size of the correlation coefficients. A four-point "scale" which was used to judge the presence or absence or degree of brain-damage in relation to all eight measures is also open to criticism, because of its arbitrariness and the loss of data caused by its application. Allowing for these reservations, the findings of the study remain (in the words of the authors) "rather disquieting"; and this is perhaps an understatement in view of the continuing popularity of these diagnostic techniques. (1) The individual diagnostic measures did not reach an acceptable level of reliability, and did not co-vary significantly. (2) Nor was there any evidence to support the concept of a syndrome of brain-damaged behaviours, as the variables involved did not co-vary. (3) Only one set of behaviours correlated significantly with both the diagnostic clusters which were found, and that correlation was in the wrong direction. On the basis of this evidence, and in terms of the indices used in this r^search, the construct of brain-damage—considered as a single entity— seems nonsensical.

Those who believe that it is more constructive for psychologists to develop and apply tests which describe and measure the functional deficits manifested by brain-injured patients, rather than searching for inclusive "diagnostic" tests of "brain-damage", will agree with the conclusions of Cruickshank et al. (1961). In a monograph describing an extensive experiment in special educational techniques with brain-injured and hyperactive children, they state that neurological diagnosis in itself can rarely be translated into a dynamic educational or rehabilation programme, whereas careful psychological assessment can.

# 4. Reaction Tendencies of the Nervous System and Problem Behaviour

THERE ARE several sensory typologies in existence which are based upon the assumption that children (and adults) vary in the characteristic "reactivity" of their central nervous pathways. These theoretical groupings of what are sometimes known as "reaction tendencies" of the central nervous system, have been formulated to account for the stable interpersonal variation in the sensory responses of individuals to given stimulus intensities. They are thought to have important implications for the development of psychopathology (Herbert and Kemp, 1969). The differentiation of nervous systems into "strong" and "weak", i.e., into opposite poles of a continuum of "intensity of the excitatory process", provides one such typology.

The brilliant work done by Pavlov and his colleagues on conditioned reflexes, led to the original formulation of the concept of strength. Pavlov was of the opinion that since man's behaviour, as well as that of higher animals, is determined and controlled by the nervous system, the "truly boundless variety" of his behaviour and personality characteristics could be reduced to a limited number of "basic properties of the nervous system". The foremost of these, he believed, is the "strength of the basic nervous processes—excitatory and inhibitory—which always constitute the sum total of nervous activity . . ." (Pavlov, 1957).

Pavlov's terminology, containing as it does neurological concepts which are not confirmed by contemporary neurophysiological research, can be confusing. The ambiguities are less serious if concepts such as excitation and inhibition are thought of as intervening variables. The operational basis of the concepts involved in his theory are purely behavioural, and the neural entities are of a hypothetical nature. As Gray (1964) points out, they are designed to make sense of the relationships which have been found to exist between various kinds of stimulation and various kinds of response.

Pavlov (op. cit.) advanced the studies of inhibition by his demonstrations that it is an active process, not just the absence of excitation. This internally acquired inhibition contributes to the delicacy and efficiency of the resolving power of the brain—its analytical power. Using "conditioning" techniques and differential reinforcement, a dog can be made to distinguish a circle from an ellipse (see page 94), 100 metronome beats per min. from 96, and a tone of 500 vibrations per s from a tone of 498 vibrations (Pavlov, 1927). According to Pavlov, inhibition is not only an important coordinating factor in the activity of the brain—singling out important signals from a multitude of stimuli that are either of no consequence to the individual or which have lost their signalling value, but it also plays another, no less important, role—protecting the highly reactive and vulnerable cortical cells when their normal condition and activity are impaired, or when they are in danger from disease or injury. Pavlov demonstrated this protective type of inhibition in the laboratory. If a dog was conditioned to salivate at the sound of a bell, by pairing the sound of the bell with the feeding of the animal, the amount of salivation would be proportional, within limits, to variations in the intensity of the sound. But when the sound of the bell became particularly intense, the conditioned reflex—salivation—would begin to decrease and perhaps cease altogether. In Pavlovian theory this observation was incorporated into the "law of strength" which states that response magnitude increases with increasing stimulus intensity up to a limiting value, beyond which further increments in stimulus intensity result in a fall in response magnitude. The stimulus appears to have become excessive (i.e., beyond the threshold of tolerance of the nervous system) and there is a danger of over-excitation of the nerve cells. It was hypothesized that when nerve cells are exposed to prolonged or intense stimulation, they cease to react or transmit information. Such a state of inactivity was termed "transmarginal" (in Russian, literally "beyond the limit") or "protective" inhibition.

This phenomenon leads us to Pavlov's definition of "strength of the nervous system" as "the working capacity of the cells of the hemispheres". What he had in mind was the capacity of the nervous system to respond appropriately to stimulation which is extreme either in its duration or its intensity without (a) passing into a state of transmarginal inhibition, or (b) breaking the law of strength—i.e., the law of proportionality between the intensity of stimulation and amplitude of response. To put it another way, the greater the level of intensity of stimulation up to which an increment in stimulus intensity evokes a corresponding increase in intensity of response, the greater is the strength of the nervous system. That level of stimulus intensity at which rises in the intensity of stimulation result not in an increase but in a decrement of response-amplitude, is referred to as "the threshold of transmarginal or protective inhibition". This threshold provides the main index of strength; those whose threshold is relatively high are "strong nervous system types", those who have low thresholds are of the "weak nervous system type".

## Dependability and Sensitivity of Nervous Functioning

A major strand of modern Russian research concerns these basic properties of excitation and inhibition; it is psychological in its technology rather than neurophysiological or clinical. During the last decade the group of psychologists, originally under the direction of Professor Teplov, extended Pavlov's theory of the physiological basis of personality so that it might be applied to humans (Teplov, 1956, 1964). Early on they faced the serious problem of how to measure strength in human subjects. In his typological theorizing (as we have seen) Pavlov defined strength of the nervous system in terms of the working capacity of the cortical cells. This involved subjecting the experimental animal to protracted and concentrated excitation so as to determine the stage at which the system passed into an inhibitory state. Strength of the nervous system as conceived by Pavlov had its referents in conditioning behaviour and in such indices as speed of formation of conditioned reflexes, the magnitude of such reflexes, and the speed of their extinction—with or without reinforcement.

A detailed account of some of the techniques evolved to translate the experimental measures into human terms is given in Gray (1964). Suffice it to say that the Russian psychologists measure special conditioned reflexes (e.g., the photochemical reflex), reaction times, discrimination skills, and visual and auditory thresholds. They test the stability of these responses while subjecting the individual's nervous system to such stresses as fatigue or distraction. It is postulated, in accordance with the law of strength, that the individual with a "strong" nervous system, i.e., a tendency for the protective inhibition to "stand off", should not show a fall-off in response in the face of long or severe excitation, while the "weak" individuals would be expected to manifest a decrement in response because inhibition "cuts in" early to protect the system.

## Reaction Tendencies of the Brain and Individual Differences

On the basis of extensive experiments, Teplov and his co-workers took the concept of strength a stage further. Their evidence (e.g., Nebylitsyn, 1960), led them to suggest that individuals vary idiosyncratically in their processing of stimulation, that is, in the amount of sensory response that is elicited by a particular level of stimulus energy. At one extreme of the dimension "strength of the nervous system", the individuals with strong nervous systems, on a wide variety of measures, do in fact withstand extreme intensities of stimulation, continuing to respond appropriately and without decrement, while those at the other extreme with weak nervous systems do the opposite. There is an interesting relationship between this quality of strength and sensitivity. The strong individuals manage to resist levels of sensory stress only at the expense of their sensitivity at lower levels of intensity. Their reactivity, in terms of their central nerve pathways, is less than that of their weak counterparts; their nervous systems act as if they damp down stimulation. The weak nervous system subjects on the other hand, act as if they amplify stimulation, are highly reactive and therefore more sensitive to the environment at low levels of intensity but more susceptible to overwork (*vide*: Gray op. cit.) This inverse relationship between strength and reactivity means that "efficiency" depends upon what end of the work dimension one is considering (see Fig. 1).

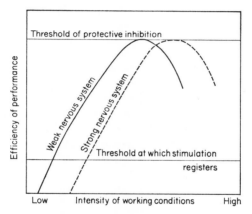

Fig. 1. Strong nervous systems can continue to work at higher stimulus intensities than weak nervous systems, but are less responsive to low intensity stimuli. Individuals vary a great deal in the stimulus conditions which give optimum performance under stress.

The high reactivity of the weak nervous system allows it to respond at full speed at a point where for the strong, but less excitable, nervous system the level of stimulation is not yet fully effective. Owing to its heightened reactivity, it is impelled into action by relatively weak stimuli. The implications of this might be that weak nervous system people, with their excellent perceptual and resolving skills, might be best on tasks requiring fine and detailed visual or auditory discrimination, where distractions are minimal. Being susceptible to stress, their superior efficiency is lost in situations which require prolonged vigilance, say, or steady concentration in the face of intense distraction. Here the strong individual comes into his own. There are many real-life situations where these individual differences may become critical: piloting a plane, observing radar displays, operating complex machinery, and so on.

There is a compelling similarity in the descriptions given by the Russians of these "idling properties" of the nervous system, elicited as they are in a Pavlovian framework, to typologies produced in quite different methodological contexts. Reason (1968) using a variety of different measures including the spiral after-effect, in his study of motion sickness, found clear-cut differences in "receptivity", i.e., characteristic variations in the way individuals transduce stimulus intensity. He was able to identify stable differences in receptivity with "receptives" at one extreme and "non-receptives" at the other. A neural basis was postulated for this dimension, and Reason states that the data suggest a close resemblance between weak nervous system types and "receptives". His receptive group, incidentally, was more susceptible to motion sickness than non-receptives.

Petrie (1967) describes three perceptual types on the basis of their sensitivity to painful stimulation and their tolerance of perceptual isolation. The group she calls "augmenters" seem akin to the weak type. Because of their automatic tendency to amplify sensory input, they are more intolerant of painful stimulation. On the other hand, they tolerate confinement and isolation relatively well. Her "moderates" do not show extreme reactions, whereas the "reducers" show notable tolerance of pain, but relative intolerance of reduced sensory situations.

The high tolerance of isolation and low tolerance of pain of the augmenters are found to be characteristics of introverts as opposed to extraverts, as described by Eysenck (1967). His investigations demonstrate similarities, in terms of experimental indices involving measures of inhibition, between the dimension of strength and the dimension of extraversion. Eysenck urges caution (1967, p. 80) in assuming—at the descriptive level—such parallels, but admits that the findings suggest (1967, p. 242) the possibility of a rapprochement between the weak nervous system (as one pole of a continuum) and introversion, and the strong nervous system and extraversion. There is evidence, for example, that the greater generation of inhibition by the extravert has the same effect of "damping down" the sensory response to stimuli as that produced by the characteristically small excitatory process in the strong nervous system. There is some experimental evidence (Herbert, 1970) of a relationship—albeit complex—between these concepts. It is perhaps significant that in four typologies, defined by different behavioural indices and built upon somewhat different theoretical foundations, all share at least two important properties in common. They all imply some characteristic interpersonal variation in the processing of stimulus-intensity, and these sensory characteristics are central (cortical) rather than peripheral.

The reaction tendencies of the central nervous system are thought to have implications for personality development, and individual differences on a variety of vigilance and perceptual skills (Gray, 1964, 1967). Disorders of thought are related by some investigators (Pavlov, 1941) to defects in the basic properties of neural activity; and variability in susceptibility to fatigue, sensory deprivation, isolation and tolerance of pain has been explained in terms of inhibitory processes (Eysenck, 1967). The characteristics of a child's nervous system (Teplov, 1956) may provide answers at least to some of the puzzling individual differences in socialization and in susceptibility to mental illness, if theorists such as Eysenck and Teplov prove to be correct in their thinking. There certainly is evidence of individual differences in the sensory responses of babies to given stimulus intensities.

## Reactive Characteristics of the Child

Any nurse who has had the care of a nursery of newly born babies or any mother who has had several children so as to be able to compare her babies, knows that they differ markedly in their actions and reactions to the environment from birth. Not all theorists seem to be aware of these differences. Zigler and Child (1969) point out that interpretations of socialization in terms of social reinforcement have shared a common model of the child as an essentially passive organism under the control of a socializing agent who dispenses rewards and punishments. However, as Danziger (1971) puts it: "This preconception led to a neglect of those factors contributing to the course of socialization which are not under the control of external agents. Such factors include maturational processes which predetermine the sequence and structure of developmental stages, as well as hereditary and congenital conditions." Among the psychologically relevant functions for which clear individual differences have been demonstrated in early infancy are autonomic response patterns, social responsiveness, sleeping and feeding patterns, sensory thresholds, motility and perceptual responses (Thomas et al., 1963).

Thomas and his colleagues demonstrated in an intensive-longitudinal study of 136 New York children (Thomas et al., 1968) just how important inborn or constitutional aspects of personality—the temperamental qualities of the child—can be in the development of normal behaviour and emotional problems. The authors observe that over fifteen years or more of experience with children, they were increasingly convinced that environmental influences could not accommodate the range and variability in the course of development exhibited by individual children, nor explain the marked differences in children's responses to similar patterns of parental care. It can best be left to the authors to state the relevance of this concept of temperament to general clinical theory. It lies, as they put it:

... neither in its sole pertinence for behaviour disorders, nor in its displacement of other conceptualizations, but in the fact that it must be incorporated into any general theory of normal and aberrant behavioural development if the theory is to be complete. Existing theories emphasize motives and drive states, tactics of adaptation, environmental patterns of influence, and primary organic determinants. The central requirement that a concept of temperament makes of such generalizations is that they come increasingly to focus on the individual and on his uniqueness. In other words, it requires that we recognize that the same motive, the same adaptive tactic, or the same structure of objective environment will have different functional meaning in accordance with the temperamental style of the given child. Moreover, in such an individualization of the study of functional mechanisms in behaviour, temperament must be considered as an independent determining variable in itself, and not as an ad hoc modifier used to fill in the gaps left unexplained by other mechanisms (Thomas *et al.*, 1968).

The present study was designed to test under controlled conditions their clinical impressions. Nine characteristics of temperament were identified, three of which are described below. The following temperamental qualities have a good deal to do with the level of arousal of the infant:

(1) *Level of Sensory Threshold:* Some babies have what is termed a "high sensory threshold". Their mothers report that they are fortunate because they can have a houseful of visitors without worrying at all about awakening the baby. Babies with a high "sensory threshold" do not startle at loud noises; bright lights don't bother them. Whether clothes are smooth or rough, wool or cotton, hot or cold, makes little difference. They are not particularly discriminating about food. Their mothers can easily disguise something the baby doesn't like by adding it to something "good". They do not react to being wet or soiled.

At the other extreme are "low threshold" babies who cry the moment they soil. There are sensitive ones who, even in the first weeks, wake up when a light is turned on in the room or a door latch clicks. Some literally shudder at even a whiff of a disliked food. A slight sound will attract their attention, and their eyes will move toward it. (One mother could always tell when her husband was home, because her six-month-old could hear his footsteps in the hall outside the apartment and would start to coo and kick). Response to pain varies. (One baby could bang his head hard against the crib bars without a whimper. For another a slight bump would bring howls of discomfort).

(2) *Intensity of Response:* One baby lets his mother know he is hungry with a loud, piercing cry. Another baby cries softly. These two examples show the range of intensity of the children's reactions. Both children are crying, but one is doing so with a considerably greater expenditure of energy than the other. When a behaviour is characterized by a high level

of energy expenditure, it is judged as intense. When the energy expenditure is low, the response is considered mild. One baby may open his mouth for a second spoonful of food he likes without any other movements. This is a response of mild intensity. On another occasion he might open his mouth, turn toward the dish, and strain actively toward the spoon with his whole body. Such a response is one of high intensity. The child of preponderantly low intensity smiles gently, but his more vigorous companion chortles, gurgles, and kicks when he is happy.

The intensity of response does not relate to whether the child is showing positive or negative mood. It refers to the energy expressed in his behaviour.

(3) *Activity Level:* Some babies are much more active from early infancy onward than other infants. Even in the period toward the end of feeding, when most babies are quiet and sleepy, they move their arms, lift their heads, kick, or—if they are on their backs—move their whole bodies till the covers are off. This goes on right up to the moment their eyes shut. Even when asleep they frequently move from spot to spot in the crib. Their mothers can never turn away for a moment when their babies are high up on, say, the bed, for fear they will squirm off.

In contrast, the quiet babies tend to lie where they are placed and move both little and slowly. Sometimes they are almost as still when awake as when asleep. Often only their eyes move.

## Arousal Theories

Gray (op. cit.) has re-interpreted the dimension "strength" as a dimension of "arousability". It is suggested that the weak individual is more highly aroused than the strong individual, when both are exposed to objectively identical physical stimulation. Several aspects of behaviour are determined by the level of arousal in the individual—the intensity with which behaviour occurs, the level of alertness, his efficiency of learning and his efficiency of performance. Gray says of this re-interpretation that:

> . . . it may be taken on a purely behavioural level, using the kind of theoretical framework developed by such workers as Duffy (1962) and Freeman (1948). Alternatively, we may give the notion of arousal level a physiological substrate by supposing that it is dependent on the degree to which the cerebral cortex is bombarded by impulses from the non-specific reticular activating system* (Gray, op. cit.).

The various strands come very close together when we note, as Gray has noted, the suggestions (Eysenck, 1967; Claridge, 1967; Corcoran, 1961) that the dimension of extraversion-introversion may be partially, or wholly, dependent on differences in arousability.

* The reticular activating system (RAS.) See: Magoun, 1963.

## Extraversion–Introversion

Eysenck (1960b, 1967) considers extraversion and introversion definable in terms of interrelationships between various primary traits such as sociability, impulsiveness, rathymia, ascendance, activity, etc. In general the extravert tends to be outgoing, sociable, impulsive, hedonistic, and of higher intra-personality variability, whilst the introvert tends to be more socially withdrawn, less impulsive, less hedonistic, and less variable in his behaviour than the extravert. Behavioural studies have shown the following characteristics to distinguish extraverts and introverts:

TABLE IV (adapted from Eysenck, 1960a).

|  | Introversion | Extraversion |
| --- | --- | --- |
| Neurotic syndrome | Dysthymia | Hysteria: Psychopathy |
| Body build | Leptomorph | Eurymorph |
| Intellectual function | Low IQ/Vocabulary ratio | High IQ/Vocabulary ratio |
| Perceptual rigidity | High | Low |
| Persistence | High | Low |
| Speed | Low | High |
| Speed/Accuracy ratio | Low | High |
| Level of aspiration | High | Low |
| Intrapersonal variability | Low | High |
| Sense of humour | Cognitive | Orectic |
| Sociability | Low | High |
| Repression | Weak | Strong |
| Social Attitudes | Tender-minded | Tough-minded |
| Rorschach Test | M% High | D High |
| T.A.T. | Low productivity | High productivity |
| Conditioning | Quick | Slow |
| Reminiscence | Low | High |
| Figural after-effects | Small | Large |
| Stress reactions | Overactive | Inert |
| Sedation threshold | High | Low |
| Perceptual constancy | Low | High |

It can be seen that the attributes which distinguish introverts and extraverts are very diverse. Eysenck has sought a common basis for this behavioural diversity in the balance of cortical excitation (or arousal) and the balance of autonomic nervous system (ANS) functioning in introverts and extraverts (see Fig. 2).

It is tempting to link the imbalances between "central inhibition" and "central excitation" which are postulated in introversion–extraversion, with imbalances in the suppressor and facilitatory functions of the reticular formation of the brain. It is postulated that in the extravert there is a tendency toward the predominance of the suppressor elements of the

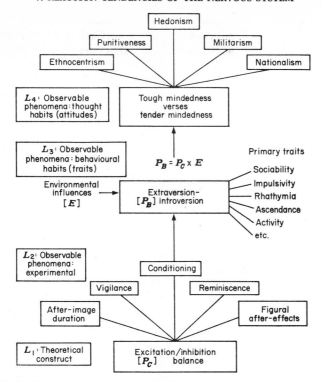

FIG. 2. Relationship between genotype and phenotype in extraversion–introversion (Adapted from Eysenck 1967).

reticular formation, whereas in the introvert there is a tendency for the facilitatory portions to predominate. In other words we might expect the development of an imbalance between the two portions (facilitatory and suppressor) of the reticular formation, in one or other direction, to be a feature influencing the appearance of extravert or introvert patterns of behaviour.

Such a tendency towards imbalance might originate outside the reticular formation and involve the interrelationship between the autonomic nervous system and central nervous system. Such speculations are inviting because of the wealth of behaviourally based evidence. Work on reminiscence, figural after-effects, conditioning and learning tend to support the excitation–inhibition hypothesis as does research tending to show the "extraverting" effect of general CNS depressants. The autonomic differences—an autonomic imbalance—between introverts and extraverts, the overactive stress responses of the former compared with the latter, the tendency of the neurotic reactions of the introvert to involve sympathetic nervous system overactivity, and the "introverting" effect of stimulant drugs, all tend to support the idea of cortical and autonomic imbalance as the neurophysiological basis of this personality dimension. Eysenck (1967) discusses these possibilities and the status of the various strands of evidence (some of which have been outlined above) in his book "The Biological Basis of Personality".

### Neuroticism

Among the factors which are thought to predispose a child to develop one sort of psychological problem rather than another are the possession of combinations of the personality characteristics extraversion–introversion (already discussed in some detail) and another dimension (mentioned only briefly so far) called neuroticism, emotionality or instability. What of the latter dimension?

The child who has a high degree of this attribute is often referred to as being "nervous", "timid", "emotional" or "highly strung", because his emotions seem to be so labile, so volatile. It has been demonstrated by experimental investigation that the emotional person displays a variety of related traits (see: Eysenck, 1957). He tends to be anxious, worried, unhappy, egocentric, quickly and easily aroused. Such traits set him apart from the "calm" individual. But we must remember that it is all a matter of degree, *not* an absolute distinction. The calm person tends to be persistent, steadfast, carefree, hopeful and contented.

The child who shows intense emotionality and anxiety is susceptible to neurotic breakdown. Such a vulnerability implies a low tolerance for stress, whether it be physical as in painful situations, or psychological as in conflict or frustration situations. There is some evidence that highly strung, overreactive attributes are in part the consequence of inherited factors (Eysenck and Prell, 1951).

### Neuroticism and the ANS

Mention has been made of the postulated relationship between ANS imbalance and introversion–extraversion. This system is thought to be vital in defining the degree of neuroticism shown by the individual. The control system—a network of motor nerve cells—plays a large part, not only in maintaining the individual's day-to-day "vegetative" functions (his internal homeostasis) but it also operates to change the economy of the body when the person is faced with stress.

The maintenance of the internal environment is largely the responsibility of the glands, blood vessels, smooth muscles, and heart muscle. The activities of these effectors are controlled by the ANS; the sympathetic division of the ANS acts to adjust the body to states of alarm or emergency, i.e., when the individual is highly emotional. It has, among others, the following effects:

(a) It increases the heart rate.
(b) It increases the blood pressure.
(c) It distributes blood to the exterior muscles.

Broadly speaking the sympathetic division accelerates those bodily processes concerned with the mobilization and/or expenditure of energy.

The parasympathetic division of the ANS tends to predominate when the individual is calm and relaxed. It does many things which, taken together, build up and conserve the body's stores of energy.

(a) It decreases heart rate.
(b) It reduces blood pressure.
(c) It diverts blood to the digestive tract.

In times of emergency the sympathetic division predominates. The effects are analogous to the priorities typical of a national wartime economy. In emergency situations some functions are more vital than others to survival. Digestion can cease, for example, while the supply of blood is increased to muscles, for if the animal does not survive by means of flight or defence, it will make little difference (in emergency situations) whether the last meal is digested. On the other hand the muscles are toned up for maximum performance.

Disturbance of these functions sometimes causes pathological conditions such as psychosomatic illnesses. Those individuals who are high on the dimension of personality referred to earlier as "neuroticism", are thought to have inherited an excessively reactive ANS, one that is biased toward sympathetic predominance.

The integrating processes which regulate the balance between the two divisions of the autonomic nervous system are located in the master control system—the brain.

## The Autonomic Nervous System and RAS

Eysenck (1967) has discussed some of the possible neural mechanisms underlying emotional activation and cortical arousal, and their relationship. Eysenck hypothesizes that:

... cortical arousal can be produced along two quite distinct and separate pathways. It can be produced by sensory stimulation or by problem-solving activity of the brain, without necessarily involving the visceral brain at all; in this case we have no autonomic arousal, but possibly quite high cortical arousal. A scientist sitting quite immobile and to all appearances asleep, but thinking profoundly about some professional problems, might illustrate this state of affairs; there is considerable cortical arousal but little autonomic activity ...

Cortical arousal can also be produced by emotion, in which case the reticular formation is involved through the ascending and descending pathways connecting it with the hypothalamus. In this case we have both autonomic arousal and cortical arousal. The fact that cortical arousal is concerned in both types of loops does not mean that these loops are identical, and it certainly is dangerous to assume, as Duffy and many others have done, that indices of cortical arousal can be used as measures of emotional involvement. It might be true to say that emotional arousal can be indexed in terms of cortical arousal, but this proposition cannot be inverted; cortical arousal can take place without any marked degree of autonomic–emotional arousal.

Eysenck contends that there is some degree of partial independence between autonomic activation and cortical arousal, and he finds parallels between the parameters which define neuroticism and extraversion–introversion respectively and those which demarcate the two categories of arousal.

## Personality and Problem Behaviour

There is evidence (Collins *et al.*, 1962; Quay, 1968) to show that the introverted neurotic child (the child with very marked introversion and neuroticism) tends to manifest the so-called "personality" problems.* This child tends to be depressed, seclusive, absent-minded, irritable, to have daydreams, inferiority feelings, mood swings and mental conflict. The extraverted neurotic child (the child with very marked extraversion and neuroticism) tends to produce the "conduct" problems; he is described as egocentric, rude, violent, disobedient, destructive; he has temper tantrums, and is given to fighting, stealing and truanting. This distinction is manifested in girls as well as boys, and it does so at various ages.

These findings have their parallel in studies of adult psychopathology. According to Eysenck's typological postulate (Eysenck, 1957) persons with strong "excitatory" potentials and weak "inhibitory" potentials will tend to develop introverted personality traits, and dysthymic disorders if subject to neurotic breakdown; persons with weak "excitatory" potentials and strong "inhibitory" potentials will tend to develop extraverted personality traits, and hysteric and psychopathic symptoms if subjected to neurotic breakdown.

* The causal links are elaborated later—on page 203.

# Part III

## Infancy
*From birth to approximately eighteen months*

# Introduction: Psychosocial Developments

WHEN HUMAN development is viewed in terms of the accomplishment of certain crucial socialization tasks, it is necessary to define the social, emotional and physical demands which the child has to cope with and master. Various theorists stress different tasks. Erikson (1965), taking a broad view, proposes that the essential task of infancy is the development of a basic trust in others. He believes that during the early months and years of life a baby learns whether the world is a good and satisfying place to live in or a source of pain, misery, frustration and uncertainty. Because the human infant is so totally dependent for so long, he needs to know that he can depend on the outside world. If his basic needs are met by the world he inhabits, he is thought to develop a "basic trust" in the world, and thus to evolve a nucleus of self-trust, which is indispensable to his later development. But how does trust show itself in behavioural terms at this early stage of life? According to Lowe (1972) it is demonstrated in the ease with which the baby feeds, in the depth of his sleep, and in the relaxation of his bowels. Later on it is shown when the infant will let his mother out of his sight without undue anxiety or rage. The baby who smiles easily is also thought to demonstrate trust in Erikson's sense.

If a major task to be achieved during infancy is the internalization of a sense of trust (derived from parental affection and the prompt satisfaction of needs), mistrust and a sense of insecurity are the emotional problems which potentially have their origins in the neglect of the child's needs during this phase of life. If parents are neglectful, he may see his world not as a manageable and benign place, but as threatening and insecure. The contrasting attitudes of trust and mistrust are very like the adult attitudes of optimism and pessimism; they colour his entire outlook on life and, indeed, his personality. A lasting sense of security or insecurity, self-confidence or inadequacy—as well as many other social and self-attitudes of vital importance for positive mental health—are thus, in this view, laid down in the early months and years. Assertions of this kind (as we shall see in Chapter 5) are difficult to prove or disprove, although they have considerable face-validity and are articles of faith for many clinicians.

Freud (1939) puts forward a somewhat similar "sensitive period" theory regarding the early and long-term antecedents of attributes such as optimism, pessimism and narcissism. He described certain character traits which are thought to be associated with either too great frustration or overly indulged gratification at each of three psychosexual stages of development: the oral, anal and phallic stages. Freud postulated, as the basis of this theory, that certain sensitive parts of the body (the mouth, anus and genitalia) become the centre of excitation and pleasure. Only the first stage of psychosexual development—the oral stage—concerns us at present. In the new-born child the mouth is the primary organ of pleasure (and Freud defined early sexual arousal very broadly as *sensuous* pleasure); it is through the mouth that he makes contact with his first object of desire —the mother's breast. Babies indulge in a great deal of non-nutritional sucking and the fingers and thumb are sometimes used as sources of gratification, or to put it in psychoanalytic terms, as substitutes for the nipple. That an interest in the mouth region is never entirely superseded is evidenced by the pleasure taken by adults in eating, smoking, kissing and the more overtly sexual acts performed with the mouth. Certain children, depending on how they are weaned and toilet trained, and how their sexual curiosity is dealt with, can become fixated at one or other of these developmental stages. The resultant oral, anal or phallic erotism, as it is called, may be repressed and emerges as character traits in adult life. According to this view, personality characteristics depend to an important extent on whether pre-genital erotism was expressed directly or repressed in infancy. Depending on the resolution of the "oral" stage of psychosexual development the infant might grow up to become:

(a) the sort of optimistic, immature individual who has the feeling that he was born with a silver spoon in his mouth. His orality is postulated to be associated with dependent attitudes and a need for nurturance which could persist even into adult life. If the child does not successfully negotiate this stage of development, he longs to continue to shelter under the comfortable and protective umbrella of care and security provided by his parents. He represents what is called the "sucking" or the "passive oral erotic" type of personality.

(b) The "biting" or "oral-sadistic" type of individual whose basic outlook is one of pessimism and the anticipation of malice. Like the oral-passive type, he feels that the world owes him a living, but unlike the passive type, he anticipates that he will not get it. He is likely to be acidulous and sarcastic in conversation, if not actively sadistic in his treatment of others.

There are basically two sets of hypotheses here: (1) that there exist certain personality constellations, (2) that these syndromes are related to child-rearing procedures and oral erotism. Psychosexual hypotheses belong to those parts of psychoanalytic theory that can be stated in a refutable form. As regards the first of these hypotheses there seems to be evidence that probably Freud's ideas are valid. The evidence for the link between these personality syndromes and child-rearing or pre-genital erotism is far less impressive. Here methodological problems undermine the validity of many studies (see: Kline, 1972; Lee and Herbert, 1970, for a review of the evidence).

Freud conceived of the baby at birth as pure "id"—a seething bundle of strivings which demand immediate gratification. This immediacy, this lack of a social or moral point of view in checking instincts, Freud called the "pleasure principle". Needless to say some of the baby's demands— as he gets older—clash with the sometimes harsh realities of his mother's needs, what she thinks is right, and eventually with what society thinks is the correct mode of behaving. In other words the "reality principle" comes into play, and out of the frustration caused by the collision of forces representing the reality and pleasure principles, there develops a rudimentary ego. According to psychoanalytic theory, the "ego" is the rational, reality-oriented component of personality. It is conceptualized as possessing a repertoire of defensive strategies (ego defence mechanisms), and the capacity for delay and detour so that it can search for id gratification while taking account of the demands of reality and of conscience (superego).

Theorists (see: Ausubel and Sullivan, 1970) usually place the emergence of the self-concept or ego between the ages of one and three; there is no apparent evidence in infants of any self awareness, whereas it is plainly discernible in the child of four or five. Until this age, there is good reason to think that the child's own perception of his personal identity is unstable. This can be observed by the ease with which the child depersonalizes himself in play and speech, and in the lack of clear definition he reveals (early on) with regard to his own body-image. A common view expressed in the literature on the development of self is that, in the early stages of life, the infant perceives only emotional significances. The baby cries from unlocalized discomfort. There seems to be only a vague global awareness of comfort or distress. It appears that he does not know that these experiences are "his". He does not yet conceive of himself as a person separate from other persons. Loevinger (1966) refers to the first phase of ego-development as the pre-social (or autistic) stage; it is inferred that the infant cannot at first distinguish between the animate and inanimate parts of the environment.

The role of the mother (and other important persons close at hand) by providing warmth, comfort and nurturance, and relief from discomfort, helps the child to discriminate the qualities of objects and the significance and separateness of others. The imposing of a routine on the chaos of the infant's early experiences, is of key importance in the process of self-awareness. Feelings which were previously undifferentiated, come to be associated with specific situations: the pleasures of mother, feeding and play, as opposed to the distress accompanying hunger, wetness and cold. Out of this cycle of "growing tension—active distress—arrival of omnipotent mother—relief—pleasure", and all its variations, develops gradually a sense of the identity of other people, of self, of time and place. The child develops an intense relationship to mother (or a surrogate). Loevinger (1966) designates this later phase of infant ego-development as symbiotic. The self is not distinguished clearly from his mother although she is eventually distinguished from the environment. That is to say she is recognized visually from about two months. Sullivan (1953) points out that the eventual development of language and the use of symbols are the most powerful cultural instrument in the child's evolution of self, his pursuit of self-esteem and security in his relationship with his fellows. Indeed, it is language which is the crucial factor (according to Loevinger) in bringing the autistic/symbiotic stage of ego-development to and end.*

Bowlby (1958) suggests that one of the most important developmental tasks of infancy is the acquisition of a bond of attachment between the child, his mother and other significant people in his environment. It is claimed that his physical and emotional survival hinge on the quality and quantity of the stimulation and interaction he receives. What constitutes "adequate" perceptual, emotional and social stimulation is not usually specified. What we do know—at a global level of analysis—is that maternal "warmth" is related to stimulating behaviour and affectionate interactions (Sears et al., 1957).

In terms of cognitive development, infancy coincides with what is called the period of "sensorimotor intelligence" (Piaget, 1954); it lasts until a child is somewhere between eighteen months and two years old. During this phase the child is a sensing–acting sort of creature as *initially* he makes only reflex, random, and diffuse mass reactions, and very little thought occurs. An analogy that has been used (see: Lazerson, 1971) is that of a low-level primitive computer which the infant has available to him. The thought and output of this computer are intuitive or emotional. The computer seems to combine and confuse messages from the internal, visceral environment with stimuli from the external environment, so that the

---

* Loevinger conceptualizes ego development in terms of stages. Each stage has its typical manifestations such as conscious preoccupations, character development, impulse controls and interpersonal relationships. These milestones for each stage are not thought to be monotonic functions of age. They increase to their peak and then diminish with growing maturity of the ego.

inside world is not clearly differentiated from the outside world. In general, the computer processes information in a crude, impressionistic way and is too crude to analyse experiences into conceptual categories. During this period, however, the foundations for thought are laid down. The child learns to identify the main features of the world about him. During these early months he seems to become intrigued (and delighted) with many discoveries and the mastery of such "simple" responses as picking up things, blowing, falling backwards on a cushion and making certain sounds. His intelligence is displayed in his actions. Piaget (1950) views intelligence as an aspect of the person's adaptation to his environment—adaptation being an individual's intellectual strivings, the mental actions ("operations") he performs in order to establish and find a state of equilibrium between himself and his surroundings. In his writings, the term intelligence has a very specific meaning, namely "the coordination of operation". At first (as we observed in connection with the self-concept) the infant has no knowledge that a world "out there" exists; he is only aware of his own feelings. Piaget (1954) called this state of affairs, in which the baby's world is centred upon himself without his being aware of himself at the centre, "egocentrism".

Piaget partitions intellectual development into stages or periods of growth on the route to adult thought. These are arbitrary divisions because development is a continuous process, but they provide a convenient way of seeing the nature of the changes in intelligence and thinking as they take place. The growth of intellect is measured by the increasing use of what he calls "accommodation", the ability to alter old strategies or make new ones to solve unfamiliar problems (Piaget, 1951). Flexibility of thinking is the key to Piaget's concept of intelligence.

Danziger (1971) observes that accommodation is one facet of a fundamental distinction between an individual and his environment. This relationship either takes the form of an *accommodation* (an alteration of the person's own activity in response to demands from the environment such as takes place in imitative behaviour) or *assimilation* (a modification of the environment to meet the individual's own purposes such as occurs in play). In the one case, the child adapts to environmental demands, in the other he superimposes his own wishes on the environment.

The Piagetian description of cognitive development in terms of the interplay of accommodatory and assimilatory processes is analogous (according to Danziger) to the interplay of "ego" and "alter" in personality development—namely, the achievement of a balance between the poles of recognizing and adapting to the needs of others and imposing self-centred demands on the social environment. An extreme lack of balance in reciprocity between self and others in either direction gives rise to unsatisfactory social relationships. As Danziger puts it: "In the one case, he overwhelms others with his demands, in the other case, he overwhelms himself by subjectively distorting and exaggerating the demands which others make on him. Quite commonly, of course, this lack of balance expresses itself in erratic swings from one extreme to the other" (Danziger, 1971).

As we shall see in this section (page 98) the model of the child as a *tabula rasa*, passively reacting to the environment, being conditioned, reinforced and so on, is very misleading. The infant is part of a mutually interacting parent–child system. He "reaches out", using his magnificent repertoire of grasping, smiles, cries, baby talk and the like, to shape his parent's behaviour. He is himself an agent of socialization and in Rheingold's telling phrase: "of men and women he makes fathers and mothers" (Rheingold, 1968). His temperament (Thomas *et al.*, 1968) age, sex and state (Moss, 1967), his cuddliness and his individual demandingness (Schaffer and Emerson, 1964a) all influence the mother; it is just these idiosyncratic features which cause her to change her methods from one of her babies to the next, or to adapt her style of mothering away from preconceived plans and theories she might have had about child-rearing. At the same time, of course, a child adapts to his mother's handling of him. Again, there is a balance in the mutual demands of parents and their offspring. Parents demand that the child should become increasingly self-sufficient and should conform to guidelines of socially appropriate behaviour.

Children demand parental support and they try to limit the restraints parents put upon their pleasures. The balance, therefore, is about a compromise between sometimes incompatible mutual demands, and about a style of life which maximizes the mutually rewarding possibilities of the mother–child relationship. This balance, if it is achieved, is done so over a long period of time. During infancy, the deference and attention shown by parents in a normal home to their helpless baby lead paradoxically (according to Ausubel and Sullivan (1970)) to feelings within himself of "omnipotence". This phase (beginning at roughly six months of age) is inferred from the rampant expressions of imperiousness and possessiveness so prevalent during the second half of infancy. These theorists believe that the infant's sense of adequacy or self-esteem depends upon his misinterpretation of his parents' subservience to his will and needs, as a result of which he exaggerates his volitional power and autonomy. He is in for a let down as he gets older and has to moderate his demands—except in the case of those mothers who do not allow their children to be emotionally weaned from them. Parents differ in the timing and the degree to which they encourage a transition of a baby from a totally "demanding" to a partly "demand-obeying" status. Danziger observes that many individuals never develop a strong commitment to the more abstract forms of reciprocity.

So much happens to the infant in our chosen time-span, he is so dramatically transformed in physical appearance and psychosocial skills from the somewhat amorphous neonate (that was) to a distinct personality of a year-and-a-half, that it seems naïve to treat infancy as a unified period. The justification for doing so is the absolute dependency of the human being during this time, and the implications this has in terms of the ability to enhance or disrupt development, which is in the power of his caretakers.

# 5. Origins of Problem Behaviour in Infancy

IN SEARCHING FOR predisposing influences in the development of problem behaviour, research workers have focused attention on the earliest period of the child's life within the family, when he *learns* his first lessons and enjoys (or suffers) so many novel experiences. As Milton puts it: "Childhood shows the man as morning shows the day". It is thought that childhood experiences are not ephemeral but influence later behaviour. The suggestion that adulthood may be viewed as the unfolding of qualities developed in childhood seems, on the face of it, reasonable enough. But this is not all; some theorists go beyond the so-called "continuity hypothesis". They suggest that the period of infancy has a special, in fact a qualitatively unique, significance for development. After all, the young are claimed to be more easily influenced than the mature. It is hypothesized that if certain environmental factors occur during this stage of life, they have an *overriding* influence on what subsequently takes place in his development—no matter what the later experiences. To mix the metaphors: it isn't just considered that "the child is father of the man" but it is also claimed that "as the twig is bent so inclines the bough"! The implication is that what is learned early in life is different from, and more important than, later learning.

Clarke (1968) observes, "most people have at least a sneaking regard to the view that . . . (early learning) . . . has a potent and disproportionate effect on later personality. Indeed those who testify to this thesis make strange bed-fellows—Freud, Watson, Ribble, Adler, Hebb, Ferguson, Klein, and Montessori are examples. While many consider that the first five years of life do have this potent effect, there is disagreement in ascribing to one period, or even to one type of learning or another, a particularly critical role."

There are three issues involved here: (i) whether there are critical periods during which the person is particularly susceptible to certain environmental experiences; (ii) whether there is an *overriding* influence of infantile experience over those of later life, in other words, a fixity about what happens during a particular phase of life—early childhood; and (iii) what the nature is of those environmental influences that do shape the person-to-be.

## Critical Periods

What is the evidence for the hypothesis that there are "critical" periods during a child's earliest years when he shows a heightened susceptibility to the effects of his environment and is therefore vulnerable (in, perhaps, an irreversible manner) to adverse experiences and learning situations? The concept of a critical period, in its original embryological context, is very precise in meaning. Timing is of the essence in the neurological or other genetic events unfolding toward a climax of maturation. We have noted in Chapter 2, that if, at a certain period during pregnancy, a woman contracts the disease rubella, irreversible damage is caused to her unborn infant. One of the critical period principles is that any phase in life when rapid organization is taking place (for example development of the embryo's bodily organs) is a critical period. This is so because the changes which are accidently produced at that time become a fixed and relatively permanent feature of the final and stabilized limb, brain or whatever other organ is being organized.

This notion has also been extended to psychology. The concept of critical periods in developmental psychology was given an impetus by its application in ethology. Lorenz (1935) found that during a restricted period—just after hatching—goslings instinctively follow the first large moving thing they see. These young creatures not only tend to follow this moving object but they come to prefer it to all others, and after a time will follow no others. In an experiment, Lorenz presented himself to some goslings during this critical period, and from their first fateful look in his direction, they followed him. Thus he, in effect, became their "mother", for once the attachment (called "imprinting") had taken place, they would not follow the natural mother. One of the interesting features of imprinting is that the attachment behaviour can develop without the infant receiving food or any other reward. There are many aspects to this phenomenon (also, at times, referred to as familiarity or exposure learning). Animals reared in a particular environment tend to show preference for features of that environment to which they have been exposed. For example, young chicks reared in a box with walls of a particular colour, or exposed to a particular colour for even short periods of time, show preferences for that colour when put in a choice situation (Taylor and Sluckin, 1968; Herbert and Sluckin, 1969).

The fascinating question that arises from such studies is whether human attachments, preferences or other behaviours are acquired (and perhaps even "fixed") during restricted phases of development on an imprinting-like basis. It is argued, for example (Bowlby, 1969), that a period in the infant's life when a major new relationship (e.g., to mother) is being formed is a vital one for determining the nature of that relationship. Not only the presence of adverse influences (e.g., a harsh, rejecting mother), but the absence of crucial stimulation (e.g., the lack of a mother or mother-substitute) disturb—possibly irremediably—the child's ability to make relationships with people. (We return to this particular issue later on.)

It should be noted that the critical period hypothesis (even in animal work) has been criticized for being of limited value in describing develop-ment (see: Sluckin, 1967). The upshot of recent research (Sluckin, 1970) is that it is misleading to think of imprinting as a unique phenomenon occurring only during a very short genetically determined critical period in early infancy, or that it is completely irreversible once it has developed. This has led to a preference for the term "sensitive periods".

Questions about sensitive periods for imprinting, socialization, or for the acquisition of specific skills are basically questions about learning. The fact that development, experience and learning are cumulative and con-tinuous makes it extremely difficult to separate them into categories such as "early" and "later". Yet this is necessary in order to answer questions implicit in the sensitive period hypothesis: that early learning differs substantially, and in crucial ways, from later learning. There are physio-logical differences between the central nervous system of the young child and that of the adult. From birth to four years there is a continuous increase in the number and size of dendrites in all layers of the cortex, in the fibres lower in the brain, and in association fibres within and between cortical areas (Tanner, 1970). This elaboration or increased "connectivity" is crucial to the exercise of more complex brain functions. Myelination of fibres is one sign of brain maturity. The enwrapping of nerve cells in myelin—which allows them to conduct nerve impulses rapidly and con-tinuously—is nearly complete only when the child reaches four years of age. Much more complex responses become possible with myelination. The fibres which link the cerebellum to the cerebral cortex—necessary to the fine control of movement—do not have their full complement of myelin until age four. The reticular formation, involved in the maintenance of arousal and attention continues to myelinate *at least* until puberty. These differences could be enlisted on the side of the Freudian argument that early learning is *critically* important for later personality development, for only during this period is the brain still in the developing and malleable state. But as Sluckin (1967) points out, it could also be argued that learning is relatively *unimportant* during the earliest years, because it occurs in an immature brain and one which is perhaps not fully capable of effective functioning.

What is the evidence—rather than the folk-lore—about these issues of early learning and their consequences? Clarke (1968) has painstakingly reviewed much of the available evidence. He concludes that at the moment valid scientific knowledge is sadly lacking. Indeed, dogmatism about either the long-term effects or non-effects of early experience is at the present time entirely misplaced. Nevertheless, it is possible to identify a few consistencies in the data.

Clarke was unable to find much evidence to support the belief that infant learning is acquired more easily than later learning. Infant learning does not seem to be better retained or more resistant to extinction. Infants and young children are strikingly inferior to adults in many dimensions of learning. There is, in fact, no evidence that environmental experiences can only have a decisive effect in early childhood (Stevenson, 1962; Stein and Susser, 1960; Rutter, 1972). Evidence suggests that *early learning* is of importance mainly for its foundational character. Development proceeds at different rates through a sequence of well-marked stages. Each stage depends on the integrity of previous stages. It seems most appropriate (see: Caldwell, 1967) to talk of optimal periods of learning in childhood. At such times, a stimulating environment which provides a rich variety of learning experiences, enhances the child's development. Where such intellectual and social "nutrients" are scarce, vital foundational skills and motivations are impaired.

An illustration of this comes from an investigation by Provence and Lipton (1962) of the early intellectual and social development of infants in institutions as compared with children reared at home. On almost every measured variable the institutional infants were below par—being less socially alert and outgoing, less curious, less responsive, less interested in objects and generally less advanced. In a study of foster children by Skeels and Harms (1948) the biological mothers all had intelligence quotients below 75, and the biological fathers were all labourers and therefore likely to be of less than average intelligence. The children were placed in occupationally superior foster homes before the age of two years. When they were five years old their average intelligence quotient was 104, compared to 62·6 for their biological mothers. The subjects in another study (by Skodak and Skeels, 1949) were children placed in adoptive homes before the age of six months. Their biological parents were of low educational and occupational status, while their adoptive parents were superior in both respects. When the children were thirteen years old, they had an average intelligence quotient of 107, compared to an average of 85·7 in the biological mothers. Thus, in both studies there is a clear difference in the average intelligence of the biological parents and adopted children, whose intelligence in each case was nearer to that of their adoptive rather than their biological parents. While it seems justifiable to infer that favourable environmental circumstances can produce unexpectedly high intelligence test scores from children with poor intellectual backgrounds, it does not follow that heredity is of little importance. In some cases the biological mothers might be dull or subnormal not because their genetic potential is low but because of secondary factors such as birth injuries, disease or poor environmental conditions. The genetic potential transmitted to the child in such cases may be within normal limits, and one would expect him to achieve normal intelligence in a satisfactory environment. There was, in these studies, a tendency also for the more intelligent biological mothers to have the more intelligent children, and two possible explanations of this fact might have operated either singly or in combination. First, genetic differences between the children might have still become manifest despite environmental influences. Second, there might have been selective placement of the potentially brighter children in intellectually superior homes, and these homes may have produced or accentuated the superiority of the children in them. In short, these studies highlight the influence of environment on intelligence, without eliminating the influence of heredity.

If the environment can influence intelligence, then one might expect significant changes of environment to be followed by changes in intelligence. This in fact occurred in some children who were transferred from a residential nursery either to a subnormality hospital, or to a cottage in a Children's Home (Skeels and Dye, 1939). The group transferred to the hospital received a great deal of attention and affection from the subnormal women patients, and also attended kindergarten as soon as they could walk. The cottages in the Children's Home each contained thirty to thirty-six children of the same sex aged under six years, and were staffed by a matron and three or four untrained and reluctant "teenage girls", so that some regimentation of the children was observed. Whereas the group transferred to the subnormality hospital increased in average intelligence quotient by 27 points, the Children's Home group lost an average of 26 points.

There is evidence that deficits arising from early environmental handicaps can, to varying extents, be made good (Skeels, 1966; Lewis, 1954; Clarke and Clarke, 1960, 1959; Clarke et al., 1958). Goldfarb's findings (Goldfarb, 1943) suggest that three years of extreme environmental impoverishment and adversity stunts development until adolescence; however, Clarke's work suggests that there is "from adolescence onward . . . a slow reversion towards what would have been the normal course, even though this may never be fully achieved" (Clarke, 1968).

Bloom (1964) has estimated, from his review of the data from several longitudinal studies, that during the first three to four years about 50% of the development of intelligence that is eventually achieved in the life-cycle, has occurred. During this period a child may find the ingredients that are nourishing to intellectual development and problem-solving skills or he may be starved of these "nutrients" (see: Kushlick, 1968; Brossard and De Carie, 1971; Starr, 1971). Bloom (1964) states that:

The effects of the environments, especially of the extreme environments, appear to be greatest in the early (and more rapid) periods of intelligence development and least in the later (and less rapid) periods of development. Although there is relatively little evidence of the effects of changing the environment on the changes in intelligence, the evidence so far available suggests that marked changes in the environment in the early years can produce greater changes in intelligence than will equally marked changes in the environment at later periods of development.

## The Overriding Influence of Early Learning and Experience

Although it is evident (Wiesel and Hubel, 1963; Turner et al., 1969) that early deprivation experiences in animals can have *some* consequences that are extremely persistent and resistent'to later influences, the evidence for humans is less clearcut (Rutter, 1972). (The ambiguities of maternal deprivation research, for example, are dealt with in Chapter 7.) Clarke concludes that psychological processes are differentially affected by adverse early experiences. For example, as indicated by the degree of recovery in children following early adversity, motor processes are shown to be the most resilient and emotional functions the most susceptible (Clarke, 1962).

The long-term effects of short, traumatic incidents seem to be negligible in young children (Schaffer, 1958; Clark, 1962; Douglas et al., 1968). The specific effects of experiences before seven months of age appear to be of very short duration. Experiences that occur after the first year of life are the ones which appear to have a longer-term effect, and even then, extinction occurs unless there is reinforcement. This is an important finding; it seems that it is only when early learning is continually reinforced that long-term effects appear; and these may well be more the result of the later reinforcement than of the original learning as such (Clarke, 1962).

One form that a critical period hypothesis takes in the case of human development, is the assumption that the child's personality traits are "fixed" in the family mould during earliest childhood and that all that happens subsequently is that they continue to grow, emerging in recognizable but more elaborate form (i.e., "in full bloom") at maturity. Some do, but there are difficulties in predicting adult personality from traits observed in early childhood.

Studies (see: Escalona and Heider, 1959; Kagan and Moss, 1962; Robins, 1966; Rutter, 1970) that follow up the development of children over long periods of time, show that there is only a modest correspondence between many specific traits seen during infancy and early childhood and adult life, although overall trends enable one to identify *some* fairly gross stabilities or continuities in personality. Among the characteristics which are most stable are the formal aspects of behaviour (temperamental qualities) and such specific attributes as achievement-motivation, passive dependent behaviour (in the case of females), and severely aggressive, antisocial acting-out behaviour. Most other traits are very poor predictors of adult personality development. The view commonly held by workers in the field of mental health that early characteristics remain relatively stable, seems therefore either to be the result of selection of evidence based on hindsight, or to be true only of a specially vulnerable section of the population (Clarke and Clarke, 1960).

These findings are somewhat out of key with the ideas held to this day by many theologians, philosophers and psychoanalysts, that the learning experiences of the first five or so years of a child's life are *all-important* in determining the sort of person he is to be and that what happens to an individual after that is merely a ripple on the surface of his already "set" character structure.

Certainly, Clarke's review of the evidence leads him to be sceptical about the rigidity of the structuring of character which is thought to occur during infancy. The fixity of the child's psychological attributes at a very tender age seems to have been exaggerated by some theoreticians. *Early* learning experiences do not appear to set the child an inevitable "tramline route" to follow in his later development.

It would seem that man is a creature of habit. This means that he relies on *learning* rather than instinct.* The higher we go up the evolutionary scale, the less dependent are species on stereotyped inherited instinctive responses. At the summit is man, the most flexible of all creatures, who (as we saw) has reached this pinnacle because of his adjustive equipment, notably his brain. He has a tremendous capacity to learn, to imitate, observe insightfully, and to change, and then to adapt to novel situations. Here is a crucial source of man's great variety—his susceptibility to many different types of environment.

But Clarke emphasizes the point that the child should not be viewed as a passive organism whose character is moulded solely by the impact of environment upon genetic predispositions. The child may himself act indirectly as a reinforcer of his own behaviour. For example, the mother–child pair (dyad) is a feed-back system, and the degree to which the

* Complex, rigid and inborn patterns of behaviour universal to a species and not reliant for their appearance on experience.

child's actions have the power to change the mother's behaviour increases with development. The child from an institution, for example, may in foster care show an irritating immaturity of behaviour which changes the foster-parent's mode of handling and makes matters worse, thus reinforcing immature or aggressive responses.

The flexible (adaptable) and healthy person is much better placed to cope with changes because his ability to learn—his openness to new ideas, his acceptance of reality—is efficient and always in a state of readiness. Not all people attain this flexibility. This raises some interesting questions: Why do some children learn inappropriate strategies for coping with life? How does this come about? What, anyway, is "inappropriate" learning? To begin to answer these questions we need to analyse the relationship between learning and the control of behaviour.

### The Stimulus Control of Behaviour

The basic elements of a stimulus-response or stimulus control analysis of behaviour include the assumption (mentioned above) that most behaviour in the case of humans is learned. Experimenters try to identify the causes of behaviour by first looking at the antecedent stimulus conditions or variables (inasmuch as they are observable and controllable) and then by looking at the consequences or terminal response events, insofar as they are observable and controllable (see: Bandura, 1965). Between input (stimulus) and output (response), various motivational states, cognitive processes, etc., can be inferred. A behavioural classification* can be specified in terms of the following four components (see Kanfer and Saslow, 1969):

(1) Prior stimulation (S). These are the antecedent stimulus events which reliably precede the criterion behaviours. They may be functionally related to the response by setting the stage for them ("discriminative stimuli") or evoking them ("eliciting stimuli").
(2) Organismic variables (O) include motives and the biological and psychological states of the organism.
(3) Response (R).
(4) Consequent events (C). Consequent events refer to the new conditions which the criterion behaviours were instrumental in bringing about. The effects of these behaviours on the person's internal and external environment are crucial determinants of whether or not the behaviour will recur. The term "contingency-related conditions" is used to refer to the temporal relationships of both antecedent and consequent events.

* This classifying process (whereby it is possible to specify environmental conditions that elicit and maintain behaviours) is usually referred to as a "functional analysis".

An important aspect of these relationships are "schedules of reinforcement" under which response-contingent consequences occur (see: Ferster and Skinner, 1957).

We can indicate the relative temporal relationships as follows: $S \rightarrow O \rightarrow R \rightarrow C$. The complete description of any behavioural sequence requires the specification of each of these elements and their interaction with each other. In the equation above, the stimulus component specifies those aspects of the environment that are related functionally to the behaviour of the individual. When two different stimuli appear together repeatedly, the responses to one of them are gradually transferred to the other. If a response to a stimulus is followed by reinforcement (a factor powerfully related to O variables), this reward increases the probability of the bonding of that response to that stimulus.

The process begins with the newborn child. Large aspects of his environment are essentially neutral in their effect on him (i.e., they exert no influence on his behaviour). As the infant grows older he acquires behaviour. He learns to crawl, walk, talk, sit at table, cooperate, read, and so on and so forth. Aspects of his environment begin to assume special properties for the child as a result of sheer familiarity and also the quality of his experience of them. Some of them have pleasurable consequences, others have painful ones. He comes to associate his mother with warmth, comfort, stimulation and many other pleasant feelings. He tries to approach her or in some other way ensure her proximity.

### Classical (Respondent) Conditioning

Some responses become functionally attached to stimuli by a process of association (or contiguity)—the process called "classical conditioning" (see: Pavlov, 1927). This is but one model illustrating how our behaviours come to be elicited by such a wide variety of stimuli. Theorists (e.g., Bandura, 1969; Lovaas, 1966) state that the person's behaviour comes to be regulated by "antecedent stimulus events"; and they call such learning the acquisition of "stimulus functions". In other words he learns to respond appropriately to particular situations. For example, stimuli associated with painful events come, by a process of conditioning to evoke fear (Kimble, 1961). The child's survival would soon be in jeopardy if he didn't acquire these functions. Sometimes these normal processes of learning—usually so adaptive—are subverted and produce maladaptive responses. In the last two decades psychologists have "rediscovered" some of the ideas being discussed in the 1920's which suggested that many psychopathological responses can be conceptualized as inappropriate responses that have been acquired through faulty stimulus-control learning.

A child may be conditioned to respond in a non-adaptive fashion to various innocuous situations. Take the experiment performed by Watson and Rayner (1920) on an 11-month-old boy named Albert. Having first ascertained that the child was not afraid of a white rat, they gave it to him to play with. Whenever Albert reached for the animal the experimenters made a loud noise behind him—a proven fear-provoking stimulus for this child. After only five trials Albert began showing signs of fear in the presence of the white rat alone. This fear spread itself to objects which had something of a resemblance to the rat, such as furry objects, cotton wool, and a white rabbit. These *phobic* reactions were still present when Albert was tested 4 months later. This demonstration seems to make it clear that phobias can be produced by a simple conditioning procedure in which a previously *neutral* object is associated with painful or frightening circumstances in such a way as to "infect" the neutral object. In this case, the rat—previously liked—acquired the fear-evoking properties of the loud noise, and furthermore the fear spread automatically to other objects which had similarities to the white rat in some way—the phenomenon of stimulus generalization.

The unconditioned response could also be shame or disgust or some other emotion. The point about such emotions is that they are largely under the control of the autonomic nervous system, not under conscious control. It is no use telling the child that such and such an anxiety is unnecessary and irrational and that he must pull himself together and stop it. It is no more under his control to switch off, no more a voluntary action than a knee jerk to a physician's mallet.

A large group of maladaptive behaviours may be caused (*inter alia*) by the fact that formerly innocuous and inappropriate stimuli can acquire the capacity to elicit highly intense emotional reactions.* Many of the obsessions, compulsions and phobias of childhood may be understandable as conditioned emotional reactions. Another group of problems includes chronic muscular tensions, intolerable anxiety reactions, and other forms of exaggerated activity of the autonomic nervous system. Symptoms may take the form of a wide variety of physical upsets such as chronic fatigue, insomnia, stomach and bowel disturbances and also breathing (asthma) and cardiovascular (fainting, blushing, etc.) disorders. (See: Ullmann and Krasner, 1969; Costello, 1970; Yates, 1970.)

The explanations of maladaptive behaviour given so far are usually grouped under the generic title of "inappropriate stimulus control of behaviour". Irrelevant behavioural responses may have become accidentally associated with consequences that are rewarding (as when a neglected

---

* An important question that arises in connection with this theoretical model is why conditioned emotional reactions persist if unreinforced, i.e., if the original trauma or cumulative sub-traumatic events are not repeated. An answer to this is attempted on page 106.

child finds that he attracts attention from his mother when he has a temper tantrum), or, as happens most frequently, learning has occurred in aversive conditions and rituals and avoidance techniques have been acquired because they prevent unpleasant outcomes. We saw in Chapter 1 that a rapidly growing area of Clinical Psychology usually referred to as "behaviour therapy" has been concerned with the application of findings from experimental psychology in general, and learning theory in particular, to the explanation and treatment of clinical problems. Critics of behaviour therapy (see: Breger and McGaugh, 1965) question the amount of consensus there is among the proponents of "modern learning theory". They are sceptical about the pride taken by the more doctrinaire practitioners of behaviour therapy in the scientific respectability of their theory and practice—especially as it has transferred from the rigorous conditions of the animal laboratory to the less precise atmosphere of the human consulting room.

There is a further source of maladaptive behaviour related to learning situations: where stimuli are ambiguous (i.e., not clearly discriminable) conflict may arise, producing vacillation, tension and a variety of emotional problems. If the stimulus control of behaviour is to go ahead smoothly, the child must be able to make accurate discriminations between stimuli.

## Discrimination Learning

The child must learn very soon in life to discriminate between what is allowed and what is not. Classical conditioning (particularly in the case of animals and preverbal infants) can lead to adaptive behaviour (i.e., responses that are appropriate and that have survival value). For example, it lays the foundations for important perceptual discriminations that the young child should learn in order to discriminate between safe and dangerous objects. Unfortunately, as we have seen—and it is the case with all forms of learning—the very process which helps the child adjust to life can, under certain circumstances, contribute to his maladjustment. Conditioning methods can be used to teach very subtle discriminations, but if conflict is introduced into the learning situation it can produce an "emotional breakdown". Conflict is an important cause of emotional problems in childhood.

Discrimination learning can be deliberately tampered with in such a way as to produce abnormal psychological reactions—the so-called "experimental neuroses" (see: Pavlov, 1957). A dog was trained to distinguish a circle from an ellipse. An ellipse with semi-axes in the ratio of 2:1 was projected among presentations of a circle. The circle was accompanied by feeding, but no reward followed the ellipse. The next stage was to gradually change the shape of the ellipse so that it began to resemble more closely the circle, thus making it more and more difficult for the dog to decide whether or not this was a cue for food to follow. The animal remained undisturbed as long as the circle and ellipse were easily discriminable. At a critical stage, however (when an ellipse of 9:8 was reached), the behaviour of the dog underwent an abrupt change in which it appeared to suffer a kind of breakdown. It began to squeal in its stand, kept wriggling about, tore at its harness and reacted violently on being taken on subsequent occasions to the experimental stand. Thereafter a fear of the total situation seemed to develop and the animal would become "neurotic" whenever it was brought into the laboratory. A point of interest was that not all dogs had such a "nervous breakdown"; only certain animals with a specific type of temperament (the "weak" nervous system type) were predisposed to develop such emotional problems (Pavlov, op. cit.). On later tests the animal's ability to make even simple discriminations had been destroyed. (A similar phenomenon has been demonstrated in children by Krasnogorski, 1925.) Other *conflict* situations have been used to demonstrate neurotic-like* behaviours in animals (Liddell, 1944; Maier, 1939).

In everyday life, children may be forced to make discriminations—such as where their loyalties lie in a divorce situation—which are beyond their powers of resolution. The same applies to "double bind" situations in which the child is faced with contradictory communications in the context of emotionally fraught situations. We take up this issue shortly.

Owing to the nature of the animal experiments upon which much of the behavioural theory of neurosis is based, emphasis has inevitably been placed on the stressful effects of direct painful stimulation such as electric shock. Noxious stimuli have been used to produce "neurotic reactions" in a variety of animals (Liddell, 1944) and in human beings (Campbell *et al.*, 1964; Watson and Rayner, 1920). In everyday human life, of course, other types of stress are more common and more likely to be important in the genesis of neurotic behaviour. Conflict, in particular, has been shown to evoke avoidance tendencies (Masserman, 1946; Miller, 1944, 1959; Maher, 1964) and is functionally akin to pain. Conflict is given great weight in psychoanalytic theory particularly when the conflict develops around a person's desire to behave in ways which he has learned to consider immoral so that the desire is accompanied by feelings of guilt. There are several types of conflict situation (see: Yates, 1962; Maher, 1966).

There is what is called the *approach–approach* conflict. In this case the child may, for example, have to decide between two attractive prospects, such as when he is asked to choose between going to the circus or visiting the fun fair. Then we have the *approach–avoidance* conflict. This occurs when the responses conditioned to a stimulus are both approach and

* There have been criticisms of the allegedly anthropomorphic labelling of such phenomena as neuroses. (See: Hunt, 1964.)

avoidant in nature. Here the choice entails deciding between a pleasant or an unpleasant outcome. Next there is the *avoidance–avoidance* conflict. In this situation the child finds it necessary to decide between two goals, both uncongenial. The child is in a situation in which two aversive stimuli are present; if he avoids one he is forced to approach the other. A child who is refusing to go to school may want to return because of painful parental sanctions, but at the same time he may be reluctant to do so, because of his fear of being bullied. A cycle of approach and avoidance is set up in which there is mounting tension as he oscillates around some point of equilibrium, until some new factor (e.g., fear desensitization therapy) enters the situation to alter the relative strength of the two tendencies. Most of the important conflicts children face are complex elaborations of these simple models. They are often of the *double* approach–avoidance kind, where there are two choices, each with both attractive and aversive properties. Such a situation is thought (Sheehan, 1953) to underlie the momentary blocking of speech experienced by a stammerer as he approaches a particular word. Two types of conflict are involved, that between speaking (approach) and not speaking (avoidance) and that between not speaking (approach) and speaking (avoidance). Speech and silence carry double approach–avoidance connotations; they both involve a desired and feared goal. To quote Sheehan:

> Speaking holds the promise of communication, but the threat of stuttering; silence eliminates temporarily the threat involved in speaking, but at a cost of abandonment of communication . . . (Sheehan, 1958).

In general, approach–approach situations are the least likely to have unfavourable consequences because the outcome in either case is attractive. Although sometimes presenting clear alternatives and relatively simple choices, approach–avoidance situations can demand exceedingly fine discriminations (see Maher, 1970). The child vacillates and this may result in a state of fairly chronic tension. Conflict increases arousal level (Berlyne, 1960), repression (Bobbitt, 1958) and displacement behaviour. Avoidance–avoidance circumstances are regarded as the greatest risk for the fostering of maladaptive behaviour. Not only is a marked degree of anxiety aroused by the prospect of punishment for whatever choice is made, but there is a tendency for the individual to avoid making any decision and the conflict remains unresolved. This can lead to chronic tension. Conflict increases adaptive striving in some individuals in the sense that they search for realistic solutions. Others retreat from the conflict situation by making use of defence mechanisms (see: Anna Freud, 1937).

The solution of many problem-solving situations requiring specific responses to certain stimuli, appears to depend upon the previous acquisition of language and verbal-symbolic discriminations (Kendler and Kend-ler, 1959; Kendler, Kendler and Wells, 1960). In some children (see Chapter 12) this acquisition is delayed and/or impaired. A child's inability to communicate, by comprehending other people and by expressing him-self meaningfully, apart from its other serious implications, contributes to the development of serious emotional problems.

Bannister (1960, 1963) and Bateson *et al.* (1956) adduce evidence that the complexities of language and logic are such that a condition as serious as schizophrenic thought disorder may be a consequence of the child having received a conflicting and in other ways confusing grounding in the consensual (linguistic) meanings of society. For example, repeated experiences—in the primary learning situation provided by the family called "double bind" experiences (approach–avoidance situations) are thought to interfere with the learning of effective or rational communica-tion and at the same time create unbearable frustration and anxiety. The parent makes demands for different and mutually contradictory responses from the child by juxtaposing injunctions (in emotionally fraught situa-tions) which are incongruent. Two distinct messages are conveyed by a communication each belonging to a different level of meaning or logical type. Whatever the child does in response is "wrong". A response of some kind is mandatory. The fundamental contradictions in the communications are concealed or denied by the "binder". These early and often repeated experiences limit or distort the child's adaptive capacities and permit him to escape from insoluble contradictions by abandoning the "meaning system" of his culture. He may take refuge in irrationality and withdrawn behaviour. (We return to these problems in Chapter 12.)

## Parent–Infant Interactions

Because psychological problems are so intricately enmeshed in the child's social relationships and perceptions, it is usually the case that when the finger is pointed in accusation (because a child is emotionally disturbed) it is in the direction of his immediate "environment". In the wake of the pervasive influence of thinkers like Freud, Pavlov and Watson (paradoxically in the case of the first two) a possibly over-exclusive atten-tion has been given to environmental influences in the development of behaviour. And, when things go wrong with the child, the major feature in his early environment, his mother, tends to receive most of the blame. As Hilde Bruch (1954) puts it:

Modern parent education is characterized by the experts' pointing out in great detail all the mistakes parents have made and can possibly make and substi-tuting "scientific knowledge" for the tradition of the "good old days". An unrelieved picture of modern parental behaviour, a contrived image of artificial perfection and happiness, is held up before parents who try valiantly to reach the ever receding ideal of 'good parenthood', like dogs after a mechanical rabbit . . . The new teaching implies that parents are all-responsible and must assume the role of playing preventive Fate for their children.

This environmentalist point of view has always been particularly strong in American psychology which reflects a rather more optimistic "philosophy" than European psychology. In a way this has proved fortunate as it has produced a rich harvest of research (Mussen 1970, Hoffman and Hoffman 1964) on the family, school and society, and their influence on child development. However, while parents undoubtedly "condition", shape and influence their offspring, it is *not* a one-way process. As Thomas *et al.* (1968) put it:

Frequently . . . problems seem to reflect poor care. On the other hand, what looks like "bad" mothering often shows up, after careful investigation, to be the mother's confused reaction to a difficult child, rather than a primary cause of the child's problems. Any conscientious young mother who has been persuaded that she is uniquely responsible for her children's healthy development is bound to feel guilty and anxious when a child is difficult. When the problems persist, her feelings sometimes explode in anger at the child. The mother then looks like the villain. Actually, the picture is a much more complex one. The problem is not the parent's, but the parent's *and* the child's, and results from a pattern of interaction between the two.

Thomas and his colleagues found, in their study referred to on page 67, that there were certain infants who, before the age of two, stood out quite clearly as "difficult children"—they have been described rather unkindly, but accurately (by mothers and research staff) as "mother killers". Those identified so early in life as particularly troublesome had a fairly clear-cut pattern of temperamental traits. Approximately 70 per cent of such infants later developed emotional problems.

## The Difficult Child

There is a cluster of temperamental traits that typify the difficult child.* The first is the predominance of *intense reactions*. These are seen in the infant who shrieks more frequently than he whines, who gives belly laughs more often than he smiles. As a three-year-old he will express his disappointment not with a whimper, but a bang. Frustration characteristically produces a violent tantrum when he gets older. Pleasure is also expressed loudly, often with jumping, clapping, and running about.

Frequently, difficult children exhibit *withdrawal behaviour* when exposed to new features of the environment. Some children react negatively to particular types of stimulation or sensory experiences such as touch or

* The clinical examples are provided by the authors (Thomas *et al.*, op. cit.).

taste. Other children are not bothered by such experiences, but react adversely to new people.

In general, difficult infants manifest a predominantly *negative mood*. This means that they cry more than they laugh, and fuss more easily than they express pleasure. Negative moods are usually evident at times when the child is experiencing new situations and new demands, especially if he reacts to them by a withdrawal response.

*Slow adaptability to change* may manifest itself in different ways at different age periods. In infancy, the baby typically withdraws from new experiences. Eventually he adapts, but only after frequent and repeated exposure to a given situation. For example, the difficult infant may kick and scream during his first bath, and for a long period of time he may continue to behave in this way each time he is placed in the water. However, if the child is bathed daily for several weeks, there will be a gradual but noticeable lessening of his negative behaviour, and eventually he will show either a quiet acceptance of the bath or a vigorous positive reaction to it with laughing, splashing, and playing. But, he may now frequently protest and cry when he is *taken out* of the water.

The difficult infant typically follows this pattern of very slow adaptability in most new situations, and reveals a need for many familiarizing exposures to them before he can make a positive adjustment. If given an opportunity to experience the new situation without being pressured for an immediate positive response, such children will in time adjust. The stranger becomes a familiar person, liked or not as the case may be; the new bed is taken for granted; riding in a car and going to public places become an accepted part of the daily routine. However, if the child is not given regular and repeated exposures, and any particularly novel experience is repeated only intermittently or after a long gap of time, then the child will tend to display his original withdrawal response.

Difficult infants tend to show an *irregularity in biological functioning*, which can show itself in a variety of ways and is particularly evident in the early months and years of life. Such infants sleep irregularly and, in many cases, seem to need less sleep in a twenty-four-hour period than the average infant of the same age. The child may awaken two or three times a night at unpredictable intervals, while at other times it may sleep for as long as five or six hours at a stretch. Such babies do not quickly develop lengthened periods of sleep. It is not at all unusual to find that during the first two or more years of such a child's life his parents were frequently awakened by his crying and could not get him to sleep through the night, no matter what training procedures they used.

Irregularity in hunger is another characteristic. In early infancy, the baby may take only half an ounce at one feeding and a number of ounces at another. He may be hungry again within half an hour, or not accept food for five or six hours. Irregularity is apparent both in the cycles of feedings and in the quantity of food consumed at each.

Patterns of elimination are also typically irregular. There is considerable variability in the timing, frequency, and size of bowel movements. Often, the only thing that is predictable is irregularity itself. As a result, toilet training procedures often do not work.

## The Easy Child

As a contrast to the difficult children, a group of so-called "easy" infants were identified in the study by Thomas *et al.* (1968). The temperamental organization of these babies was such that it usually made early care remarkably uncomplicated. They were mainly positive in mood, very regular, low or mild in the intensity of their reactions, rapidly adaptable, and unusually positive in their approach to new situations. They frequently enhanced their mothers' sense of well-being and of being "good" and effective parents. Mothers tended to characterize such infants as "easy" babies. Most of these "easy" children did not develop behaviour problems. However, as the authors point out, the exceptions make it clear that no pattern of temperamental traits can guarantee against a child developing emotional problems. Even these easy children, who generally thrived on the widest variety of life situations and demands, could, under special circumstances, find themselves vulnerable to adverse influences. When they adapted to inconsistent and unpredictable maternal demands, their easy adaptability, usually a temperamental asset, could become a liability.

Whatever the child's temperament, the ups and downs of life are inescapable. Eventually he has to face the problem of assimilating unpleasant, frustrating and frightening events as well as enjoying more benign experiences. Much has been made (particularly in the psychoanalytic literature) of the allegedly disruptive effects on infant adjustment of different child-care practices—notably feeding, weaning and toilet-training procedures. What, in fact, is the evidence?

## Specific Techniques of Child Rearing

We have no conclusive evidence about whether breast feeding, for a long or short time, has more favourable consequences than bottle feeding; whether early weaning is disadvantageous compared with later weaning; whether feeding from a cup is better than the sucking type of feeding; or whether unscheduled feeding is superior to schedule feeding. In fact it is the conclusion of many research reports (see: Caldwell, 1964), that *no* clear adjustment or maladjustment patterns have been demonstrated to result from any aspect of the infant's feeding experience, nor are personality traits shown to be related to such matters as type and schedule of infant feeding.

Behrens (1954) studied both specific maternal infant-rearing practices and general maternal attitudes to child-care. Her subjects were twenty-five lower middle-class families who were attending a mental health clinic. She investigated infant-rearing practices with regard to feeding, weaning, and toilet training and their relationship to the adjustment of these children at the age of three. She found no correlation between the three infant-rearing practices and the children's adjustment. This study confirmed other studies using the same approach in the sense that the findings were negative (see: Orlansky, 1949; Caldwell, 1964; Maccoby and Masters, 1970).

Behrens also investigated what she called the "total mother person", her term for general maternal attitudes and conduct. She differentiated three components: the mother's underlying attitudes, the manner of meeting the maternal role demanded of her, and observed conduct toward the child. This last component refers to maternal consistency, overprotection, and adaptation of her behaviour to the child's needs rather than to specific practices.

Behrens found, in essence, a very high degree of association between these various dimensions of the "total mother person" and the children's emotional adjustment. In other words, specific child-rearing practices were not related to adjustment, but overall, global scores of maternal attitudes were predictive of adjustment.

The generalization that seems to emerge from the literature (Caldwell, 1964) is that what is important in child-rearing is the general social climate in the home—the attitudes and feelings of the parents which form a background to the application of specific methods of child-rearing. For example, the mother does best who does what she and the community to which she belongs believe is right for the child. This implies a relaxed and confident mother.

Elimination training—the method and age of initiating toilet training—has been linked (because it is assumed to be frustrating) with the development of problem behaviours such as aggression. While there may be short-term differences in a child's reactions to different types of bowel and bladder training (coercive and punitive methods may result in bowel and bladder malfunctioning), there is no apparent relationship to different personality characteristics, either favourable or unfavourable. In those cases, for instance, where toilet training does affect the child negatively, it is clear (see Caldwell, 1964), that it is not toilet training, as such, that makes a difference to the youngster, but a whole set of severe parental attitudes and practices which accompany rigid toilet training.

## Parental Illness

There is a relationship between the incidence of physical and mental illness in parents and the presence of emotional problems in their offspring (Rutter, 1966). In Rutter's study it was found that, of the children with neurotic and behaviour problems attending a child psychiatric clinic, one in five had a psychiatrically ill parent. This was three times the incidence found in the parents of a control group consisting of children attending a dental clinic. Also, the children under psychiatric treatment whose parents had a history of psychiatric disorder, had more severe and extensive problems than other problem children at the same clinic. Not all, by any means, of the children of mentally ill parents develop emotional problems; many grow up to be healthy adults. Nevertheless, children in this situation are at risk. The children of psychotic parents are less vulnerable than those with parents manifesting personality problems such as neurosis and psychopathy.

There appears to be little relationship between the specific type of illness in the parent and the type of problem displayed by the child. What does seem to make a child most susceptible is his direct involvement in the mother's or father's symptoms. He is particularly at risk, for example, if the parent has delusions about the child, paranoid feelings, obsessional fears of harming him, morbid anxiety concerning his development or hostile feelings towards him. Affective symptoms (that is to say disturbed emotions such as hostility and depression) are particularly associated with the development of problems in the offspring.

Childhood problems are more likely to be associated with psychiatric illness in the mother than in the father. When both parents are psychiatrically disturbed, the child is particularly vulnerable as there is no one, except possibly brothers and sisters, to act as a buffer between himself and the parental illness. A longitudinal study (Graham *et al.*, 1973) of three- to seven-year-old working-class London children, each of whom had at least one mentally ill parent, identified 41% as abnormal. A year later the same *proportion* were judged to be abnormal. The disturbed children were the ones who, at the outset of the investigation had "adverse temperamental characteristics" (ATC) similar to those described as "difficult" by the New York research group. There was a significant relationship between maternal criticism of the child and two of the temperamental characteristics. The authors hypothesize that ". . . certain ATC (perhaps marked irregularity) may make it more difficult for parents to deal with the transient disturbances that commonly accompany stressful experiences. Accordingly, what in another child might be a passing problem of little consequence becomes a more persistent and more handicapping disorder."

# 6. Instrumental Learning and Problem Behaviour

ANXIETY HAS A directly disturbing effect on the nervous, hormonal and muscular systems, which, as we saw on page 72, interferes with normal efficiency, particularly in demanding situations. Distress also has a motivating effect in that the sufferer seeks ways of evading the disturbing situation; such avoidance responses, if maladaptive, are labelled neurotic symptoms.

Many kinds of problem behaviour (especially the exaggerated fears called phobias) have such an avoidance ingredient. Little Albert, whom we discussed on page 93, acquired not only a "classically conditioned" fear of rats and similar furry objects, but also certain "instrumentally conditioned" avoidance behaviours to keep the feared objects at a safe distance.

If a child was not sensitive to the consequences (or outcomes) of his behaviour he would be in grave difficulties. Normally, a youngster's responses are comprehensively controlled by their immediate results. Actions that have painful consequences (or which are unrewarding) tend to be extinguished.

The principles underlying instrumental (or operant) conditioning help to explain the question we posed above concerning the persistence of some psychological disorders which are unreinforced, and which to make it even more puzzling, seem (in some cases) to be quite the opposite of rewarding to their owners. How could a handicapping phobia like a fear of social situations, or a fear of heights or lifts, be anything but painful and embarrassing (i.e., aversive) to the victim? Let us look first at the nature of reinforcement consequences, in particular the effects of positive reinforcement: it has been found that response stability is increased by intermittent reinforcement, that is, by not rewarding the response on every trial. There are several schedules of reinforcement which have been investigated experimentally (see: Ferster and Skinner, 1957):

(a) Variable-interval schedule: a programme used in instrumental learning situations whereby the individual is reinforced after an interval of time which varies around a specified average.
(b) Variable-ratio schedule: here the individual is reinforced after a number of responses which varies randomly around a specified average.
(c) Fixed-interval schedule: a schedule of partial reinforcement in which a response made after a certain interval of time is reinforced.
(d) Fixed-ratio schedule: a schedule of partial reinforcement in which every $n$th response is reinforced.

Variable schedules result in stable response rates which are difficult to extinguish. A variable-ratio intermittent reinforcement schedule produces maximum stability of learned responses. Many behaviours manifested by children are inadvertently rewarded on variable schedules of reinforcement. Bandura (1969) points out that the "one-armed bandits" (fruit machines) are shrewdly programmed on variable schedules of reward.

It has been found in the laboratory that experimental techniques involving aversive stimulation, produce persistent forms of avoidance behaviour (see: Eysenck, 1968; Watson and Rayner, 1920; Campbell *et al.*, 1964) even when unreinforced. This is all very well, but normally, learned responses will gradually extinguish when reinforcement is not forthcoming. We see this occurring in the case of conditioned emotional responses which are maladaptive. The fact is that approximately two out of three people with neurotic problems can be expected to recover "spontaneously"— that is to say, without receiving any formal treatment. Levitt (1957) calculated that the overall improvement rate for 160 cases who withdrew from the clinic waiting-list before receiving treatment was 72·5%. This spontaneous remission rate was calculated from two reports in which disturbed children who had received no treatment, were reassessed one year later in one study and 8–13 years later in the other study. Further data on the spontaneous remission of children's fears is provided by Holmes (Table V).

Spontaneous improvements were commonly manifested by children in the MacFarlane study (MacFarlane *et al.*, 1954). In their survey of the behaviour disorders of normal children, they found that the frequency of most disorders declined with increasing age. But not all problems remit. So what are the conditions under which the stability and retention of learned responses (adaptive or maladaptive) are facilitated and maximized? When does behaviour persist without external or overt reinforcement, or for that matter under the apparently paradoxical reinforcement conditions which we mentioned at the beginning of the chapter?

Let us take the absence of external reinforcement first. This matter of

TABLE V. *Percentage of children showing fear in experimental situations.* (From Holmes, 1935, Child Development Monograph, No. 20.)

| | Percentage showing fear | | | |
| | 2–3 yrs. | 3–4 yrs. | 4–5 yrs. | 5–6 yrs. |
| --- | --- | --- | --- | --- |
| I Being left alone | 12 | 15 | 7 | 0 |
| II Falling boards | 24 | 9 | 0 | 0 |
| III Dark room | 46 | 51 | 35 | 0 |
| IV Strange person | 31 | 22 | 7 | 0 |
| V High boards | 35 | 35 | 7 | 0 |
| VI Loud sound | 22 | 20 | 14 | 0 |
| VII Snake | 34 | 55 | 43 | 30 |
| VIII Large dog | 61 | 43 | 43 | 12 |
| Averages | 32 | 30 | 18 | 5·2 |

behaviour remaining stable without reinforcement is of importance not only for clinical theory, but also for the normal socialization of the child. As Aronfreed (1968) observes, an act might be considered to be internalized to the extent that its maintenance has become independent of external outcomes—that is, to the extent that its reinforcing consequences are internally mediated, without the support of external events such as reward and punishment.

Solomon, Kamin and Wynne (1953) have demonstrated resistance to extinction under conditions of non-reinforcement. They investigated the effect of shock on the learning of dogs. Their work illustrates the fact that responses can be strengthened by the avoidance/removal of punishing consequences. Each dog was placed in one compartment of a shuttle box with a gridded floor, and received a high intensity shock ten seconds after a buzzer sounded. After very few trials, the animal learned consistently to hurdle the barrier between his compartment and an adjacent shock-free compartment on the occurrence of the buzzer alone. Usually a stable latency of about 1·6 s was established. The authors concluded that fear had replaced shock as a drive. One dog which received only eleven shocks in the acquisition of this response had still failed to extinguish after 490 shock-free trials. It was found that in order to produce extinction it was necessary to introduce a "reality-testing" procedure (preventing the dog's jumping response by erecting a total glass barrier between the compartments) or a "punishment-of-response" procedure (shocking in the previously shock free compartment).

The strength of active avoidance learning is such that it may persist and even increase in frequency when punishment is made contingent on its performance rather than its non-performance (Brown, Martin and Morrow, 1964). It is suggested that as the initial response seems to reduce anticipatory anxiety, punishment of the response itself serves to increase generalized anxiety and thus to provoke more strongly and frequently the anxiety-reducing response, at least over a period.

What about the question of the apparently paradoxical pattern of reinforcement in disabling neurotic conditions? The paradigm of aversive conditioning proposed by Mowrer (1960) is of interest because of its attempt to integrate the classical and instrumental conditioning models into one superordinate theory of learning. Aversive stimulation is thought to produce a state of emotional arousal in the organism which becomes classically conditioned (on the contiguity principle) to external cues and/or proprioceptive cues immediately preceding the punishment. This conditioned autonomic reaction functions as a "drive", with the consequence that there is increased activity by the organism. Its behaviour usually includes responses which are instrumental in escaping from the aversive situation thereby reducing the fear or anxiety drive. Consequently these responses are selected and stabilized, being regularly elicited whenever the organism is confronted by the warning cues from the stimulus situation. Escape or avoidance behaviour is learnt whenever the organism is directly stimulated until the adaptive response is discovered or it suffers unavoidable aversive stimulation and is allowed to discover escape routes only under the motivation of conditioned anxiety.

The rewards in those neurotic fears of social situations, heights and lifts (to which we referred earlier on) arise out of escape from or avoidance of, the activities which cause the distress. It is *immediately* rewarding—a relief—to escape the painful shyness experienced at a party by leaving early or to escape the confined space of a lift which creates suffocating anxiety. It is this immediate relief—a form of drive-reduction—which maintains the strength of maladaptive actions. It is of little consequence that in the long-term such maladaptive behaviours are socially crippling. If the consequences of some action are too distant from the actual behaviour itself, then such consequences cease to influence that behaviour at all.

Of course, there are situations from which there is no retreat, particularly for children (e.g., a harsh teacher). Confinement tends to increase the disruption of behaviour consequent on fear. Experiments by Campbell *et al.* (1964) have established that really intense fear in confining situations can elicit conditioned emotional responses in humans which are extremely resistant to extinction.

Techniques of aversive stimulation produce more persistent forms of behaviour more readily than do techniques using positive control (Miller, 1959). Under optimum conditions (which depend upon such factors as the strength and timing of punishment, ease of discrimination among preceding stimuli and availability of non-punished alternative forms of behaviour) aversive stimulation causes rapid and highly stable learning, which may be either the inhibition of on-going behaviour (passive avoidance learning) or the performance of behaviour leading to escape (active avoidance learning).

## Symbolic Rewards (Social Reinforcement)

Positive reinforcers in the day-to-day socialization of the child usually take the form of words of praise and encouragement and even a nod or smile of approval. They all have the property, if they follow a particular behaviour, of making that behaviour more likely to occur on future occasions.

One of the most important of the child's acquisitions is the establishment of these so-called "symbolic rewards" or "conditioned reinforcers". Some of the aspects of the child's environment—a mother's smile, voice and physical proximity—which previously had no meaning for the newly born infant, acquire the properties of being able to strengthen or weaken behaviour.

The presence (or absence) of these social influences function rather like primary reinforcers (food, pain, etc.). At one time it was considered that nonsocial reinforcers were primary, and social (or conditioned) reinforcers secondary. The latter were thought to be derived from association with the former. However, recent research has made this view very hard to sustain. There is evidence that the stimulation of another's expressive behaviour, mediated by the distance receptors, can be as primary in its reinforcing effects as food (Walters and Parke, 1965).

There is a substantial body of research on the effects of social reinforcement. Most studies have been designed to show that children's behaviour can be shaped by verbal expressions of approval. They have used operant conditioning procedures, positive reinforcements, and strangers as the reinforcing agents. From the developmental point of view, the effect of social reinforcement has been demonstrated in babies during the first year (Rheingold, 1956) and in children from the age of three onwards (Stevenson, 1965). From the age of five years, certain developmental trends have been observed: a cross-sex effect appears, women being more effective with boys, and men with girls, strangers tend to be more effective than parents; peers increase in importance as sources of social reinforcement; and there is some evidence that "disliked" peers are more effective than "liked" ones.

The point about these symbolic rewards or social reinforcers is that they regulate behaviour. The child, for example, will be willing to obey distasteful rules because he wishes to have his parents' approval or avoid their disapproval. The trouble, when it comes to treating some children who have been deprived of affection and grossly maltreated, is that they may not respond to the same "social reinforcements" as other children.* They have never known the normal rewards and encouragements, and kind words are viewed with suspicion. The reinforcing function of a particular event depends on the social context in which it occurs. The rewarding or aversive effects of expressions of approval or disapproval vary with the sex, age, social class and race of the child, the sex of the experimenter, and the preceding experimental procedure (Stevenson, 1961, 1965).

Parents are generally the most potent source of social reinforcements affecting learning, attitudes and values when children are still young, and it is their influence which often precipitates and maintains deviant behaviour in their offspring.

Lovaas (1966) observes that what we are confronted with is an enormous variety of behaviours which are regulated by a prodigious number of social, interpersonal, or intellectual consequences which have the property of rewarding or punishing particular actions. He states that it is difficult at first to appreciate the great complexity of this interaction between behaviour and environment, and that reinforcement theory illuminates, rather than reduces this complexity.

Lovaas examines deviant development in the light of reinforcement theory. He says that emphasis can be placed firstly on the *actual deviations of behaviour*. For example, one might define a certain deviation, or abnormality, in terms of the failure in the acquisition of speech behaviours, or the acquisition of excessively aggressive behaviour. Secondly, one might approach deviations in terms of distortions in the so-called *stimulus functions*, and particularly in terms of disturbances in the acquisition of symbolic rewards. For example, a child may develop in such a way that a smile does not function as a symbolic reward. Or it has a meaning or function different from that which society initially intended it to have. Since symbolic rewards regulate behaviour, it would be difficult to observe a deviation in the acquisition of such rewards without simultaneously observing deviation in behaviour.

If it is assumed that normal behavioural development depends upon the acquisition of a large variety of symbolic rewards, then it follows that the child who has failed in the acquisition of such rewards, is likely to

* Baron (1966) has presented a conceptual scheme to account for the effects of social reinforcement history. He suggests that experience of social reinforcement generates a "social reinforcement standard" which is that familiar sequence of reinforcing responses in the adult or peer which the child actively seeks to evoke because he feels most at home and secure with them. Substantial discrepancies from this standard, *in either direction*, induce discomfort, and lead to action designed to restore the standard. This raises the interesting possibility that, for children who have habitually experienced negative social reinforcement, types of reinforcer usually judged to be positive may in fact be negative in their consequences.

demonstrate a deficiency in the behaviours which typically terminate in such rewards. In the extreme case of complete failure in the acquisition of such symbolic rewards, the child would display little, if any, social behaviour. That is, the child should fail to attend to people, fail to smile, fail to seek human company, to talk, and so on, because his environment did not provide him with the rewarding consequences for such behaviours.*

Next Lovaas looks at the behaviour of autistic children who appear to manifest this complete or partial failure in the acquisition of conditioned reinforcers or symbolic rewards. Among the most frequently occurring behaviours in these children are self-stimulating, or auto-erotic actions. They take the form of rocking, spinning, flapping of the arms, fondling oneself, etc. Lovaas' studies indicate that as the disturbed child acquires new behaviours, such as appropriate social behaviours, the self-stimulatory behaviour diminishes. This decrease in self-stimulation is independent of any direct intervention on the part of his clinical team. He points out that even when normal children are in a situation, such as a totally empty and silent room, where there are no cues for intellectual or social behaviours they engage in self-stimulation, which is virtually identical to that exhibited by autistic children. Similar types of self-stimulation can be observed in small babies prior to the acquisition of other behaviours. Adults, when idly sitting and waiting also tend to exhibit such behaviours. Lovaas concludes, on the basis of such observations (several of which have been carried out in highly controlled studies) that there exists an inverse relationship between self-stimulation and other kinds of behaviours. When other kinds of behaviour are high, self-stimulation is low, and vice versa.

Lovaas argues that activity as such is rewarding (reinforcing) for individuals, therefore a certain minimum level of activity must be maintained. If the child does not obtain these reinforcing stimuli as a result of interacting with people in his environment, he obtains them by stimulating himself.

He states that the second major type of behaviour characteristic of autistic children is destructive behaviour and tantrums. The destructive behaviour is often directed toward himself and it can become so severe as to necessitate the use of physical restraints for the protection of his health. These self-destructive behaviours involve head banging, biting and scratching himself, etc. The following case of a severely disturbed child illustrates Lovaas' theme. Beth, who was thirteen, had been self-destructive from the time she was four, initiating her self-destructive behaviour by placing her hair in a wall heater and igniting it. It was clear that environmental stimuli were crucial in maintaining self-mutilation. When a

* Charles Ferster (1961) has theorized that such is the case in autism, and probably, in varying degrees, in childhood schizophrenia. Explanations of this failure in communication and meaning are explored in Chapter 12.

sympathetic comment or a token of affection was given by someone in response to such behaviour, the behaviour increased in intensity. For example, when the staff assured Beth during her self-destructive episodes that she was not a bad girl, the behaviour rose in intensity. If the child was isolated from such personal responses when she displayed her self-destructive behaviour, the behaviour decreased and eventually disappeared. There was, however, an initial increase in intensity of the self-destructive behaviour immediately following this intervention.

Lovaas describes the clinician's dilemma and, in essence, the origins of his now well-known attempts to help autistic and schizophrenic children (see Chapter 12). He says:

We learned much from Beth, but two things were of particular importance. First, we could teach her by using food instead of social rewards; she could learn. Within a couple of months, we had taught her a 50-word reading vocabulary. Second, when we placed demands on her, however gentle, she became, in clinical terms, increasingly psychotic. We observed an immediate increase in bizarre behaviour, and in the intensity of self-destructive behaviour. She left sessions with us in a psychological mess, and we were frightened by her behaviour. We sought professional advice on conventional methods of dealing with self-destruction, and found that no objective study had been reported on the effect of such methods on the patient, although such advice was offered to the parents. We applied these methods in a controlled study, and were surprised to observe the patients become worse. We were faced with two alternatives: to remove all demands, or to find other ways to terminate her self-mutilation. My training as a clinician would have led me to remove the demands. The students working with me were clinically naïve, but very interested in Beth, and somehow they persuaded me to try ignoring her self-destruction. Surprisingly, it worked; after a few months, Beth adjusted to the new demanding environment without simultaneously becoming more psychotic. In short, we learned that these children kept us at a distance by being psychotic, and we would have reinforced the psychotic communication had we maintained the distance (Lovaas, 1966).

Lovaas states that self-destructive behaviour appears to be triggered by situations in which the child has been previously, but is no longer, rewarded. Technically speaking, the self-destructive behaviour takes place during extinction; it is cued by reinforcement withdrawal for another response. Therapists have observed that the children are very discriminating about the situations in which they will or will not engage in self-destructive behaviour. These discriminations appear to be based on the child's prior learning of the situations under which he will or will not be reinforced for self-destructive behaviour. Lovaas concludes, on the basis of children his research group investigated, that there is every reason to believe that self-destructive behaviour in autistic children follows the laws of other learned behaviours; the self-destructive behaviour is regulated by the consequences that such behaviour has upon the environment. It is of interest to note that when a child engages in self-destructive behaviour, he should have a better prognosis than one who is involved merely in self-stimulation, since the self-destructive child is being affected by at least a limited range of symbolic rewards. The therapists have had to resort to the use of physical pain in the form of electric shock in the case of dangerous self-mutilating behaviour. This was applied in addition to isolating the child. Such a controversial procedure was judged to be necessary in cases like Marilyn and Jim (two more autistic children treated by the Lovaas team) who conceivably could have killed themselves by their self-destructive behaviour.

## Shaping

The problems of children are more likely to involve the building up of deficient habits and controls than the removal of inappropriate responses. Behavioural techniques have been particularly useful for establishing skills and habits in children who have not had the opportunity to learn socially-adequate behaviours because of the absence or dereliction of parents, or for other reasons. They are especially helpful with problems like brain damage and mental subnormality where communication by language and abstract thinking are impaired and restricted. The therapeutic use of instrumental conditioning principles for this purpose involves three elements: choosing a reward that is really effective for the child; delivering the reward (reinforcement) on a precise and scheduled basis when the child manifests the desirable behaviour; and ensuring that a reward is possible. The therapist does this by working out the successive steps the child must and can make so as to approximate more and more closely to the desired final outcome. This last element, called "shaping" or the principle of "successive approximation", is an important one in behaviour modification; it involves taking mini-steps towards the final goal. The therapist starts by reinforcing very small changes in behaviour which are in the right direction even if somewhat far removed from the final desired outcome. No reinforcement is given for behaviour in the "wrong" direction. Gradually the criteria of the individual's approximation to the desired goal are made more stringent until, in the end, he is only rewarded for the precisely correct behaviour.

# 7. Separation Problems

THE BABY'S FIRST social achievement, in Erikson's view, is his "willingness to let the mother out of sight without undue anxiety or rage, because she has become an inner certainty as well as an outer predictability" (Erikson, 1965). One of the most potentially damaging events of childhood occurs if the infant is separated from his parents by death or abandonment and this loss is not mitigated by adequate substitute care. There are, of course, other forms of "separation"—the disruption of psychological bonds— brought about by parental neglect, rejection and hostility. The unloved child may find his self-confidence and self-esteem as adversely affected as the physically deprived child.

There is a range of separation anxieties shown by children—from the normal protests they make when parents go out, to the morbidly fearful preoccupation at all times with mother's whereabouts. The sort of child who fits into the latter category is often referred to as "clinging" or "over-dependent". (We take up this problem in the next chapter.) Theorists have long been interested in the development of bonds or attachments between children and their mothers. They have also studied the weakening of these bonds—the period of psychological "weaning" from the parents— whereby children become persons in their own right. Another area of research concerns the fear of separation which, when it persists, is thought to be central in many neurotic conditions. From the clinical point of view, the evidence (Rutter, 1972) suggests that psychological distress of a kind commonly termed neurotic results (at least in part) from the early *disruption* of bonds, whereas affectionless psychopathy probably arises because stable attachments *fail to develop*.

## The Development of Bonds

The beginning of the baby's "separate" or independent existence takes place, of course, at birth when he ceases to receive all his sustenance through the umbilical cord. But at this stage he is not psychologically separate, emotionally or intellectually differentiated, from his mother. The infant does not conceive of himself as a person; he and his surroundings merge and he does not distinguish "things out there" from internal impressions or feelings. The crux of the matter is that the child has no self-awareness. It's a strange paradox that in order to become a *person*, he must first become attached to the mother (or other significant persons) by the all-important bond we call dependency and love. Disturbances of this "dependency" relationship have long been thought by diverse theorists (e.g., Freud, 1916; Storr, 1968; Bowlby, 1951; Levy, 1943; Alexander and French, 1948) to be a vital ingredient in the genesis of psychopathology.

There is fairly conclusive evidence that the infant in western society first acquires an attachment to his mother at some point during the second half of his first year of life. Humans have a long period of helpless infancy— longer in relation to their life-span than any other species. It is crucial that child and parent should become attached to one another. The newly-born infant is totally dependent for survival on the nurturance and the loving and stimulating presence of his mother. He develops a bond of love— binding himself to his mother and her to him—by a combination of reflexes such as smiling, crying, clinging and so on and by a slow learning process whereby she comes to be seen as indispensable for the gratification of his physical needs. Gradually, he realizes that his emotional security depends on the presence of his mother.

Theorists of both the "psychoanalytic" and "social learning" schools of thought believe that this tie evolves out of the feeding situation. The idea here is that the infant's experience of nursing at the breast or bottle, is the earliest experience in social participation and that this is the occasion for the baby to learn to like to be with others—the basis for sociability. A widely accepted account of the genesis of dependency needs and behaviours is that provided by social learning theorists. This stresses the development of secondary drives—i.e., dependency motives—in association with primary drive reduction. The child begins to be socialized as he learns to value his mother as an agent who alleviates and reduces tensions associated with hunger, thirst and physical discomfort. (Dollard and Miller, 1950; Stendler, 1952; Mussen, Conger and Kagan, 1969.)

Because of the child's helplessness he depends totally on his mother for the gratification of his biological needs. He soon learns to associate her presence with the relief of painful tensions (e.g., hunger). Not only does he depend on her to satisfy these primary needs but eventually he comes to depend on her for the satisfaction of his emotional needs. The child's early love, in other words, is a form of "cupboard love" which is learned.

There is evidence that much social learning depends on reinforcement—

rewards and punishments (see: Bandura and Walters, 1963). But as Sluckin (1967) points out in his review of the evidence, although all later social learning may depend ultimately on the reinforcement of approval and disapproval, recent studies of infants indicate that the earliest social learning is different in character.

Walters and Parke (1965) show that the baby's social responsiveness, and the special attachment to his mother result from the impact of sensory stimulation, i.e., from the sheer familiarization with the physical environment, in which the mother is a primary feature. Schaffer and Emerson (1964b) conclude that attachments may derive from repeated encounters with an object not necessarily ever associated with feeding or contact comfort. Whether such apparently unreinforced exposure learning occurs only or mainly at the earliest stages of the life cycle is still a matter of speculation.

Bowlby, in Britain (Bowlby, 1969) and Ainsworth, in the U.S.A. (Ainsworth, 1969, 1970) have criticized the social learning model as an oversimplification. A child, they say, is *not* just a passive recipient of love and stimulation. Researchers (e.g., Schaffer and Emerson, 1964b) have noticed how children often seem to dictate their parents' behaviour by the insistence of their demands. Quite a few mothers report that they are forced to respond far more than they really consider desirable. Babies don't wait passively for things to be done to them; they reach out actively to their surroundings for stimulation and social contact. In his early months, a baby smiles, laughs, reaches out and coos at his mother. Later, when he is able to, he greets her and approaches her and does delightful things which ensure that she will continue to do the things he likes, such as making funny noises at him, tickling him, playing games, and so on. Every mother has an enormous influence on her child's behaviour; by encouraging some activities and discouraging others, she shapes his personality. But in all sorts of subtle ways her behaviour is also shaped by the child. In the crucial business of becoming a person, there is a two-way traffic in the relationship between mother and child.

## Theories Concerning the Development of Attachment

Bowlby (1969) has moved beyond the two main theories of attachment—learning theory and psychoanalysis. Bowlby sees attachment behaviour as the operation of an internal control system. The child is biologically predisposed to form attachments. It could be said that he is biased to respond to social situations; almost every baby enjoys human company. He displays social forms of behaviour (e.g., smiling, crying, clinging, and so on) from the beginning of his existence up to and beyond the point in time that he makes a focused attachment to parental figures.

Bowlby, in his monograph "Attachment and Loss" (1969), states that the evidence we have—and it is still incomplete—shows that the child (like other animals) can become attached to his mother without the rewards of food, warmth and so on. In other words, human attachments have imprinting-like features. A child is born with physical and psychological equipment—one might say he is "programmed" by his heredity—so that he is sensitive to certain types of stimulation in his surroundings. The human face in movement, for example, "triggers" a smile in young babies. Even in the first days of life, as Bowlby points out, a baby is soothed and quietened by social contact—being caressed, rocked, talked to, or just picked up. A baby attracts and keeps his parents' attention by crying, smiling, babbling and laughing. And the more attention he gets, the more he will babble and smile. He responds to people even though he can't discriminate one from another. If anyone approaches, he changes his position, tracks them with his eyes, grasps a finger, reaches out, and stops crying when he catches sight of a face or hears a voice. The rate of emission of smiling behaviour in infants can be increased by reinforcing it with social contact (Brackbill, 1958). All these kinds of interaction encourage attachment.

What is new when a child becomes attached, is not the display of new forms of behaviour or new intensities of social responses, but a pattern of organization of these responses in relation to one significant person. Virtually all the elements in the child's behaviour repertoire become capable of being functionally linked to a controlling system or plan which is hierarchical in its organization and target-seeking in its effect. The "target" is defined as the maintenance of proximity to mother, and the hierarchical nature of the organization is revealed in the fact that a particular response can serve a number of different functions in maintaining this proximity.

Bowlby's conceptualization of attachment seems to offer more fruitful ways of looking at attachment; it stresses such features of attachment as its goal-seeking qualities, the way in which almost any behaviour can be enlisted in its service, and the fact that behaviours compensate each other and can be alternative routes to the same goal. It suggests new ways in which attachment systems can be compared. Instead of thinking of children as simply being more or less attached ("dependent"), their attachment systems can be compared according to the nature of the favoured strategies they employ, how strongly they are established, the degree of elaboration of alternative strategies, and the nature of their setting, i.e., the closeness of the proximity they are set to maintain.

Ainsworth (1963) recommends the use of multiple criteria of attachment because of observed individual differences in the way such behaviour is organized and manifested—differences that seem to be related to differences among mothers in their infant-care practices (Ainsworth and Wittig, 1969). Both accumulated clinical evidence and recent research data (Ainsworth and Wittig, 1969; Ainsworth and Bell, 1970; Bell, 1970) suggest that qualitative differences in infant–mother attachment relationships are associated both with qualitative differences in antecedent behaviours and different behavioural outcomes in the child. Interpretations of a child's dependent behaviour can only be made in terms of inferences about the significance for him of what his mother is doing at the same time. (These considerations, if valid, make much of the clinical literature on dependency problems and separation experiences difficult to evaluate.) As Bowlby (1969) puts it:

> It seems clear that the strength of attachment to one or more discriminate figures is itself altogether too simple a concept to be useful (just as the concept of a unitary dependent drive has proved to be). New concepts are needed, but to develop them will take time, and can hardly be done until the relative phenomena are more systematically described. One step in that direction might be to regard a child's attachment in terms of a number of different forms of behaviour as they occur in a number of specified conditions.

The following criteria of attachment behaviour commonly appear in the literature and have implications for the study of the development of emotional problems in children.

### Differential Smiling, Vocalization and Following

Most infants are already reacting differently to their mothers as compared with other people by about four months of age. The baby will smile and coo and follow her with his eyes more than he will other people (Ainsworth, 1963). But although he may be able to recognize her, this is not the same thing as saying there is a bond which makes him behave in a way that ensures his proximity to her in particular—the essential meaning of attachment.

### Introduction of a Stranger

Until he is about seven months of age, a baby will generally show little concern about being with strangers, but beginning from between about seven and twelve months of age a new emotional response appears and then gradually vanishes. It shows itself as a shyness with, or even fear of, strangers (Schaffer, 1966). Maccoby (1971) found clear changes with age in the child's behaviour during the free-play period before a stranger entered the room. The younger children (age two) stayed closer to their mothers than when they were older (ages two and a half or three). With the entrance of the stranger, however, the children went closer to their mothers at all three ages. The frequency of touching the mother or clinging to her (in this situation) did not change with age. At all three ages the child was less likely to look, smile at or speak to the mother when the stranger was present than when they had been alone. The younger the child, the more likely he was to be upset when left alone or left with the stranger. Acceptance of the stranger varied with age. At the youngest ages the children were more likely to stay close to mother, but there was a good deal of ambivalence in this behaviour. By the age of three, the most common reaction to the stranger was to greet her and resume active play with toys. Proximity seeking to the mother when the stranger was present was the index which predicted whether the child would cry when mother left the room.

### Use of the Mother as a Secure Base from which to Explore

In an unfamiliar situation the mother's presence is, for most infants, a necessary condition for the activation of exploratory behaviour (Rheingold, 1969; Ainsworth and Bell, 1970). The child uses mother as a secure base from which to explore. For example, Ainsworth and Bell (1970) found that while the presence of the mother encouraged exploratory behaviour, her absence depressed exploration and heightened attachment behaviours. There were large individual differences, however, in these behaviours. Messer and Lewis (1970); Goldberg and Lewis (1969) report sex differences in behaviour in strange situations. Girls appear to be more dependent, show less exploratory behaviour and a quieter style. Girls show more attachment behaviour than boys and this difference cuts across social class. Mothers' behaviour towards boys and girls differs, reinforcing sex-appropriate behaviour.

### Separation Anxiety

Ainsworth (1963, 1967) used separation protest, among other measures of attachment, in her studies of early attachment behaviour and came to the same conclusions as Schaffer and Emerson (1964b), and Yarrow (1963, 1967), in placing the mean age of the onset of attachment in the third quarter of the first year, and particularly between the ages of 6–8 months. Schaffer and Emerson (1964) used separation protest in minor everyday situations as the criterion for judging the age of onset of attachments. They studied 60 Scottish children in their attempt to find out when the tie between child and mother comes about. Attachment was defined in terms of separations in which the baby cries or tries to follow mother and is no longer placated by just *anyone* else. The researchers interviewed the mothers of these infants during the period from the children's birth until over 12 months of age. They were particularly interested in the baby's reaction to being left alone by mother, for example when left alone in a room, left in a cot at night and other day-to-day situations. They measured the intensity of the protest (if any) expressed by the child at these "temporary desertions". They found that one-third of the babies showed attachment behaviour (separation protest of a fairly consistent sort) by six months of age and three-quarters by nine months. One infant showed this kind of behaviour as early as twenty-two weeks, while two failed to display specific attachments until after the age of one. During the month after the children first showed evidence of an emotional bond, one-quarter of them were showing attachment to other members of the family, and by the time they were a year and a half, all but a few children were attached to at least one other person (usually father) and often to several others (usually older children).

The formation of additional attachments progressed so rapidly in some infants that multiple attachments seemed to appear simultaneously with the first specific attachment that was observed. The number of persons to whom the child became attached was a function of the number of people who interacted with him. The most stimulating individuals—not always the caretakers—tended to become attachment figures.

It has been found that in separation episodes, behaviours such as crying and searching are increased; in the reunions, proximity seeking and contact-maintaining behaviours are heightened (Ainsworth and Bell, 1970). Coates, Anderson and Hartup (1971) found that visual regard, touching and proximity to the mother were more frequent following separation from the mother (in 10, 14 and 18 month-old infants) than before separation. Crying and orientation to the locus of the mother's disappearance were more frequent both during and following separation than before separation. Rheingold (1969) was able to show that when infants are placed in a strange environment *alone* with a familiar toy or with a relatively unfamiliar adult, exploratory behaviour is inhibited and they exhibit clear signs of distress. If the mother is there, however, even in a thoroughly passive role, there is no distress and the child explores the strange setting freely.

## Disruption of Early Attachments

Young primates show clinging patterns and fear of separation. Harlow (1958) has demonstrated this very clearly with young Rhesus monkeys. Under normal circumstances, a baby monkey, which is startled while at play, will rush to its mother and cling to her chest until the danger has passed. Harlow showed that if such baby monkeys were brought up by artificial mothers of two kinds—one made of wire mesh, and the other of wire covered with a soft terry cloth—when alarmed they would always fly to the cloth mother for comfort. Furthermore, this soft, comforting type of mother was essential to the young animal's social progress. If totally deprived of such solace from birth, a young monkey would be unable to learn to play, or to defend itself, and would show signs of extreme nervousness and discontent.

It is also clear from studies (Heinicke and Westheimer, 1966) of how two-year-old children behave during and after a period in a residential nursery, that the very experience of being with strange people in a strange setting promotes anxiety, both during the separation and also after it. During the course of the stay, children show, among other disturbances, bouts of crying, refusal to eat followed by overeating, periods of inactivity and occasional outbursts of violence. After they have returned home, they tend to become apprehensive and clinging. The same is true of youngsters who are threatened by their parents with being sent away from home.

Psychologists have come to realize that prolonged separations from mother or an adequate substitute mother-figure, especially in the first two years of life when the child is becoming a social being, can have serious consequences for his personality development. Studies (Robertson and Bowlby, 1952) of the behaviour of healthy children in their second and third years of life who have been separated from their parents for one reason or another tend to show a fairly predictable, though not invariable, sequence of behaviour. In the first stage—of so-called "protest"—the child reacts to the separation with tears and anger. He demands his mother back and seems hopeful he will succeed in getting her back (the stage may last several days). Later he becomes quieter; but it is clear he is as much as ever preoccupied with his absent mother and still yearns for her return, but hopes have faded. This is called the phase of despair. Often the stages alternate: hope turns to despair and despair to renewed hope. Eventually a greater change occurs. The child seems to forget his mother so that when she comes for him he remains curiously uninterested in her and may seem even not to recognize her. This is called the stage of detachment. In each of these phases the child is prone to tantrums and episodes of destructive behaviour. The child's behaviour on returning home depends on the phase reached during the period of separation. Usually for a while he is unresponsive and undemanding; to what degree and for how long, depends on the length of the separation and the frequency with which he received visits in hospital or wherever he was. For example, if he has not been visited for a few weeks or months and has reached the early stages of detachment, it is likely that unresponsiveness will persist from an hour to a day or more. When at last it breaks, the intense ambivalence of his feeling for his mother is made manifest. There is a storm of feeling, intense clinging and the expression of acute anxiety and rage whenever his mother leaves him. Bowlby (1951) is of the opinion that if the separation lasts for more than six months for the young child, there is a danger that the detachment will become permanent. He interprets this sequence of events as analogous to adult mourning. The difference lies in the fact that the very young child cannot understand what is happening so he may fail to come through the experience properly, remaining "frozen" in a state of emotional detachment. All psychoanalytic schools regard mourning as the normal analogue of depression.

Freud, in his monograph "Mourning and Melancholia" (1917) compared the normal emotion of grief and its expression (following bereavement) in mourning, with the psychosis melancholia. He based this comparison upon the general picture of the two conditions as well as upon the external precipitating causes which he felt to be the same in both cases. According to the argument, the loss of a loved object gives rise to feelings and behaviours which are collectively referred to as mourning; these psychological processes are always set in train by the disruption of a precious attachment and they commonly lead to the *relinquishing* of the loved object.

Mourning is typically accompanied by identification with the lost object, and seems to fall into three stages: (i) *Denial* or *protest* in which the bereaved individual tries to repudiate the reality of the loss of the loved person, refuses to believe it, gets angry, reproaches himself, the deceased person and any medical consultants who failed to "save" his life. (ii) *Acceptance, rejection* or *despair* in which the bereaved person admits the reality of the loss and sorrow and grief take their course. (iii) *Detachment* in which the survivor relinquishes the object, adjusting himself to life without the loved one. If mourning takes its normal course the person gets over the tragedy and is capable of making a new attachment. It might also, in the case of some people (subsequently suspected of a pathological disposition) give rise to a deep-seated depression or melancholia. In melancholia the symptoms are:

(a) Painful dejection
(b) Loss of interest in the external world
(c) Inhibition of activity
(d) Loss of capacity to love
(e) Loss of self-esteem hence self-reproach and delusional expectations of punishment.

In mourning the same "symptoms" are observed with the exception of the fall of self-esteem and the expectation of punishment.

In both mourning and melancholia—according to Freud—the precipitating cause is the same: the loss of a loved object on which the libido was sublimated/cathected. It need not involve a person; it may concern something which has taken the place of the loved object such as a father-land, liberty or an ideal. Both mourning and melancholia are marked by departures from normal behaviour. However the grief of mourning is not regarded as a pathological condition; no one thinks of sending the mourner to a psychiatrist. It is anticipated that time will cure the grief, and usually people think that grief should be left alone to take its course.

Freud's theories about the function of mourning inspired clinical theorists (e.g., Bowlby, 1951; Spitz, 1945, 1946) to find applications in the realm of child development. According to Bowlby (1951, 1961) infants and children react to separation from their mothers by mourning processes which predispose them to psychiatric illness in later life. Spitz (1946) made a study of 123 unselected children in a nursery setting; however, this was unusual in being an institution for women offenders with babies. The infants stayed in the nursery from their 14th day of life until the end of their first year and in a few cases until the end of their eighteenth month. All shared the same environment, care and food. When the infants were somewhere between their sixth and eighth months, their mothers were removed from them for a practically unbroken period of three months. During this time the infants did not see their mothers at all, or at best, once a week. Before the separation the mothers had full care of their babies and spent more time with them than is probably usual in an ordinary home. A striking syndrome was observed in the babies. The principal symptoms composing this syndrome were not all necessarily present at the same time, but all of them were noticeable at one point or another in the clinical picture, which consisted of:

(a) Apprehension, sadness, weepiness.
(b) Lack of contact, rejection of environment, withdrawal.
(c) Retardation of development; of reaction to stimuli; slowness of movement.
(d) Dejection; stupor, frozen immobility.
(e) Loss of appetite; refusal to eat; loss of weight.
(f) Insomnia.

To these is added the facial expression which Spitz finds difficult to describe, but which in an adult, would be described as depression. This syndrome developed in the course of four to six weeks following the mother's removal. No child, whose mother had not been removed, developed the syndrome.

The proposition put forward by Spitz is that it occurred only in those children who were deprived of their love object for an appreciable period during the first year of their life. On the other hand not all the children whose mothers were removed developed the same syndrome. Hence, the author suggests that maternal separation is a necessary but not a sufficient cause for the development of the syndrome referred to as "anaclitic depression".

Spitz (1945) compared 69 of the children staying in the Nursery with 61 infants from a Foundling Home and a control group of 34 infants leading a normal home life. The background of the children in the two institutions did not favour the Nursery group; on the contrary, it showed a very marked advantage for the Foundling Home children. A number of children came from socially well-adjusted, normal mothers whose only handicap was their inability to support themselves and their children. This was expressed in the average of the developmental quotients (DQ's) of the two institutional groups during the first four months, which favoured the Foundling infants. The housing conditions in both institutions were described as excellent, the food good and varied. In the Foundling Home, however, the cubicles opened onto a bleak deserted corridor; nothing much went on, each child was screened in a deep cot with sheets over the bars. They could only see the ceiling and they lay in solitary confinement. Due to lack of stimulation, babies lay supine and even at ten to twelve months old they lay on their back playing with all they had got—their toes.

It was found that the developmental curves of the Foundling and Nursery children crossed between the fourth and fifth month. Foundlings, originally above the Nursery children in DQ level, fell below them. The impoverished environment of Foundlings, devoid of humans, leads (in Spitz's view) to a severe restriction of psychic capacity by the end of the first year. This restriction was progressive. By the end of the second year, the DQ sank to 45 (i.e., a mental age equivalent of 10 months (severely subnormal)). Spitz concluded that the mother–child relationship is vital for the development of the child during the first year. If it is intact, all sorts of other deprivations can be compensated for.

The Foundlings all showed manifestations of what Spitz calls "hospitalism"—an exaggerated form of anaclitic depression. Despite impeccable hygiene they showed extreme susceptibility to infection and illness. *All* personality factors appeared to be undermined. Many showed psychiatric phenomena such as stereotyped motor patterns and bizarre behaviour. In the last third of the first year a change in their reaction to strangers was observed. Their behaviour varied from extreme friendliness combined with anxious avoidance of inanimate objects, to generalized anxiety expressed in blood-curdling screams that could go on indefinitely. The Nursery group (as we saw earlier) developed well until the traumatic break from their mothers.

This study is described in detail because its impact together with Bowlby's publication (Bowlby, 1951) on theory and practice in connection with institutions, maternal care and attachment behaviour, was immense. It led to a great deal of research which has tended to moderate some of the wilder claims and to inhibit the more naïve oversimplifications of the earlier work in this field.

The work of Spitz has not escaped criticism. Pinneau (1955) mounted a devastating attack on the methodology and interpretations of the investigation. Nevertheless, the fears aroused by the publication of this study and the exaggeration (in subsequent clinical reports) of the dangers of "maternal deprivation" were probably salutary in the sense of bringing about reforms in the placement and care of children in institutions.

Rutter (1972), in an invaluable review of the literature on maternal deprivation, demonstrates how the pendulum has swung. He contrasts Bowlby's 1951 conclusion that ". . . mother love in infancy and childhood is as important for mental health as are vitamins and proteins for physical health" and that of Casler (1968) that ". . . the human organism does not need maternal love in order to function normally." If anything, the pendulum has swung too far back in the direction of complacency.

Like so many other clinical would-be explanatory concepts "maternal deprivation" is over-inclusive and too imprecise to be of any predictive value. It is used as if it described a unitary phenomenon. In fact, there are many modifying influences which determine the seriousness of the consequences for the child. The following have been found to be important:

(1) Sex (Stacey *et al.*, 1970)
(2) Age (Schaffer and Callender, 1959).
(3) Temperament (Stacey *et al.*, 1970).
(4) Previous separation experiences (Ainsworth, 1962; Vernon *et al.*, 1965; Stacey *et al.*, 1970).
(5) Previous mother–child relationship (Vernon *et al.*, 1965).
(6) Duration of separation experience (Heinicke and Westheimer, 1965).
(7) Separation experienced within a strange environment (Douglas and Blomfield, 1958).

The effects of early maternal separation are not always permanent (e.g., Hellman, 1962). Each and every separation situation is a unique, complex and many-sided matter, requiring painstaking analysis. Studies of the effects of separation, though they tend to support the assumption of an increased risk of later disturbance, raise a number of problems. It is difficult to isolate the effects of separation from other adverse side-effects. To what extent are the ill-effects of a child's separation experience (brought about by, say, a divorce) the result of the discord between his parents, or the disruption of bonds, or both? In an institution, the child commonly suffers *other* kinds of deprivation which add to the burden of his grief over a separation. Frequently, a shortage of residential staff means that the intensive care required by each child cannot be given. And the rapid turnover of staff means that the child's separation experiences are repeated over and over again until he cannot trust himself (or adults) to make the emotional commitments most people take for granted.

Factors like these make the outcome of early separations difficult to predict. Some institutions are excellent, some children are remarkably robust.

## Broken Homes and Long-term Consequences

An important distinction which is not always made clear in the literature, is that between long-term and short-term consequences of maternal separation. Rutter (1972) concludes that short-term distress (protest, despair, detachment) is probably due to a disruption or distortion of the attachment process—but not always, or necessarily, in relation to the mother. The syndrome of developmental retardation is probably a consequence of the child being deprived of adequate social, perceptual and linguistic stimulation. The evidence for long-term effects is much more tentative. The syndromes of "deprivation dwarfism", intellectual retardation, antisocial behaviour, delinquency, and affectionless psychopathic personality are among the problems for which maternal deprivation has received some blame.

The evidence concerning long-term consequences apart from being very meagre, is difficult to evaluate. One of the most thorough investigations of adult mental health, the Midtown Manhattan project, (Srole *et al.*, 1962; Langner and Michael, 1962) revealed that people who had experienced a broken home in childhood had only a *slightly* higher risk of developing psychiatric problems than those from stable homes. For those from a comfortable economic background, there was no difference at all in the risk factor. There is, indeed, evidence that children from broken homes may fare better than youngsters from *unhappy* unbroken homes. The McCords (1959) showed that broken homes resulted in significantly less juvenile delinquency than did unbroken but neglectful and quarrelsome homes.

If a child is unavoidably separated from his parents the quality and continuity of substitute care are vital if potential harm is to be mitigated. This was demonstrated in studies by Goldfarb (1945, 1947). He compared a group of children who had been fostered during the first few months of life with another group who had lived in an institution until they were fostered at the age of three years. When examined intensively at the age of twelve, the early fostered group had developed reasonably well whereas the late-fostered group showed general emotional improverishment, hyperactivity and inability to concentrate. The children in this group tended to demand affection without being able to give it much themselves. They also did less well on tests of conceptual attainment.

These findings, however, do not allow any complacency. The relatively reassuring information about the effects of broken homes on psychiatric illness in later life is not repeated in the area of delinquency. Here, the influences are more malign, given certain circumstances. A study (Gibbens, 1963) of Borstal boys showed that one-third of the inmates had experienced a breakup of their home before the age of fifteen. This however, is only a contributory influence, along with factors such as overcrowding, too large families, poor educational opportunities, and so on.

The generalities about the consequences of broken homes do not take account of the individual suffering involved. Whatever the long-term statistical trends, we are still left with the intense and immediate (even if temporary) grief, confusion and apprehension affecting many children in the period leading up to and following divorce, death or desertion. For some children, the disruption of a divorce may be minimized by parents who somehow arrange that they are protected from the more unpleasant and discordant features of the deteriorating marriage.

When homes are broken up because of the death of a parent (or for some other reason), the disruptive effects do not always show themselves immediately. There is sometimes what is called a "sleeper effect", in which the adverse consequence—say a depressive illness—appears after the passage of time in adulthood (Brown, 1961; Gay and Tonge, 1967; Hill and Price, 1967). Ill effects are thought to be likely for the child if it is the mother who dies when he is very young; the father's death is more likely to have adverse effects if it occurs when the child is older.

The problem of delinquency presents only a slightly higher risk for those youngsters who have lost a parent by death compared with children from intact homes (Gregory, 1965; Rutter, 1972). Delinquency is less associated with the decease of parents (despite the finality of the separation) than it is with parental divorce, where attachments are often maintained. It seems to be the distortion of relationship rather than the disruption per se, which has the most damaging consequences (Rutter, 1972).

## Maternal Deprivation Studies

Yarrow (1961) has emphasized the point that it is a mistake to equate maternal deprivation (such as exists in institutional environments) and maternal separation. The data reveal that short cyclic interruptions of mother-child contact culminated by reunions do *not* have the same effect as prolonged disruptions, even though—in quantitative terms—at the end of a specified period the amount of time spent without the mother might be equal for the two experiences.

The existence of a single term "maternal deprivation" which stands for a variety of experiences has led to much confusion in the literature because of its implication of a specific syndrome with unitary causation (see Ainsworth, 1962). The ideal study—a factorial design experiment which isolates the subtle relationships and interactions between various independent variables and their effects on such dependent variables as the child's personality—is, of course, impossible.

Rutter (1972) in his excellent review of the literature on the consequences of different types of maternal deprivation has done the next best thing; he has attempted to tease out the significant mechanisms causing most damage by posing particular questions and then weighing up the evidence. Thus he asks in connection with the long-term consequences of maternal deprivation, whether they are mainly due to:

Disruption of bonds or change of environment?
Disruption of bonds or deprivation of stimulation?
'Sensory privation' or 'social privation'?
Emotional privation or nutritional privation?
Social privation or nutritional privation?
Failure to form bonds or disruption of bonds?
Failure to form bonds or failure to form bonds with mother?
Privation or deprivation?
Disruption of bonds or distortion of relationships?
Distortion of relationships or deviant model?
Distortion of relationships or ineffective discipline?

Rutter concludes this exhaustive analysis as follows:

Distorted intra-familial relationships involving both lack of affection and hostility or discord are associated with the development of later antisocial behaviour and delinquency. Although the presence of a deviant parental model and inefficient discipline may be contributing factors, the lack of a stable, persistent, harmonious relationship with a parent appears to be the crucial variable.

Less is known about the syndrome of "affectionless psychopathy", but the little evidence available suggests that the most tenable hypothesis is that a failure to develop attachments (or bonds) in early childhood is the main factor. A bond to one or other parent, usually the mother, is the strongest attachment formed by most normal young children. However, the evidence suggests that what is needed is a bond. Whether this is to the mother seems irrelevant in this connection and indeed it is doubtful whether it even has to be to an adult. Nevertheless, *which* person it is with whom bonds form is important for other reasons. Although the necessary facts are lacking it is probable that bonds with both men *and* women are advantageous for optimal psychosexual development.

Stress during the first six years (often but probably not necessarily involving parent–child separation) is a factor in the genesis of enuresis. However, some aspect of an institutional upbringing also appears important in that enuresis is common among children in a wide range of institutions. Which aspect of institutional care is pertinent in this connection is not known.

Loss of an attachment figure, although a major factor in the causation of short-term effects, seems of only minor importance with respect to long-term consequences, in spite of many previous claims to the contrary. Such a loss may play a part in enuresis, as one of several stress factors. Also, it may have a more specific connection with depression in adults. However, in this case the association is more with parental loss during adolescence than with loss in early childhood. Loss may be a minor contributory factor in other types of outcome, but so far as can be judged from the evidence it is not the main influence.

Indeed, the evidence strongly suggests that most of the long-term consequences are due to privation or lack of some kind rather than to any type of loss. Accordingly the "deprivation" half of the concept is somewhat misleading. The "maternal" half of the concept is also inaccurate in that, with but few exceptions, the deleterious influences concern the care of the child or relationships with people rather than any specific defect of the mother (Rutter, 1972).

# Part IV

# Early Childhood: The Toddler Stage
*From eighteen months to about three years of age*

# Introduction: Psychosocial Developments

THE CHILD'S striving for mastery and control often reaches a peak between the ages of two and three years of age. He is struggling with conflicting needs within himself and against parental controls. The "terrible two's" are notorious for displays of negativism, temper-tantrums and ambivalence. The major developmental task of this phase of life according to Erikson (1965) is the attainment of a sense of autonomy; the child begins to view himself as an individual in his own right, separate from parents although dependent on them. The major hazards are conditions—social and physical —which interfere with the child's achieving a sense of personal adequacy or which hinder his learning of skills such as locomotion, speech and the control of elimination. In learning competencies and self-control the child gains a lasting sense of autonomy; whereas failure leads to a loss of self-esteem and a pervasive sense of doubt and shame. Loevinger (1966) refers to this period as the "impulsive" stage of ego-development because the child is confirming his separate existence from mother by the exercise of his own will. She sees the child's interpersonal relationships as being predominantly exploitive and dependent. People are seen as sources of supply. However, parents are prepared to nurture and indulge the child to a massive degree only as long as he is totally helpless and vulnerable. The age deemed appropriate for terminating what Ausubel and Sullivan (1970) call "the stage of volitional independence and executive dependence" (viz. infancy) varies between two and four years of age in different cultures—and nearer to two in Western society. During the toddler stage parents become somewhat less tolerant, attentive and deferential toward the child. As Ausubel and Sullivan (1970) put it:

They comfort the child less and demand more conformity to their own desires and to cultural norms. During this period the child is frequently weaned, is expected to acquire sphincter control, approved habits of eating and cleanliness, and to do more things for himself. Parents are less disposed to gratify his demands for immediate gratification, expect more frustration tolerance and responsible behaviour, and may even require performance of some household chores. They also become less tolerant toward displays of childish aggression. In short, all of these radical changes in parent behaviour tend to undermine environmental supports for infantile self-perceptions of volitional independence and omnipotence. ... As a consequence of ego devaluation, the situation is precisely reversed: increased *executive* independence is required along with greater *volitional* dependence.

Language develops apace during this phase of life (see: Lewis, 1951; Bar-Adon and Leopold, 1971). A high point in the verbal labelling of the self-concept is reached at about 27 months when the child uses the personal pronoun "I" (Gesell and Ilg, 1943). Rees (1973) observes that "language mediates an appreciation of self and non-self, and body image. Thus ... a child can control powerful feelings by the insightful, externalizing effect of putting such feelings into words. The growth of ego functioning is facilitated by the acquisition of language, which helps the child 'programme' his emotional reactions and behaviour and allows him to distinguish between reality and phantasy". Much of the frustration of this phase of life may be due to the child's inability to express his demands and ideas as quickly or as adequately as he would wish. His speech is not yet flexible enough for all his purposes. Frustration gives rise to anger, anger to temper tantrums.

Much research effort is currently being devoted to the study of how children acquire language, and in particular how they acquire grammatical utterance. Yet a developmental step of major importance—social control through language—has been neglected. It is, after all, that point in development when the child's behaviour is capable of being shaped and controlled by the verbal commands, directions and requests of adult caretakers, and when physical intervention becomes unnecessary, that he is well on the way to becoming a social being. The subsequent socialization of children depends heavily upon verbal control and will suffer if this control is imperfectly established. Luria (1961) suggests that the impelling function precedes the inhibitory, and that control by others is a precondition of self-control—that point in development when the child himself takes over the control previously exercised by others. During early childhood, however, control of impulses is lacking or at best undependable. Rules are not recognized as such; an action is bad because it is punished. The child's conscious concern with sexual and aggressive drives is high. Mastery is often centred on such developmental tasks as the control of emotional outbursts (e.g., anger), curiosity (e.g., sex play) and physiological functions (e.g., defaecation).

The toddler is beginning to develop a rudimentary conscience by internalizing rules. Obedience of rules—whether they are laid down by convention, codified in laws, or internalized in the form of conscience—is a prerequisite of social living. All parents and teachers are beset at one time or another by the problem of instilling obedience in the children in their care. The earliest signs of obedience began to appear during the previous stage of development—i.e., in the last quarter of the baby's first year of life. They consisted of heeding and complying with the mother's simple commands and prohibitions, such as "Come here!" and "No, don't do that!" Some infants may, on occasion, display an inner-directed obedience to commands given previously by the mother. A baby shows such primitive self-control when he stops himself in the act of reaching out for the forbidden wall plug, perhaps accompanying his act of self-denial with a shake of the head (imitating his mother) or a vocal "No! No!" (Stayton *et al.*, 1971).

The child's increasing cognitive maturity, for example, his cognitive differentiation of self from others, allows the toddler to recognize causal relationships in a more realistic manner. Among the realities he perceives is his relative impotence in the power structure of the home. This is postulated by Ausubel and Sullivan (1970) to contribute to the devaluation of his ego. But it also transforms what Kohlberg refers to as his assimilation of the interesting into a definite desire for power and control over things and people (Kohlberg, 1963). This motivation, and the differentiation of self from others, are thought to be essential for the perception and subsequent imitation of the behaviour of models. When the adult does something fascinating, the child wishes to see if he can also do it. According to Ausubel and Sullivan the next best thing to being omnipotent (which the child cannot be) is to be a satellite of people who are. The child has to accept volitional dependency, becoming subservient to the will of his parents. This demand for the subordination of the child's will, counterbalanced by demands that he display more executive independence, plus the factor of increasing self-awareness, characteristically lead to the negativistic crisis referred to above. We now get a situation in which the child who has previously accepted help without any fuss, insisting (sometimes excessively from the parents' point of view) that he display his competence by managing on his own. So it doesn't take long for what parents might perceive as "problems" of disobedience to appear. These are not simply difficulties due to the child "not listening"—an absence of obedience; they are more likely to be wilful acts of rebellion, a deliberate countering of the mother's will. Negativism is an exaggerated form of resistance, occurring when a child becomes stubborn and "contrary", often doing quite the opposite of what the mother wishes. To put it graphically, the child goes through a stage of sheer "bloody mindedness'. This begins at about eighteen months and reaches its zenith at about three, after which it rapidly declines.

Parents and teachers are more sensitive to the breaking of certain kinds of rules than others. On the one hand there are the conventional rules of good manners and of correct behaviour, and on the other hand there are the rules concerning sympathy and respect for others, keeping faith, honesty and so on. The latter—moral issues—are given greatest lip-service, but the conventional rules are sometimes treated as if they were sacred moral principles. Gorer's survey (1955) of English attitudes revealed that aggressive acts were the ones which parents felt most strongly it was their duty to uproot, eradicate or control.

Training of sexual impulses is one of those life tasks which are universal in child-rearing. All children have to learn to place certain restraints on their sexual impulses and to behave in certain ways thought appropriate to their gender. "Sex-typing" is the process by which the child learns the behaviour and attitudes culturally appropriate to his sex. The foundations of a child's "gender identity" are laid down with more emphasis during the toddler stage than has been the case during the previous phase of development. After the consolidation of training in the next preschool period, gender identity is established pretty well irreversibly.

An important developmental task for the toddler is the achievement of continence in toilet functions. All societies insist on this training; parents of whatever culture, demand that their offspring must learn not to evacuate the body's waste products within the immediate living area. The control of elimination means the inhibiting of processes which are, at first, completely involuntary. The baby's muscles must mature until they are strong enough and coordinated enough to hold back the waste products that are trying to emerge from his body. Of all the muscles in the trunk region, those which control the organs of elimination are the slowest to come under voluntary control. This is perfectly understandable because the finer muscles are involved.

Ordinarily, bowel control comes after the child can walk (somewhere between the ages of one and two); bladder control comes somewhat later. Many babies acquire the "dry habit" during the day between the ages of two and two-and-a-half, although they have frequent lapses when they are excited or tired. As much as another year may pass before the child is dry at night, and this, too, is subject to many lapses. The difficulty of this exercise in self-control depends on the child's degree of maturity when training begins. There are fashions concerning the age of initiating toilet-training, just as there are in other child care practices (notably whether to breast feed or not). In 1935 an American survey (Fries, 1935) found that the average age for initiating bowel training was six months. A 1957 survey (Sears, Maccoby and Levin, 1957) put it at eleven months, and yet another (Heinstein, 1966) carried out in 1966 found that 57% of mothers were patient enough to have postponed toilet training until after eighteen months. There is a wide (and normal) range of differences in children's acquisition of the "dry habit" and wide variations in parents' threshold of tolerance of incontinence. This makes for problems in certain families. Unfortunately, some parents are very competitive, and the "fact" that "little Johnny next door" is trained while "our Jimmy" (three months older) is not, becomes a source of embarrassment, resentment or anxiety. The potting situation has been aptly described as follows:

. . . like every other early coupling situation (it) is full of an unspoken language in which a system of minimal cues plays its part. The mother requires to learn the natural rhythms of her child, the rate at which food moves along his alimentary tract, the filling and emptying capacities of his visceral organs and the sensitivities of the thresholds concerned in giving signals that herald a need. The average mother learns this language without much difficulty. . . . In the normal training situation, the mother's prompt response to the child's physiological cues and her own communications during the process gradually make the child aware of his own cues, so that he is able, eventually, to take over mother's role in the potting situation and thereby become autonomous (Anthony, 1957).

Severe toilet training is thought by psychoanalysts to produce problems of adjustment. When anal erotism is repressed it is thought to give rise to the anal character—the classical triad of attributes being obstinacy, orderliness and parsimony (see: Beloff, 1957; Hetherington and Brackbill, 1963; Jones, 1948).

A high order of skill at discriminating cues is required of the toddler in the toilet training situation. The same applies to his learning to discriminate between these situations in which it is appropriate to show dependent behaviour and those in which it is not; between those objects which he can touch and those which he cannot; and those times when he is being "manly" or "a real personality" when he stands up for his "rights" and those when his aggressiveness is chastized for being "naughty". We take up this issue of discrimination learning again in the chapter on self-restraint.

The toddler stage spans roughly the first part of what Piaget calls the *"preoperational representation* period", a phase of symbolic thought development (Piaget, 1951). This phase of cognitive development begins with a "preconceptual stage" that lasts from about two years of age until a child is four years old or thereabouts. He learns the basic use of language for simple communication. The child's acquisition of language (first symbols and then concepts) now proceeds to dominate his mental life. When the child begins to speak it is possible to distinguish two categories of conversing; egocentric speech and socialized speech. In the former, according to Piaget, the child does not bother to know to whom he is speaking nor whether he is being listened to. He does not attempt to place himself inside the point of view of the listener as he does with socialized speech. During this stage the child is continually investigating; he discovers new symbols such as how a stick can represent a gun. As yet his thought is not organized into concepts and rules. During this phase several systematic errors in basic logic appear in the child's thinking. One of these—the error of realism—refers to the conviction of youngsters that everything they see is seen in the same way by other individuals.

The love and affection of parents for the child during this difficult and conflict-full period of life, their unfolding attitudes toward him as he copes with his impulses and failures, are of importance in the more and more sophisticated evolution of his self-image. The expressed attitudes and behaviour of the various individuals in the family provide him with information about his mastery, goodness and worth. Living up to parental expectations (or always failing to do so in the case of over-critical or hostile parents) and the consequences of such endeavours become part of his self-concept.

# 8. Dependency Problems

STRECKER (1946) writes that every woman who bears children is confronted by a dilemma from which there is no escape. As he puts it:

The future social behaviour of a child has its beginning and is patterned in the conflicting sensations and emotions that arise from the early relationship between the mother and child. For the child, the mother is not only the great Dispenser of pleasure and love and the great Protectress, but also the source of pain, the ruthless Thwarter and Frustrater. So the dilemma of the mother is likewise the dilemma of the child. It is a delicately balanced conflict of clinging and rejecting and, depending on which way the balance is tipped, the child either learns to meet successfully the larger give-and-take aspects of mature living or he doesn't. If the give-and-take capacity is not developed, the child will fail to adjust himself to his own life and to society. As a result, the child never grows up. He remains emotionally immature.

The interdependence of all people is an inescapable fact of life so that what constitutes problematical dependency (especially in the case of children) is a highly imprecise judgement. Ordinarily, dependency is not considered a problem; in fact it is a necessity, for, compared with the young of other species, the human infant is ill-prepared to fend for himself.

Antonovsky (1959) defines dependency as behaviour whose goal is seeking help or attention. She used three measures of dependency responses:

(a) *seeking help*—a measure of dependency in which the child seeks help from the mother,
(b) *affectional contact*—a measure of dependency in which the child seeks the mother's attention by making affectionate responses toward her,
(c) *noninteractive play*—a measure of independence in which the child plays by himself, ignoring the mother's presence.

At what point does dependent behaviour become problematical? Beller (1955) suggests that excessively dependent behaviour shows itself particularly in the needless seeking of help. Rather than showing initiative, the child keeps going to an adult for assistance. He requires aid not only when he comes up against some real obstacle, but even when the task is of a routine nature. Physical proximity—the need to stay close to an adult—is yet another behaviour suggestive of dependency. It may take the form of continually seeking physical contact. The child may always want to sit on his mother's lap or hold tenaciously on to her. Attention-seeking behaviour is a further clue; here the child habitually wants the adult to watch him, talk to him, or look at something he has made. Finally, the child who seeks frequent reassurance and approval is manifesting his inability to rely on his own competence.

The term "dependency" is unsatisfactory and it has been tellingly criticized by Bowlby (1969) and Ainsworth (1970). They prefer the more neutral term "attachment"—a word not without its own difficulties. Nevertheless, the concept of dependency is so pervasive in the clinical literature, that we have to consider it. The criteria of what can be considered dependency "symptoms", naturally change with age. Thus the defining behaviours described by Antonovsky and Beller are quite normal (i.e., appropriate or usual) in a young infant and can hardly be thought of as pathological. The peak period for "clinging" behaviour is difficult to specify because there is a shortage of longitudinal information about attachment behaviour after the age of two. However, it would not be unusual to find a good deal of dependency behaviour between the ages of six months and three years.

Lee, Wright and Herbert (1972) differ from Ainsworth (1970) and Bowlby (1969) in the sense of not rejecting the term "dependent" out of hand. It is thought to be useful for describing certain aspects of attachment behaviour. A proviso is that it must be balanced by its converse of "independence" for the grouping of items of mother-oriented or mother-based behaviour. The authors carried out a longitudinal study at the University of Leicester to examine the attachment behaviour of 27 children of both sexes at 12 months and again at 24 months. This investigation was an attempt to refine the kind of "attachment" measures used by researchers like Ainsworth and Rheingold. In addition to attachment behaviour, the intention was to study behaviour consequent upon secure attachment (exploration, approach to or avoidance of strangers, reaction to social reinforcement, etc.).

Each mother–child pair was observed in a laboratory situation (a) for some 120 minutes when the child was 12 months old, and (b) for about 40 minutes at 24 months. Various "episodes" were introduced in each session at each age, to vary the social situation (e.g., open-field situation, entry of a stranger, mother leaving child alone). All sessions were recorded on videotape, each session being later analysed in terms of attachment responses (of the kind mentioned earlier plus many others). Background details of the child's ordinal position and milestones of development, parental rearing techniques and philosophy, etc., were obtained from his mother in an extensive interview, as were details of the infants' daily routines. The pattern of intercorrelations and tests of mean differences led the authors to conclude that:

(1) Measures of attachment were stable between children by "split half" and "repetition" procedures, and intercorrelated logically with each other.
(2) The basic attachment measures proved amenable to classification into variables of "dependent attachment", and "independent attachment". This classification proved an invaluable basis for the assessment of the various episodes. The authors felt constrained by their data to handle even "early "and "simple" attachment behaviour at one year of age in terms of "independence" and "dependence" measures, i.e., as subclasses *within* the superordinate framework of an overall attachment system existing between mother and child.
(3) Significant sex differences appeared early, boys being much more exploratory, "object-centred", and "independent" than girls at one year of age.
(4) At two years of age, both sexes appeared to show "dependent" characteristics to a much greater extent, but girls became, very often, the more "independent" of the sexes; at this age, boys were more "dependent" and less exploratory.
(5) The degree of motor development of the child did not appear to appreciably influence attachment behaviour, at any age, but later weaning to solid foods was associated with earlier maturation and more "independent" behaviour in the child.
(6) After the first few episodes, the researchers found it possible to "predict" a variety of social behaviours by the child in later and varied episodes.
(7) Mothers who sought physical proximity to their children, when the latter were one year of age, tended to be, throughout the episodes, those mothers whose children were more "dependent".
(8) Throughout the research it became more and more apparent that *motivational* rather than maturational factors were immediately responsible for the main attachment acts of the child.

What became increasingly evident as this study proceeded was the complexity of the "language" of attachment—a fact to make one cautious about accepting some of the simplistic generalizations about dependency in the clinical literature.

Smith *et al.* (1963) placed infants in a playpen in such a way that each infant could see his mother, a stranger, or a neutral stimulus on a television screen. The playpen revolved slowly, so that the infant could, by crawling, keep the image in view. Results showed that infants between 10 and 20 months of age would spend about 35 seconds per minute of an experimental period crawling to keep in visual contact with the image of the mother, in contrast to about 30 seconds for a stranger, and 15 seconds in the control condition. At 22 to 26 months of age, infants spent 52 seconds in visual contact with the mother image, 45 seconds with the stranger, and 16 seconds with the control. When infants passed 26 months of age, the orienting behaviour toward the mother continued to increase, whereas the interest in the stranger dropped off somewhat. The experimenters observed that the marked increase in attempting to keep in contact with mother that occurred between 22 and 26 months, coincided with the age at which crying at environmental changes reaches a peak.

Stendler (1952) states that there are two "critical" periods during which the preschool child might become excessively dependent as a consequence of frustration. The first period occurs near the end of his first year of life. The child, with his glimmering awareness of his absolute dependence on mother, tests out her responses toward him. It is as if he is working out the extent to which he can rely on her. It is thought essential to meet the infant's dependency needs during this phase of development. If separated from the mother during this period, the infant (as we saw in Chapter 7) is likely to experience anxiety which he will later attempt to resolve by making intense demands on the mother.

The second critical period (or more accurately, "sensitive" period) is thought to come between the ages of two and three when a child is expected to relinquish some of his dependent attitudes and behaviours. The human infant during the third year of life becomes fearful and anxious when the mother leaves him temporarily. Arsenian (1943) noted that infants and young children placed in a strange room without their mothers showed anxiety; those whose mothers were present played adaptively. The mother's presence seemed to induce a sense of security; her absence evoked anxiety, thus indicating the presence of dependent attachment. Disturbances of a serious nature in the child's dependency needs at this time, may arouse insecurity in his relationship with his mother, thereby exacerbating his dependency drive. The Newsons report this interview with a Nottingham miner's wife:

Ever since I left her that time I had to go into hospital (two periods, 17 days each, child aged two years), she doesn't trust me any more. I can't go anywhere— over to the neighbours or to the shops—I've always got to take her. She wouldn't. leave me. She went down to the school gates at dinner time today. She ran like mad home. She said, "Oh, Mam, I thought you was gone!" She can't forget it. She's still round me all the time. I just sit down and put her on my knee and love her. Definitely. If I don't do it, she says "Mam, you don't love me any more"; I've *got* to sit down (Newson and Newson 1970).

By about $3\frac{1}{2}$ years most children will separate from their mother, at least for a reasonably short time and especially if they know the adults to whom they are entrusted. Before this age it is a somewhat hazardous matter labelling the child's dependent behaviours as maladjusted.

The object of a child's dependency strivings may shift with age. This raises the issue of the persistence and generality of dependency. Danziger (1971) puts it this way:

The naïve and unreflecting tendency of human beings is to see their interaction in terms of agents endowed with permanent and constant properties . . . As long as we are personally engaged in a relationship, this is a useful way of introducing some order into our experience of other people; it is also a useful way of identifying some of the problems we meet in our daily interaction with others. But if we want to play the role of scientist or psychologist and to gain some knowledge of the other as he really is, we need to step outside the confines of a particular relationship and look at the person in *all* his important relationships. When we do this, we generally find that what we had taken to be a reliable, general personal quality is no such thing, but only appears in certain types of relationship. We may find that . . . a particular child is called 'overdependent' only by female teachers. In other words, we have no right to expect that the labels attached to individuals by particular classes of others correspond to any truly general personality characteristics that will reliably manifest themselves no matter what the circumstances.

What can be said about the persistence of dependent behaviour? Kagan and Moss (1960) carried out a longitudinal study on 27 males and 27 females from birth through adolescence, at the Fels Research Institute. Their findings suggest that passive dependent behaviour remains stable over time for the dependent female but not for the dependent male. Their results are interpreted as supporting the importance of cultural influences which operate to reinforce the sex roles. The social pressures work in such a way that the small boy is encouraged to become self-reliant and independent, while the small girl is directed toward the stereotype of relative passivity.

## Independence Strivings

Almost as soon as the infant learns to seek help, he begins to learn to manage without it. Independence becomes an end in itself. Young children take great pride in being able to do things for themselves. Rheingold and Eckerman (1970) observe that as soon as the infant is able to move, he begins to separate himself from his mother. At first, he does so by inching along on his belly. "Later he creeps, and then walks away from his mother. He goes out the door and enters another room. In time he walks out of the house, plays in the yard all morning, goes to school, goes still farther away to high school, and then to college and to work. . . . Eventually he sets up his own home and produces infants who, in turn, repeat the process".

Rheingold and Eckerman note that the infant's separation from his mother is of crucial psychological importance, because it greatly widens his opportunities to interact with the environment. The universe can only be explored and understood if the infant becomes separated from the mother. As long as he is in physical contact with his mother, his universe is limited to her person and the adjoining environment. There are limits to what even the most attentive and indulgent mother can bring to an infant.

It makes considerable difference whether the separation is done voluntarily or not. As we saw in the previous chapter, human infants who are separated from their mothers after the age of six months or thereabouts manifest fear or resentment. They enjoy separation from their mothers only if they are in control so that they can initiate it and can return to home base (mother) at will.

Rheingold and Eckerman (1970) placed mothers and their ten-month-old infants in one of two adjoining rooms. About two-thirds of the infants were at the crawling stage, and of the remaining third, half could creep on their stomachs while the other half were already toddling. The experimental treatments consisted of placing one or more toys in one of the adjoining rooms. They were connected to each other by an open door. Should the child decide to explore the second room he could see his mother through it. Even when there were no toys in the second room, infants spent about a third of the ten-minute observation period in it. When a toy was placed in the second room, the infants spent a little more time there, often bringing the toy back to the first room. Infants who visited the second room did not stay there, but instead went back and forth, as though testing the situation and their "independence".

In the next phase of the experiment, infants who had participated in the first phase without the toy were now retested with a toy in the adjoining room. The familiarity of the experimental environment was apparently re-assuring, because they now spent considerably less time with their mothers and about half of the ten-minute observation period in the second room. Those infants who had experience with the toy in the first observation did not increase their time in the second room on the second trial when one toy was present, but did increase it considerably when three toys were available.

The results confirmed the hypothesis that infants are attracted by novelty and seek to maximize their stimulation, at least under conditions where they can maintain visual contact with their mothers and feel free to return to them at any time.

## Self Help

If dependency is conceptualized (Sechrest and Wallace, 1967) as a strategy which occurs when a child relies too readily on others to solve his problems for him, then a child's independence can be measured, in part, by the degree to which he can help himself. The level of self-help that parents expect of their children depends not only on their individual notions but on the society in which they live. The threshold for judging at what point this strategy becomes maladaptive in childhood—a time of normal dependency—is probably lower in American society than many other cultures. It is a central issue of American child-rearing philosophy that independence-training should come early and be fairly comprehensive.

In some cultures, mothers continue to breast feed, fondle and cuddle young children for longer periods than in others. The Newsons' study (1970) of children brought up in Nottingham, provides information about the amount of self-help expected of children in urban working-class and middle-class cultures. Their survey of four-year-olds shows that at this age, 79% of the children studied could make purchases in shops, although their mothers often waited outside while the purchase was made. Seventeen per cent of the children dressed themselves completely in the mornings and 39% took responsibility for undressing themselves at night; 34% would clear up their own playthings. As regards physical dependence, the Newsons found that 97% of the mothers positively encouraged cuddling at this age, although in some cases the child did not seem to enjoy this experience. This may be quite a normal expression of the child's developing sense of his independent personality. There were few differences between working-class children and middle-class children in the amount of self-help expected.

Self-help skills and other indices of independence sometimes vanish temporarily when a child suddenly finds that he has to share the affection and attention of his mother with a new baby sister or brother. His jealousy is often accompanied by behaviour which reveals a return to more infantile strategies of adjustment. He may become tearful and whiny, clinging to his mother's skirts, going back to baby talk and even returning to incontinence. Such "regressive" attention-seeking behaviour may indicate that the child feels threatened and rejected and has concluded that he can only compete for his previous monopoly position by becoming a baby again.

Many parents and teachers, in their eagerness to promote independence in children, fail to appreciate that dependence is a prerequisite of independence. The child can become independent only after he has learned that he can depend on his parents' acceptance, approval, and support. If his dependency needs are frustrated, he may lack sufficient support and nurturance to progress successfully through the experiences culminating in independence. Frustration of basic dependency drives is quite apt to occur in our culture because of the society's emphasis on early independence training and because of the economic and personal (career) pressures on women to return to work. The mothers whose babies tend to cling between the ages of twelve and eighteen months tend to be the mothers whose children can separate without too much fuss for brief periods at about three years of age (Bowlby, 1969). This may be the age when the child has to make his first big move away from mother. He may go to a playgroup or nursery school.

## The Genesis of Dependency Problems

Sears, Maccoby and Levin (1957) have attempted to isolate some of the antecedents of (*inter alia*) dependency behaviour in their monograph on the child-rearing methods of 379 American mothers. The mothers of five-year-olds were chosen from those living in two suburbs of a large metropolitan area in New England. One suburb was primarily residential and the occupants were mostly of middle-class occupational level, whereas the other suburb contained considerable heavy industry with the population mostly working-class people. Eight schools supplied the sample. Standardized interviews were conducted by ten trained women interviewers. Various dimensions concerning the mother had to do with (1) her disciplinary technique; (2) her permissiveness; (3) her severity in applying techniques; (4) her temperamental qualities; and (5) her positive inculcation of more mature behaviour in her child. These were based on interview schedules or rating scales. Analysis of the interviews was made to decide on the ratings to be given; ratings were made by ten advanced graduate students. Each interview was rated independently to test the reliability of rating. Final scores were on pooled judgements of the two raters.

Sears *et al.* (op. cit.) report the following intercorrelations among child dependency measures:

| Scale | 2 | 3 | 4 | 5 |
|---|---|---|---|---|
| (1) How much attention wanted | 0·50 | 0·21 | 0·20 | 0·71 |
| (2) Wanting to be near; clinging | | 0·27 | 0·17 | 0·63 |
| (3) Earlier tendency to cling | | | 0·16 | 0·29 |
| (4) Objection to separation | | | | 0·43 |
| (5) Over-all rating of dependency | | | | |

To digress for a moment, Yarrow, Campbell and Burton (1968) attempted to replicate the Sears' findings. Dependency (and aggression) were assessed by questionnaires and interviews with mothers and by teachers' ratings—conducted with regard to the same nursery-school children. The intercorrelations among maternal questionnaire responses (ranging between 0·22 and 0·38) were very much lower than the intercorrelation among the responses to interviews covering the same questions. The higher correlations in the interview material could, of course, be artefacts produced by coding procedures and their susceptibility to halo effects. The correlations between mothers' questionnaire and mothers' interview responses only amounted to 0·39. The correlation between independent ratings of a child's dependency by two teachers was 0·47. This compared with a correlation of 0·29 obtained by an analysis of overall measures of the child's dependency derived from two independent sources, namely parent and teacher. In the latter case, if there was a general personality factor involved, it accounted for less than 9% of the variance in the children studied and in the case of the former, less than 23%. Sears, Rau and Alpert (1965) used trained observers to obtain five different measures of dependency behaviour in nursery-school children. They obtained correlations ranging from −0·24 to +0·23 for boys and −0·03 to +0·71 for girls.

The point about this digression is that with such unimpressive correlations to support the concept of dependency as a general trait, it is difficult to move on with any confidence to a review of evidence on child-rearing antecedents of dependency behaviour. Sears and his colleagues were sceptical about the possibility that there is any single direction of cause-and-effect relationships in the child-rearing process. As they put it:

True, the mother's personality comes first, chronologically, and she starts the sequence of interactive behaviour that culminates in the child's personality. But once a child starts to be over-dependent—or is *perceived* as being so by his mother—he becomes a stimulus to the mother and influences her behaviour to him. Perhaps, within the present group of mothers, over-dependency of their children increased the mothers' rejective feelings, made them more angry and hence more punitive for aggression. The whole relationship could be circular. An enormous amount of painstaking research will be required to untangle these phenomena (Sears *et al.*, 1957).

What research there is tends to be disappointingly meagre in the way of statistically significant and consistent findings (see Yarrow *et al.*, 1968).

## Child-rearing Practices and Attitudes

In an earlier study, Sears and his associates (Sears *et al.*, 1953) found that severe weaning practices in infancy were associated with dependent patterns of behaviour during the pre-school years. Furthermore, dependent behaviour in pre-school girls was also related to mothers' insistence on rigid feeding schedules during infancy. Some theorists have postulated a relationship between the severity of frustrations suffered by infants and later manifestation of excessive dependency strivings. Although the dependent tendencies are those learned in earliest childhood, their effects are thought to be most apparent when the child is somewhat older—at the pre-school or school-going age. Contrary to what might have been expected, however, the investigators found no relationship between dependency tendencies and the severity of toilet training the children had experienced as infants. The later study (Sears *et al.*, 1957) did not confirm the results—concerning infant feeding and weaning—of this investigation. No general connection between severity of weaning and dependency could be elicited. No relationship was found between rigid feeding schedules and dependency in girls, but boys fed on self-demand (nonrigid) scheduling were more dependent.

The study revealed no apparent relationship between the display of regular and excessive dependent behaviour in a youngster at five years of age and the warmth his mother had given him when he was a baby. General dependency at age five could not be linked to either breast or bottle feeding, to the age at which weaning began or ended, or to any other common infantile frustrations. Although such frustrations frequently caused dependency at the time they occurred, this effect was only temporary. Almost half the mothers studied were quite responsive to their babies' crying, usually (or in some cases, always) picking up the baby immediately. Such responsiveness was *not* associated with later dependency in the children.

The authors found that the mother who had an accepting and tolerant attitude toward dependent behaviour, was also likely to be, in general, affectionately warm toward her child; to be gentle in toilet training, permissive about sexual interests shown by him, unlikely to use physical punishment for dependent behaviours, and tolerant when he was angry and aggressive toward his parents.

### Reaction to Feelings of Helplessness

Horney (1945) believes that early feelings of helplessness and isolation engender a profound anxiety which gives rise to dependency strategies. The findings of Sears *et al.* (1957) lend a little support to this idea. More than one-third (36%) of the mothers studied were often irritable and punished their children when they hung and clung to them. It was found that their irritable scolding while pulling themselves away from their clinging children only increased the frequency of such dependency. The most dependent children of all belonged to mothers who, for a time, irritably rejected dependency demands, but eventually gave in to them, thus rewarding the child by intermittent reinforcement.

We have seen how the mother, as the agent for meeting the child's needs, becomes, in operant conditioning terms, a source of reinforcement. She is the configuration of stimuli that is consistently associated with the reduction of his needs—she changes him when he is wet, and feeds him when he is hungry. He learns to be dependent on her as the instrument for meeting his needs, i.e., he acquires a form of *instrumental dependence* (Heathers, 1955). The infant also learns to seek help from others.

There is another aspect of dependence—*emotional dependence*—which is illustrated by the events that occur after instrumental dependent tendencies have begun to be learned. After the first few days or weeks an infant will cease crying when picked up before his primary need, e.g., hunger, is relieved. His mother's mere presence has acquired reward value for him. The goal here is more than mere help; it is about *relationship*. Her comforting presence has become a secondary drive in itself.

In most families the child, as he grows up, will tend to obtain a mixture of rewards and punishments—and not always in a consistent pattern—for dependent behaviours. He will be required to be independent in some situations and allowed (or even encouraged) to be autonomous in others. The question of whether a child remains dependent or becomes relatively independent is likely to be contingent upon parental rewards and punishments for dependent and autonomous behaviours. Indeed the frequency of dependent behaviours displayed by the child has been found to be associated with direct permissiveness for, and reinforcement of, such behaviours (Heathers, 1953; Bandura, 1960; Finney, 1961).

Given such findings, it might be predicted at a highly generalized level, that a nurturant parent who is characteristically interested in, and encouraging, rewarding and supportive toward her child, would tend to enhance his dependence on her, and possibly others. Such a global dimension of parental behaviour (called "maternal warmth") has proved to be a poor predictor of dependency in children. Parental warmth is not related *per se* to the intensity or breadth of infantile attachment behaviour (see: Maccoby and Masters, 1970). And the weight of the available evidence is against any relationship between parental warmth and dependency in children of various ages. Sears *et al.* (1957) found (as we saw earlier) that maternal warmth was unrelated to children's current dependency, i.e., at kindergarten age. Finney (1961) found the same lack of relationship between maternal nurturance (defined as equivalent to warmth) and dependency in 31 boys aged five to sixteen who were patients at a mental health clinic. Cairns (1962), in a study of 60 second- and third-grade children, demonstrated an absence of relationship between maternal and paternal warmth and the child's responsiveness to social reinforcement. Baumrind and Black (1967) and Hatfield *et al.* (1967) found a relationship between parental warmth and *independence* in pre-school boys and nursery-school boys and girls respectively. Siegelman (1966) investigated children's dependency in the school setting. A small but significant negative relationship was found between mother love and child dependency. However, Bandura and Walters (1959) found that parental warmth *was* associated with dependency (and nonaggressiveness) in adolescence, while Bandura (1960) found it to be related to high levels of dependency in pre-adolescent boys.

The methodological problems in the area of research into child-rearing in particular, and socialization in general, are legion (see: Danziger, 1971; Maccoby and Masters, 1970). The unreliability of retrospective reports (see: Robbins, 1963), the difficulty of distinguishing between "socializing variables" and "relationship variables" (Schaffer and Emerson, 1964b), the problem of separating the effects of early parental behaviour from concurrent practices (Kagan and Moss, 1962) and the formidable task of measuring subtle parent-child two-way interactions (see: Mussen, 1960) are but a few of the reasons why it is not surprising if researchers are often unable to replicate each other's findings. In the case of parental warmth and dependency there is almost a consensus about the lack of relationship between them. This is somewhat unexpected given (on one side of the equation) the high level of abstraction and the relatively undifferentiated nature of an attitudinal concept like maternal warmth, and on the other, the concreteness and manysidedness of dependent behaviour in children. Warmth, in fact, may be positively related to dependency when it interacts with other socialization conditions such as parental restrictiveness. (The effects of such interacting variables are illustrated in Fig. 3, page 153.)

Smith (1958) found that maternal rejection (the polar opposite of warmth) was positively related to observed dependency in pre-school children. Marshall (1961) showed that parental "interpersonal distance" from children is related to high frequency of teacher-contacting among nursery school-aged girls. Tharp and Wetzel (1969) have demonstrated the modification of dependent behaviour by means of behaviour therapy techniques. They show incidentally that teachers can be very helpful "behaviour therapists" for children with school problems. A good example of this was a three-year-old child whose behaviour was excessively dependent, in the sense of being almost exclusively oriented towards the grown-ups in her school. This is how Foxwell (1966) described the situation: she tagged along after teachers, spoke to them almost exclusively, only participated in activities which teachers were conducting or watching closely. She became more entrenched in this pattern as the weeks went by. Observation indicated that the girl indeed spent only about three per cent of the typical pre-school session in interaction with other children; by contrast, she spent nearly twenty per cent of her time interacting with the teachers. Social reinforcement of the child's interactions with other children was begun. At the same time, eradication (extinction) of her adult-orientated interactions was instituted. Thus, the teachers attended to the girl only when she played with other children, but virtually every time she did so. When she attempted to interact with the teachers, they turned away, often with a friendly but brief excuse, but nevertheless ceasing to provide social stimulation for adult-orientated behaviour.

An auxiliary technique, called "priming", was also used by the teachers. In order to provoke some interactions with other children, which they could then reinforce, the teachers prompted other children to approach the girl, perhaps with an attractive doll or other piece of play equipment. If an interaction ensued between the children, the distant but alert teacher immediately moved in to admire both children, thus reinforcing the girl for her behaviour involving the other child. Such promptings increased the number of interactions observed each day, but did not immediately produce very lengthy or complex social behaviour in the girl. By the seventh day, the combination of reinforcing her interactions with other children and extinguishing her interactions with adults had produced a marked decrease in adult-orientated behaviour. Her child-orientated behaviours quite suddenly increased in both frequency and duration. Six more days of reinforcement with no further priming produced a very high rate of interactions with other children (40% of the time available). Adult-orientated interaction decreased at the same time to 5% of the typical session.

Eventually the teachers had managed to encourage the girl's interactions with children to an average of nearly 50% of each session. Then, they began a quite gradual reduction of their reinforcement practices; they reinforced fewer and fewer of the girl's interactions with other children. As this went on, the quality of the child's play with other children increased in such a way that she received a growing amount of social reinforcement from them. As this was seen, the teachers withdrew more quickly, and found that they could eventually forget the case, as such. The child was now firmly in the reinforcing hands of her peer group. She had developed a repertoire of behaviours, rather new for her, which produced stimulus consequences from other children of a reinforcing kind. Observations, five, six and seven weeks later, showed that the child's number and quality of social interactions remained quite high, despite the fact that the teachers were planning no special contingencies for her at all.

## Rejection

We discussed problems arising from the physical separation from parents in chapter 7. There is also a form of psychological "separation" brought about by rejection of the child. For some children, rejection means callous and indifferent neglect or positive hostility and cruelty from the parents. The cruelty does not always take a physical form; it may be emotional and subtle so that the child comes to believe he is an unmitigated nuisance; that his very existence makes his parents unhappy so that he is something to be devalued.

Among the important clinical implications of extreme rejection are the severely punitive parental attitudes toward and sanctions for dependent behaviour on the part of the child. One would predict that if rejecting parents tend to punish dependent behaviour, their children would eventually suppress such behaviour. Bandura and Walters (1959) indeed found that aggressive boys who have undergone a good deal of parental rejection show much less dependent behaviour than non-aggressive boys who have been accepted by their parents. But there is an exception.* If the parents withhold or are meagre with their attentions and care, but don't actually punish dependent behaviour, they are likely to *intensify* the child's needs for attention and care. The more a child is "pushed away" (figuratively speaking) the more he clings for dear life (Hartup, 1963; Bowlby, 1969; McCord *et al.*, 1962; Wittenborn, 1956).

If rejection is not extreme, both reward and punishment may occur and the effects of rejection will depend on which pattern predominates. Sears, Maccoby and Levin (1957) report (as we saw) that parents who irritably rejected their children's requests for dependency but who eventually succumbed to such demands (a form of intermittent reinforcement) produced the most dependent children.

The trouble with dependency needs is that every child has some awareness of the pleasure and comfort of being cared for; even the most reluctant mother has to attend to certain of her child's basic wants. So the child knows what it is missing and craves for more—especially if he isn't specifically discouraged by punishment. This is where dependency training differs from training in sexual matters which is likely to be consistently punished, or at least, ignored (i.e., never rewarded). In the case of dependency, because of his sheer helplessness, the child will be occasionally rewarded with some signs of nurturance.

## Maternal Overprotection

Bandura and Walters (1963) suggest the variables of maternal warmth and demonstrativeness as possible antecedents of dependency behaviour. Clinicians, generally, have been concerned about the effects on children of an excess of mothering. Maternal nurturance, in other words, may be a

---

* It is difficult to predict behaviour at the best of times; it is particularly foolhardy to make predictions about the consequences of *punishment* for human actions. (See: page 155.)

vital ingredient for the child's healthy development, but there can be too much of a "good thing".

Levy (1943) investigated 15 cases of overprotective mothers in depth. Their child-rearing methods ensured excessive mother–child contact. In a typical example, the child slept in the same room as his mother for years. She tended to fondle him excessively, watch over him constantly, and prevented him from taking risks or acting in an independent manner. She would fuss a lot about his health by over-medicating and over-dressing him. His mind was made up for him, more often than not. She tended to indulge his every whim in return for absolute obedience. Levy interpreted this transaction as an attempt on the part of the mother to prolong his childhood and keep him tied to her apron strings. Over-protective mothers frequently alternated between dominating the child and submitting to him. According to Levy, such over-protection may lead to excessively dependent behaviour on the part of the child. Certainly, the children in his study tended to be dependent, passive and submissive. It is thought that if the child is discouraged from acting independently, exploring, and experimenting, he acquires timid, awkward, and generally apprehensive behaviours. It is important to remember that what is being referred to here is really extreme maternal behaviour which either involves maternal indulgence (spoiling), domination (restrictiveness and nagging), or a combination of both.

There would seem to be *a priori*, a balance between the over-protective mother, who produces an insecure, clinging child because she never allows him to try things out for himself, and who cannot allow him to "wean" himself from her emotionally, and the rejecting mother who creates an anxious, clinging child because she seems to threaten him with abandonment or makes it obvious that he is a burden. What is the evidence? Symonds (1939) published a comprehensive review of findings—based on many years of experimental and observational research—concerning parent–child relationships. Two major dimensions—acceptance-rejection and dominance-submission—emerged from all this work. Children of submissive parents appeared to be more aggressive, stubborn and disorderly, although more self-confident than the offspring of dominating parents. Dominating parents tended to produce children who were more sensitive, submissive, orderly and polite, better socialized but more dependent. Children who were accepted seemed to manifest characteristics which are generally thought desirable, while those who were rejected were reported to be more neurotic, rebellious and delinquent.

Much of the clinical literature of that era concentrated on the benefits or ill-effects of the extremes of authoritarianism, libertarianism, over-protection and rejection in parents. Gibson (1968) notes that most of the earlier studies had been applied to abnormal parents and abnormal children, and for that reason did not provide a balanced guide to the nature and consequences of the normal variations in parent–child relationships. In addition, most of the studies were based on clinical impressions rather than any sort of objective measures. As Gibson cautions, the kinds of questions which are asked and the way in which the clinician interprets the answers depend on his theories about child development. Not surprisingly what has been referred to as the "folk lore" of parent–child relations tends to be self-validating.

## Parent–Child Relationships

More recent studies of parent-child relations have been made reasonably precise by the application of special psychological instruments (see: Straus, 1969). Factor analytic and computer techniques have also been used in order to reduce the rich variety of childhood and parental behaviours to a few main dimensions. Two main underlying components of parental attitudes and behaviours emerge from many of the studies:
(1) Attitudes which are "warm" (or loving) at one extreme, and "rejecting" (or hostile) at the other;
(2) Attitudes which are restrictive (controlling) at one extreme, and permissive (encouraging autonomy) at the other.

Schaefer (1959) describes parental behaviour in terms of the interactions of the two main attributes, thus a "democratic" mother is one who is both loving and permissive; an "antagonistic" mother combines hostility and restrictiveness; a "protective" mother is one who is both loving and restrictive, and so on. (Fig. 3 below.)

Schaefer's dimensions in the figure below have been combined with the table describing the sort of behaviour and problems produced by different combinations of parental attitude (as summarized by Becker, 1964). The outcomes of these combinations—trends, of course—appear in the inner quadrants.

According to Baumrind (1966), the restrictive or "authoritarian" parent (as she emerges from detailed investigations) is one who attempts to shape, control, and assess the behaviour and attitudes of the child according to a set standard of conduct, usually an absolute standard, motivated by theological considerations and formulated by a higher authority. She values obedience as a virtue and favours punitive, forceful measures to curb self-will at those points where the child's actions or beliefs conflict with what she thinks is proper conduct. She believes in indoctrinating the child with such values as respect for authority, respect for work, and respect for the preservation of traditional order. She does not encourage verbal give and take, believing that the child should accept her word for what is right.

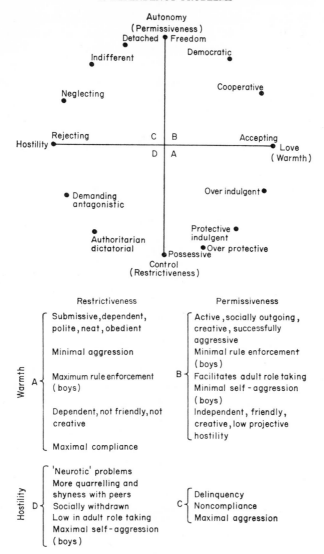

FIG. 3. Empirical relationships between parent variables (Schaefer, 1959) and child behaviours (Becker, 1964).

There is evidence (Becker, 1964) to suggest that strict, autocratic (undemocratic) adult domination and restrictiveness will produce a conforming child, but will handicap him in initiative. Such a child may turn out to be rather passive, colourless, unimaginative and incurious—burdened, in addition, with shyness and a sense of inadequacy. The children of domineering mothers usually lack self-reliance and ability to cope realistically with their problems, and later on fail (or are slow) to accept adult responsibilities. They are apt to be submissive and obedient and to withdraw from situations they find difficult.

According to Baumrind (1966) the technical meaning of calling someone a "permissive parent" is that the parent attempts to behave in a non-punitive, accepting, and affirmative manner toward the child's impulses, desires, and actions; to consult with him about policy decisions and give explanations for family rules; to make few demands for household responsibility and orderly behaviour; to present herself to the child as someone to call upon for help and company as he wishes, not simply as an active agent responsible only for shaping or altering his ongoing or future behaviour; to allow the child to regulate his own activities as much as possible; to avoid the excessive exercise of control, and not encourage him to obey absolute, externally-defined standards; to attempt to use reason but not overt power to accomplish her ends.

This empirical analysis is very different from the popular usage of the word "permissiveness", which tends to be restricted to the extreme end of the dimension with its connotations of "*laisser faire*". The emotional background to this pattern of unbridled licence or "lax discipline" is only too often outright indifference.

Reviews of research (Becker, 1964; Baumrind, 1971) into child-rearing techniques suggest an empirical basis for the notion that there is a "happy medium", that the extremes of permissiveness and restrictiveness entail risks. A blend of permissiveness and a warm encouraging and accepting attitude fits the recommendations of child-rearing specialists who are concerned with fostering the sort of children who are socially outgoing, friendly, creative and reasonably independent and self-assertive. Warm loving, and consistent discipline, in which (when the child can understand them) reasons are given, is thought to produce the rational sort of "obedience" rather than the blind and emotionally dependent following of orders.

The balance is perhaps best illustrated in the philosophy of what Baumrind (1971) calls the "authoritative parent". This kind of mother attempts to direct her child's activities in a rational manner determined by the issues involved in particular disciplinary situations. She encourages verbal give-and-take, and shares with the child the reasoning behind her policy. She values both the child's self expression and his so-called "instrumental attributes" (respect for authority, work and the like); she appreciates both independent self-will and disciplined conformity. Therefore, she exerts firm control at points where she and the child diverge in viewpoint, but does not hem in the child with restrictions. She recognizes her own special rights as an adult, but also the child's individual interests and special ways. The "authoritative parent" affirms the child's present qualities, but also sets standards for future conduct. She uses reason as well as power to achieve her objectives. She does not base her decisions solely on the consensus of the group or the individual child's desires; but also does not regard herself as infallible or divinely inspired. Baumrind found that authoritative parents are most likely to facilitate the development of competence and self-reliance in young children by enhancing responsible purposive and independent behaviour.

There are many inconsistencies, even contradictions, in the literature on parent–child attitudes and relationships and parental child-rearing practices. The isomorphism between parental *attitudes* as measured and specific *behaviours* is limited. Global assessments of such independent variables as parental warmth, hostility, rejection and the like, are too abstract and too coarse to capture many of the subtle nuances of parental behaviour. They lack also sufficient contextual anchorage; that is to say, they do not specify the variations in behavioural interactions between parents and children which occur in *particular* situations and which are necessary to define precise relationships between independent and dependent variables. This applies especially to the fund of dependent variables clinicians are interested in, namely, moral behaviour, delinquent reactions and so on. To quote Danziger:

Extremely hostile and rejecting parents are more likely to have delinquent children, but within the normal range the value of a given reward or punishment depends on its relation to the overall level of nurturance. The same effective reward and punishment can, therefore, occur under quite different overall conditions of nurturance. Behavioural conformity to specific norms in particular situations is more likely to depend on situation-specific sanctions than on the general pattern of parent–child relationships (Danziger, 1971).

## Punishment

We have spoken of inconsistencies in the area of child-rearing research. Nowhere are they more apparent than in that emotionally fraught topic of discussion—punishment (see: Solomon, 1964). Definitions of punishment tend to be tautological. Liberman (1972), for example, states that "spankings . . . are punishments only if they produce a reduction in the behaviour on which they are contingent . . ." Punishment is usually regarded as but one of the forms of negative reinforcement; the latter generally refers to any intentional action by one individual which has aversive emotional consequences (such as anxiety, fear, embarrassment, guilt, disappointment, pain and so on) for another, and which the other is subsequently motivated to avoid. (The problem with this definition is that some people may seek punishment, for example, if it terminates feelings of guilt.)

Walters *et al.* (1972) point out that it is unfortunate that in the discussions of punishment, it is so often the case that it is the painful, extreme, and perhaps rare effects that are emphasized, while the "thorns and little shocks" that occur daily and which may ceaselessly, slowly and effectively change habits and, indeed, destinies, are ignored. Even the most permissive of parents, intentionally or unintentionally, punish their children in the course of bringing them up. To quote Walters *et al.*:

If virtue is its own reward, the acquisition thereof is fraught with inherent punishment. Parents not only whip, spank and beat children, they scold, shout at, isolate and withdraw love from their children, sometimes at the slightest provocation. Many permissive parents who would never dream of beating or otherwise hurting their child may frequently utter a harsh word or send the child from the room for misbehaving. Such actions may cut as deep or more deeply than all but the most violent of thrashings. In no sense are shouting and isolation punishers necessarily secondary to more "fundamental" pain-producing stimuli. Although a number of theorists have implicitly or explicitly defined punishment as a "pain-producing stimulus" the majority of apparent punishments experienced in everyday life are not, strictly speaking, painful.

A review by Marshall (1965) of research on the effects of punishment such as blame, reproof, failure, the word "wrong" and the removal of positive reinforcers (but not including physical punishment) on children, reveals that, in general, it tends to improve learning and performance of various scholastic tasks. However, there is no simple, clearcut relationship between negative reinforcement and performance. Factors found to influence the consequences of negative reinforcement include intellectual and achievement level, complexity of the task, delay of reinforcement, instructions, the subject's and experimenter's personality, and atmosphere in the home or classroom. It is small wonder, when there is such a complex interaction of factors, that investigations do not always appear to replicate each other's findings.

Parents and teachers are, of course, interested in broader implications of the use of punitive types of discipline. Many philosophize regretfully that in a better world we could do without punishment, but "human nature being what it is . . .!" McCandless (1969) has little doubt about the evidence. His view is that *other things being equal* (a phrase that, in the light of the dissimilarity between real life situations and controlled experiments, recurs alarmingly in the literature) it is almost certain that a child learns faster if he receives both positive and negative reinforcement. Positive reinforcement tells him what he may and should do, and negative reinforcement tells him what he may not and should not do. Thus, if he receives both types of reinforcement, he is more fully informed than if he receives only one.

So much, of course, depends upon the nature, intensity, timing and dispenser of negative reinforcement. Sears, Maccoby and Levin (1957) are quite clear about the aspect of severity of punishment in their research. They say:

Punitiveness, in contrast with rewardingness, was a quite ineffectual quality for a mother to inject into her child training. The evidence for this conclusion is overwhelming. The unhappy effects of punishment have run like a dismal thread through our findings. Mothers who punished toilet accidents severely ended up with bed-wetting children. Mothers who punished dependency to get rid of it had more dependent children than mothers who did not punish. Mothers who punished aggressive behaviour severely had more aggressive children than mothers who punished lightly. They also had more depressed children. High physical punishment was associated with high childhood aggressiveness and with the development of feeding problems. Our evaluation of punishment is that *it is ineffectual over the long term as a technique for eliminating the kind of behaviour toward which it is directed.*

The background to punishment is all-important. Punitive methods *persistently* used against a background of rejecting, hostile parental attitudes lead, in the long term, to trouble. These methods are often referred to as power-assertive; the adult asserts dominant and authoritarian control through physical punishment, harsh verbal abuse, angry threats and deprivation of privileges. There is a positive relationship between the extensive use of physical punishment in the home by parents and high levels of aggression in their offspring outside the home (see: Becker, 1964). It would seem that physical violence is the least effective form of negative reinforcement when it comes to *moulding a child's behaviour*. All the evidence to date (Johnson and Medinnus, 1965; Brown, 1965) shows that physical methods of punishment (the deliberate infliction of pain on the child) may for the time being suppress the behaviour that it is meant to inhibit, but the long-term effects are less impressive. Violence begets violence. What the child learns is that might is right. Delinquents have more commonly been the victims of adult assaults—often of a vicious, persistent and even calculated nature—than non-delinquents. Boys who have been caned at school for smoking are more likely to increase their smoking than those not caned.

The evidence we possess about punishment as a disciplinary technique is fragmentary; experiments have scarcely begun to tap the subtlety or diversity of punitive situations which arise in parent–child relationships. Experiments (Aronfreed and Reber, 1965; Walters *et al.*, 1965) have shown that, other things being equal, the closer punishment is to the moment a forbidden act is to be performed the more effective it is in inducing inhibition of the act. (This work is described more fully on page 284.) Generally speaking, the more severe the sanctions are, the more effective are their inhibitory short-term consequences. A proviso is that discrimination between punished and non-punished acts must be relatively easy to make (Aronfreed, 1968). When discriminations are difficult, severe punishment over-arouses the child and interferes with learning. Children can be deterred from committing certain acts by watching others being punished (Walters and Parke, 1964; Walters *et al.*, 1965) although probably not as effectively as by direct punishment. There is evidence (Parke and Walters, 1967) that even a semblance of a positive relationship between an experimenter and child increases the effectiveness of punishment in inhibiting behaviour. Aronfreed (1968) has demonstrated that when punishment of a relatively moderate type is accompanied by explanations it is more effective in producing later resistance to temptation. If it is explicitly associated with a general rule in the child's mind, its effects tend to be more lasting (Parke, 1969).

The trend in research on punishment and its long-term consequences (see: Hoffman, 1970) is toward a recognition of the vital role of cognitive structuring of "wrong" actions. The explanation of why certain acts should be inhibited carries greatest weight when the prohibiting or instructing adult has a warm relationship with a child such that he is liked, respected and listened to.

# 9. Elimination Training

THE PERIOD OF elimination training is not only an important phase in the socializing of the child but also (according to Freudian theory) one of the more sensitive periods of childhood. This is due to the anxiety and conflict which are potential accompaniments of the key learning experiences of this phase. Within a relatively short space of time the toddler must learn, under pain of losing his mother's esteem, "to attach anxiety to all the cues produced by excretory materials—to their sight, smell and touch . . . to deposit faeces and urine only in a prescribed and secret place and to clean its body. It must later learn to suppress unnecessary verbal reference to these matters . . ." (Dollard and Miller, 1950).

The control of elimination means that the child has to inhibit processes which are, at first, completely involuntary. The baby's muscles have to mature until they are strong enough and coordinated enough to hold back the waste substances that are periodically evacuated by his body.

## Bowel Control and Encopresis

Ordinarily, bowel control comes after the child can walk—somewhere between one and two years of age. The *total time* required to complete bowel training has been found to be less (as is the case with weaning) when it is initiated relatively late (Sears *et al.*, 1957). When mothers began bowel training before the child was five months old, nearly ten months (on average) were required for success. But when training was begun later (at twenty months or older), only about five months were required. Children whose toilet training was begun between five and fourteen months or after nineteen months, manifested fewest emotional problems during training. We have already seen that where toilet training does have an adverse effect on childhood adjustment it is not due to rigid toilet training *per se*, but the consequence of a series of associated attitudes and practices on the part of a generally severe mother (Beloff, 1957; Hetherington and Brackbill, 1963).

One of the problems associated with elimination training is encopresis, a disturbance in the regulation of bowel evacuation, involving, usually, involuntary defaecation which is not directly attributable to physical illness. Anthony (1957) defines the problem as the regular passage of a formed motion of normal or near-normal consistency into the bedclothes, clothes or receptacle not intended for the purpose. Occasionally, soiling is associated with the hiding of faeces or the smearing of the walls with excreta. Pringle *et al.* (1966), found that 1·2% of the 1958 National Cohort of British Children were encopretic at the age of seven years. The problem occurs more often in boys than in girls (Rutter *et al.*, 1970).

Unfortunately, as Yates (1970) points out in his detailed discussion of elimination problems, virtually nothing is known of how voluntary initiation of defaecation or its inhibition is achieved. Certainly, there is no uniform aetiology for all cases of encopresis. The search for antecedent variables which may be linked with the problem, produces a list of influences ranging from mental subnormality and phobic anxiety connected with the toilet, to neglected or coercive training in toilet habits.

Encopresis is not, in fact, a unitary symptom. It is a syndrome of which soiling is but one manifestation. Anthony (1957) identified at least three types in his investigations:

(1) *Continuous*—children whose soiling was but one aspect of a general lack of concern with being clean;
(2) *Discontinuous*—children for whom the soiling contrasted sharply with overt attitudes towards regularity and cleanliness in other aspects of living, and
(3) *Retentive*—children with persistent constipation and only occasional encopresis.

It is postulated (Anthony, 1957) that many children in the continuous group have suffered neglectful training, and children in both the retentive and discontinuous categories tend to have had severe and coercive training experiences. Either mothers are too lax in their training methods, so that defaecation remains a pleasurable act, or they are too coercive, so that extreme disgust is associated with the act.

Yates (1970) contends that the continuous encopretic suffers from *a failure to acquire* internal control of the defaecatory act whereas the discontinuous encopretic has *lost* internal control because of externally imposed environmental stress. It is suggested (Anthony, 1957) that the continuous encopretic is in need of habit training rather than psychotherapy. The discontinuous encopretic is thought to have a more serious problem needing psychotherapy for himself and counselling for his parents.

Operant conditioning techniques have been used successfully in the treatment of the continuous type of encopresis in the case of fourteen-year-old Anthony (Gelber and Meyer, 1965). A combination of positive and negative reinforcement was used to modify the chronic encopresis and smearing. After hospitalizing the boy in order to gain "contingency control", the therapists made time off the ward the reinforcer for appropriate toilet behaviour. The negative reinforcer consisted of being confined to the ward; this aversive condition was terminated following a desired response. Punishment for undesirable response also involved limiting Anthony's time off the ward. The most effective positive reinforcer for the boy was the privilege of walking around the hospital grounds. (The therapists stress the need for discovering an appropriate reward, because what is reinforcing for one child may be aversive to the next. They make the point that only careful assessment can ensure the effectiveness of reinforcers.) The total time required to treat Anthony was 62 days. A six-month follow-up revealed only minor relapses and no evidence of symptom substitution.

These operant techniques have been applied successfully by several therapists (Giles and Wolf, 1966; Peterson and London, 1964; Neale, 1963). Sluckin (1973) successfully treated four cases of encopresis attending an out-patient child guidance clinic. Mothers of the children were instructed to reward them for passing a motion in the lavatory. Laxatives (senekot) were prescribed in order to ensure regular and painless bowel movements. A psychological and somatic approach is often required in the case of encopretic problems.

## Bladder Control and Enuresis

Bladder control comes somewhat later than bowel control. Many babies acquire continence during the day between the ages of two and two-and-a-half. Usually, but not invariably, some time must pass before the child is dry at night. At $2\frac{1}{2}$, about 60% are dry in the day. 57% at night and 41% dry both day and night. By the age of 5, the figures for studies in different countries are usually in the 90% plus region. In each year from the age of 5, out of the children still not continent at night, about 15% become dry (De Jonge, 1971). By the age of twelve about 2% of children are still enuretic at night (Blomfield and Douglas, 1956).

Is there a sensitive period for toilet-training the child? If such a concept is defined by a high rate of emergence of a particular behaviour during a particular period, and a lower rate of emergence in the periods preceding and following it, then between $1\frac{1}{2}$ and $4\frac{1}{2}$ (and particularly the third year) is a sensitive period for acquiring the dry habit at night. Not surprisingly, enuresis is defined (Michaels, 1955) in terms of an age factor, viz. as uncontrolled, unintentional voiding of urine at one expulsion usually occurring during sleep, if it occurs past the age of three. Others regard four as a liberal age for control of urination to have been established in so-called normal individuals and refrain from using the term enuresis until then (Hallgren, 1957). The problem is more common in boys than girls (Shepherd *et al.*, 1971). Rutter *et al.* (1970) reported that enuresis is also a problem for about two out of every five encopretics. One in eight of the enuretic children were also soiling.

Morgan and Young (1972) say of enuresis that it:

is one of the most widespread disorders of childhood, and is a problem frequently encountered by most social workers. It is a source of embarrassment to the sufferer, often invoking ridicule or punishment, and can place an intolerable burden upon intrafamilial relationships—especially in those large families living in overcrowded conditions, where several children may wet the bed. For the majority of enuretics, to be a bedwetter carries adverse emotional consequences, and many exhibit some degree of reactive disturbance. Even when this is not apparently the case, enuresis imposes a limit on the child's choice of activities; few enuretics can happily go camping or to stay with friends. In residential establishments, the daily wash of bed-linen is unpleasant and onerous. Because of its widespread, offensive, embarrassing and potentially disturbing nature, the problem of the management and cure of enuresis should be of concern to any caseworker or residential worker involved with an enuretic child; all too often both natural parents and house-parents are forced into a fatalistic acceptance of, and accommodation to, enuresis as an inevitable correlate of child upbringing.

Parents often expect perfect control as soon as the child has apparently mastered the skill of inhibiting nocturnal urination. Like the acquisition of any other new skill, the progress of this one follows the normal curve of acquisition. This means, of course, that lapses are quite usual, and that perfect bladder control is achieved over a period of time rather than suddenly.

Enuresis sometimes represents a behavioural deficit and is called "primary enuresis". The child has never gained control of nocturnal wetting. In "secondary enuresis" he reverts to bedwetting after a period of dryness. The child's control may, anyway, have been tenuous at best. A period of stress may produce the regression; we know that behaviours acquired under stress are particularly prone to break down under emotional strain. A further distinction can also be made between children who are "regularly" and those who are "intermittently" enuretic. In the latter case fluctuating control may point to a psychogenic aetiology. Some children wet the bed in times of stress.

There is, at the best of times, a wide (and normal) range of differences in the ages at which babies and toddlers develop control over their organs of elimination and communicate their needs. From birth onwards, the child becomes dry for gradually increasing periods. At about fifteen months he will point to wet pants and puddles. He may wake at night and cry to be changed. He usually has a word which is used for both urine and faeces. By between 18 months and two years of age most children report to mother when they have soiled their pants. Their vocabulary now distinguishes between urine and faeces. By $2\frac{1}{2}$, 91% of girls and 79% of boys make known their need to urinate. By about 3 years of age, children commonly go to the toilet by themselves. The difficulty of the exercise in self-control depends on the child's degree of maturity when training begins. Once the child has had a dry night then we know that the necessary physical control mechanisms are present. After a month of completely dry nights it is fairly safe to assume that the maturational and training processes are complete.

Enuresis may begin as a relatively "simple" matter of faulty learning. Emotional problems are sometimes superimposed when the child is made to feel acute shame at his "babyish" ways. Only too often he has to endure punishment, scorn and ridicule at home and school. It has been estimated that 10% of enuretic problems in childhood are associated with some organic (physical) disorder of the urinary system. Such cases require urological treatment (Crosby, 1950). The problem may have a multiple aetiology requiring somatic and psychological attention. It is markedly persistent when there is a background of familial disruption (Stein and Susser, 1967). Enuresis frequently but not invariably occurs in association with other behavioural or psychiatric problems (Rutter *et al.*, 1970).

Various treatments involve what is called "symptom suppression". The mother (perhaps on the doctor's advice) may try limiting the child's intake of fluids in the late afternoon and evening. She may also wake the child at night to urinate so that there is no accumulation of an appreciable quantity of urine in the bladder. Drugs are also used to inhibit kidney function. The fallacy of theories based upon restriction of fluids or inhibition of kidney action lies in the failure to understand that the essential feature of the enuretic condition is the failure of the bladder to fill in the normal way. Incontinence will occur during sleep in the case of persistent enuretics even when there is extremely little urine (as little as one fluid ounce) in the bladder. Therefore an essential part of therapy for enuretics is to train them to tolerate a greater and greater quantity of urine in the bladder before the physiological capacity is reached. Treatments which drastically restrict the fluid intake of the child in the late afternoon and evening, make it difficult for the enuretic to achieve continence in sleep because he never becomes accustomed to tolerating a normal volume of urine in the bladder while in the sleeping state. Other symptom-suppressing treatments include interference with the depth of sleep, which is thought to be particularly deep in many bedwetters.

There is a widely held assumption that the enuretic symptoms are subject, somehow, to the conscious will of the child or are unconsciously motivated. When the former notion is held, rewards and punishments are sometimes used as incentives to make the child try harder to control himself or to desist from a habit which it is assumed affords him some sort of satisfaction, or which he is too "lazy" to overcome. Conscious modelling or imitation has also been postulated as an explanation for many aspects of the acquisition of continence. Children may learn appropriate behaviour by observing how other children ask to go to the toilet, adopt the correct position for micturition and arrange their clothing. Some children seem quite suddenly to become aware of the inappropriateness of their behaviour, especially when mocked by their peers. This sometimes produces a dramatic "cure". It is as if latent learning has occurred and performance awaits a final "push" from the environment.

The theory of unconscious motivation leads to speculations about the meaning, or psychodynamic significance, of enuresis. Some theorists believe that enuresis is a disguised expression of hostility towards parents which the child does not dare to express openly. Because (as we saw earlier) there is a natural and rapid decline in the incidence of enuresis as children get older, any sort of treatment, no matter how wildly unrelated to the aetiology of a particular case of enuresis, will seem to produce a proportion of "cures" if carried on for long enough. The remission of symptoms, in such cases, may have no relation to the specific treatment or theoretical rationale.

It can be said that a great deal of abnormal behaviour represents a failure to manifest expected skills; treatment, in such cases, can be thought of as the teaching of new and more effective skills, more appropriate responses to stimuli. Mowrer and Mowrer (1938), taking this view of enuresis, devised a special training pad which was placed under the child when he was tucked up in bed. The pad, when moistened (with urine) during the night, closed a circuit and rang a bell. It was arranged that when this happened, someone would wake the child, take him to the toilet, and change him. This "conditioning" technique was very effective. The children were actually encouraged to drink water before going to bed as opposed to the old method of avoiding liquid. Lovibond (1964) is critical of the classical conditioning model of treating enuresis. He put forward an alternative model based on instrumental avoidance conditioning, and also developed a more sophisticated apparatus, incorporating a twin signal, and used it in a manner to apply intermittent reinforcement. The object of the alarm systems is to train the enuretic to exercise in sleep exactly the same control over bladder function that he exercises during the day. The purpose is not, as is sometimes stated, to train the child to awaken easily to bladder pressure although this may occur during the training procedure. Once a stable conditioned response of inhibiting urination during sleep is established by means of the alarm, the bell or buzzer is superfluous and the child reacts to bladder pressure like the normal person.

The training period to achieve an initial improvement criterion of fourteen dry nights rarely exceeds eight weeks and, on average, is as low as four to six weeks. It has been estimated, on the basis of a survey (Yates, 1970) of 352 enuretics, that a success rate of 90% to 95% can be obtained in this way. The enuretics in this survey remained dry at least six nights per week, and maintained this for at least a six-month follow-up period. When the follow-up period extends to two years or more, the relapse rate is a disappointing 35% to 40%. Another review of published studies (Turner, 1974) found an initial success rate of nearly 80% within eight to ten weeks of treatment; the relapse rate being approximately 11% following termination of treatment.

Enuresis is sometimes a symptom of a general anxiety problem. Youngsters who were previously toilet trained may become incontinent when going through a period of maladjustment. Treatment, in such a case, will have to be more widely conceived than in terms of habit training. A monograph "Recent Advances in the Knowledge of Bladder Control in Children", edited by Kolvin, MacKeith and Meadow (see: Turner, 1974) is an invaluable guide to the problems discussed in this section and source of normative data.

# 10. Problems of Self-restraint

CHILDREN HAVE to learn to check their impulses—irrational, sexual, aggressive and acquisitive. They are forbidden sexual play, and not allowed to hit and hurt other children or to steal. They are also forbidden the means of "defending" themselves when they are caught out in misdemeanours or in some other way threatened. For example, they are forbidden to lie and cheat. These issues raise the whole question of self-control. How does a self-centred, wilful infant come to act in accordance with the rules and values of his society? How does he become a reasonably self-controlled, inner-directed and altruistic member of his community?

If the individual fails to achieve a certain minimum level of self-control so as to adjust his needs to those of the other members he is censured, punished, or even removed from society. He may be placed in one form of institution or another—a community home (approved school) or a Borstal in the case of antisocial or criminal behaviour. Of course such a drastic step only occurs in extreme cases. There are many degrees of loss of self-control and a variety of sanctions open to those who are given the task of training children. Children have to be inducted into the codes of their society by a long and complex process of learning, or socialization. The apparently asocial infant is required to develop, through interaction with caretaking adults, into a mature adult, who accepts the norms of his society, and who will act upon them without continual supervision. He, in turn, will transmit these norms to his own children. In addition he should be able to understand the function of rules so that he is able to contribute to their modification and development. The human species is unique in having as its main mechanism of social regulation a system of conceptually formulated rules, values and conventions. These norms of conduct, of course, vary widely from culture to culture.

According to contemporary theories, a child, through learning and identification, acquires both the content of his parents' moral code *and* a willingness to act in accordance with the rules. Stayton *et al.* (1971) point out that usually no distinction is made between the process of learning the rules of society and that first (and most important) step in the socialization of the child, which occurs when he develops a *willingness* to do as he is told. What he learns will depend on the nature of the parents' demands, but the development of an initial disposition toward compliance may be critical for the effectiveness of all further attempts at training the child. If the child lacks this tendency he will remain, in many ways, a stranger to his society, unidentified with it, regarding its rules and values from an external point of view.

Another assumption is called into question by Stayton and his co-workers. The basic question in the theory of socialization is put as follows: "What must be done to a child in order that he will act in accordance with the rules of his society?" The implication here is that the 80 or 90% of the child population who are normally socialized have become so only as a result of specific adult interventions designed to foster learning or identification. Deviant or unsocialized children (among them our so-called conduct problems) are seen as instances in which the socialization process has failed. Stayton *et al.* reverse the question: "What must be done to a child in order to estrange him from his society?" As they point out, when the question is posed in this way, it turns attention from the problem of socializing the majority to ways of preventing or correcting the failures of socialization in a deviant minority.

The authors touch on another assumption which is often taken for granted. In most treatises on socialization, it is implied that there is a fundamental antagonism between a child and his society, between natural behavioural tendencies and cultural constraints. As they put it: "Some writers regard society as inimical to the wholesale development of man's true nature; others consider society as necessarily inhibiting the anarchic impulses of the individual for the good of the whole". Alternatively, they believe (and experimental evidence is presented in support of this view) that man has evolved *as* a social species, that infants are genetically biased toward certain social behaviours; that the family is a microcosm of society for which infants are preadapted; and that children are social from the beginning. In other words, a disposition for obedience and compliance —in fact for socialization in general—is the product of proper social development rather than the result of a rigorous and specialized training regimen. Many a parent with a disobedient child (not to mention teachers) may be surprised to hear this, but Stayton *et al.* add: "Clearly, as a child matures increasing parental intervention will be necessary. A child will not conform 'naturally' to all the rules of his parents or society, no matter how benevolent the home environment may be. It is the initial disposition to comply with which we are concerned, and this seems to be a 'natural emergent'".

## Agencies and Techniques of Socialization

The family, like other socializing agents of society (among them schools and churches) uses various techniques to teach and control the child in its care. Among those used are material and psychological rewards, praise, reproof, corporal and psychological punishment, example, giving or withholding love, approval, and explanations of rules.

Social learning theorists view the family as being particularly significant in the moulding of the child because it is the first and most frequent agent determining which social stimuli will be presented to the child, what he will be taught, which behaviour patterns will be rewarded and consolidated, which will be punished and inhibited.

The theoretical model is clear enough: certain categories of experience tend to reinforce particular personality traits, and the more often these experiences are repeated the more enduring the traits become. Through a system of rewards and punishments, patterns of behaviour are shaped. For example, happy social experiences encourage the child to want to repeat the experiences. By comparison, too many miserable social experiences tend to reinforce negative attitudes towards other people and social interaction. Thus, early social experiences play a large part in determining sociable, outgoing (i.e., extraverted) patterns of behaviour—or their opposite. Then again, a child subjected to repeated and violent beatings early in life may learn that, by complete submission, the painful experience can be avoided. Subsequently, he may develop a generally submissive manner in dealing with all other people. As a result of similar experiences, an individual with a different combination of environmental influences and genetic constitution, may believe that beating is the only way to produce a desired behaviour in others, and so he may become a strongly aggressive character.

This sort of model is, *a priori*, very plausible; the model has face validity. And we all have our pet theories and prejudices about the particular and significant consequences of early childhood experience. McCandless (1969) expresses the article of faith as follows: "On the basis of our actual contact as parents, teachers, and professional workers both with individual children and groups of children, we 'know in our hearts' . . . that children's lives and adjustment do vary according to their families' treatment of them. These variations may be temporary—a function of some family crisis or improvement of family condition—or they may be long enduring." When one considers the intimate and protracted nature of parents' relationships with their children, it seems self-evident that the *quality* of such relationships must have a vital bearing on the development of the child's personality. Possibly this assumption explains much of the heat generated by controversies over parental discipline, and child-rearing issues such as methods and schedules of breast-feeding (or bottle-feeding), weaning and toilet-training. People with the responsibility of children to bring up feel intuitively that a lot is at stake. Mothers of children attending child guidance clinics frequently express fears of having made "mistakes" in their relationships with their children.

Unfortunately, in science, we cannot rely on the emotional convictions McCandless refers to above. This is our cue to look at the evidence we do have. Yarrow and her co-authors of the book "Child Rearing" (1968) admit that questions of child-rearing have not yielded easily to scientific study. They conclude from their own investigations and extensive review of the available evidence, that "we are still searching for the specific conditions in the child's cumulative experience with his parents that evoke, strengthen, or modify his behaviour".

## Conduct Problems

There is (see: Peterson, 1968) a category of problems—the so-called "conduct problems"—which includes behaviours such as temper tantrums, fighting, disruptiveness, profanity, and other signs of open defiance of authority usually involving aggression and limited self-control. In the case of "conduct disorders" the child's impulses are given direct expression and it is those who make up his social environment who chiefly suffer, whereas in the case of the personality problems, impulses are inhibited and the child is the chief sufferer from his "symptoms". Among the most formidable acts of self-restraint required of the child are those which occur when he feels angry and he has to stop himself hitting out and hurting. In other words, when he has to control his aggressive impulses.

## Anger and Aggression

There are many definitions of anger and aggression in the literature. They depend to a large extent on underlying assumptions about the mainsprings of aggression. Thus for Lorenz (1966) it is the universal fighting instinct in man. Many social scientists (e.g., Suttie, 1935; Rosenzweig, 1944; Scott, 1958; McCord et al., 1961; Berkowitz, 1962) conclude that studies of aggression in individuals and societies (e.g., the Trobriand Islanders) invalidate the concept of an instinctive impulse to violence within man. Aggression, in their view, is a learned habit or appetite. Danziger (1971) has some cautionary words about labelling children as "aggressive". As he puts it:

The individual who is seen as being rather more assertive than the situation warrants is labelled "aggressive", as though the aggressiveness resided in him and not in our relationship. We are apt to forget that in another relationship, perhaps with his mother, this same individual may act in ways we would be more inclined to label "meek" or "timid" . . .

Spielberger (1966) has emphasized with regard to anxiety, the necessity of drawing a distinction between "trait" and "state" constructs. The same applies to aggression—a complex pattern of physiological and cognitive responses—which can be conceptualized either as a *sample* of a person's reactions to frustration under specific stimulus conditions (state) or as a *sign* of an individual's predisposition toward manifesting hostile reactions in a variety of stimulus contexts (trait).

Goodenough (1931) analysed records of angry episodes by 45 children from one to seven years of age. Their mothers kept daily diaries of any angry incidents, recording the time, place and duration of outbursts, their causes, and the kinds of behaviour manifested. A total of 1,878 angry outbursts were recorded over 4 months. Goodenough listed the following forms of expression of anger: kicking, stamping, jumping up and down, throwing oneself on the floor, holding one's breath, pulling, struggling, pouting, frowning, throwing objects, grabbing, biting, striking, crying and screaming. Each child had his own particular repertoire with a preference for some but not for others. With time he would change the repertoire of behaviours used in expressing anger. The author classified expressions of anger in terms of the direction of energy expended:

(1) *Undirected energy*—anger not directed toward any end except that of emotional outlet, such as in kicking randomly, holding the breath, and screaming;

(2) *Motor or verbal resistance*—anger expressed in opposing doing what was asked, such as verbal refusal or resisting being held; and

(3) *Retaliation*—anger expressed in motor or verbal attempts at revenge, such as biting the agent or giving him a verbal scolding.

Figure 4 below shows the frequency of anger outbursts by age and sex.

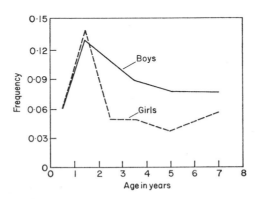

FIG. 4. Frequency of anger outbursts per hour of observation for a sample of young children. (Adapted from Goodenough 1931.)

A rapid decrease in outburst occurs as the child gets older after the peak age of one-and-a-half years. Boys consistently show more anger outbursts than girls.

As the children increased in age from two to five, there was a steady diminution in random directionless discharges of expression of anger, and an increase in retaliatory behaviour aimed at someone or something. As the child gets older his motor resistance decreases as his verbal resistance increases. Fewer than one-third of the outbursts lasted for as long as five minutes. The immediate causes of anger could be divided into the following categories which accounted for 70% of all incidents reported:

30%—Problems of social relationship (e.g., being denied attention, incomprehension of child's desires, etc.).

20%—Conflicts over routine physical habits (e.g., going to bed or the toilet, etc.).

20%—Conflicts with authority (response to punishment, prohibitions, etc.).
Goodenough found that problems of social adjustment constituted the most frequent single source of anger outbursts among children.

Dawe (1934) set out to study the quarrels of pre-school children as they arose in a relatively uncontrolled social environment—the morning free-play period at nursery school. Forty boys and girls (25–60 months of age) were observed using the behaviour sampling method. A total of 200 quarrels were analysed. Dawe summarizes her findings as follows:

(1) The average duration of the quarrels, 23 seconds, is surprisingly short. Quarrels of the older children last longer than those of the younger. The brief duration of the quarrels seems a true characteristic and not a function of teacher interference, although the teachers do terminate quarrels indoors more quickly than quarrels outdoors.

(2) Boys quarrel more frequently and are more aggressive during quarrels than girls.

(3) Quarrelsomeness tends to decrease with age; at least quarrels of the type studied do.

(4) The youngest children start the most quarrels but take the less aggressive role during the quarrel. As children grow older aggressiveness and retaliation increase.

(5) A very slight negative relation is found between IQ and frequency of quarreling.

(6) Children quarrel most often with those of the same sex, who are, however, either older or younger than themselves. The latter difference seems influenced by opportunity.

(7) The majority of quarrels are started by a struggle for possessions. The number of quarrels of this type decreases with age but still holds the lead over other types at all ages.

(8) Pushing, striking and pulling are the most common motor activities. The older children indulge in the more violent forms more often. In only three quarrels is there no motor activity.

(9) Crying, forbidding and commanding are the most common forms of vocal activity, although silence is a more frequent reaction than any single activity. Talking during a quarrel increases with age but reciprocal conversation is rare. There is some indication that quarrels of the argumentative type increase with age.

(10) The average number of quarrels per hour is three to four, although this is probably an underestimation of the total quarreling of this group. There seem to be more quarrels indoors when the children are crowded together.

(11) The children settle the majority of the quarrels themselves, most frequently by one child's forcing another to yield. Most often the younger child is forced to yield to the older; and most often it is the older who yields voluntarily to the younger.

(12) The great majority of the children recover after a quarrel very quickly and show no evidence of resentment.

Brown and Elliott (1965) state that "there are many theories which try to explain aggression in young children. Probably most are partly true and perhaps the simplest is the best. One simple one is that many fights, etc. occur because they bring with them a great deal of fuss and attention from some adult". They demonstrated how teachers can dramatically reduce physical and verbal aggressive responses in 27 males (aged 3 to 4) by systematically ignoring aggressive behaviour and attending to cooperative interactions.

There is no denying, of course, that there are inbuilt physical factors such as hormones and brain mechanisms mediating the aggressive behaviour of animals and humans. These are activated and bring about the adaptive bodily changes which occur during the "emergency emotions" rage, fear, excitement and pain. In man, rage and anger are regulated by the highly developed cerebral cortex which both inhibits or gives release to hostile behaviour. Many theoreticians believe that it should be possible to lessen the likelihood of aggressive conflicts between people by decreasing the occurrence of severe frustrations and by minimizing the gains to be won through aggression. They believe that social (and learned) more than biological (and innate) characteristics determine the aggressiveness and belligerence of individuals and nations.

There appear to be two broad groups of environmental factors which determine aggressive acts:

(1) Previous learning experiences, and
(2) Contemporary circumstances, which either (a) instigate aggression

(viz., physical or verbal attacks, deprivation, frustration, conflict and exposure to aggressive models) or (b) maintain aggression (viz., direct, vicarious and self reinforcement).

A prominent theory (Dollard *et al.*, 1939; Miller, 1941) about the origins of aggression is the "frustration-aggression" hypothesis. Frustration is the internal state of feeling or emotional disturbance experienced when a more or less insurmountable obstacle gets in the way of the individual satisfying a need or of fulfilling a goal to which he aspires. Whether violent behaviour ensues, and what form it takes, depends upon the habits acquired during upbringing, temperamental qualities moulded during the formative years, exposure to aggressive models (such as aggressive parents), and the indulgence or punishment meted out when the child manifests anger in particular situations. Obviously, people differ in their experiences of frustrations, privations, and mishaps; and a lifetime of conditioning or sensitization to particular frustrations is thought to create differences in thresholds of frustration- and anger-tolerance.

Buss and Durkee (1957) distinguish, by factor analysis, several different forms of aggression: the tendency to be physically assaultive, indirect hostility, irritability, negativism, resentment, verbally expressed anger and guilt regarding hostile impulses and attitudes. These different forms represent an approximate continuum from "anger out" to "anger in" responses. Rosenzweig (1948) suggests that while there are several tactics for dealing with anger and "blame" in frustrating situations, three basic patterns can be observed: the extra-punitive, or "anger out" reaction, in which the tendency is to blame others aggressively for misfortunes; the intropunitive, or "anger in" response, in which the tendency is to look within oneself for the responsibility for frustrations and to accept the blame; and lastly the defensive impunitive reaction, in which the frustrating situation is glossed over, its existence denied, and no blame attributed.

Yarrow, Campbell and Burton (1968) assessed aggression by means of questionnaires and interviews with mothers and by teachers' ratings— conducted with regard to the same nursery-school children. The correlation between mothers' questionnaire and mothers' interview responses only amounted to 0·29. The correlation between independent ratings of a child's aggression by two teachers was 0·65. This compares with a correlation of 0·33 obtained by an analysis of overall measures of the child's aggressiveness derived from two independent sources, namely parent and teacher. Sears, Rau and Alpert (1965) compared reports and observations of direct and indirect aggression at home and at school in nursery-school children. The correlations ranged from −0·20 to +0·36.

As in the case of dependency, there is so little evidence for the reality of a general trait of aggression, that it would seem rather ingenuous to hope for the formulation of reliable cause–effect equations linking child-rearing variables and aggressive behaviour. Nevertheless, there is a somewhat surprising consensus—and a confidently expressed one—that aggressive behaviour in children can be related to long-term attitudes and child-rearing practices. To summarize the findings (see: Becker, 1964): it is suggested that a combination of lax discipline combined with hostile attitudes in the parents produces very aggressive and poorly controlled behaviour in the offspring. The lax parent is one who gives in to the child, acceding to his demands, indulging him, allowing him a great deal of freedom, being submissive and inconsistent, and in extreme cases, neglecting and deserting him. The parent with hostile attitudes is mainly unaccepting and disapproving of the child; she fails to give affection, understanding or explanations to the child. She tends to use a lot of physical punishment but not give reasons when she does exert her authority, something she does erratically and unpredictably. Over a long period of time this combination produces rebellious, irresponsible and aggressive children; they tend to be disorderly in the classroom, lacking in sustained concentration and irregular in their working habits. The evidence (Bandura, 1965b, 1969b) suggests that children *model* their behaviour on that of their parents. So it is not surprising to find that hostile parents tend to have aggressive children.

## Social Imitation (Observational learning)

This brings us to another crucial type of learning. We referred to imitation in the introduction (page 133) because of its centrality at this stage of life. As with other forms of learning, maladaptive as well as adaptive patterns of behaviour may be acquired through the child's imitation of the people, real and imagined, whom he observes and hears about. Bandura and Walters (1963) claim that the development of novel responses cannot be satisfactorily explained on the basis of the principles of operant or instrumental conditioning. They describe the acquisition of novel responses through the process called "observational learning"; it is considered to be the cornerstone of social learning. The concept of vicarious conditioning is central to their thinking. As Bandura (1969) states:

Virtually all learning phenomena resulting from direct experience can occur on a vicarious basis, through observation of other persons' behaviour and its consequences for them. Thus, for example, one can acquire intricate response patterns merely by observing the performances of appropriate models; emotional responses can be conditioned observationally by witnessing the effective reactions of others undergoing painful or pleasurable experiences; fearful and avoidant behaviour can be extinguished . . .

A basic distinction is made between the acquisition and the performance of the imitative response. Acquisition is thought to result mainly from the contiguity of sensory events. Bandura describes what happens when the observer performs no overt imitative response at the time of observing the model. He can acquire the behaviour only in cognitive representational form. As Bandura puts it:

Observational learning involves two representational systems—an imaginal one and a verbal one. After modelling stimuli have been coded into images or words for memory representation, they function as mediators for subsequent response retrieval and reproduction. Imagery formation is assumed to occur through a process of sensory conditioning ... modelling stimuli elicit in observers perceptual responses that become sequentially associated and centrally integrated on the basis of temporal contiguity of stimulation.

Performance is thought to be influenced by the observed consequences of responses, or more generally operant conditioning. Bandura demonstrated the separability of these two processes in an experiment where children observed a film-mediated model perform aggressive acts, with rewarding, punishing or no consequences, (Bandura, 1965b). While response consequences to the model clearly affected subsequent imitative behaviour in the children, attractive incentives offered to the children to reproduce the aggressive behaviour completely wiped out these performance differences, revealing an equivalent amount of learning or acquisition.

Aronfreed (1968, 1969) in trying to deal with the acquisition of imitative behaviour rejects those simple "learning by contiguity" explanatory models which do not take into account the affective value of the stimulus context in which the model's behaviour is observed. He makes a distinction between two major types of contingency for observational learning; those in which affective value is directly transmitted in the observed behaviour, and those in which affective value is transmitted by outcomes of the behaviour. Aronfreed observes that when the affective value of observed behaviour is inherent in the behaviour, then the child's affectivity will be governed quite closely by intrinsic stimulus features of the behaviour itself, rather than by the instrumentality of the behaviour in producing outcomes. He uses the term "cognitive template" to refer to the child's apparent ability to form a rapid symbolic or representational structuring of the observed behaviour, to which the affective value of the stimulus situation becomes attached. The problem of observational learning is to account for the motivation to form a cognitive representation of behaviour and the degree of fidelity with which it is reproduced. The concept of imitation (according to Aronfreed, 1968) has maximum utility when it is restricted to the type of observational learning which produces a high degree of fidelity in the child's replication of another individual's behaviour. The child attends to cues intrinsic to the structure of the modelled behaviour. In contrast to the situation in which there is direct transmission of

affective value by the behaviour which the child observes, "the transmission of affective value by the outcomes of observed behaviour does not
lend itself so readily to the child's representation of the precise form of the
behaviour" (Aronfreed, op. cit.).

When behaviour has been imitated by the child he is often rewarded by
praise and encouragement and approval—in other words social rewards—
from the "model". Such modelling, particularly on the mother, is important for the development of conforming patterns of social behaviour. It
is a popular clinical conception that parents (consciously or unconsciously,
explicitly or implicitly) encourage and thereby reinforce aggressive
behaviour. There have been reports in the literature (see: Yarrow *et al.*,
1968) of a low positive correlation between childhood aggression and
maternal permissiveness towards the expression of aggressiveness. But
Yarrow and her colleagues found only one significant correlation out of
36 relevant to such an association.

Some mothers find it difficult to tolerate their children's hostility and
strictly suppress all signs of it. This may make for over-submissiveness—
the fear of anger. Ultimately, an affectionate and tolerant atmosphere in
which the child knows the limits beyond which he definitely cannot go is
the best long-term antidote against aggressive behaviour. There are
sanctions which specifically discourage childish acts of aggression, but
they do not take an aggressive form.

There are several methods (see: Bandura, 1973) of coping with aggressive problems. Jehu (1974) lists the following approaches:

### Reducing Discriminative Stimuli for Aggression

The absence of, say, the teacher in the nursery-school playground may
be a cue for some children that threatening or hitting other children is
likely to gain them certain advantages, e.g., the best playthings. In other
words, certain stimulus conditions provide signals to the child that
aggressive behaviour is likely to have rewarding consequences for him.
Several treatment programmes could be planned to reduce discriminative
stimuli for such aggression; one way would be to provide adult supervision of play until such time that it is no longer necessary.

### Providing Discriminative Stimuli for Non-aggressive Behaviour

A "time-out" or "response-cost" programme (see page 229) provides
stimulus conditions which signal to the child that his aggressive behaviour
is unlikely to have rewarding consequences or, indeed, is likely to lead
to negative effects. The provision of such discriminative stimuli as part of
a treatment programme may bring aggression under control while more
acceptable alternative behaviour is being acquired.

### Reducing the Exposure to Aggressive Models

We have already seen that there is evidence that exposure to other people behaving aggressively may facilitate the imitation of such behaviour by the observer (see page 174). An attempt to reduce the exposure of a child to such aggressive models is likely to decrease the likelihood of him behaving similarly.

### Providing Models of Non-aggressive Behaviour

Acceptable alternatives to aggression may be enhanced by exposing youngsters to people who manifest such alternative behaviours, especially when they are instrumental in obtaining rewards for these models.

### Reducing Aversive Stimuli

Aggressive behaviour may be instigated by a large variety of aversive stimuli; by physical and by verbal assaults of a painful, threatening or humiliating nature, and by deprivation of proper nurturance, rights and opportunities. Reduction of such aversive stimuli may be accompanied by a reduction in aggression. Another technique involves the defusing of aversive stimuli by diminishing their power to arouse anger in the child. This is achieved by desensitization procedures. (E.g., Rimm et al., 1971; Evans and Hearn, 1973).

### Skills Training

Many children, because of unfavourable life experiences, lack some of the critical skills required to function in a satisfactory manner. Consequently, they may behave aggressively in response to a variety of frustrations and humiliations. If such children can be helped to become more competent, then they may have less recourse to aggression (see: Staats and Butterfield, 1965; Browning and Stover, 1971; Gittleman, 1965; Kaufmann and Wagner, 1972). A particular example of providing skills is "assertive training" aimed at helping the individual to protect his own rights in a capable and confident manner, but without denying the rights of others by being aggressive or neglectful towards them (Alberti and Emmons, 1971).

### Differential Reinforcement

We saw on page 172 that aggressive behaviour may be maintained by its reinforcing consequences. The purpose of differential reinforcement regimes is to reverse this situation by attaching neutral or negative consequences to aggression while positively reinforcing more acceptable alternative behaviour with either social or material rewards (see: Patterson, 1973).

A clinical illustration (Hawkins, *et al.*, 1966) of the positive reinforcement of problem behaviour is provided by the case of a four-year-old boy Peter S. Peter had been brought to a university clinic because he was extremely difficult to manage and control. His mother told the staff that she was helpless in dealing with his frequent tantrums and disobedience. Peter often kicked objects or people, removed or tore his clothing, called people rude names, annoyed his younger sister, made a variety of threats, hit himself and became very angry at the slightest frustration. He demanded attention almost constantly, and seldom cooperated with his mother. He was found, on examination, to have what is called borderline intelligence; he tended to be over-active, and was thought to be possibly brain-damaged. The psychologists, observing the mother and child in the home, noted that many of Peter's undesirable behaviours appeared to be maintained by *attention* from his mother. When Peter behaved objectionably, she would often try to explain why he should not act in such a way; or she would try to interest him in some new activity by offering toys or food. Peter was occasionally punished by having a misused toy or other object taken away, but he was often able to persuade his mother to return the item almost immediately. He was also punished by being placed on a high chair and forced to remain there for short periods. Considerable tantrums usually followed such disciplinary measures and were quite effective in maintaining mother's attention, largely in the form of verbal persuasion or arguments.

The psychologists divided their treatment programme into several "differential reinforcement" stages; it made use of both rewarding and punishing contingencies. During the first period, Peter and his mother interacted in their usual way and this was observed and recorded by the experimenters. Prior to the next (experimental) stage, the mother was informed of nine of Peter's objectionable behaviours which would be treated. She was shown three signals which indicated how she was to behave toward Peter. Signal "A" meant she was to tell Peter to stop whatever objectionable behaviour he was manifesting. Signal "B" indicated she was immediately to place Peter in his room and lock the door. Thus, every time Peter behaved objectionably, Mrs. S. was either signalled to tell him to stop or to put him in his room. When she saw signal "C", she was to give him attention, praise, and affectionate physical contact. This signal was given by the experimenter when he noticed that Peter was playing in a particularly desirable way. When placed in his room Peter was required to remain there for at least five minutes. In addition, he had to keep quiet for a short period before he was allowed to come out. Since all objects likely to serve as playthings had been previously removed from the room, he had little opportunity to amuse himself.

The rate of objectionable behaviour in the experimental periods dropped dramatically. Data obtained during the follow-up period showed that Peter's objectionable behaviour remained low in rate after the passage of a twenty-four day interval. His mother reported that Peter was well behaved and much less demanding than he had previously been. Mrs. S. stated that she felt more "sure of herself" and could not remember how she had previously behaved toward her son. It was apparent that Mrs. S. now gave Peter firm commands when she wanted him to do something and did not "give in" after denying him a request.

## Sex Training

Most industrialized and monotheistic cultures train children not to masturbate. The fact that this training in self-restraint almost universally breaks down at adolescence and even before then, particularly in the case of boys, might be thought to support the popular concept of sex as an instinct. However, scientific studies (see: Beach, 1948, 1965; Wright, 1970a) indicate that the wide individual differences in human sexual responses are less a consequence of biological influences than of psychological and particularly learning experiences. This view of sexual behaviour as predominantly a learned or acquired appetite rather than a rigidly determined instinctual pattern, is essentially an optimistic one, as it implies that the child who is exposed to relaxed, healthy attitudes about sex is likely to be relaxed and happy in his sexual relationships rather than fearful, anxious or aggressive. It is also optimistic in the sense that unsatisfactory sexual habits or negative attitudes which have become attached to the sex drive may be unlearned—remedied by therapy or advice, or by the individual's own efforts. Another important issue is raised by Wright (1970a) in discussing the appetite theory of sex; this concerns the nature of the emotions society judges appropriate to sexual arousal. Among the emotions that are currently associated with sex in the mass media are the desire for social status and success, aggression and cruelty, self-contempt, fear and guilt.

Wright suggests that if sex is to be fully human and personal, then it ought to be linked with affection, tenderness and awareness of the feelings of others. He believes that this is the outcome of a warmly affectionate and reasonably permissive upbringing. He sums up as follows: "Rather than lament the fact that sexual appetite is now being encouraged, we might more profitably spend our time trying to ensure that the emotions that are integrated with it are the ones we approve of. To condition sexual arousal to moral feelings of guilt and obligation may destroy the ties with affection as effectively as conditioning it to cruelty or disgust".

## Sex Play

Conditioning of emotions and attitudes to the sex drive often begin at the time when the mother observes her child playing in a sexual manner. Sex play with other children often takes the form of undressing or exploring the friend's body while playing doctors or mummies and daddies; it is quite common by the age of four, and even more so in nursery school. In a survey (Ramsey, 1943) of heterosexual play in boys, it was found that the incidence rises from nearly 5% at five years to a third of the boys at eight years. As many as two-thirds had indulged in sex play by the age of thirteen. The rates of sexual activity in girls are lower than in boys, but also show an increase with age. Sexual interest and behaviour in these immature youngsters is intermittent, casual, in fact rather unintense. Homosexual play—sex play between children of the same sex—also rises in incidence as youngsters get older. It usually takes the form of children handling each other's genitals. This occurs (Ramsey, 1943) in 30% of thirteen year-old boys, and the figures for girls are comparable. Homosexual activities are very much commoner in boys' and girls' boarding schools than in day schools (Schofield, 1965a). But there is no convincing evidence that this transient phase of homosexual activity has any bearing on *long-term* adult homosexuality. What can be said is that the child's setting and the presence or absence of opportunities for heterosexual contacts influence the manifestation of homosexual activities.

## Masturbation

Pre-school children—during the two to five-year-old phase—show increasing interest in their genitals. Masturbatory activities occur in about 55% of the boys and 16% of the girls (Sears *et al.*, 1957). About 80% of boys masturbate by their thirteenth year (Ramsey, 1943). A study of parental attitudes to masturbation showed that there is considerable emotional reaction from mothers (Sears *et al.*, 1957). Although most modern mothers have heard, read, or personally experienced the fact that masturbation is harmless and that it does not stunt growth, cause insanity, sterility or impotence, they feel anxious when their children do it. Fewer than one-fifth of the mothers interviewed felt that a certain amount of playing was to be expected; while one half considered it wrong or harmful. Some said masturbation "might not do anything if it happened just once", but that, all the same, they wouldn't like it to happen.

Like most behavioural patterns—even innocuous ones—masturbation, if carried to an extreme, becomes a problem—or is symptomatic of an already existing problem. Many children who are deprived, unhappy and poorly adjusted, turn as a source of solace and compensation to masturbation.

What can we infer from all this sexual experimentation in childhood and the later pre-adolescent phase of development? It seems that Freud was wrong in claiming that there is a virtual cessation of sexual activity after the age of six or so (the so-called "latency" period). What is clear is the fact that we cannot suppress children's sexual interests and explorations, even if we want to do so. The adults who reported their sexual behaviour in the Kinsey studies (Kinsey *et al.*, 1948, 1953), were brought up in a far less sexually permissive atmosphere than exists today; it was a period when the deeds they were recalling were likely to be severely punished. However, repression of their childhood sexuality was singularly unsuccessful in its aim. Fifty per cent of the men and women reported sexual contacts with peers before adolescence. It has been argued that the only effect of extreme efforts at suppression is to drive the behaviour underground and to permeate it with a sense of shame and an aura of furtive excitement. In girls, the repression of sexuality during childhood and adolescence is one of the major factors in adult frigidity.

## Sex Typing

Apart from the attitudes and emotions which will attach to the child's sexual arousal and curiosity, largely engendered by the atmosphere— relaxed or tense—when sexual matters are discussed or acted out, there is the vital process by which he learns the behaviour and attitudes culturally appropriate to his sex. This is the process called "sex-typing". The child learns, in other words, certain "sex-role standards", those psychological characteristics which are considered appropriate to one sex in contrast to the other. He acquires "gender identity". This refers to whether the individual feels himself to be male or female. Physical gender is decided at conception. But the evidence suggests that, from a psychological point of view, the newborn human is not, in any essential sense, sexually differentiated. Gender identity and sexual role standards are acquired during childhood; in fact, by the age of six a child is passionately committed to shaping his behaviour to the cultural mould of what is "appropriate" to his biological sex. He manifests anxiety, and even anger when accused of acting in ways regarded as characteristic of the opposite sex.

As early as the second year of life, the child *begins* to distinguish between what is "masculine" and "feminine". Preference for one sex role or the other also begins to emerge early in life, probably by the third year. By school-going age, he has thoroughly learned the concepts "male" and "female", he has divided the world into male and female people and is preoccupied with boy–girl distinctions (Hartup and Zook, 1960; Kagan, 1964). Studies (Money, 1965; Hampson and Hampson, 1961) have shown that it is difficult to bring about a major realignment of sex role and gender identity after three years of age. Once the standards of sex-role behaviour are learned, they are not easily altered. The die is cast, pretty well, by the age of six if not earlier.

Studies of abnormalities of physiology and anatomy suggest that prenatal or postnatal genetic or hormonal influences play only a secondary part in the process; upbringing and indoctrination into a sex role have the overriding influence. Hampson and Hampson (1961) found, in a sample of 20 hermaphrodites who had been assigned to, and reared, in a sex contrary to their chromosomal sex, that every individual had a gender role in keeping with his assigned sex and rearing experiences rather than his chromosomal sex. The researchers found, in a series of 30 individuals in whom the sexual status of the gonads was out of keeping with the assigned role and rearing practises, that in all but three instances the gender role was fully concordant with the sex rearing. The gender role was ambiguous in the three exceptions.

Among the attempts which have been made to account for the way in which the child acquires sex-typed patterns of behaviour, several theories have emphasized the role of identification. The concept of identification refers to the process or processes whereby one person models himself upon another. It differs from the concept of imitation in certain ways. It suggests a relatively long-lasting relationship between subject and model, and focuses attention on the fact that some models exert more influence over the subject than others—although the reasons why they do so are not adequately explained in the literature (see Danziger, 1971). A subject is said to be identified with a model if he is more likely to match that model's behaviour than other models' behaviour. Also, the matching behaviour is more extensive than that implied in the notion of imitation. The subject behaves as if he were the model in situations other than those in which he has seen the model, and in a relatively comprehensive manner. That is to say, he adopts the model's values, beliefs, attitudes and style of life, as well as matching particular forms of behaviour.

The view of many social learning theorists (e.g., Kagan, 1958a; Mischel, 1970; Bandura 1969) is that the child's experience with parents (particularly same-sex parents) critically determines the nature of his subsequent learning of social roles. The empirical results of the many studies which have been carried out present a somewhat confusing picture, and there is not space to review the theoretical debates in detail here. However, according to the anaclitic theory of identification, the child imitates and identifies with the behaviour of the parent who is warm and nurturant

(Kagan, 1958a; Kohlberg, 1967). There is some evidence in support of this theory. In a series of experiments (Payne and Mussen, 1956, and Mussen and Distler, 1959; 1960) it was found that boys were more likely to identify with their fathers (in the sense of seeing them as similar or in the sense that they themselves were "masculine") if their fathers were warm, affectionate and rewarding to them, and (for reasons that are less clear) if they were also somewhat strict. Cooper and Blair (1959) found that children who valued their parents highly were more likely to share their ideologies. Heilbrun (1965) found that perceived similarity to fathers was related to good psychological adjustment in male students.

Danziger (1971) is unimpressed by the available evidence. He states that there is certainly no clear and simple relationship between the readiness of the child to adopt a given adult as a model and that adult's degree of warmth of nurturance. As he puts it:

It may well be that once a certain minimum level of nurturance has been established, this fact becomes essentially irrelevant to the socialization process. It may also be that the functional relationship between nurturance and readiness to imitate the model has the shape of an inverted U, with both highly nurturant and highly depriving adults being essentially failures as models. In any case, an examination of the research literature in this area suggests that there is no direct proportionality between the 'warmth' of the model and tendency to imitate.

Likewise he feels that it is by no means certain that the assumption of an appropriate sex role depends on a special relationship with a particular parent figure. Such a relationship may facilitate positional identification but it is neither a necessary nor a sufficient condition for its occurrence.

Another type of identification—"defensive identification"—involves what is called "identifying with the aggressor" (Kohlberg, 1963, 1967, Bandura, 1969). The child adopts his parents' style of life through fear of punishment. Parental warmth may be more important in fostering appropriate sex-typing in girls than in boys, while dominance and power of the father may be more critical for the boy's sexual identifications. Hetherington (1965, 1967), in an experiment with young children, obtained measures of parental dominance and warmth and of the child's imitation of the parents in a controlled experimental setting. Whereas there was some general tendency for boys to imitate their fathers most, and girls their mothers, the warmth and dominance of the parents were important factors. The more dominant or warm the parent, the more he was imitated. There was some evidence, however, that dominance was rather more important for boys and warmth for girls. There is also evidence that mothers with punitive and non-permissive attitudes tend to inhibit certain aspects of masculinity in their sons but promote femininity in their daughters; boys from homes in which fathers are dominant display more masculine sex-role preferences and are more highly identified with the father than are boys from mother-dominant families. Highly masculine boys also view their fathers as more powerful than feminine boys do. A dominant father may also accentuate the femininity of his daughters (see: Sears *et al.*, 1965; Mussen and Rutherford, 1963; Mischel, 1970).

The Freudian theory of the Oedipus complex fits into the theory of "defensive identification". Freud gave the names "Oedipus Complex" and "Electra Complex" respectively to the psychosexual events taking place when boys or girls are five or six. In the case of boys they are thought to recapitulate, at a figurative level, the Sophoclean tragedy in which Oedipus is horrified to discover that he has unknowingly murdered his father and married his mother. The metaphor refers to the mutual attraction between mother and son and between father and daughter, and also for the corresponding rivalry and hostility between father and son and between mother and daughter. It is hypothesized that the young son in the Oedipal situation is faced by an apparently insoluble emotional conflict between his envy of his father as his "rival", and his awareness of how impotent and dependent he is in terms of the father's power. The usual outcome of the child's fear of retaliation by his father (the projection of his hostile feelings directed against the father) is a sequence of events in which the child represses his erotic desires toward his mother and identifies with the potential aggressor. Such family romances and dramas have been observed, not only in the analyses of neurotic patients, but also by many perceptive parents in their wholly normal homes. The theory of the Oedipus complex is one which stands up well, in Kline's view (Kline, 1972), to the light of the available evidence.

A problem in this area of research into sex roles is the fact that nearly all these studies have been of a correlational kind in which inferences about the directions of cause and effect are speculative and inconclusive. The direct measure of identification most often used is the degree of similarity between the subject's concept of himself and his concept of the model. The subject rates himself and the model on some personality measure, and if the two ratings are similar, the subject is said to be identified with the model. There are variants to this procedure, such as taking the similarity between the subject's concept of himself and the model's concept of himself. A detailed critique of these methods has been given by Bronfenbrenner (1960). The general problem they raise is just how the measure should be interpreted, and whether it is really measuring identification as theoretically defined.

Parents (especially fathers) place great emphasis on the manly virtues. Boys have a more inflexible sex-role to play than girls; they have the added difficulty of being required to shift initial identification with the mother to the father, in order to acquire the appropriate masculine attributes. The girl's model remains the same. This question of a boy's gender-identity is also of concern to those mothers who through force of circumstances, have to rear boys in the absence of their husbands. What they are worried about is whether he identifies himself as a male. They may also worry about their child being homosexual. It is here that confusion arises because the issues of gender-identity problems and homosexuality are often mistakenly thought of as one and the same thing.

Homosexuality, transvestism and sexual inversion are independent (although sometimes overlapping) phenomena, and the failure to draw this distinction causes much misunderstanding (see: Rutter, 1971). For example, only a small percentage of adult transvestites are homosexual (Randall, 1970), and only a minority of homosexuals are transsexuals. The direction of the individual's sexual interest—the choice of a sexual partner —is very rarely explained by chromosomal or hormonal anomalies. On the other hand, genetic factors may be important in certain cases of homosexuality (see: Kallmann, 1952; Weinberg and Bell, 1972). Early life experiences seem to play a part in many cases of homosexual inclination; poor relationships with parents, particularly the parent of the same sex, are thought to be a contributory factor (Kenyon, 1970; West, 1968; Bancroft, 1970). When one considers how many strongly heterosexual individuals have had poor relationships of this kind, such a theory is robbed of most of its explanatory value. Nevertheless, there remains strong evidence that early family relationships are, in some way, involved in homosexuality, and in other deviations, but the precise "hows" and "whys" remain a mystery.

# Part V

# Early Childhood: The Preschool Stage
*From three to five years approximately*

# Introduction: Psychosocial Developments

ERIKSON (1965) considers that the major developmental task in this stage is the achievement of "initiative"—vigorous reality testing, imagination, and imitation of adult behaviour. The major hazard to this achievement is thought to be overly strict discipline and the concomitant internalization of rigid ethical attitudes which interfere with the child's spontaneity and reality testing, and lead to excessive guilt. Guilt is but one of several facets of moral behaviour. It is this aspect which we deal with in Chapter 11. Guilt is the emotional discomfort or remorse we ascribe to our consciences when we have transgressed the rules. Another facet is the inhibitory mechanism which leads the child to resist temptation. Prior to the present stage of development the child has certainly felt "bad" when he has transgressed, but primarily because he fears external parental punishment or disapproval. Now, at about four or five years of age, the locus of anxiety or fear comes from within and the child feels guilt when he has transgressed. Hoffman (1970) observes that:

> ... the guiding concept in most moral development research is the internalization of socially sanctioned prohibitions and mandates. One of the legacies of Freud, and the sociologist Durkheim as well, is the assumption now prevalent among social scientists that the individual does not go through life viewing society's central norms as externally and coercively imposed pressures to which he must submit. Though the norms are initially alien, they are eventually adopted by the individual, largely through the efforts of his early socializers—the parents—and come to serve as internalized guides so that he behaves in accord with them even when external authority is not present to enforce them. That is, control by others is replaced by self-control.

From three to five years of age, as the child becomes increasingly aware of his own limitations and the relativity of his competence, imitation and susceptibility to suggestion or instruction become even more important than in previous years. The Freudian concept of identification, in which the child incorporates his parents as an ego-ideal, has its parallel in this increase in the child's global imitation of them. Adults are selected as models for reasons which (as we saw in the previous chapter) are still imperfectly understood. The difficulties in this area of research are many. Danziger (1971) observes that:

> There is one crucial difference between the psychologist who sets himself up as a model to be imitated by his child subjects and the parent who has to cope with his own children. The parent must accommodate to the demands of the child, while the experimenter can afford to ignore them. That is why experiments on imitation yield a very poor simulation of real-life parent-child interaction. The paradigm that equates the parental role with that of the model and the child's role with that of the follower simply does not fit the facts. What mother does not imitate the sounds and smiles of her infant? And who could deny the modelling role of adolescents, at least in respect to dress and speech? In real life the roles are often reversed and it is the child who finds himself in the role of the model or socializing agent to an imitating parent.

There is reason to think that, in social development, the end of the phase we are considering—approximately five years—is something of a watershed. After five there is a decline in the amount of imitation and a change in the child's interactions with his parents. We deal with these changes in Part VI. According to Piaget, the age of five to seven marks the transition from preoperational thinking to operational thinking, and hence the decline in social as well as in perceptual and cognitive "egocentricity". Prior to this age the child is becoming fully exposed to wider cultural influences through the mass media, visiting friends' homes and (perhaps) attending a playgroup or nursery school.

Loevinger (1966) describes this stage of ego-development as the "opportunistic stage". There is a marked shift away from the earlier massive dependence on mother. The child understands that there are rules, but they are obeyed in terms of immediate advantage. Thus the morality is purely an expedient one. The child's interpersonal relationships are still thought to be, to some extent, manipulative and exploitive. However, there is an increase in empathic behaviour as the child's cognitive egocentricity diminishes. Learning how to respond empathically may be a precondition of truly *social* behaviour in the child. He needs to develop the capacity to "see a situation through the eyes of another", and to respond "as if" he were the other person. This is the sort of behaviour which is referred to as imitation or sometimes as identification.

It is possible to distinguish two aspects of empathic behaviour. The first concerns communication. In order to communicate effectively to another, it is necessary to understand the other's point of view and accommodate the communication to it. The second aspect is illustrated by the child who, in the absence of his mother, acts as if he were his mother. There has been a great deal of clinical and informal observation of this phenomenon, but little systematic study of the conditions under which it arises, or, of what precisely is happening when the child does play the role of a parent.

We have seen that the child's range of social contacts is widening fast. The number of friendly contacts between children becomes more pronounced between the ages of two and five; attachments to friends and the peer group begin to evolve. During these years, the first friendships are generally, but not exclusively, with others of the same sex. Friendship patterns change dramatically with age. Between the ages of two and five the number of friends increases; after this age, the development is towards closeness of attachment to a few special children.

In studies of nursery school children affiliation is a predominant tendency of the little girls. They spend the greatest proportion of time in social interaction of one kind or another, while boys are more frequently engaged in some physical activity (running, chasing, etc.). The girls are also more cooperative especially to *younger* children. Hutt (1972) observes that "these differences in fact reflect the predominant tendency of the girls to perform a care-taking and protective role—aiding younger infants in carrying heavy objects, helping button pinafores or tie aprons, etc."

Popular children can actually be distinguished as early as the nursery-school phase. The popular children are frequently sought out as playmates, while others are consistently avoided and shunned by their peers. The interaction of these preschool or nursery school children are more characteristically friendly and cooperative than hostile, competitive or unfriendly. The friendships at this age are casual, transient and unstable, and in the view of Mussen (1963) they probably have few important or enduring effects on a child's personality.

The preschool and early school years of four to seven coincide with a phase of *"intuitive thinking"* (Piaget, 1950), during which the child wrestles with problems regarding the interpretation of his environment. He is using language in a more complex and subtle manner. The parents transmit to the child the essential adaptive techniques of the culture including this uniquely human one of language. Youngsters learn the basics of communication—language and logic—at their mother's knee. That is to say, children obtain their fundamental training in "consensual meanings"—the concepts and symbols used by society, the generally accepted meanings of words, nuances of expression such as emotional gestures and glances, and other forms of communication—within the family. A great deal is at stake as we shall see in Chapter 12.

The child is intuitive about relationships because he cannot give reasons for them. He is still without true concepts. There are still many limitations to his development of logical thinking, consistent explanations and coherent arguments. He is susceptible to conflict and confusion caused by the illogicality of communications from parents who are irrational in their thinking and behaviour (see Chapter 12). The child is also vulnerable, in a stage of massive imitation and identification, if parents are indifferent or hostile to their children thereby creating poor "models" for the child to identify with. Observations of children in social case records reveal grimly the way "history repeats itself". The unwanted child knows only the life he is born into and the chill of indifference seems to blight his sense of self. This may produce, in turn, another rejecting parent. If his ability to feel deeply, to feel empathy for others has been impaired he may find it impossible to accept and love his children. The case records are filled with recurring patterns, accounts of destructive, bitter, suspicious children—youngsters whose view of the world has been such as to make them apathetic, depressed and silent, or intensely hostile, non-conformist and rebellious. The McCords have this to say about the potentially very grave consequences of lovelessness:

Failure to develop a conscience flows logically from lovelessness. Almost all social scientists believe that the internalization of moral controls takes place primarily through the child's acceptance of his parents. The child and the parents strike an unconscious bargain: in return for the child's conformity to social restrictions, the parents give the child love. If the child fails to conform, disapproval follows. In time, the child looks ahead to the consequences of his acts. If he is about to misbehave, a gnawing fear warns that his parents might stop loving him. Thus, the inner anxiety eventually results in internalization of the parent's morality. The child has developed a rudimentary conscience (McCord and McCord, 1964).

The McCords observe that there is a constructive aspect in this development of inner controls; the child fears withdrawal of his parents' love, and at the same time identifies with them. To quote the authors again:

He wishes to emulate them . . . Children who fear the loss of love develop the concept of "must", but the "ought" of behaviour comes only through identification with parents and other moral symbols. In a rejectant environment, love, the central element, is missing. Because the rejected child does not love his parents and they do not love him, no identification takes place. Nor does the rejected child fear the loss of love—a love which he never had—when he violates moral restrictions. Without love, the socializing agent, the psychopath remains *asocial* (McCord and McCord, op. cit.).

This problem is discussed in Chapter 11.

Piaget (1932) defines the essential core of morality as the tendency to accept and follow a system of rules which regulate interpersonal behaviour. The child's early moral behaviour (from four to seven) is termed "egocentric", a stage on the way to the mature phase of "genuine cooperation".

These stages take the child from what Piaget calls "moral realism" to a "morality of cooperation"; he is shifting from a morality essentially based upon authority (and as such external to the child) to an internalized form of morality. The immature conception of rules is that they are absolute, fixed and unchangeable. The force that produces moral change is at first constraint; the child believes himself to be inferior to the adult and he accepts the adult value system even though he does not understand it. Piaget conceives of moral development as an inevitable consequence of growing up; on the one hand it is a result of the maturation of intellectual functions, and on the other it is due to increased experience of mutual respect among peers, as contrasted with the unilateral respect for adults which prevailed in the earlier years.

After the age of ten a morality of cooperation develops in which the child realizes not only that there are rules but that they evolve out of the reasonable needs of society. All of this has yet to come. Towards the end of the preschool age-range the child enters what Loevinger (1966) calls a "conformist" stage. Rules are partially internalized. They are obeyed just because they are the rules. The chief sanction for transgression is shame.

Reasonable conformity, then, must be contrasted with unreasonable or blind, conformity—as a socializing force that enables the child to learn the patterns of behaviour that will guarantee social acceptance. As such, it will lead to good personal as well as good social adjustments. Nonconformity, on the other hand, is just as prejudicial to good personal and social adjustments as extreme conformity. The child who refuses to conform to the accepted patterns of behaviour of the group, regardless of his reasons for not conforming, finds himself a social outcast. He is deprived of the satisfactions of belonging to a group and of the learning experiences which can come only from belonging.

A precarious balance is required by our society—a balance which is often difficult to perceive, and difficult to achieve for a child. It is difficult enough for adults. It was in a series of experiments carried out by Asch, that a disturbing discovery emerged. He found conclusive evidence that adult human subjects conformed to a judgement that they knew was contrary to fact, contrary to what they perceived, or both (see: Asch, 1952, 1956). Children, also, bend to these group pressures or feel anxious when they try to resist them (Berenda, 1950).

Lidz (1968) observes that the youngster of three or four is beginning to assemble his major resources for managing his life through his ability to communicate and manipulate symbols. Interference with the child's attempts to satisfy his curiosity by exploring the world he lives in and by trying to find solutions to problems for himself, can retard the development of language. Discouragement of the free play of discussion (see page 277) also impedes development. Lidz has this to say:

The child's reality testing will depend upon the slow sorting out of his experiences and the learning of what works and what does not that started during infancy; but this will, in turn, also depend upon the consistency and reliability of the behaviour of his tutors, primarily the members of his family. Verbal communication assumes increasing importance as the child emerges from his family. Members of the family had, through long experience, been able to understand and even anticipate many of his needs without his verbalizing them. Still, the child's trust in language—and what can be conveyed verbally and what responses his words will elicit—develops in the home setting. Here he learns how effective words will be: whether they concur with the unspoken communications; whether they are apt to match the feelings that accompany them; whether they subserve problem solving or are just as often a means of masking the existence of problems. The child's trust in verbal communication depends upon whether the words of the persons who are essential to him help solve problems or confuse, whether they prove more consistent signals than nonverbal cues, and whether the child's use of words can evoke desired responses. Difficulty can arise when parents' words contradict their nonverbal signals, as, for example, when the mother's words of affection are accompanied by irritable and hostile handling of the child; or when the mother's instructions for the child to obey his grandmother are accompanied by her obvious delight when the child disobeys and becomes a nuisance to the grandmother. The value of words is also diluted or negated when erroneous solutions are habitually imposed, as when the child who cries because he wants attention is told that he is hungry and is fed. Predictive values of communication are undermined when promises rarely materialize (Lidz, 1968).

# 11. Problems of Over- and Under-Socialization

ONE OF THE child's major acquisitions on the road to becoming a social being is the development of conscience—the "internalization" of standards of conduct and morality. Erikson (1965) comments as follows on this momentous achievement: "Man's childhood learning, which develops his highly specialized brain–eye–hand coordination and all the intrinsic mechanisms of reflection and planning, is contingent on prolonged dependence. Only thus does man develop conscience, that dependence on himself which will make him, in turn, dependable; and only when thoroughly dependable in a number of fundamental values (truth, justice, etc.) can he become independent and teach and develop tradition" (Erikson, 1965). Erikson recognizes that there are risks attached to this vital aspect of socialization for the individual. As he puts it: ". . . this dependability offers a problem because of its very origin in childhood, and because of the forces employed in its development . . . the immature origin of his conscience endangers man's maturity and his works: infantile fear accompanies him through life", (Erikson, op. cit.). Some individuals appear to remain fixated at an immature level of moral awareness.

Piaget's finding (Piaget, 1932) that young children act as though the rules are sacred and untouchable in their games, that any departure from the sacred rules makes the game unfair and unthinkable, is reminiscent of the rigid character-structure of some adults (see: Adorno *et al.*, 1950). There must be implicit *obedience* to authority. Such obedience is always right; a moral absolutism thus prevails. Sadly, it seems that some parents insist on this attitude to games' rules in the business of life as the child grows older, and they make it difficult for him to shift to a more mature morality. As a result of Piaget's studies (Piaget, 1932), we possess some useful generalizations about the "immature" moral approach. The immature conception of rules is that they are unchangeable, being absolute and fixed. They are handed down from authorities of a semi-mystical kind.

The immature concept of wrong acts takes no account of intention or motivation behind actions in judging their wrongness. The criteria which are applied, take into consideration the degree of disobedience of authority involved and the seriousness of the punishments normally decreed for the action by the authorities. The literal deviation from the rule and the amount of damage committed are also taken into account. The function of punishment is essentially viewed as retributive; wrong acts must be balanced by punishment, no matter what form it takes. In fact the severer the punishment, the better it is. The immature concept of punishment fails to perceive injustice when a group is punished for the misdeeds of an individual (collective responsibility). Accidental mishaps which follow wrongdoing are interpreted as punishment for it (imminent justice).

## The Development of Conscience

The mother cannot always be on the spot to check her child and enforce the rules. Eventually (to use a popular metaphor), her voice and other voices (which speak for society) are taken inside the "psyche" of the child so that what he now "obeys" is his own voice of conscience.

Hoffman (1970) provides an invaluable review of the literature on moral development. He makes the point that all disciplinary encounters have a great deal in common, regardless of the specific technique used. The techniques are not unidimensional or mutually exclusive. They all have three components, one or the other of which may predominate. The three components are: power assertion; love withdrawal; induction.

(1) *Power assertion.* Hoffman contends that the most reliable finding in the parent–child area of research is the negative relationship between power assertion and various indices of moral behaviour. It holds up for both sexes and the entire age range of childhood.

(2) *Love withdrawal.* Hoffman admits that the most surprising result of his research is the poor showing made by this technique, which runs against the commonly held view (see page 192) that anxiety about threatened withdrawl of parental love is the major contributing factor to the child's internalization of parental values. Hoffman's findings call this hypothesis into question. However, there is evidence that love withdrawal may contribute to the inhibition of anger (Hoffman and Saltzstein, 1967). It produces anxiety which leads to the renunciation of hostile and possibly other impulses. However, although Hoffman recognizes the contribution of love withdrawal in making the child more susceptible to adult influence, he maintains that this does not necessarily have a bearing on moral development (i.e., guilt and internal moral judgement).

(3) *Induction*. This is the type of discipline Hoffman finds most conducive
to moral development. It involves pointing out the effects of the child's
behaviour, giving reasons and explanations. (The cognitive structuring
of wrong acts is elaborated on page 284.)

To be effective the disciplinary technique must enlist already existing
emotional and motivational tendencies within the child. In other words, a
basis of affection must fuel the child's need for approval and hence his
readiness to attend to and heed what is being conveyed to him. All three
disciplinary techniques listed above communicate some negative evaluation
by the parent and are thus likely to elicit the child's need for approval.
This description, so far, is fragmentary.

It is not possible in the space available to describe, in anything but
superficial detail, the reasons why certain children find it easier to resist
temptation than others, or why certain parents foster strong or obsessive
consciences in their offspring while others don't. Fortunately this has been
done very fully by several writers (e.g., Piaget, 1932; Kohlberg, 1963,
1970; Aronfreed, 1961, 1968; Wright, 1971). There seems to be substantial
agreement about the conditions which are conducive to the acquisition of
internalized standards of morality. They include:

(i) Strong ties of affection between parents and children;
(ii) Firm moral demands made by parents upon their youngsters;
(iii) The consistent use of sanctions;
(iv) Techniques of punishment that are psychological rather than physical
     (i.e., methods which signify or threaten withdrawal of love);
(v) An intensive use of reasoning and explanations.

On the issue of conscience formation, it is suggested (see: Wright, 1970b)
that one of the most effective sanctions available to the mother is any
action which threatens or implies the withdrawal of her love. It provokes
intense anxiety in the child, as distinct from aggression. There is evidence
that punishments which evoke anxiety are likely later to result in self-
control, while those producing an aggressive reaction are not—although
they may well make a child wary of being caught. For this reason, physical
punishments are among the least effective as far as the development of the
child's conscience is concerned.

The normal reaction to any physical assault is anger and aggression,
though the expression of anger may be inhibited by fear. It by-passes the
more subtle sense of anxiety which leads to the resisting of temptation
through self-control rather than through wariness of punishments. We
know that in general, extremely hostile and/or rejecting parents are likely
to produce aggressive (and possibly delinquent) offspring (Feshbach,
1970). However, these child-rearing variables are influenced by moderator

variables and cannot be considered in isolation. There are several crucial interactions at work in the case of aggression. Kagan and Moss (1962) show that maternal restrictiveness with older boys is associated with high levels of aggression but this does not hold for young boys or for girls. In the case of paternal punishment, Eron *et al.* (1963) show that the consequences depend on their occupational level. Punitive fathers with high-status appear to be much more likely to have aggressive sons than low-status punitive fathers.

It is a fairly reliable generalization that punishment leads to self-control only when the child is on the side of the person punishing. Since he loves his mother, the child is partly on her side. Because of this identification with her, he will join in her condemnation of himself. Although such attachment is a condition which makes the development of conscience possible, it also gives the mother a power which can be detrimental to the child. And this brings us to one of the problems of over-socialization. If a child is strongly and exclusively attached to a mother who sets impossibly high standards and is deeply "hurt" when her child fails to live up to them, it is extremely probable that he will acquire a sense of conscience so severe and restrictive that his spontaneity, and emotional life will be crippled, and much of his creative energy remain unused. On the other hand, warm, loving, and consistent discipline in which reasons are given (when the child can understand them) are thought to produce the reasoning sort of "obedience" rather than the uncritical and emotionally dependent subservience to authority.

Learning theorists (e.g., Mowrer, 1960; Eysenck, 1960a) base their investigations of conscience-development upon the assumption that there is nothing about moral learning to distinguish it qualitatively from other forms of learning. Principles which derive from the study of anxiety conditioning on the one hand, and instrumental learning on the other, are used to explain resistance to temptation. To describe the process in synoptic form: the infant who commits a prohibited deed is punished in some way. Anxiety is aroused by the punishment and becomes associated with the configuration of external and internal stimuli being manifested at the time. This learned anxiety will be elicited on future occasions in similar situations. Being a powerful response it inhibits other responses, and once learned, is resistent to unlearning. There is, however, a problem of discrimination. The internal and external stimuli present in a situation are often virtually the same for both prohibited and permissible behaviours. For example, a young child who has been taught to share might find it difficult to distinguish between borrowing a friend's toy with permission and taking it home without consent. The situations have to be cognitively structured to bring out the differences. These often involve subtle nuances such as the distinction between "white" lies and other, presumably "black" ones. Effective moral instruction depends upon the young child (who is being punished for some intended misbehaviour) having the situation verbally labelled and cognitively structured for him. Eventually, through the processes of generalization and discrimination, the label (or concept) itself becomes capable of evoking the anxiety response. On subsequent occasions, the way that an individual cognitively structures the situation will determine whether or not anxiety is elicited, thereby inhibiting the immoral act. Guilt is interpreted as anxiety which has been conditioned to the events occurring after a transgression of the rules. Learning theorists consider that behaviours indicative of guilt such as confession, self-criticism and apology, are learned responses which have been found to be instrumental in reducing post-transgression anxiety.

Wright (1971) points out that social learning theorists share the basic orientation of learning theorists, but would claim that certain extensions of that theory are required in accounting for moral behaviour. The learning theorists model does not account sufficiently for the fact that moral behaviour develops exclusively in a two-person situation. Within the theory, there is no basis for differentiating punishment and reward mediated by human agents from those which are the impersonal consequences of behaviour. Yet it appears that the nature of the reinforcing agent, and of the individual's relationship to this agent, are crucial factors in moral development. Additional principles—some of them controversial —like introjection (Argyle, 1964), imitation (Bandura and Walters, 1963) and identification (Kagan, 1958) have been introduced.

Piaget (1932) points out that the morality prescribed for the individual by society is not homogeneous because society itself is not just one thing. Society is the sum of social relationships, and among these relationships two extreme types can be distinguished: relationships of constraint (whose property is to impose upon the individual from outside, a system of rules with obligatory content) and relationships of cooperation (whose property is to create within people's minds the consciousness of ideal norms underlying all rules). The pursuit of altruism, idealism and other moral virtues is explained by learning theorists in terms of instrumental learning. Because honesty and helpfulness have in the past been rewarded by parents, they become established habits; and since the concepts which structure such behaviour have also been associated with positively reinforcing experiences, the individual's recognition of his own honesty becomes rewarding. And, of course, strong habits of "good" behaviour themselves have an inhibitory effect upon the corresponding but incompatible "bad" behaviour. Hartshorne and May (1928–1930) found that altruistic behaviour on one test tended to be associated with similar behaviour on other tests, and a small, positive association ($r = 0.33$) was found between overall measures of helpfulness and of honesty.

## Conformity

We saw that Loevinger (1966) refers to part of the pre-school-going stage of ego-development as a "conformist" stage. Children brought up in Western society have to deal with the paradox of an ideology which insists on a marked degree of conformity while paying lip-service to individualism.

The Buckinghamshire study (Shepherd *et al.*, 1971) showed that children who always obey the rules are rather rare. Just as children who are too individualistic can be a problem, so can children who are too conformist, or to put it another way, too submissive. Shepherd *et al.* observe that the paragons who always did as they were told comprised only 10% of the girls and 8% of the boys, not a low figure if Kanner's view—that "complete obedience" is the expression of pathological submissiveness resulting from suppression of spontaneity and initiative—is accepted. A further 10% of the girls and 13% of the boys were reported as "usually resisting when asked or told to do things": and approximately 80% of the children were considered by their parents "about as obedient as most children". The age and sex trends within the pattern were unremarkable.

It has been suggested that there is a *general* trait or predisposition for some people to be more conformist than others, i.e., that there are consistent individual differences in susceptibility to social pressure no matter what the particular situation (see: Berg and Bass, 1961). Related characteristics such as persuasibility, acquiescence and suggestibility have also been investigated. The evidence suggests that there are general factors of responsiveness to social influence, such that one can speak of a "conforming personality".

Researchers (see: Mann, 1959; Crutchfield, 1955) have found marked personality differences between conformers and non-conformers. Interestingly, overly conforming people tend to be poorly adjusted (in the *general* mental health sense), lacking in dominance, and they are inclined to manifest depressive tendencies, rigidity, social inadequacy, and an inability to express aggression. In addition, they are described as lacking in self-confidence and self-esteem, as less intelligent, lacking in originality, lacking in incentive to achieve, conventional with a strong need for social approval, and authoritarian minded.

It is not surprising that, for pragmatic reasons, the non-conforming child is labelled a "problem child" and possibly referred to a child guidance clinic for treatment. However, the dilemma posed by society's demands for "adjustment" to norms is not to be escaped by giving in too readily to the pressures to conform. Such a child may also be considered a problem child; as with most attributes, a balance is required by our society.

There is evidence (see: Campbell, 1964; Secord and Backman, 1964) about group influences which provides us with certain generalizations. Within any longstanding group of children, some members have more influence over a particular child than others. As a rule, the greatest influence comes from the leader and the least from the lowest-status members—those who are least popular with the rest of the group. The more solidly the group is formed and the more secure the child's status within that group, the greater its influence over him will be. The influence of the group on a child varies according to the strength of what is called the child's "affiliation motive"—that is to say the degree to which the child is anxious to be accepted. The stronger the child's affiliation motive, the greater his susceptibility to influence from group members will be, especially those who are in positions of high status in the group. His motivation to gain status is influenced, too, by his own status in the group. Children with high status have a stronger motivation to be popular than those with such a low status that they have no hope of winning acceptance.

There are several determinants of conformist patterns of behaviour. It is necessary to ask whether the child has identified with a dominant or passive parent. It is also important to know whether the parent suppresses attempts at domination by the child and rewards his submissiveness, or in other words, whether the child-training methods used in the home punish the child for non-conformity and reward him for conformity to parental wishes.

The influence of the peer group is also critical. Campbell's (1964) review of peer relations in childhood, suggests that information on the role of age and sex presents a somewhat inconsistent picture. What does emerge is the predictable finding that younger children are more susceptible to the views of others than are older children, and (in keeping with cultural stereotypes) girls are more likely to yield to group pressure than boys. Susceptibility to pressure by one's peers increases up to about the age of fifteen, and thereafter declines. Some children are excessively devoted to the peer group. Wright (1971) describes the conformist character as giving himself entirely to his group so that its norms become his morality as long as he remains a member. The distinctive characteristics of the conformist character arise from the fact that during upbringing attachment to the peer group takes precedence over attachment to parents. When the peer group takes over some of the functions of parents, the child's attachment to it tends to be pathological. If his allegiance to his group changes, his morality will change as well.

Every child growing up in his community will experience a great many social-pressure situations, varying from the trivial to the serious. The child's characteristic way of responding to social influence will be determined by the interplay of his psychological needs and the extent to which his culture inculcates conformity-proneness in its members. Anthropologists (e.g., Margaret Mead, 1935) have shown that societies differ in their demands for social conformity. The quality of the child's experiences within the family (see Fig. 3, page 153), the conformity pressures of his milieu, and the personal resources he brings to the situation in evolving strategies so as to "be himself", eventually produce a "life-style" or "habit" of conforming or of resisting pressures.

Not all acts of conforming are identical in psychological meaning. In the case of what is called "expedient conforming" (or "compliance") the individual outwardly agrees with the group while remaining in inward disagreement; in "true" conformity the individual is brought to agree both inwardly and outwardly (see: Berg and Bass, 1961). Several studies have shown that if the individual cannot leave the group—and one thinks of the maltreated child who cannot escape his situation—then there is usually compliance from the individual. However if he wants to be in the group then there is likely to be private acceptance as well as outward conformity. Conformity is likely to be at its greatest when the limits of the society's tolerance and the penalties for deviance are clearly defined.

The child's expectation of acceptance depends on the degree to which he believes he possesses the attributes that his peers value—qualities such as skill, strength, beauty, verbal facility and so on. His actual body-build and attractiveness are of critical importance as well. The more accepted the child is by the group the more willing he is to conform; the more willing he is to conform, the better accepted he will be. Willingness to conform is especially strong in the later part of childhood (getting on towards adolescence) when the desire for social acceptance reaches its peak. This raises the question of the general socializing influence of the child's peer group—an issue we shall return to on page 296.

## The Authoritarian Character

There is a variation of the excessively conformist type of person—the so-called authoritarian character. Racial and other kinds of prejudice and bigotry are associated with the possession of authoritarian traits (Adorno et al., 1950). Morality for the authoritarian character is a function of contemporary social relationships rather than of individual reasoning and decision. His is an imperfectly internalized morality; his behaviour is controlled by the expectation of others. The authoritarian character is preoccupied with status and power; he wants to feel there are those he can look up to uncritically and those he can look down upon as inferior. He finds democratic relationships difficult. Morality is a matter of obeying rules that are sanctioned by authority and tradition. Because self-esteem is founded upon social position, he is strongly motivated to conform.

The authoritarian character tends to come from a home in which a rather stern and distant father dominates a submissive and long-suffering, but morally, restrictive mother. Discipline consists in the harsh application of conventional rules. Relationships are conceived in terms of power rather than love.

## Emotional Problems due to Surplus and Deficient Social Conditioning

In Chapter 4 we looked briefly at Eysenck's model of personality and its theoretical link with the conduct and personality disorders of childhood. We did not go into how this comes about. Eysenck (1957) distinguishes, as a learning theorist, between two broad categories of emotional disorder. According to the model (Fig. 5). normal and abnormal subjects are distributed with respect to behaviour and test performance over a two-

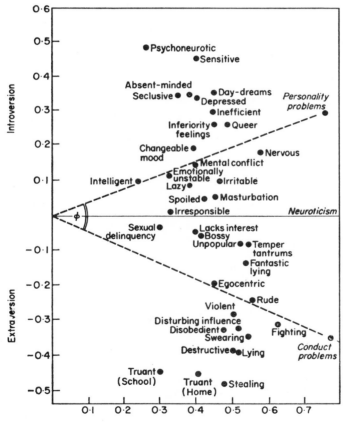

Fig. 5. Results of a factor analysis of various conduct and personality problems shown by children. (Adapted from Eysenck 1960b.)

dimensional factor space. The continua of neuroticism–normality and extraversion–introversion form the axes.

A child who is high on neuroticism and extraversion will show a distinct tendency to be labelled as a "conduct problem"—perhaps "hysterical" or "psychopathic" by an examining psychiatrist; a youngster who is high on neuroticism and introversion is more likely to be labelled as having a "personality problem"—one of the dysthymic disorders such as "anxiety state". How does Eysenck explain such a taxonomy?

If conditioning is as crucial in learning maladjusted (e.g., neurotic) behaviour as is claimed, then it would be very significant if human beings differed in their capacity to be conditioned. It would not be surprising if this were the case, as individuals differ in their speed of learning and the strength or retentiveness of what is learned.

In fact, there is evidence (see: Eysenck, 1967; Franks, 1956, 1960) to suggest that there are individual differences in the speed and strength with which conditioned responses are formed. It follows from this, that other things being equal, the acquisition of a "conditioned emotional response" like fear, will be facilitated in children who form conditioned responses rapidly, strongly and lastingly. Those youngsters who condition ineffectually tend to be less susceptible to the impact of the environment; they are less likely to acquire maladaptive behaviour patterns. Introverts do seem to form conditioned responses more rapidly and lastingly than do extraverts.

Being somewhat impervious to the impact of the environment is not, however, totally advantageous. The relative absence of conditionability may have unfavourable consequences according to theorists who propose that classical conditioning plays a crucial role in the socialization of the child. Eysenck observes that in such a person socialization would proceed only to a very limited degree, and if his failure to condition were to be particularly severe, then he would grow up into a psychopath or more generally a "conduct problem". This theory about the significant role of conditioning in socialization which is strongly supported by experimental research (see: Eysenck, 1967) is only one strand in the complex story of social learning. Nevertheless it is a significant theme, and has serious implications for the child who can only form conditioned responses weakly and slowly.

Extraversion–introversion is not the only dimension on which people vary in a way that has implications for learning maladaptive behaviour. People also differ in their emotionality or neuroticism. These differences (as we saw in a previous chapter) are in part due to the inherited sensitivity or reactiveness* of the autonomic nervous system, and in part due to the

* A tendency of the autonomic nervous system to react strongly and lastingly to stressful situations.

quality of the experiences an individual is exposed to during the course of his life; the net result of the interaction of these hereditary and environmental influences is that certain children are easy to arouse emotionally as compared with others. Children (and adults) whose autonomic nervous systems possess this excessive sensitivity are much more likely to develop neurotic disorders than are those whose nervous systems are stable. Intense emotional reactions (trauma) can be disruptive by themselves as was seen in cases of "shell shock" as they used to be known in World War I. But there is also another consideration. Drive is an important factor in learning. There is evidence that emotion, in a broad sense, acts as a drive (Spence, 1958; Taylor, 1956). Emotionality, as an attribute of certain children, produces stronger drives in such children when they find themselves in emotionally laden situations. Such emotions acting as drives in times of stress may, up to a point, facilitate learning (and this includes maladaptive learning).

So what we have, according to Eysenck, are two broad categories of disorder. The first group involves surplus conditioned responses. The child has learnt the moral and other lessons of society too well (i.e., he is overly conscientious or conformist). We have already looked at this type of problem. Another child may too easily acquire maladaptive feelings and behaviours (e.g., phobias, depressions, obsessions and compulsions). The second group of disorders involve a failure or deficiency in the conditioning process which would normally produce socially desirable habits.

Rosen and Gregory (1965) tabulate (Table VI below) typical clinical differences between the extreme representatives of the two groups of disorders as follows:

TABLE VI. Characteristics of the typical antisocial sociopath (psychopath) and neurotic. (From Rosen and Gregory, 1965.)

| Antisocial Sociopath | Neurotic |
|---|---|
| Predominantly male (approx. 3:1). | Predominantly female (approx. 3:2). |
| First psychiatric contact in adolescence or as young adult. | First psychiatric contact at any time in adult life. |
| Concentration in lower socioeconomic classes. | High frequency in all socioeconomic classes, but concentration of treated cases in middle and upper classes. |
| Defective or absent superego. | Rigid superego. |
| Minimal or no guilt or depression over serious antisocial behaviour. | Frequent guilt and depression over minor or imagined misdeeds. |
| Uninhibited acting out of impulses, with inability to postpone gratification of future reward. Reckless nonconformity. | Excessive inhibition of sexual or aggressive impulses in anticipation of long-range advantages. Conformity with standards of society. |

TABLE VI—*continued*

| Antisocial Sociopath | Neurotic |
|---|---|
| Amoral, unreliable, irresponsible. Pathological liar, cheat, swindler, thief. May be promiscuous, violent or addicted to alcohol or drugs. Confident and carefree. Indifferent to religion. | Moral, reliable and responsible, but lacking in self-confidence and often indecisive. Religious or conflicted over religion. |
| No long-range plans or efforts. Freedom from worry or anxiety. | Ambitious plans and striving for future goals. Intangible ideals with much doubt, fear, anxiety and apprehension. |
| Indifferent to others' opinions except when these frustrate immediate needs. Incapable of true affection. Superficial charm and plausibility used to manipulate others. | Insecure and sensitive to criticism. Frequent feelings of inadequacy. Capable of affection and has strong need for affection, but latent or unconscious hostility often interferes with ability to maintain deep relationships. |
| Transient, uninhibited sexual behaviour with wide variety of partners. | Sexual impulses and behaviour perceived as dangerous or disgusting. Frigidity or impotence. |
| Tendency to express hostility directly and violently except when direct expression would interfere with momentary goals. | Hostility not permitted direct expression but may be expressed indirectly or displaced. |
| Frequent EEG abnormalities. | Autonomic lability. |
| Tendency to mesomorphic body build. | Tendency to ectomorphic body build (except in conversion reactions). |
| Frequent history of sociopathy in parents and siblings. | Frequent history of neurosis in parents and siblings. |
| Parental deprivation, discord, deceit, lack of supervision, occasionally overindulgence. | Parental deprivation, discord, domination. |
| Association with delinquent peers or siblings. | Restricted relationships with siblings and peers. |
| Truancy, job instability and nomadism (pathological roaming from place to place). Record of conflict with police or military authorities. | Often high achievement in school and occupation. |

## Psychopathic Personality

We have looked at problems of over-socialization—excessive social conditioning. At the other end of the scale we get the so-called psychopathic personality problems. Franks (1956) says of the psychopathic personality: "He may steal, swear, lie, truant, be destructive, disobedient and egocentric. These traits are all characteristic of the psychopathic delinquent, and all have in common a high degree of under-socialization, of not having learned the socially approved modes of behaviour."

The psychopath has been described as an antisocial, aggressive, highly impulsive person, who feels little or no guilt and is unable to form lasting bonds of affection with other human beings. McCord and McCord (1964) describe the child psychopath as having the embryonic personality characteristics of the adult psychopath. His delinquencies and tantrums betray his aggressiveness, his truancy, the impulsiveness of his nature. He is cruel to other children and to animals. He tends to be asocial as well as anti-social, showing little or no remorse for his brutal and usually purpose-less deeds; there is an inability to make any sort of deep and meaningful relationship with other children or adults.

There are few generally accepted explanations of why psychopaths behave in the manner just described. Eysenck (1957) considers the psycho-path to be an extremely extraverted individual who has had a life-long history of maladjustment and anti-social acts. He has all the impulsiveness of the extravert. He fails to think before he acts. It is a long-established observation that the psychopath appears to be deficient in learning avoid-ance responses. According to Eysenck, the characteristic personality traits of the psychopath are due to an excess of cortical inhibition, affecting his ability to learn the lessons of life—at the basic level of reflex aversion to certain antisocial acts. Eysenck (1960, 1964) postulates an inherited factor "conditionability" as having a critical influence on human avoidance learning and socialization. Lykken (1957) found that prisoners labelled as psychopathic showed less anxiety on a self-report questionnaire, less G.S.R. reactivity to a conditioned stimulus paired with shock and less effective avoidance learning in a punishment learning paradigm. There seems to be a distinct possibility that a low reactivity of the sympathetic nervous system could be an inheritable factor leading to a lack of internal-ized control over behaviour. Hare (1960, 1965) found some evidence that the psychopath is deficient in acquiring anticipatory anxiety in the presence of the cues for punishment. He was able to demonstrate that the gradient of anxiety for the psychopath does not begin to rise as soon as in the normal person. Solomon, Turner and Lessac (1968) found distinct differences among their dogs in degree of resistance to temptation according to breed.

Franks (1956) points out ways in which the psychopath resembles the hysteric with respect to traits such as emotional immaturity—which is another way of saying that they have not formed the socially approved conditioned emotional responses. Another group who condition poorly, are the brain injured. Hysterical and psychopathic reactions are not uncommon following prefrontal leucotomies, and it is following organic illnesses, especially those involving the cortex, that hysterical symptoms often occur. Other theorists have pointed out the fact that diseases such as encephalitis lethargica, which damage certain regions of the brain, can—and often do—result in the occurrence of many psychopathic symptoms.

In discussing these organically based interpretations of the deficient socialization of psychopaths, it should be remembered that animal studies have shown that early experiences of intense unavoidable aversive stimulation may disrupt or completely suppress the animal's capacity for active or passive avoidance learning later on in life. Many of the individuals who are labelled "psychopathic" have an early history of severe and prolonged rejection (Bowlby, 1944, McCord and McCord, 1964).

McCord and McCord (op. cit.) hold the view that brain injury or malfunction plays a part in the development of psychopathy, but they also stress environmental factors. They summarize the organic aetiological picture as follows:

Injury to the frontal lobe region or the hypothalamus results in aggression and antisociality.

Many psychopaths exhibit physical signs of brain disorder.

Proportionally, more psychopaths than normal people have a history of early brain diseases.

The psychopath's physiology responds more quickly to physical changes in the environment.

The environmentalist research reviewed by McCord and McCord (op. cit.) indicates that:

The vast majority of psychopaths have been rejected in childhood.

Aggression is the dominant reaction to rejection.

Rejected or institutionalized children often, but not invariably exhibit the psychopathic syndrome. They lack normal guilt feelings; they are impulsive, aggressive, pleasure-seeking, and they seem incapable of relating to other people.

The overall causal patterns fall into three types. As the authors put it:

(1) Severe rejection, by itself, can cause psychopathy.
(2) Mild rejection, in combination with damage to the brain area (possibly the hypothalamus) which normally inhibits behaviour, causes psychopathy.
(3) Mild rejection, in the absence of neural disorder, can result in psychopathy if certain other influences in the environment fail to provide alternatives.

# 12. Developmental Problems of Speech and Communication

WE HAVE ALREADY referred to the fact that communication in spoken language is the latest, most complex and probably the most vulnerable of man's evolutionary achievements. To communicate is to convey meaning from one individual to another in an intelligible code. Such a code is provided by language. In learning a language, the baby is assimilating his culture's conceptual categories for thinking, perceiving and reasoning. The basic needs of children are fulfilled by interaction with adults and other children; successful adaptation to the environment requires an ability to communicate. Not surprisingly, serious emotional problems flow from a child's inability to express himself meaningfully or to comprehend others. This also applies to vital extensions of communicative skill such as reading. Reading backwardness is strongly associated with maladjustment (Rutter *et al.*, 1970; Douglas, 1964).

The investigation of verbal and pre-verbal communications in young children has been complicated by confusions of terminology. However, attempts have been made to design a set of accurate symbols for the basic speech sounds (e.g., the International Phonetic Alphabet) and to formulate other units of observation (e.g., the breath unit), in order to study the beginnings of speech (see: Irwin, 1960). The infant's prelinguistic communication* reaches a peak at about 16 to 20 months. Meaningful words appear towards the end of the first year or the beginning of the second year of life. At first they constitute a very small proportion of the infant's vocalization, but during the later part of the second year they become prominent. Thereafter as his spoken language improves, nonverbal communication tends to decline, although he continues to use it.

Irwin (1949) finds no fundamental group differences in the inherent

* Consisting of body-movements, facial expressions and emotionally charged vocalizations such as gentle coos, whimpers, urgent screams, attention-seeking calls, soft chuckles and loud laughter, gestures, etc.

phonetic equipment of human beings. But by the time they begin to form word patterns, some sex differences begin to manifest themselves. Irwin provides some developmental data:

At a year and a half, girls exceed boys in the ability to use consonants at the beginning, in the middle and at the end of a word. The mean number of consonants used by girls in the initial position is 8·7 as against 7·7 for boys. For the medial position, the mean for girls is 7·9 and for boys 6·9. In the final position, girls use 2·9 consonants while boys use 2·4.

The average 8-month-old child is unable to use words. At 10 months he probably will have one word; at 12 months, about three words. At a year and a half, his vocabulary may be 20 words. During the next three months it will jump to over 100, and at two years it may contain as many as 250 words.

The ultimate language problem for the growing child is to relate words into meaningful sentences. His first sentence may be a single word; for instance, he will use the word "do" to obtain many of his demands. From a single word grows a variety of longer sentences. The average child's first sentence appears soon after the 15th month. At two years the average length of his sentences is 1·7 words. At five it has expanded to 4·6 words. The 10 words most often used in constructing the first sentence are: "I", "is", "it", "you", "do", "a", "this", "not", and "the". Nouns and verbs at first are used more frequently than adjectives and connectives.

There is insufficient space to give more than a brief comment on a few of the language and communication problems.

## Stuttering

This problem—also referred to as "stammering"—is a disorder of speech rhythms. Kanner (1953) states that "the flow of speech is disrupted by blocks and tensions which produce hesitations and repetitions or prolongations of sounds. The continuity of diction is broken by clonic and tonic spasms of the muscles which participate in the mechanism of speech". Stein and Mason (1968) are critical of definitions of stammering which emphasize the lack of fluency in speech because they see stammering as a disorder of communication not of speech. They define persistent stammering as "a neurosis manifest in progressive dissolution of communication. The disorder is expressive of a disharmony in the interrelation between psychic processes and the linguistic encoding process irrespective of possible neuropathological conditions." A majority of cases have their onset between the ages of three and five years. Andrews and Harris (1964) in a survey of over a thousand school children found an incidence of 3%. This figure rose to 4·5% if cases of transient stammering lasting up to six months were included.

It is well known that emotional factors can affect the speech mechanisms; normal speakers occasionally stutter with strong emotion and stutterers may experience a particularly severe blockage in speech in times of distress.

In fact, at the best of times, there is a considerable degree of overlap to be observed in the speech features of persons classified as stutterers and those classified as non-stutterers (Johnson, 1956). Three categories of stutterer have been identified by Andrews and Harris (op. cit.):

(1) Developmental stuttering, being of early onset (2–4 years) but lasting only a few months.
(2) Benign stuttering, characterized by late onset (mean age $7\frac{1}{2}$ years) but tending to spontaneous remission after about two to three years.
(3) Persistent stuttering, with an onset between $3\frac{1}{2}$ and 8 years.

There is a massive literature on this topic (see: Hahn, 1956; Beech and Fransella, 1968; Hill, 1944) and a multiplicity of aetiological theories and therapeutic techniques are catalogued therein. Psychoanalysts view stuttering as the outward and visible manifestation of conflicts over sexual or hostile instinctual impulses (Fenichel, 1945; Santostefano, 1960). There are a variety of physiological explanations of the speech defect. Cherry and Sayers (1956) contend that the stutterer suffers essentially from an auditory perceptual defect in the sense that he continually receives false or misleading information (feedback) concerning the progress of his emitted speech. A learning theory model (Brutten and Shoemaker, 1968) and in particular a conflict paradigm (Sheehan, 1958) has been used to explain many of the known characteristics of stammering (see page 96).

Ullmann and Krasner (1969) view stammering as learned behaviour, and, where there is no definite physical defect, as a behaviour pattern that may be directly retrained by a variety of behaviour-orientated techniques. These include aversive response-contingent procedures (Flanagan *et al.*, 1958); negative practice (Case, 1960); removal of positive reinforcement of the stutter (Sheehan, 1951); distraction (Cherry and Sayers, 1956); and systematic desensitization.

## Elective Mutism

Some children, when they begin school, maintain a degree of silence which usually disappears within a year of school entry. Elective mutism is an emotional problem which is an exaggeration of this sort of election not to communicate with certain people. The youngster is capable of speaking perfectly normally (usually with his parents and siblings) but he maintains a silence with other individuals. The problem usually occurs in early or middle childhood, mainly in girls and mainly in introverted children who dislike change and who manifest a predominantly negative mood. It often occurs in an overprotective or coercive environment. Kanner (1953) reports cases of children whose silence is in part a reaction to forceful attempts by their parents to make them conform. He describes perfectionist parents who determine that their offspring should talk at the earliest possible age. They urge and correct them ceaselessly, becoming impatient with their inevitable developmental mispronunciations and failures in fluency. Some youngsters develop a negative attitude toward speech and remain or become silent. Sometimes elective mutism is associated with an actual (rather than developmental) articulatory defect or some other minor speech disorder.

It is only too easy for parents and teachers unwittingly to reinforce and maintain this childish strategy of voluntary silence. The problem has been successfully treated by means of behaviour therapy (see: Sluckin and Jehu, 1969).

## Developmental Aphasia

Disturbances in the ability to produce and comprehend speech are referred to as *aphasic* conditions (aphasia). Much of the information that enables the individual to understand and express himself in speech appears to be stored in the left parietal cortex in right-handed people (Penfield and Roberts, 1959). The use and understanding of language may be impaired in several ways, and such impairments lead to associated difficulties in mastering that all-important skill of reading. Penfield and Roberts (1959) are of the opinion that there are no really pure forms of language defect. However they present evidence that relatively small lesions may in some cases produce impairments where one aspect of language is much more disturbed than others. The commonly quoted examples of this are expressive impairments of speech associated with lesions in the region of the Rolandic fissure, and dyslexia, usually accompanied by dysgraphia, associated with parieto-occipital lesions.

## Executive Aphasia

It is fairly common for there to be a developmental delay in language expression in the case of intelligent children with unimpaired comprehension and normal adjustment. There is usually a good prognosis in such cases of developmental speech retardation. Many of these children will enjoy normal speech by six years of age. However, this sort of problem shades into the more serious syndrome of executive aphasia. Here there is usually evidence of perceptual difficulties indicative of brain-injury. The comprehension of language may be normal or relatively less impaired than the ability to speak.

## Receptive Aphasia

This "syndrome" is rare in its more serious form. The milder form of impairment may involve an inability to localize sounds although the child can respond to some of them in an undifferentiated and gross manner. Such a deficit makes it impossible for the youngster to process the complex series of sounds which make up language. At the other extreme are those individuals who are "word deaf" and, in fact, totally inattentive to sounds, although special techniques indicate that there is no peripheral or cochlear hearing loss to account for their deafness. The problem may occur in early childhood following or preceding a series of epileptic attacks.

These children with receptive and executive aphasia often have the kinds of language disorder and present other handicaps—perceptual and behavioural—which are reminiscent of infantile autism (Rees, 1973; Wing, 1966). Rees (1973) observes that there are children whose clinical features reveal them to be in the "hinterland between autism and aphasia" and there are aphasic children who, under stress, temporarily preoccupy themselves with the same obsessive rituals and avoid making interpersonal relationships in a manner analagous to autistic children. Aphasic children shed these habits on removal from stressful conditions, unlike autistic children. He notes that both the autistic and aphasic syndromes have clinical features generally considered to be the result of brain dysfunction or even overt brain damage, and almost never simply due to pathological child-rearing. However, Rees contends that the main reason for classifying the aphasic and autistic conditions together, is that they can best be remedied to some extent by the same type of diagnostic teaching method which identifies their perceptual and cognitive difficulties. The main aim of therapy is directed towards teaching language, using the most intact sensory system, either auditory-vocal or visuo-motor.

## Early Infantile Autism

The major characteristics of this syndrome as described by Kanner and his colleague (Kanner, 1943; Eisenberg and Kanner, 1956) are as follows:

(1) A profound withdrawal of contact from other people ("aloneness");
(2) Failure to use language for communication;
(3) Obsessive maintenance of the status quo—"sameness"—in the environment;
(4) Skill in fine motor movements, especially with regard to objects; as opposed to
(5) Inability to deal with people;
(6) Very high cognitive potential as manifested by "islets" of performance.

Kanner regards infantile autism as a variation of childhood schizophrenia. It would be easy to get bogged down in a differential diagnostic riddle as to the precise meaning of infantile autism and its boundaries relative to childhood psychosis in general or childhood schizophrenia, mental subnormality and brain damage in particular (see: Van Krevelen, 1962, 1963; Bender, 1969; Mahler 1952; Rimland, 1964; Rutter, 1965; Yates, 1970). Hermelin (1963) suggests that "childhood psychosis" like "mental subnormality" or "brain damage" is too general a term to be of much value in planning precise experimental investigations. She points out that whereas "schizophrenia" is the name given to a group of mental illnesses which usually develop after the age of puberty, and which have a characteristic pattern of clinical symptoms, and a characteristic course and outcome, there is no justification for finding analogies between it and between infantile autism—a condition of maldevelopment in childhood— which simply has as one of its features (like schizophrenia) social withdrawal. This characteristic is shared with many other psychotic conditions, and may be secondary in childhood autism to difficulties in language and communication. It is this serious deficit in communication which makes it possible to follow Rees' lead (Rees, 1973) and discuss autism in the context of disorders of language development.

Before proceeding, however, it is perhaps worth noting the characteristics which Rimland (1964) has tried to abstract from a vast and confusing literature, as differentiating infantile autism from childhood schizophrenia. His comparisons appear in Table VII.

The question of how valid these distinctions are awaits answers from many more carefully controlled experimental investigations. Rosen and Gregory (1965) find that early infantile autism is so similar to childhood

TABLE VII. Differential characteristics of childhood schizophrenia and early infantile autism.

| Early Infantile Autism | Childhood Schizophrenia |
|---|---|
| Present from birth | Early development normal |
| Good health/appearance | Many ailments/frail appearance |
| EEG usually normal | EEG often abnormal |
| No physical moulding when carried | Physical moulding possible |
| No social interaction | Dependency on adult |
| Preservation of sameness | Variability |
| No hallucinations or delusions | Hallucinations/delusions occasionally |
| High level of motor skill | Motor skill poor/bizarre movements |
| Language disturbance (pronominal reversal, affirmation by repetition, delayed echolalia, metaphoric language, part-whole confusion) | Language development, but may be abnormal |
| Idiot-savant performance | No special skills |
| Unoriented, detached | Disorientated, confused |
| Not easily conditionable | Easily conditionable |
| Occurs in both of monosygotic twins | Does not occur in both of monozygotic twins |
| Stable, professional home background | Unstable home background |
| Low family incidence of psychosis | High family incidence of psychosis |
| Lack of affective contact and warmth in relations | More appealing/responsive in human relations |

schizophrenia in its manifestations that sometimes the two disorders cannot be differentiated except on the basis of historical data. This refers to the view held by some clinicians that the childhood type of schizophrenic reaction represents a regression from some higher stage of development, while the infantile autism involves grossly atypical development from birth. Rimland (op. cit.) regards infantile autism as a unique psychosis which is part of a brain damage syndrome. Rimland believes that the basic defect is cognitive—an inability to relate new stimuli to remembered experience—and that the defect is due to a malfunctioning of the reticular system. A clinical picture which is indistinguishable from infantile autism may develop after a brain disease such as encephalitis when it occurs in early childhood (Rutter, 1965). There is other supportive evidence (see: Rutter, 1968). However, against brain damage as a general explanatory or causal hypothesis is the absence of evidence of cerebral injury in at least half the cases of autism.

The autistic child's abnormal responses to stimuli and his lack of response to sounds (Anthony, 1958; Rutter, 1968) has excited speculation that autism involves a defect such as relative inability to comprehend sounds (Rutter, 1965a; Wing, 1966). Like the child with "developmental aphasia" the autistic patient has a fundamental difficulty in the comprehension of language and in addition, experiences disturbance in the organization of perception (Stroh and Buick, 1961). If the mechanisms in that part of the brain responsible for processing and structuring (i.e., integrating) the visual and auditory stimuli which enter the eyes and ears of the child, were faulty, it would make sense of several observations concerning the autistic youngster. A failure to achieve order and meaningful structure from the incoming messages the child is receiving from the environment would explain his withdrawal, his limited span of attention, his intensely violent emotional reactions when he receives certain forms of stimulation, and his obsession with sameness. Hermelin (1966), and Hermelin and O'Connor (1964) have conducted a series of experiments on the hierarchical organization of sensory systems and sensory dominance in the development of autistic children. The background to their work is explained as follows: the developing child goes through a number of sequences, in the course of which alterations in the nature of the hierarchical structure of avenues of senses occur. Thus interoceptive and visceral sensations are dominant in the infant, and this dominance is gradually superseded first by tactile and kinesthetic, and then by the auditory and visual sensory systems. Thus, in an organism in which vision represents the predominant sense mode, the other avenues of sensory input are utilized as background information against the pre-eminent visual stimulus. Once a certain stage of development has been reached, it is the meaning rather than the modality of stimuli which determines their place in the hierarchy. As Luria (1960) has put it, the second signalling system concerned with meaning and language comes to dominate and direct the first which is concerned with the organization of direct sensory input. The hierarchical organization of sensory systems therefore functions to a very large extent to determine which aspects of the environment constitute figure and which aspects constitute background. One would expect that the organization of behaviour would depend on whether and how such a hierarchical structure of sensory systems has developed.

The experiments performed by Hermelin and O'Connor (1964) demonstrated that this development is relatively orderly in most nonpsychotic subnormal (imbecile) children. At a mental age of about four to five years visual dominance is established in the sensory hierarchy of the first signalling system. However, this visual dominance is suppressed if it competes with meaningful verbal stimulation, which then in turn assumes dominance. In undisturbed mongol children a hierarchical structure of sensory systems, with vision as the dominant sense avenue has also developed. However, even if words are the competing stimuli, mongols remain primarily responsive to the direct visual signals coming to the first signalling system.

In autistic children, even within the first signalling system, the structural hierarchy seems to be insufficiently developed. Variables such as intensity or reinforcement schedules, rather than sensory modality seem to determine response behaviour. Their behaviour appears more random and less predictable than subnormal controls. In short, the authors demonstrated that imbecile children respond most often to words, mongol children to light and autistic children most often to the most intense signal regardless of its modality or meaning. Hermelin (1963) proposes that failure to achieve auditory dominance may be a factor in the impaired speech of autistic children.

The fact of the matter is that in the present state of research no one can be certain about the nature and cause of the condition. The prognosis for autistic children is a rather bleak one. Therapy at present can only be said to be ameliorative rather than curative—training the children to acquire language and certain social skills and to cease other undesirable (even dangerous self-mutilating) behaviours.

## Childhood Psychosis/Childhood Schizophrenia

A working party (Creak, 1961) has formulated the following points as basic to "childhood psychosis" or "childhood schizophrenic syndrome":

(1) Gross and sustained impairment of emotional relationships with people;
(2) Apparent unawareness of his own personal identity to a degree inappropriate to his age;
(3) Preoccupation with particular objects or part of his own body;

(4) Sustained resistance to change in the environment or routine, and a striving to maintain or restore sameness;

(5) Apparent abnormalities of special senses in the absence of any detectable physical cause;

(6) Abnormalities and inappropriateness of mood, such as acute, excessive and seemingly illogical anxiety;

(7) Absence of speech or presence of speech disturbance;

(8) Disturbance of movements and the general level of motor activity (e.g., hyperkinesis, immobility, bizarre posturing, or ritualistic mannerisms);

(9) Apparent islets of ability against a background of varying degrees of intellectual retardation.

These criteria are not without their critics (see: Wolff and Chess, 1965a and b). It is always stressed that no single behavioural item is diagnostic of psychosis when taken in isolation. Some of the items could be manifested in other emotional or organic disorders. Bender (1969) contends that autism is neither synonymous with the generic term "psychosis", nor does it indicate a specific type of mental illness. The evidence she adduces from her investigations suggests to her that autistic behaviour represents a primitive and chronic manifestation of a normal developmental process, one which has a protective role—that of a withdrawal in the face of anxiety. The anxiety arises from disorganization. Such an extreme defensive strategy is conceived of as being secondary to a wide variety of serious conditions such as brain damage, emotional traumata, severe emotional deprivation or schizophrenia.

In the case of childhood schizophrenia, Bender (1947) identified a distinct group of children in whom the disorder develops between the ages of three and four-and-a-half years, preceded by apparently normal development. Others showed an early onset, i.e., from birth. Faretra and Bender (1962) found supportive evidence for the concept propounded by Knoblock and Pasamanick (1962) of a "continuum of reproductive casualty" underlying many of the developmental disorders of childhood. They (Faretra and Bender, op. cit.) discovered that maternal bleeding and toxaemia during pregnancy, and especially prematurity of birth, occurred frequently enough to be considered aetiologically significant in childhood schizophrenia. It is part of Bender's formulation of childhood schizophrenia (Bender, 1969) that a pre- or perinatal defect, trauma or a "physiological crisis" constitutes the stress that decompensates the genetically vulnerable child and produces a clinically recognizable picture of childhood schizophrenia.

Bender (1966, 1969) views "plasticity" of function and behaviour as the specific characteristic of schizophrenic disorders. She sums up the concept as follows:

Evolutionary processes in development of the human brain, mentality, and behaviour may represent causes for stress in the child in the process of maturation. Undetermined pluripotential plastic states appear to be characteristic for those brain functions specifically human and last in evolutionary development and still evolving. Clinical experience has shown that in all maturational lags in children, primitive plastic phenomena of an embryonic nature is the characteristic dysfunction. Childhood schizophrenia is such a maturational lag with a pattern of behavioural disturbance in all areas of central nervous system functions, characteristically plastic at an embryonic level.

This explains the common underlying pattern of disturbance in schizophrenia, in the visceral or autonomic functions, in perception, mentation, language, in motor activity and emotional-social behaviour. It also may make understandable the great variety of clinical pictures and symptomatology which are presented by schizophrenic children. It accounts for the response to physiological and pharmacological therapies which have aimed at reducing the plastic patterning in homeostasis, in the tone of the vascular bed of viscera and in the motor system, in perception and the affective and social behaviour. It explains the schizophrenic tendency for regressions, remissions, and even accelerated, precocious, and creative capacities and the reverberating anxiety which is at the core of the schizophrenic experience (Bender, 1969).

Danziger (1971) comments on some of the psycho-social factors which have a bearing on the psychological disorganization (in particular the lack of a clear and autonomous sense of ego-identity) in schizophrenic children. As he puts it:

One may speculate that the primary effect of patterns of parental demand and support lies in the establishment of ego boundaries, that is, in the creation of a zone of self-expression bounded by a clearly perceived social reality. In the absence of such boundaries there is confusion between self and non-self; impaired appreciation of external reality and impaired autonomy of the self are mutually complementary (Laing, 1961). The development of effective ego boundaries depends on both the demands and the supports for which socialization agents are the source. A boundary is, of course, a relationship. To establish the kind of relationship between "inside" and "outside" which we associate with normal personality functioning, parental demands must establish wide but firm limits within which generous support is extended to the growth of autonomous ego functions.

Wynne and Singer (1963) regard a stable and coherent environment—one which provides opportunities for the child to test reality in a variety of roles during development—as a prerequisite for the formation of a healthy ego. However, it is postulated that the families of schizophrenics lack these attributes of stability and coherence. According to Lidz, Fleck and Cornelison (1965) there is a blurring of age- and sex-roles in these families, and the combination of instability at home and ambiguous role-relationships hinder the development of appropriate forms of behaviour and a stable sense of identity in the child.

The findings from several studies appear to demonstrate the disruptive effect produced by parents of schizophrenic children in crucial areas of their psychological development (e.g., Lennard et al., 1965; Mishler and Waxler, 1965; Lidz et al., 1957; Laing and Esterson, 1970; Bateson et al., 1956). These findings are relevant to our discussion of problems of language and communication, as there is a fairly consistent tendency of the parents of schizophrenic children to deny communicative support to their offspring. Verbal interactions between parents and child tend to be stereotyped with almost no outlet for spontaneous expression. Frequently they fail to respond to their child's communications or to his demands for a recognition of his own point of view. Their own statements tend to be intrusive and take the form of interventions rather than replies to the child. The replies they do make tend to be selective, being responses to those of the child's expressions which have been initiated by themselves rather than to any expressions originated by the child. The child's spontaneous utterances and self-expression are restricted as if he were being denied the right to an independent point of view. There are theorists who contend that the complexities of language and logic are such that a condition as serious as schizophrenic thought disorder may be a consequence of the child having received a faulty grounding in the consensual (linguistic) meanings as well as other instrumentalities of society. These deficiences limit his adaptive capacities and permit him to escape from insoluble contradictions by abandoning the "meaning system" of his culture. He takes refuge in irrationality and withdrawn behaviour.

Bateson et al. (op. cit.) believe that repeated experiences—in the primary learning situation provided by the family—called "double bind" experiences, interfere with the learning of effective or rational communication and at the same time create frustration and anxiety. The "double bind" as described by them involves a recurring situation in communication in which there is a "primary negative injunction" and a "secondary injunction" in conflict with it. What does this mean? The "binder" makes demands for different and mutually contradictory responses from the other person at one and the same time, but on two levels of communication, as by voice and by action. The injunctions are not always conveyed by words but also by gesture, attitude and expression. The basic idea of two conflicting communications may be illustrated with the example of the mother who gives the following sarcastic injunction to her child: "Don't be so obedient!" Jackson (1960) uses this as a simple model of the double bind situation. The binder (in this case the mother) places the child in an impossible paradox. If he obeys the injunction, he is disobedient; if he disobeys he is obedient. Either way he is a loser.

The "double bind" is more than just conflicting communication. It implies that either of the child's alternatives of responding will meet with rejection, disapproval, punishment or some threat to well-being. (You are damned if you do; you are damned if you don't.) The double bind as originally formulated occurs repetitively in a situation of two or more people involved in an intense relationship in which escape is impossible. The child is so dependent on his parents that he is strongly inhibited against pointing out or acknowledging the contradiction; yet he cannot ignore or fail to respond to the paralysing injunction.

It is suggested that after enough "double bind" experiences the total environment begins to be perceived in double bind patterns, and that the child learns to react to any part of what seems to be a double bind sequence with panic or rage; and eventually withdrawal and illogical thinking. The concept of the double bind is an interesting one, being one of the few explanatory "mechanisms" that has been interposed by clinical theorists between global independent variables (e.g., "disturbed families") and fairly specific dependent variables (e.g., the mosaic of thought disorder). However, the idea has been subjected to heavy criticism (e.g., Schuham, 1967) because of its vagueness, the disagreements about the criteria thought necessary to produce double bind situations and the lack of empirical support for the far-reaching claims that have been made for it. It's specificity has been questioned by Berger (1965). A 30-item scale designed to reveal inconsistency of the type described by the double-bind hypothesis did differentiate between normals and schizophrenics. However, only 5 of the 30 items discriminated between schizophrenics and a maladjusted, non-schizophrenic group.

The background to the supposedly pathological communications inflicted on schizophrenic children, are a variety of extremely disturbed and disturbing family relationships. Lidz (1968) maintains that a coalition between the parents is necessary not only to give unity of direction to the children but also to provide each parent with the emotional support essential for carrying out his or her cardinal functions. In one type of family situation which is frequently found (Lidz *et al.*, 1957; Wynne *et al.*, 1958) as a background to the development of schizophrenic withdrawal, the members are torn by a "schismatic conflict" between husband and wife, so that the family is divided into two hostile factions. The children become involved in an emotional tug-of-war. This destructive situation— a complete negation of a parental coalition—may go on and on. Although a divorce would probably end everybody's misery, it does not occur, and a state of what is called "emotional divorce" persists—a corrosive situation pervaded by continual bickering, mutual recriminations and venomous hatred. If the child shows affection to one parent, this is regarded as betrayal by the other.

In another disturbed familial pattern, called "marital skew", one parent dominates the roost, and his (or her) psychopathology—abnormal thinking, bizarre style of living and abnormal manner of child-rearing—is passively accepted by the spouse. Suspiciousness and distrust of outsiders amounting to paranoia may prevail, and these deluded attitudes, together with other irrational interpretations of life, may be conveyed to the children. Such parents provide faulty models for their offspring to emulate; they transmit faulty modes of thinking to their children. Both these types of environment immerse the child in an irrational family atmosphere which is thought to negate the development of a healthy ego.

These theories have been highly influential. However, the conditions described in the home situation are by no means unique to the parents of psychotic children (see: Frank, 1965). Bender and Grugett (1956) point out the diversity of personalities among parents of schizophrenic children. While some of the investigations mentioned above are concurrent or longitudinal studies, much of the work on the psychosocial background to psychosis is retrospective. Life histories are among the most popular methods used in clinical research, but data based on life histories retrospectively obtained can be fraught with error and difficulties of interpretation. Schofield and Balian (1959) investigated the life histories of 150 psychiatrically normal subjects by means of extended clinical interviews. They collected information on the basis of a research schedule which had been used previously in a study of the histories of 178 hospitalized schizophrenics. Selection of the "normals" was made so that they were drawn from the same general population as the psychiatric patients and they were matched with the schizophrenics for age, sex, and marital status.

The purpose of the study was

(1) To determine what the life histories of "normal" persons look like if examined through the spectroscope of a comprehensive psychiatric history interview as conducted and recorded by a skilled clinician, and
(2) To determine in what ways such histories may be distinguishable from those of schizophrenics.

The basic hypothesis was that the life histories of "normal" (i.e., nonpsychiatric patients) will be readily and clearly differentiated from those of psychiatric patients if equally complete and carefully collected history data are available for both.

Separate statistical analyses were made of the reliability of the differences between the distribution of the normals and schizophrenics on 35 major aspects of early history and adjustment. Of these 35 variables, 13 (or 37%) failed to reveal a reliable difference between the two samples. On 5 of the 22 variables which yielded reliable differences, the normals were characterized by greater frequency of the undesirable or pathogenic factor. Specifically, the "normals" had a greater frequency of poverty and invalidism in their childhood homes, poorer heterosexual adjustment and adequacy of sexual outlet, and a greater incidence of an intellectualized, ritualized orientation toward religion. Additionally, the greater frequency of divorce in the childhood homes of the normals approached reliability.

The personal history characteristics which were predominent in the schizophrenics were in line with the general description which has been made in the clinical literature of the pre-schizophrenic personality. However, as the authors point out, the extent to which the same characteristics were found in closely approximate proportions in the histories of the normals suggest the need for great reservation in interpreting the isolated schizophrenogenic potency of such factors as the mother–child relationship. They state that the finding of "traumatic" histories in nearly a quarter of the normal subjects suggests the operation of "suppressor" experiences or psychological processes of immunization.

Rutter (1968) offers what seems to be the most reasonable summary of an extensive literature on infantile schizophrenia and infantile autism. He acknowledges that only tentative conclusions are possible, but in his view:

> . . . infantile autism is *not* anything to do with schizophrenia, and it is *not* primarily a disorder of social relationships. The presence of mental subnormality is not sufficient to account for autism and it seems unlikely that psychogenic or faulty conditioning mechanisms are *primary* factors in aetiology, although they may be important in the development of secondary handicaps. The importance of genetic factors remains unknown. The role of "brain damage" in the genesis of autism is also uncertain, but organic brain abnormalities appear to be primary influences in some cases—in how many is not known. In any case the concept of "brain damage" is too general to be of much help in understanding the genesis of autism. The determination of the relevance of abnormalities in physiological arousal awaits further research. Of all the hypotheses concerning the nature of autism, that which places the primary defect in terms of a language or coding problem appears most promising. It is suggested that many of the manifestations of autism are explicable in terms of cognitive and perceptual defects.

While admitting the good response of some autistic children to operant conditioning methods of treatment (see: Leff, 1968; and page 109 of this book), Rutter cautions against the fallacy of extrapolating from the effectiveness of therapy to the nature of causation. The theory (Ferster, 1961; Ferster and De Myer, 1961) that lack of positive reinforcement (especially parental attention) is the fundamental agent in the production of many autistic deficits, has yet to be convincingly validated.

# Part VI

# Middle Childhood: The School-age
*From about five to eleven or twelve years of age*

# Introduction : Psychosocial Developments

ERIKSON (1965) sees the major developmental task of this period of life as a sense of duty and accomplishment—laying aside of fantasy and play and undertaking real tasks, developing academic and social competencies. The crises are related to "industry" versus "inferiority". Erikson has this to say:

Children at this stage do like to be mildly but firmly coerced into the adventure of finding out that one can learn to accomplish things which one would never have thought of oneself, things which owe their attractiveness to the very fact that they are not the product of fantasy but the product of reality, practicability, and logic; things which thus provide a token sense of participation in the real world of adults.

The child therefore is probably as amenable at this stage as he is ever likely to be to learning, and direction and inspiration by others. What gets in the way of such readiness or subsequent achievements are maladjustment, excessive competition, personal limitations, or other conditions which lead to experiences of failure, resulting in feelings of inferiority and poor work habits. If the child fails to develop skills and social competencies he is likely to suffer a sense of inadequacy or inferiority. There is evidence (Dubin and Dubin, 1965) that the child accepts into his self-image what he believes to be his parents' view of him and this has consequences for his behaviour. If the youngster appraises his parents' view of him (perhaps incorrectly) as negative or rejecting he may exhibit feelings of insecurity.

The ever-increasing importance of social and extra-familial influences in the child's life has been discernible in the first three developmental phases. In order to achieve trust, autonomy and initiative it was necessary for the child to make contact with increasing numbers of people. Now by going to school his social universe is significantly extended. For a large part of each weekday, the child lives and works in his classroom with a much wider circle of children and adults than he has previously known.

Where previously the parents and family were the main agents of the child's socialization, in middle childhood, teachers, friends and peers now become important social influences. There are fairly crucial implications in the balance of power between parents and peer-group in the socializing of the child, as he grows older (see page 296). Children at this stage tend to choose friends from those who live in the same neighbourhood or who are in the same class at school and who are about the same age. Even at this tender age children tend to choose friends who have the same status as themselves. In choosing friends, primary school children (after the age of 8 or so) prefer members of their own sex.

Lippitt and Gold (1959) suggest that each classroom has its own social and emotional structure; the child finds his position in the structure of the class, and this position is postulated to have a bearing on his social and academic adjustment. Glidewell et al. (1964)* find the child who tends to do well in the classroom is the one who enters the classroom possessing the following combinations of attributes: he is a middle class child with vigorous health, intelligence, and well-developed social skills. He is likely to have a good opinion of himself, and the ability to gauge accurately his effect on others, to perceive correctly the quality of the approaches and responses of others to him.

Such a child is likely to begin making cautious attempts to mix socially with others—especially the most obviously respected children and the teacher. He is willing to take some social risks, but, at first, only moderate ones. He is likely to be quite sensitive to the reactions he gets from others when he makes his first experimental overtures. If they are positive, he will probably judge them as positive, and be likely to repeat his approaches to others. If the responses are negative, he will see them as negative and is likely to try new tentative overtures. He will probably avoid being too obvious in his first experiments. He is also likely to make good use of his intelligence.

As the skilful child gains more acceptance, power, and competence in the classroom, his self-esteem is enhanced. Under some conditions, he also develops more willingness to take risks by trying new approaches to people and tasks. His new approaches can change his position in the system. As the risks—large and small—turn out to be fruitful, his self-esteem is further enhanced, and his status in the social system becomes even more gratifying. What Glidewell et al. call a "circular, self-perpetuating interaction process" thus becomes established. In plain English: "Success breeds success!"

At the other extreme, we have a working-class child who enters the classroom with less vigorous health, with limited intellect, and inadequate social skills. He is likely to be relatively anxious and to have rather low self-esteem. The evidence indicates that he tends to make awkward over-

* This review appears in Hoffman and Hoffman, 1964, Vol. 2.

tures to his peers and the teacher, and he is likely to provoke reactions which are, at best, of restrained embarrassment, or at worst, of hostile ridicule. He will probably feel humiliated, and is quite likely to react with either aggression or withdrawal, or both in alternation. If he responds aggressively, he is likely to invite some form of passive rejection or counterwithdrawal. The "low-status" boys—often aggressive and troublesome—invite more criticism from the teacher than do their "high-status" classmates; whereas the "low-status" girls—often overdependent and passive—receive more emotional support from their teacher. The teacher's reaction tends to increase a boy's hostility and a girl's dependency.

The response of the other members of the classroom to the awkward child's social overtures are not likely to build up his self-esteem or his social skills. He is liable to distort his perceptions of their behaviour by denial or projection in order to protect whatever small residue of self-esteem has survived his rejection by the others. He does not make use of his full intellectual capacity. Again, a self-sustaining circular process is established. Failure breeds failure! Rejection breeds defensiveness and perceptual distortions; this leads to a reaction of further aggression or withdrawal from the other children, which in turn, reduces the child's self-esteem. Finally, the child displays intense aggression or withdrawal, provoking further counteraggression or passive rejection, thus completing the circle. Symptoms of emotional conflict and disturbance may also follow.

This phase of life we are dealing with begins with the child of five at a stage where temporarily, as his self-critical capacity develops, he is observed (Gesell *et al.*, 1940) to lose some of his confidence and exuberance. For a while he is more dependent upon adult emotional support. This dependency declines as his social horizon (at school and elsewhere) widens.

During the early school-going years (i.e., from five on) there is a decline in the child's imitative behaviour; he increasingly differentiates "good" and "skilful" aspects of adult behaviour. He is better able to abstract what is "role-appropriate" behaviour from what he observes. He is now aware that there is something beyond mere conformity to parental demands, that the parents themselves conform to a set of rules which are not embodied in the behaviour of any one person. At this stage the child becomes capable of acting and assessing his own competence in relation to principles of "good" and "right". Freudians refer to the psychosexual developments taking place at the age of five or six as the phallic stage. The resolution of the Oedipus complex crisis at this time is thought to bring in its wake crucial developments in the formation of the superego and the establishment of moral standards (see: Healy *et al.*, 1930).

The child of five tends to be relatively quiet and conforming. Indeed as we saw with regard to the overlap between the last phase and the early part of this school-going phase of life, it is called the "conformist" stage of ego-development (Loevinger, 1966). Rules are partially internalized being obeyed just because they are the rules. The chief sanction for transgression is shame. The child's interpersonal relationships are based on reciprocity and are rather superficial. Piaget refers to the period of moral development coinciding with the child's first years at school as the "egocentric stage" and to the following period of development as the stage of "incipient cooperation" (ages 7 to 11). Observing two boys in the earlier "egocentric stage" (4 to 7 years) playing marbles, he concluded that each child was merely playing an individual (i.e., egocentric) game and did not really need the other. This stage was very much bound up with egocentric speech and parallel play. The child is centred upon himself and does not take account of the other person's point of view. Later on the game of marbles begins to acquire a definite social connotation. The youngster cooperates and competes with his partner. There are arguments. Nevertheless there is some accommodation to the other's opposing point of view. Toward the end of middle childhood the stage of "genuine cooperation" commences—i.e., approximately at the age of 11 or 12. By this time the child has achieved mastery of the rules and tries to win in a manner that is based upon mutual agreement about those rules. Piaget also states that the "mature" understanding of rules goes with an ability to keep them. Mature children make motive and intention a critical factor in their evaluation of misdeeds. They do not perceive that disobedience of authority is necessarily wrong; they are much less influenced in their judgements by the sanctions that authorities have prescribed.

The social and moral developments we have been outlining above are paralleled by the cognitive events described as the "*concrete operational thinking*" stage (Piaget, 1926; 1952a and b). The child had begun to think in language in the previous stage, but now he manages to see events from different perspectives. He has acquired concepts involving complex relationships. Very important is the fact that he now has a mental representation of a series of actions. The youngster now has the mental capacity to order and relate experience to an organized whole, but at first only in relation to objects which form a familiar part of his experience. Returning to the computer analogy (see: Lazerson, 1971; and page 80) it might be said that somewhere along the way, but in a gradual fashion, a second-order computer becomes predominant. This computer, unlike the first, is well ordered and rational. It processes information in an objective rather than a subjective way. Unlike the first-order computer, this one can systematically integrate and synthesize information and experiences. It enables the child to deal with information in the present and to relate this information back to past experiences. With the emergence of this computer, the child's behaviour begins to show organizing, planning, and inhibiting capacities.

Because the child is able to integrate and synthesize experiences, he can plan strategies for solving problems and can inhibit irrelevant behaviour. Getting on toward seven years of age the child begins (as we saw) to solve problems concretely, using a variety of methods, and it is at this point that the differences between the second-order and the lower-order computer become most evident. It is no accident, then, that the child can cope with school at about the same time as the rational computer takes the dominant responsibility for his conduct (see: Inhelder and Piaget, 1964).

By the end of middle childhood we begin to see the fundamental difference between concrete operational thinking and the cognitive capabilities of the next stage which Piaget calls *"formal propositional thinking"*. The difference is essentially to do with the real and the possible. It is during adolescence, roughly the years from 11 or 12 to 15 that the child begins to free his thinking from its roots in his own *particular* experience. He becomes capable of *general* propositional thinking, that is to say he can propose hypotheses and deduce consequences. His language is now fast and versatile (Inhelder and Piaget, 1958).

There are some interesting differences in the nature of intellectual functioning in boys and girls, although it is difficult to separate out heredity and environment as causes of these differences. Intellectually, girls get off to a good start—being slightly ahead of boys on intelligence tests during the first four years of life. They literally have the first word (on average) and, one might note, because of the longevity of females, the last one too! They are more articulate. They learn to read more easily (girls are also on a quicker physical developmental timetable than boys). The intellectual differential soon vanishes at school, although girls still excel on verbal fluency tests—using more words, telling longer stories and in fact giving support to the stereotype that females talk more than males. It is not until high school that boys draw ahead of girls on mathematical skills. Boys do better than girls on tests of spatial ability and to some extent on abstract, analytical types of reasoning (see: Hutt, 1972).

Mussen (1963) observes that the friendships of middle childhood are fairly unstable; interests change easily at this period and "old" friends may no longer satisfy the needs of earlier times, and as a result friendships are ended and others substituted. The capacity for lasting friendships gradually increases during childhood and adolescence. As the child gets older interests become focused and friendships therefore are more likely to be enduring. Girls are more socially active than boys below the age of 11 or 12 and they tend to establish more intimate and confidential relationships with each other. By the end of the period we are considering (12 years of age), the capacity of the child to form friendships and to maintain them on the basis of meeting others' needs as well as his own is thought to be a strong indication of the development of social maturity.

# 13. Problems of School-children

GOING TO SCHOOL is the first experience of prolonged separation from home for most children. For long periods each weekday, the child is removed from the familiar, comfortable routine of his home, from a playful existence with a nurturant mother near at hand, and is plunged into the more exacting disciplines and the rough and tumble of school life. The child has been transferred from what one might call a relatively "closed" system, where the rules and requirements are understood and predictable, to an "open-ended" system where, for at least a few weeks, life is full of the unexpected, the unpredictable, and sometimes the unpleasant. During these hours there is no appeal to mother's protection and comfort; the mantle of authority has been handed over to strangers. The demands and stresses of the new situation, real or imaginary, are many; a child requires a good deal of flexibility and self-control to cope with them. For a number of children—perhaps 3 or 4 (10%) in the average classroom of 30 to 40 children—the developmental demands are too great and they show emotional problems, requiring professional clinical guidance (see: Glidewell and Swallow, 1968; Bower, 1960; Rutter *et al.*, 1970). We have already looked in rather general terms in Chapter 1 at the diagnostic problem of deciding when "normal" developmental problems have escalated beyond the stage of being contained and helped by understanding parental support, to an intensity demanding professional attention. This dilemma is even more acute in the school-going child whose problems are highly visible in the school setting and whose teachers have to decide how and when to intervene. So we need to look further at the diagnostic judgement at this stage of life. We have already seen that if you take a group of school-age clinic attenders and a non-attending control group (Wolff, 1967), it is difficult to distinguish between them.

Shepherd's epidemiological studies (Shepherd *et al.*, 1971) are worth looking at in more detail. The authors describe their approach as follows:

Our starting point was an attempt to acquire systematic information about certain items of behaviour of more than 6000 children, comprising a 10%

representative sample of the state school population aged between five and fifteen years in the county of Buckinghamshire. The items were chosen because of their bearing on children's mental health and the data were obtained by questionnaire. The more detailed information was provided by the parents, principally the mothers, whose reports have been shown by other workers to constitute a reasonably reliable source of data . . . In our study the nature of the sample permits us to assume that any parental bias would be equally distributed among the various age-groups of the children (Shepherd *et al.*, 1971).

The team made an intensive study by interview of a smaller group of children. They state that these were regarded as being emotionally disturbed by virtue of their attendance at a child guidance clinic. It was found to be difficult to distinguish the behavioural anomalies of these children from those of a group of supposedly normal children.

The public (teachers and others) shows a very uneven willingness to refer its problematic or mentally ill children and adults to the various institutions designed for their diagnosis and treatment. The basis for the recognition of problems by parents, teachers, family doctors and others who refer children to clinics is uncertain and highly subjective. Shepherd *et al.* (1966) found, for instance, that the reason for referring a child to a child guidance clinic is as closely related to the reactions of parents (that is, whether they are anxious, easily upset, and lacking in ability to cope with children) as to whether he has a clinically confirmed problem. Kanner (1953) observes that "the high annoyance threshold of many fond and fondly resourceful parents keeps away from clinics . . . a multitude of early breath-holders, nail-biters, nose-pickers and casual masturbators who, largely because of this kind of parental attitude, develop into reasonably happy and well-adjusted adults".

The tendency to equate normality with untroublesome behaviour has led the quiet, withdrawn ("well-behaved") child with emotional problems to be overlooked in the classroom and sometimes in the home setting as well. Teachers have responsibilities to many children; they have to cope with group situations and disciplinary problems. Thus it is not surprising that surveys in the past (Wickman, 1928; Epstein, 1941; Griffith, 1952; Laycock, 1934; Schrupp and Gjerde, 1953) of teachers' attitudes toward the behaviour problems of children have shown that teachers are most concerned with children's patterns of behaviour that are aggressive, disruptive of school routines, or generally reflecting lack of interest in school activities. In addition, teachers are, or used to be, less worried about withdrawing and other such non-social behaviours—which clinicians are inclined to emphasize as maladjusted. However, the differences in teachers' and clinicians' attitudes toward abnormality have decreased since the 1920's when they were at their most marked (Beilin, 1959). Despite a convergence of views, studies (Rutter *et al.*, 1970) still show differences of emphasis which reflect the different roles and duties which teachers and clinicians have to discharge. The teacher is primarily task-orientated, having to teach the child a series of skills, while the clinician is principally adjustment-orientated, being concerned with the individual patient.

There is even a disparity between the views of primary and secondary school teachers on the nature of problem behaviour, which also results from such differences in role. The secondary-school teacher is much more subject-matter orientated than the primary school teacher whose philo-sophy, in recent years, has become much more child-orientated. That is to say he is more concerned with teaching the child than with simply teaching subjects. This is reflected in the similarity between the attitudes of primary teachers and clinicians towards the notion of adjustment (Beilin, 1959).

Stewart (1949) rejects the notion that teachers are wrong in reacting as they do to childrens' problems. His work shows that they have more insight than they are credited with if surveys ask them the right sort of questions, and that they are quite capable of distinguishing between problems that are "school problems" and problems that are "whole life" problems.

These points of difference in the perceptions of not only teachers and clinicians but also parents, are worth looking at in more detail. This is provided by a survey (Graham, 1967; Rutter, *et al.*, 1970) carried out on 10- and 11-year-old children living on the Isle of Wight. An attempt was made to look at the inter-relations of psychiatric, educational and physical disorders.

In 1965, about 100 teachers and about 1,950 parents of the 2,193 children in this age group were asked to complete behaviour questionnaires about them. The teachers' questionnaire was in the form of 26 behavioural descriptions. For each description the person filling in the form was required to say whether the child did not show the behaviour, whether the description applied "somewhat" or whether it "definitely applied". The parental questionnaire was very similar. The questions included items on whether or not the children stole things, whether they had twitches, mannerisms or tics of the face or body and whether they were tearful on arrival at school, etc. Experience had shown that if the child scored above the cut-off point (i.e., had more than a certain number of symptoms rated as present) on either questionnaire, he was quite likely to show psychiatric disorder on more intensive investigation but not at all likely to show such disorder if rating less than this number (Graham and Rutter, 1968).

Two hundred and eighty-four children who scored over the cut-off points on either questionnaire were selected for more intensive study. In this second phase of the investigation the parents (usually the mothers) were interviewed and the children given psychological testing and a psychiatric examination. In addition teachers were asked to give their free comments about these children and complete a second questionnaire. After the 284 children had been intensively investigated by means of parental interview, psychiatric examination, and the obtaining of further information from teachers, a rich store of information was available on each child. This was assessed by psychiatrists involved in the study and a decision was made as to whether the child showed psychiatric abnormality and, if so, what diagnosis should be attached to the disorder shown. Three broad diagnostic distinctions were made; children were classified as suffering from neurotic disorders (characterized by unusual fears, frequent crying or unhappiness, worrying and withdrawn behaviour), antisocial disorders (characterized by aggressiveness, stealing, truancy, disobedience) and mixed neurotic/ antisocial disorders in which features of both the first two were present but neither was predominant.

Of the 284 children selected for intensive study, there were 138 children (89 boys and 49 girls) who were found to have psychiatric disorder needing treatment or further investigation. This constituted about 6% of the total population of 10- and 11-year-old children initially screened (Rutter and Graham, 1966).

Children identified on the basis of information in the parents' questionnaires were equally likely to be rated as abnormal on this overall assessment by the psychiatrists as those identified on the basis of the teachers' questionnaires. Psychiatrists therefore agreed equally well with both parents and teachers in this respect. Approximately equal numbers of neurotic children were picked out on both questionnaires, although more antisocial boys were picked out by the teachers'. There was very little overlap between the children chosen from the parents' questionnaires and those chosen from the teachers' questionnaires. Of the 284 children selected, only 19 (10 boys and 9 girls) were selected on *both* questionnaires. By chance about half this number would have been expected, so although there was somewhat greater agreement than might have been expected by chance alone, in general the questionnaires selected different children.

How did the two groups differ? Rather more girls backward in reading, and rather more boys eventually found to be antisocial, were included amongst those children selected on the basis of information provided by teachers. The only other striking difference was related to the size of the families from which the children came. The teachers' questionnaires identified significantly more children who came from larger families than did parents'.

One reason put forward by Graham for this is that the parent of a large family would often be preoccupied with the problems of whichever child happened to be causing the most concern at the time and would measure the other children's behaviour using the most disturbed child as a yardstick. Interviewers in fact often had to let the mother describe the child about whom she was most worried before they could go on to question her about the selected child.

The reasons for the lack of overlap between children selected on the basis of information in the teachers' and in the parents' questionnaires could be due in part to *inadequacies of the questionnaires*. Graham admits that the response that parents and teachers made in completing the questionnaire might not adequately reflect disturbance in the child. However, the questionnaires have been found in other surveys as well as in that carried out on the Isle of Wight to distinguish reliably between children attending child guidance clinics and those in the general population, so that it is unlikely that defects in them represent an important source of error. There may, of course, be real behaviour differences at home and in school. A high proportion of children, indeed, were described as showing disturbance either only (or mainly) at home or solely (or mainly) at school and this is probably one of the reasons why the children picked out on the basis of the parents' questionnaires differed from those picked out on the teachers' questionnaires (see Mitchell and Shepherd, 1966). The number of children described as showing disturbance in the one context but not in the other may be explained by the fact that the *symptoms* of disturbance that children show at home often differ from those shown in school. Bedwetting is an obvious example but others are less obvious.

Graham (1967) comments that the survey would have missed large numbers of children if it had relied only on parents or only on teachers for information and the same fallibility must be true of any psychiatric department or child guidance clinic which neglects investigating both of the child's worlds. As he puts it:

This is not to suggest that children who are disturbed at home must also be disturbed at school for we found some evidence that this is quite frequently not so. However, although a child who shows disturbance in one situation may be helped adequately by measures related only to that situation, satisfactory assessment of a child's emotional and behavioural state will most often require information from those who know and understand him best both at home and at school.

## Social Class

It is sometimes stated that teachers, representing (as often they do) a part of the middle or white-collar class, evaluate children's behaviour in terms of the norms expected of their own class. Glidewell *et al.* (1959) found that teachers agreed best with upper class parents in the number of symptoms they reported in children and least well with working class parents. They found intermediate levels of agreement between teachers and middle class parents. But they point out that the reason for this does not necessarily lie in differences in perception between teachers and working class parents; it is possible that working class children really do show greater differences in behaviour at home and school than upper class children.

In the Isle of Wight survey (Rutter *et al.*, 1970), it was found that the teachers' questionnaire did not identify a higher proportion of working class children than did the parents'. Nor did the class distribution of those children eventually found to be definitely maladjusted differ from that of the randomly selected control group.

# 14. Reluctance and Refusal to go to School

THERE IS A BIG contrast between the life of the pre-school child—a playful existence with a nurturant mother near at hand—and that of the school-going youngster. Even in today's more informal primary and nursery schools, he is faced with exacting disciplines and intellectual demands which can constitute quite an ordeal. The stresses of the new situation are often too much for the overly dependent child. During these long hours in the classroom there is no appeal to a nurturant mother. The child is forced to rely on his own resources although he may (if the teacher lets him) relate to her in a clinging manner, as a surrogate mother.

In a study of the difficulties of ordinary children in adjusting to school, Moore (1966) kept track of 164 children (attending a large number of different London schools) from the ages of six to eleven. The children's mothers were asked at various stages whether, during the past year, their children had told them about any problems or difficulties connected with school or shown any reluctance to go.

*Reluctance to go to school:* The basic question in connection with this problem was: "Has your child shown any dislike of school at any time in the past year?" This commonly elicited a statement of the child's general attitude, whether positive, indifferent or negative, and sometimes specific problems as well.

A reluctance to go to school affected, at one time or another, a majority of the six-year-olds. This unwillingness decreased at seven, rose to a secondary peak at eight (when there was a transfer from infant to junior school) and then dwindled steadily until the children's eleventh year. Even then, one boy in three was still showing some reluctance. In all, a vast majority of the children studied were found to experience difficulties in the infant school. Nearly one half suffered problems of moderate or marked severity. At every age level, boys showed more negative attitudes than girls. Boys who were "only" children tended to have most problems in adjusting to school. Moore questions whether boys, being more active, find it harder to accept the immobility enforced, much of the time, in most schools. Perhaps they rebel against the curtailment of their freedom of choice, while girls conform more readily.

Moore found that certain types of difficulty, especially where the child was reluctant to go to school but could give no specific explanation why, or where he had difficulty in mixing with other children and showed a dislike of physical education, were associated with overdependency. He speculates as to whether, as Levy (1943) found, there are more boys than girls whose relationships with their mothers are so mutually dependent that they find it difficult to exchange the safety of home for the hurly-burly of school life?

*Difficulties with Teachers* were elicited by the question "Has he (i.e., the child) changed his teacher this year? How did he take the change?" supplemented as necessary by enquiries into past and present relationships. Some complaints came from children who had incurred punishment, but at least as many from the relatively innocent who shrank under discipline intended to impress the recalcitrant few. Shouting, smacking and grumbling; favouritism and reprimands perceived as unfair; failure to make work interesting and failure to explain clearly were among the commonest complaints. (Moore points out that children's dislike of unsuccessful teaching was easily matched by their enthusiasm for the teacher who succeeds in capturing their interest and affection). The peak for complaints about teachers came at eight years, when they were reported from one child in three; the incidence never fell below 20%, although serious disturbances were fewer. There was no significant difference between boys and girls, or between social classes.

*Difficulties with other children.* Specific enquiry in this area was made only if the child had been transferred to a different group; but mothers could be expected to report any real problem in discussing adjustment to school generally. Moore states that trouble with contemporaries is commonly experienced by the overdependent child, especially the boy who lacks a repertoire of strategies for coping by himself.

Difficulties were reported for 16% of the boys and 13% of the girls at the peak age of seven years, they fell sharply between nine and ten, and ended at around 6% at eleven, when the children are the oldest in the primary school and have generally had several years to find a *modus vivendi* with their group. The boys' curves remain consistently higher than the girls.'

Most parents have had to cope—and successfully, by and large—with the occasional *reluctance* of their children to go to school. But there is a group of children whose determination goes beyond mere reluctance to set off for school. They dig their heels in, and no one can budge these adamant refusers. Others pretend to go to school and then slip away and spend the school hours elsewhere. The child who persistently refuses to attend school is an increasingly common problem in child psychiatry. If non-attendance persists for long, it may result in educational backwardness with far-reaching effects upon emotional, social and occupational adjustment in later school-life and in adulthood.

Unlawful absence from school without the parents' knowledge is referred to as truancy. "Truant" is an old French word meaning "an assemblage of beggars". In earlier centuries it had the connotation of "a lazy, idle person, especially a boy who absents himself from school without leave . . . one who wanders from an appointed place and neglects his duty or business". The association of truancy with vagrancy and villainy lingers on in modern thinking as it is still referred to as the kindergarten of crime.

Hersov (1960) was interested in a group of children who are persistent non-attenders at school but who are not truants within the strict legal meaning of the word. That is to say they are absent from school *with* the full knowledge of at least one, if not both, parents. He tested the following hypothesis: Children who are referred for the treatment of persistent non-attendance at school fall into two broad groups:

> Those in whom this behaviour is a manifestation of a psychoneurotic syndrome which includes such conditions as Anxiety Reactions, Obsessional Disorders, and Hysterical Reactions.

> Those in whom this behaviour is a manifestation of a conduct disorder. This implies disturbed behaviour of a sort that invokes social or moral condemnation. (These groupings do overlap; as always in clinical work there are mixed cases to be found.)

Hersov predicted that there would be significant differences between the two groups in respect of:

(a) Environmental circumstances.
(b) Pattern of parent–child relationships.
(c) Personality and intellectual level of the child.

Three groups of cases were selected from case records of the children's unit at the Maudsley Hospital, London.

*Group N* consisted of 50 children referred for their refusal to attend school. There were further criteria for selection:

> The non-attendance was of at least two months' duration.
> The refusal was persistent and absolute in spite of pressure by parents.
> The child preferred to remain at home when not at school.

*Group T* consisted of 50 children in whom truancy was a major feature but not the only manifestation of disturbance. Further criteria:

The non-attendance was of at least two months' duration.

There was no strong preference on the part of the child to remain at home when not at school. His whereabouts when not at school was unknown to parents who first heard of their absence through the School Authorities.

*Group C* consisted of 50 children acting as a control group. They were made up of youngsters between the ages of five and sixteen, randomly selected from all first attendances during 1955 and 1958. Cases of epilepsy, brain damage, childhood psychosis and mental subnormality were excluded. Any cases in which truancy or school refusal had occurred at any time were also excluded.

Hersov found significant differences between the two experimental groups—differences sufficiently marked to require the treatment of the two types of non-attendance as separate clinical problems. Some of the differences he found were as follows:

A significantly greater number of group N children were in the superior range of intelligence; a higher proportion were from the middle and upper social classes. A significantly higher number had been overprotected by their parents as against a significant amount of rejection in the background of the group T children.

The N group children showed better behaviour at school. Their reading attainment was commensurate or greater than their chronological age. The T group children tended to be backward in school attainments. The N group children had a higher incidence of neuroses in their family history. They themselves were assessed as nervous, timid, inhibited and dependent personalities. The T group children showed a greater amount of gross parental disharmony and inconsistent handling as part of their background picture. The children themselves manifested various conduct disorders and a high frequency of enuresis. The N group children did not show the history of "maternal lack" before and after five years of age that was so frequently found in the T group children.

## School Phobia

Johnson *et al.* (1941) coined a label for the type of refusal to go to school which we have seen differentiated from truancy—viz., the term "school phobia". A phobia is an intense, unreasonable fear, usually directed at some specific environmental object. So the diagnosis of "school phobia" seems to imply a strong unreasonable fear of some aspect of the school situation. Obviously there are several possibilities inherent in the circumstances of school life, any of which is capable of making a child fearful for quite objective and *reasonable* reasons.

Some of the sources of children's anxiety at school are: the size and routine of the school, examination stresses, experiences of classroom failure, disturbed relationships with teachers and schoolmates, parental pressures and expectations, and intellectual disability. Sixth-grade American schoolchildren, aged eleven, worry about the following school situations, in order of frequency: failing a test, being late for school, being poor in spelling, being asked to answer questions, being poor in reading, getting a poor report card, being reprimanded, not doing as well as other pupils, being poor at maths and drawing. Chazan (1962) found that many school phobics were experiencing educational difficulties. Out of 24 children, 4 were slightly backward and 13 (mean IQ 98·7) were very backward in the sense that they were experiencing great difficulty with their work and were in need of special educational treatment. The point about a phobic reaction such as refusing to go to school is that it is disproportionate, and often completely inappropriate to, the objective "distressing" situation. It has the appearance of being irrational as it involves "maladaptive" responses to particular situations—responses which have unfavourable consequences and are self-defeating. The child's refusal to go to school (and it is *not* just the occasional reluctance expressed by most children, or the odd attempt at malingering to get out of something unpleasant at school) is accompanied by intense emotional and physical symptoms, which make it one of the most worrying problems a parent may have to cope with.

Parents' anxieties are threefold: their concern at the child's palpable unhappiness and their impotence to alleviate his apparent dread of school; their worries about the effect of prolonged absence on his school work (an important consideration in a competitive educational system); and their apprehension over their legal responsibility to ensure the child's attendance at school.

A parent found guilty of failure to secure the regular attendance of a child in a British school is liable to a fine or, in the case of further offence, to a term of imprisonment. A more disturbing possibility to the (usually) conscientious parents of the school refuser is the fact that a child, brought before the juvenile court for persistent non-attendance, may be deemed "in need of care or control" and sent to a Community Home, or placed on a supervision order. So, it is not difficult to imagine the pressures, at various levels, which build up in problems of this kind.

Parents who are still trying unsuccessfully to get the child to school find that he is obdurate in the face of entreaties, recriminations and punishment. Not even weighty authority, in the person of the school welfare (attendance) officer, will budge the adamant child. In addition, the child is suffering from unreasonable anxiety in connection with a number of topics that other children cope with fairly well; the anxiety, like quicksilver, is apt to move about, changing shape—now attached to one object now jumping to another, and then another. The focus of the child's apprehensions (as he describes them) seems to be changeable, and they do not respond to reassurance. Lastly, the child has recurrent physical symptoms for which no adequate cause can be found, and these, again, are inclined to be changeable.

The school refusal crisis, well under way, is apt to affect the entire family; and the breakfast scene (on school days) is likely to be tense if not harrowing. Parents display varying degrees of anxiety, anger or despairing resignation. If they are still trying to cajole or in some other way pressure the child to go to school, he is likely to present a very unhappy picture. He may be pale, weepy and tremulous, and other physical signs of his intense distress may be present (e.g., tics). He may have to go to the toilet frequently to urinate, or he may suffer from diarrhoea. He usually complains of physical malaise and a variety of ailments, most particularly abdominal pains and headache. He is likely to be off his food—particularly breakfast—and to feel nauseous and perhaps have bouts of vomiting. In severe cases, the child may have hysterical or obsessional symptoms. Obviously the parents must have the physical complaints checked by the doctor, but in the case of the category of school refusal we are discussing these generally prove to have no organic basis. They are inclined to subside at weekends and during school holidays or, even, shortly after the parents have resigned themselves to keeping the child at home.

It is not known precisely how frequently the problem occurs in the community of children (one estimate suggests one child in a thousand) but impressions that it is on the increase probably arise out of the growing awareness of the disorder and greater vigilance on the part of all concerned. There is greater appreciation that this is a very real emotional disturbance and that it is not simply a moral or disciplinary problem concerned with malingering; nor is it just the elusive physical illness which tends to mask it.

Why do only certain children carry their reluctance to go to school right through to the point of refusal? There are no precise answers to this question. Much will depend on the intensity of the stresses in any particular school situation, but the normal range of stressful school situations, whatever they are, precipitates drastic reactions in a minority of children only. A multitude of influences can produce a child who is predisposed to perceive a situation as more threatening than it actually is, and who lacks the ego-strength (Barron, 1953) to cope with it. In Chapters 2 and 3 we considered some of the factors, genetic, perinatal, familial and others, that might sensitize a child to "break down" when the going is tough. It does not require great imagination or empathy with children to see that certain situations at school are likely to be particularly challenging to the sensitive, labile child. But having emphasized these *negative* aspects of school life, it is necessary to maintain some perspective. Larger numbers of school-goers do *not* become refusers, because for most children—a pretty robust species anyway—school fulfils several important needs, providing a stimulating and reasonably happy environment most of the time.

Despite the inevitable complaints and the occasional reluctance (expressed to mother) which are part of the predictable ups-and-downs of any aspect of life, surveys show that most children enjoy school life once the routine becomes established. Usually nearly two-thirds like school; about a quarter are indifferent; and some 10% dislike it. Not only is it a minority that dislikes school, but strangely enough even though school refusers may be afraid of some aspect of leaving home or going to school, it is rather uncommon for these children actually to dislike school. In fact, the matter of simply disliking school does not seem to be a sufficient cause, in most cases, of absenteeism. Mitchell and Shepherd (1966) reported that in Buckinghamshire about 5% of boys and 3% of girls under the age of twelve disliked going to school; yet their attendance was very little different from those who liked school. They say that "this would seem to indicate that, during the primary school years children may achieve regular attendance under firm parental pressure and regardless of their own inclinations".

How does school refusal begin? Parents, on being questioned, are inclined to describe the onset of the refusal as sudden and dramatic—almost an overnight occurrence. Some cases do begin in this way. But, more often than not, a case-history—carefully recording the child's past attendance at school—brings to light evidence of transitory episodes of school refusal and other indications of emotional and physical upsets. The onset is rather gradual; a build-up of tension, in the form of irritability, restlessness, disturbed sleep, vomiting and abdominal pain—the so-called "prodromal symptoms"—precedes the full manifestation of the problem. And from the initial attitude of unwillingness on the part of the child, hedged around by varying excuses and complaints, the problem grows to the proportion of a frank and outright refusal.

We know that school refusal tends to follow, not infrequently, a legitimate absence from school. Some subjects (e.g., arithmetic, mathematics) are hierarchical in structure; that is, one step is logically preceded by, and dependent upon, another. So the child who misses a series of lessons (particularly the child who has chronic recurrent illnesses) may experience great difficulty in catching up. Subjects like these, which tend anyway to attract negative emotional attitudes, may (in the absence of an understanding teacher) become the focus of intense anxiety for the vulnerable child.

The children Hersov (1960) studied gave different explanations for their refusal; the commonest (34%) was a fear of some harm befalling mother while the child was at school; next in importance were fear of ridicule, bullying, or harm from other children (28%); next, fear of academic failure (28%); then—rather less frequently—the fear of a strict, sarcastic teacher (22%). Hersov found overt anxieties about menstruation in six girls and concern about puberty and masturbation in three boys. Other reasons for absence were fear of vomiting or fainting during school assembly. In some children more than one of these reasons was given by the same child while others could not give a lucid explanation other than that "something" stopped them from going to school.

There was a high incidence of neurosis in the families of the school refusers, the symptoms being most often those of an affective disorder. This factor might well have had an influence on the children in terms of genetic endowment and environmental rearing. These children had experienced less maternal and paternal absence in infancy and childhood than the truants, and the control group. Other findings concerning their environments were: 50% of the mothers were rated as overindulgent and dominated by their children; 28% were described as demanding, severe and controlling. In 22% of the cases, the mother's attitude was rated as reasonable. More than half of all the fathers were assessed as inadequate and passive, good providers in the material sense, but participating little or not at all in home management of children and unable to cope with the rebelliousness of puberty and pre-adolescence. In those families (28%) where the fathers played a firm, dominant role, the mothers were more often than not insecure and dependent personalities who overindulged their children to offset the father's firmness, thus adding a disturbing element of inconsistency to the home situation.

The children themselves were assessed for their behaviour at school and at home. They were significantly better behaved, with a higher standard of work, as compared with the control group, but a large number showed poor social adjustment. The majority of children (74%) were timid, fearful and inhibited away from home, 18% were alert and friendly and 8% domineering and aggressive. The reverse behaviour was shown at home in that the majority (74%) now were wilful and demanding at home, whereas only 26% were passive and obedient. This sort of finding should be a warning against the tendency of clinicians to ascribe specific undifferentiated "personality types" to each clinical problem; Clyne (1966) concludes that there is no one characteristic personality typology applicable to school refusers. Hersov (op. cit.) gives the following picture of parent–child relationships and behaviour patterns, which, again, should make the reader wary of the frequent claims for specificity of parental behaviour in particular psychological and psychosomatic conditions. He found (a) an over-indulgent mother and an inadequate, passive father dominated at home by a wilful, stubborn and demanding child who is most often timid and inhibited in social situations away from home, (b) a severe, controlling and demanding mother who manages her children without much assistance from her passive husband. The child is most often timid and fearful away from home, and passive and obedient at home, but may become stubborn and rebellious at puberty, (c) a firm, controlling father who plays a large part in home management and an over-indulgent mother closely bound to and dominated by a wilful, stubborn and demanding child, who is alert, friendly and outgoing away from home.

The reported incidence of emotional problems in the parents has important implications for the sensitization of the child to fear. It is crucial to investigate this factor in all cases of school refusal, as the development of fears in children is influenced by their history and the setting in which distressing stimulation occurs. Eysenck and Rachman (1965) point out that children are less likely to develop fears when in the company of trusted and reassuring adults than when they are alone, and they are less likely to become fearful in the presence of unafraid children than in the presence of fearful children. They also point to the evidence of the social facilitation or inhibition of fear in children, brought about by the mother's emotional state at the time. There is a substantial association between the frequency of fears in the children of the same family, and the correlations between fear displays by siblings range from 0·65 to 0·74 (May, 1950); while the correlation between the gross number of fears manifested by children and the number exhibited by their mothers is 0·67 (Hagman, 1932).

There is evidence that in fear-provoking experiments, the fact of confinement (if it exists) reduces the animal's or person's chances of making an adjustment to the difficulties being faced. Psychological restriction may be no less injurious than physical confinement. Eysenck and Rachman (1965) point out that the barriers which prevent a child from carrying out a particular response may as easily reside within himself as in the external situation. They give the example of the sort of psychological confinement that may be found in the relations between a child and her school-teacher. "The number of responses which the child may make in reply to a scolding is very limited. She cannot shout back, nor can she kick, scream, bite, or run away. If she is subjected to frequent verbal attacks of this kind, the child is likely to develop social anxiety."

What of some of the other background factors that are mentioned in the research literature? There are differing opinions as to the vulnerability of the sexes to school refusal problems. Some say the incidence is about equal, but most studies report that boys are more liable than girls to refuse to go to school, and this appears to be the case at all school-going ages. School refusal does not seem to occur disproportionately in any one social or economic class; the children are on average of normal intelligence, with a wide range from the educationally subnormal to the very superior levels; the impression that some workers have—that school refusal is more common among only children—is not supported. They come (in Hersov's group) from families in which the mothers were on average 43·8 years of age (Range: 33–55) and the fathers 47 (Range: 35–46) with a fairly substantial proportion (16%) being brought up by unusually elderly parents. In Hersov's study again, a high proportion of mothers (48%) had experienced a disturbed childhood in terms of a broken home, harsh and rigid upbringing or parental alcoholism. On average the families of the school refusers contained 2·3 children.

When it comes to a discussion of the causal theories of school refusal one finds a fairly wide range of views—often an indication of our lack of knowledge and/or an indication of multicausality. As with other emotional problems, the aetiology of school refusal is probably multifactorial; which is to postulate that a variety of influences, a network of precipitating and predisposing factors, contribute to the development of the problem. Psychoanalysts claim that the fear may have been displaced from the true conflict (or object of the child's concern) onto some easily rationalized aspect of the environment, such as a "harsh" teacher. In turn, the behaviour therapist would describe the phobic anxiety as a *conditioned* emotional response, and the refusal as an *instrumental* avoidance reaction. The irrational, bizarre aspects of phobic fear are accounted for in terms of conditioning and stimulus generalization. (This account is elaborated in the section on phobias (page 255).) Tyerman (1968 cautions against the attempt to classify persistent non-attenders as either truants *or* school phobics. He believes that this dichotomy is an oversimplification, that except for a minority of cases children who refuse to go to school do not fall clearly into either category. "These two conditions are extremes which shade into each other. In every case a full study should be made and appropriate measures prescribed. These measures will vary from one child to another." The advice to consider every child who will not go to school as an *individual* case in need of help is, of course, incontrovertible. However, the evidence (see: Prince, 1968) does suggest that there are large enough numbers of children at the extremes of the continuum to be treated as special problems, especially as there may be implications for specific forms of treatment. School phobia has been described as the introvert response to school difficulties; truancy is viewed as the extravert reaction to school problems (Eysenck and Rachman, 1965).

Hersov (1960) analysed his case-record data according to a 124-item schedule, covering many areas of childhood development and family environment. The most common precipitating factor of school refusal are a change to a new school, the illness or death of a parent, or an illness, accident or operation which necessitates the child going to hospital or staying at home. When the children themselves are asked to give reasons why they cannot go to school, they commonly mention, *if* they give any coherent explanations (see: page 242), fears which indicate a deep-seated separation anxiety or insecure ego-development (i.e., lack of self confidence). A teacher, sensitive to the warning signals listed above—and the periods when certain children are particularly vulnerable—may provide emotional support which prevents an incipient school attendance problem.

There is sometimes a difference of opinion between parents and teachers (on the one hand) and clinicians (on the other) over whether to get the child back to school promptly or not. Most clinicians feel that the pressure should be taken off the family by immediately issuing a medical certificate for the child; then, after treatment has commenced, perhaps a graduated re-entry programme can be worked out.

"Desensitization techniques" offer a promising compromise between the difficulties of enforcing an immediate reintroduction of the child into school and the dangers of further delays. An example of this (Garvey and Hegrenes, 1966) is provided by the case of 10-year-old Jimmy who suffered from a school phobia. He and his therapist would go to the school early in the morning when no one else was present. Jimmy was asked to report any feelings of apprehension. As soon as he did so the therapist immediately took Jimmy back to the car and praised him for what he had achieved so far. The therapist and the child approached the school together in a series of steps graded from the least anxiety-provoking situation (sitting in a car in front of the school) to the most anxiety-provoking condition (being in the classroom with the teacher and other pupils present). At the end of a twenty-day period of desensitization treatment, Jimmy had returned to school completely. The presence of the therapist (with whom Jimmy had a good relationship) was considered as a strong positive stimulus evoking a positive emotional response. The graduated re-entry into school-life was so designed that Jimmy's confidence in the therapist would counteract fears aroused by each new step forward in the treatment programme.

Cooperation of parents and school is, of course, of great importance. The type of individual therapy programme to be instituted will be determined by the exact nature of the child's disturbance. The information revealed by a thorough psychological and psychometric investigation will suggest that procedures should be followed. Remedial education can be provided when necessary, a change of class or school can be arranged, and individual therapy can be applied.

As with other emotional disorders of childhood, the long-term prognosis for school refusers is generally good. But some school refusers who have been untreated, or inadequately treated, have become work refusers in adolescence or adulthood. In very young children the problem is generally short-lived; in older children the problem may be more worrying and disabling, but again the prognosis is a good one (Nursten, 1963). In a few very severely disturbed children, not infrequently those presenting the problem at adolescence (Warren, 1960; Coolidge *et al.*, 1960), the problem has proved insoluble despite all efforts at treatment.

The earlier the treatment is initiated, the better the outcome and the quicker the disappearance of the symptoms. Quick intervention is usually wise, as neurotic disorders, with their secondary gains for the child and undesirable side-effects on the family and school, are inclined to "spiral". The child's anxieties make the parents anxious, which in turn increases the child's fears . . . and so on. A basic objective of treatment is to progress from external behavioural support (e.g., the therapist's presence in the case of Jimmy) to internally mediated reinforcement and self-control. Children can be trained to regulate their activities by deliberate self-management of reinforcement contingencies. Self-reinforcement can occur at a symbolic level (e.g., self-approval, assurance and esteem), indeed ". . . the highest level of autonomy is achieved when behaviour has self-evaluative and other self-reinforcing consequences" (Bandura, 1970).

## Truancy

The truant was defined earlier as a child who absents himself from school without a legitimate cause and without the permission of his parents or the school authorities. Boys truant more frequently than girls. Truancy is a problem which increases steadily in incidence the older children get and is most frequent at age thirteen. However, as we saw, a good deal of truancy goes on at the junior school level. One of the startling facts about serious cases of male truancy in primary school is the finding (Robins, 1970) that 82% were frequently absent during their first two years at school. Robins considers that the concentration of clinicians in the past on improving adult chances by trying to do something for high school dropouts is directed at the wrong age group; excessive absence being a phenomenon of the very young. Truancy continues into high school, but it certainly does not start there.

Studies of truants (see Tyerman, 1968; Hersov, 1960) show that this pattern of behaviour is seldom just the light-hearted or roguish contrariness of that famous absconder, Tom Sawyer. The attitude and behaviour of truants are often aspects of a more general "conduct disorder". Truants characteristically manifest problems such as enuresis, lying, wandering from home, stealing and aggression. Many delinquencies (such as shoplifting, stealing from cars, and so on) are committed by boys when they are roaming the streets during school hours. Hersov (1960) found a greater incidence of Juvenile Court appearances in these children compared with controls. In general, a child's attendance record at school is a very good predictor of his adult adjustment (Robins, 1970).

Investigations of truants (Hersov op. cit.; Tyerman, op. cit.; Robins, 1966) have uncovered certain features in the personality and behaviour of the children, and in their home life, which stand out because of their frequency. Often, home conditions are intolerable for the truant. Marital disharmony makes for rows and tension. Homes tend to be overcrowded and dirty, and parents may have little interest in their children's welfare. The families tend to be large. Their offspring may even lack adequate clothing. They are often kept out of school for no good reason. Many of them have been rejected and thus lack affection or a close tie with a parent who will demonstrate good standards. Many have slept out at night or run away from home. The homes themselves, tend to be concentrated in uncongenial slum settings. Children who truant tend to feel lonely and miserable, becoming unsociable and unable to persevere at anything.

The truant has learned, over a period, that the best strategy for avoiding tensions at home—so often the source of harsh punishment and the scene of rows and rejection—is to escape. So he wanders away from school (where he is often bored beyond words and anyway feels he is disliked by teachers and children alike) in the way he wanders from home (where he also often feels unwanted). He may amuse himself as a solitary; or may look for congenial companions who also crave excitement and a distraction from their feelings of depression and discouragement.

At the back of the truant's dislike for school lies a history of failure, often both academic and social. There have usually been several changes of school. Children who are poor at schoolwork (and truants tend to be in the dull range of intelligence) and who are constantly criticized by their teachers and called stupid, find school a demoralizing experience. If they are kept down a year, they are likely to find school boring, lonely, and embarrassing. They are stuck with younger children and are repeating work they have little feeling for and even less understanding of—a situation to escape from as soon as possible. Because over-age children generally fail to get social acceptance in the class, the repeater makes few friends, a factor which increases his rejection of school. Robins (1970) found that truancy is as powerful a deterrent to High School success as a low IQ. In any event, truants, on average, are below the majority of their schoolmates in mental ability and educational attainment. A few truants are of exceptional intelligence.

# 15. Emotional and Physical Problems Associated with Fear

THERE IS A positive as well as negative aspect to the emotional processes called fear. These subjective and physiological responses which a child experiences to events which are threatening to his personal security can be highly adaptive. Apart from toning him up for maximum effort in emergency situations they play a role in his socialization. Mothers make use of the child's fear in training him to avoid dangers. A modicum of fear can also be adaptive in preparing him to cope with testing situations (examinations, athletic contests) which require peak efficiency. An analysis of children's fears at various age levels suggests that certain types of situation tend to evoke more worries at one particular phase of development than at another. For example, the fears of three-year-olds are more often reality fears; as children get older, a majority of fears tend to be vague anxieties rather than focused fears of realistic dangers. In deciding whether a child's fearfulness amounts to an out-of-the ordinary emotional problem, it is obviously necessary to be familiar with the normal fears that children experience while growing up. A large number of fears are "outgrown" in the way that the child outgrows many childish toys, games and interests. See Figure 6.

Jersild *et al.* (1933) interviewed 400 children in order to investigate their fears. There were 25 boys and 25 girls in each age or year group from 5 to 12 years. They considered that a child showed fear when he admitted he felt afraid or when he cringed, retreated, withdrew, cried, trembled, protested, appealed for help, cowered, clung to his parents, or showed rapt or frightened attention in a particular situation. Only 19 children denied that they had any fears. Fear of the occult, of magic, giants and ogres, corpses, witches, and mystery and ghost stories were admitted most frequently. Fears of animals were the next most common fears, then fears of strangers and being alone. Next came personal bodily injury and then nightmares and night apparitions. Fears of bad people, robbers, kidnappers,

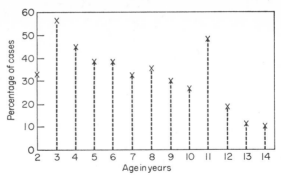

Fig. 6. The fears of normal children: percentage frequencies by age. (Adapted from Macfarlane *et al.* 1954.)

etc., were admitted by 7·3% of the children, and least frequent were fears of unusual gestures and noises. Eleven and twelve-year-olds admitted more fear of the occult, of the dark, of strange and unfamiliar places and persons, of being alone, of strange noises, lights, shadows, of deformed and mutilated people, of nightmares and night apparitions than did the five or six-year-olds. The older children also admitted more fears of being scolded or embarrassed or of not doing the right thing. Five- and six-year-olds admitted more fear of animals and of bad people. Boys admitted more fear of personal bodily injury than girls and denied having any fear more often. Girls admitted more fear of the dark, of solitude, of strange sights and noises than boys.

Studies of the fears of childhood indicate that they are so common that it might be said to be "normal" for children to be fearful about one thing or another at different stages in their development. Many investigators (e.g., Lapouse and Monk, 1958) find that it is commonplace for a majority of their samples of non-clinic-attending children to report having one or more fears. Obviously, if a degree of fearfulness is widespread during childhood we have to judge the seriousness of a particular child's anxieties by the consequences they have in his day-to-day life. At eleven, children exhibit an increase in fear. Among eleven and twelve-year-olds worries connected with *school* are nearly half as many again as worries about home matters. In Britain, eleven is that awkward phase in a child's life when the change from junior to senior school is being made. It may not be coincidental that it is also the age at which school phobias are at a high peak. Why the child should be particularly fearful at this stage is uncertain, although one might speculate about the possible effects of the pubertal changes (physical and emotional) that are beginning to occur for many children at this age. Parents often devise their own methods of dealing with the fears and phobias of their children. Jersild and Holmes (1935) made a study of the practices used by parents and teachers to overcome children's fears and tried to assess their success.

## ADULT HELP

Methods found most effective in helping the child to overcome his fears included:

(1) Helping the child to develop skills by which he can cope with the feared object or situation.
(2) Taking the child by degrees into active contact and participation with the feared object or situation.
(3) Giving the child an opportunity gradually to become acquainted with the feared object or situation under circumstances that at the same time give him the opportunity either to inspect or to ignore it.

Methods that were sometimes helpful in enabling the child to overcome his fears included:

(1) Verbal explanation and reassurance.
(2) Verbal explanation plus a practical demonstration that the feared object or situation was not dangerous.
(3) Giving the child examples of fearlessness regarding the feared object or situation. (Parents frequently quote the example of other children who are not afraid.)
(4) Conditioning the child to believe that the feared object was not dangerous but pleasurable.

Methods that were practically useless included:

(1) Ignoring the child's fear.
(2) Forcing the child into contact with the feared object or situation at frequent intervals.
(3) The removal of the feared object or situation or the offer of palliatives to the child.

## SELF-HELP

It was found that even without help, children could overcome fears, either as part of the process of growing up or by using the following techniques:

(1) They could practise overcoming their fear by enlisting the help of adults or favourite toys.
(2) They could talk with other people about the things they fear.
(3) They could argue with themselves about the reality or unreality of the dreaded imaginary creatures or fantasized events—say death—that they fear.

## Learning to be Fearful

The development of fear is, of course, influenced by the child's history and the setting in which the fear-provoking situations occur. The tendency of a child to over-react with fear is closely related to the inherited sensitivity of his autonomic nervous system. Very early environmental influences, even those going back to the child's first environment—the mother's uterus—are thought to sensitize the child to over-react (see Chapter 2). We saw it suggested that if the mother is under considerable stress during pregnancy, this may make her child more reactive and highly strung than he would otherwise be. Postnatal experiences of a very frightening kind can condition a child to feel acute apprehension in similar situations later, and this conditioning can persist (Watson and Rayner, 1920). In other words, anxiety is "learnt" by the association of unpleasant experiences with particular situations.

It is of interest to see how ancient these ideas are. Descartes (see: Errera, 1962) has this to say:

> . . . For it is certain that there is an affinity between the motions of the mother and the child in her womb, so that whatsoever is displeasing to one offends the other; and the smell of roses may have caused some great headache in the child when it was in the cradle; or a cat may have affrighted it and none took notice of it, nor the child so much as remembered it; tho' the idea of that aversion he then had to roses or a cat remained imprinted in his brain to his life's end.

## Nightmares and Night Terrors

Nightmares and night terrors are often referred to as nocturnal anxiety attacks. The term "night terror" is defined by Anthony (1959) as follows:

> At some late hour in the night, the child is found in a bizarre, crouching posture in bed or rushing about in a state of great agitation and apprehension, screaming in terror, and staring at something in front of him with wide open eyes and dilated pupils. He is not fully awake, does not recognize people and is disorientated in time and space. He will, however, reply to questions and gradually respond to soothing suggestions of reassurance. In the morning he has no recollection of the nocturnal event. The attacks tend to resemble each other and to show a periodicity. The condition does not appear to be related to other sleep disturbances, although it shares a similar background of anxiety, insecurity, instability, overstimulation and traumatization (reaction to shock).

Freud (1900) said of children's dreams: "The dreams of small children are simple wish-fulfilments and therefore, in contradiction to the dreams of adults, of very little interest. They are no puzzles, but are naturally of utmost importance as proof that in its core every dream is a wish-fulfilment." This view has been criticized as an over-simplification. While there are many dreams of this kind, it is difficult to see the frequent fear-dreams as wish-fulfilments.

It is thought (Kimmins, 1920) that the nature of a child's dreams is influenced more by his personality type than anything else. Aggressive children tend to have more aggressiveness in their dreams than do less hostile children. Neurotic children tend to have negative themes which disturb their dreams. Children who have suffered fairly prolonged separations in hospital from their mothers (four weeks or more) tend, subsequently, to suffer more nightmares than children who have been separated but have stayed in their own homes. Unpleasant dreams tend to increase when the child is in poor health, and themes such as death and other morbid topics may appear in vivid nightmare form. Children experiencing emotional and neurotic problems may suffer from recurrent nightmares—sometimes repetitive themes being present. These themes may provide a pointer to the underlying problem.

Nightmares often set in for shortish periods when the child—particularly the sensitive child—is unsettled or worried by a change of school, a move to a new town or the trial of examinations.

In the MacFarlane studies (MacFarlane et al., 1954) disturbing dreams became something of a problem for boys and for girls at about the ages of ten and eleven. This means that one-third or more of the children in this American sample were manifesting the problem. There is another peak in the incidence of nightmares in the case of girls at six or seven years of age. About one girl in ten, between the ages of seven and ten, will experience disturbing dreams (not as severe as nightmares—but nevertheless distressing) two or three times a week. They diminish in frequency as the girl gets older. According to the Buckinghamshire study (Shepherd et al., 1971) the proportion of British children with nightmares declines as they get older.

## Phobias

We have already discussed an example of phobic disorders in the chapter dealing with "school phobia". A phobia is an extreme and recurrent fear which is unreasonable (even to the victim); it is a reaction which is disproportionate to the circumstances or object which produces it. It is necessary to be cautious in applying the term phobia to some of the anxieties and fears of childhood. Many of these appear to be irrational or disproportionate to adult eyes, but (as we have seen) are so common in children at particular ages, that they must be regarded as normal developmental fears. Phobias are patterns of behaviour or response which are maladaptive—they serve no useful purpose. The child's fear of really dangerous situations is adaptive; for example, he learns to avoid touching hot things. In the case of school phobia, the child's avoidance is clearly not adaptive—it leads to his missing school, handicaps him when he eventually returns, and so on.

Some 200 phobias have been listed. Dixon *et al.* (1957), in a factor analysis of a wide variety of fears and phobias, found a general factor of fearfulness and a second factor which subsumed two broad categories of phobias—those relating to fears of separation, and those relating to fears of injury, hurt or pain. Phobias can also be highly specific, appearing singly in the individual (the so-called monosymptomatic phobias).

Phobias appear more often in females than males; they can occur at any age, and all social classes seem equally subject to them (see: Berecz, 1968). Certain phobias, such as fear of birds, are palpably unreasonable, whereas others, such as fear of trains, lifts or even heights, will bear a certain amount of rationalization or justification. Many people, of course, have circumscribed and relatively insignificant phobias such as fears of confined spaces, spiders and snakes. Such fears are common. Whether or not a child requires treatment depends on several considerations. The clinician would need to discover whether the phobia itself was seriously disabling in some way, and whether other emotional problems were preventing the child from leading a reasonably contented and productive life.

Psychoanalysts regard phobias as the visible upshot of unconscious causes (Fenichel, 1945). The symptoms are the outward manifestations ("compromise formations") of a conflict between intrapsychic forces— ego, id and superego. According to this view, the person with a phobia is really afraid of giving away to the temptation to express deeply rooted, unconscious wishes. These wishes are primitive and forbidden. Phobias often have a defensive function; they develop to protect the individual from situations in which repressed aggressive or erotic impulses are aroused. He does not wish to give way to these impulses but they tempt him. So he displaces or transfers the anxiety they cause in him to some associated object—such as a fear of venereal disease (in the case of sexual temptation) or of water (in the case of suicidal impulses). A person with unconscious or barely perceived homicidal impulses might develop a phobic avoidance of knives and other "killing" objects. The phobic symptom is sometimes thought to represent a symbolic, and therefore compromise, expression of the unconscious wish.

Several theorists in the field of experimental psychology and psychiatry, writers like Eysenck (1960a) and Wolpe (1958) reject such psychoanalytic interpretations and hold the view that learning theory contains many of the answers to the genesis of phobic problems and other neurotic behaviours. While they agree with psychoanalysts that anxiety has a central role in the development of phobias, for them the symptoms are in fact the neurosis.

They discount the notion that symptoms represent a sort of metaphorical "story" about underlying conflicts and unconscious impulses; the neurotic symptoms, the phobias, are acquired according to a learning paradigm.

According to one version of the theory (Eysenck and Rachman, 1965), certain children are predisposed to acquire dysthymic disorders in general, and phobias in particular. Given an extreme position on the personality dimension extraversion–introversion (which has implications for the individual's conditionability) and a labile or reactive autonomic nervous system (a high rating on neuroticism), the child is thought to be particularly susceptible to the acquisition of maladaptive patterns of behaviour. Take a hypothetical situation, in which a youngster is dealt with harshly by a bullying teacher during the maths lesson. The fortuitous association of the subject-matter, the classroom, and possibly other factors, with the humiliating and frightening experience, causes the child to feel anxious during maths lessons, and even when he is in the classroom, in the absence of the maths teacher. The anxiety may generalize so that he feels anxious when he approaches the school, let alone the classroom. Nevertheless, he has to make the effort to approach the classroom. But he begins to feel panicky. Avoidance of the area leads to relief from anxiety, and it is in this way that the habit of avoidance can become reinforced ("drive reduction"). The attachment of fear to the previously unfeared classroom-situation is thought to proceed on the basis of a classical conditioning paradigm—contiguity of classroom (CS) and bullying teacher (UCS). The genesis of phobic anxiety may be due to a single traumatic incident or a series of sub-traumatic events. In the latter case it might be daily criticisms and punishments from a sarcastic teacher. There is much more to a phobia than a passive conditioned emotional response. There is a strong and active avoidance element. It is postulated that motor responses of an avoidance type are acquired and reinforced on the basis of instrumental conditioning and drive reduction.

An initial fear reaction may become *more intense* over a period of time, even if there is no repetition of the frightening events ("incubation of anxiety") (see: Eysenck, 1968). The youngster's anxiety may be exacerbated by what amounts to "confinement" in the distressing school environment. In addition, it may spread to more and more aspects of the school situation ("stimulus generalization"). It can develop to a point in which only avoidance of the entire school situation brings the child relief from intolerable anxiety. The anxiety, *conditioned* as it is to various stimuli but *not* under conscious control, comes into action despite the child's best efforts to combat it. Ideas and attitudes (conveyed in children's idle, exaggerated chatter) can become the source of aversive reactions to various facets of school life ("higher order conditioning"). A child may acquire a fearful attitude without directly experiencing the fear-provoking stimulation, but by seeing (say) another child being severely punished. "Vicarious learning", as it is called, is a common source of anxieties in young children. The proponents of a learning theory of maladaptive behaviour claim that just as problematical patterns of behaviour can be acquired in terms of the laws of learning, they can also be extinguished according to the same laws. An extensive methodology for modifying behaviour now exists (see: Ullmann and Krasner, 1965; Tharp and Wetzel, 1969). One of the earliest accounts of such an approach was published by Mary Cover Jones in the 1920's.

Jones (1924) reported on the treatment of a child's animal phobias. Three-year-old Peter's fears of rats and rabbits were uncannily like those of Albert. She treated one of the fear-objects by a process of counter-conditioning—countering the rabbit with a pleasant reaction such as that resulting from eating. (She also utilized the presence of unafraid children at times to help combat Peter's fears.) This is how Jones described the treatment: During a period of craving for food, the child is placed in a high chair and given something to eat. The fear-object is brought in, starting a negative response. It is then moved away gradually until it is at a sufficient distance not to interfere with the child's eating. While the child is eating, the object is slowly brought nearer to the table, then placed upon the table, and finally as the tolerance increases it is brought close enough to be touched. Peter was treated by this method daily or twice daily for a period of two months. An analysis of her notes on Peter's reactions indicated the progressive steps in his tolerance of the phobic object.

(1) Rabbit anywhere in the room in a cage causes fear reactions.
(2) Rabbit twelve feet away in cage tolerated.
(3) Rabbit four feet away in cage tolerated.
(4) Rabbit three feet away in cage tolerated.
(5) Rabbit close in cage tolerated.
(6) Rabbit free in room tolerated.
(7) Rabbit touched when experimenter holds it.
(8) Rabbit touched when free in room.
(9) Rabbit defied by spitting at it, throwing things at it, imitating it.
(10) Rabbit allowed on tray of high chair.
(11) Squats in defenceless position beside rabbit.
(12) Helps experimenter to carry rabbit to its cage.
(13) Holds rabbit on lap.
(14) Stays alone in room with rabbit.
(15) Allows rabbit in play pen with him.
(16) Fondles rabbit affectionately.
(17) Lets rabbit nibble his fingers.

Jones pointed out how delicate the whole process is. It is essential to introduce the feared object little by little. For as she observed, a careless manipulator could readily produce the reverse result attaching a fear reaction to the sight of food.

According to Bandura and Walters (1963) counter-conditioning (or "systematic desensitization" as it is now more commonly known) "involves eliciting in the presence of the fear-arousing stimuli responses that are incompatible with anxiety or fear reactions; through the classical conditioning of these incompatible responses to the fear-arousing cues, anxiety is eliminated or reduced".

## Anxiety and Stress

Fear and anxiety wreak their havoc, not only in such psychological manifestations as dread, apprehension and feelings of tension, but also in the form of physical illness. The term "stress syndrome" is often used to categorize all these problems. Stress—an engineering term prior to the 1940s—was taken over by psychologists and psychiatrists during the Second World War and used to describe any state of emotional overload where the human being has been pushed to his limits. Stress is an elusive concept when it comes to precise definition because individuals differ so markedly in their reactions to "difficult" situations. For example, examinations may be stressful for some pupils but not for others. The identification of stressful situations always requires an analysis of the particular stimulus conditions and the individual's reaction to them. Whether stresses are immediate and extreme, or whether they are the chronic and seemingly petty threats, frustrations and conflicts of modern life, they erode the person's emotional and physical well-being in much the same way.

Perhaps the major physical stresses that people have to face today are overcrowding and noise. We know that, in both animals and humans, these irritations produce psychological and physiological effects, including aggression, anxiety and fear. So do the psychological stresses inherent in a highly competitive and success-orientated society. The changes in behaviour which people go through under stress are also matched by changes in the body. Selye (1952, 1957) has investigated these physical changes. The general effects seem to be the same for a wide variety of stresses, whether mental, like fear or anxiety, or physical, like extreme physical effort, exposure to heat or cold, injury or lack of sleep. In each case the body goes through three stages: the alarm reaction, the stage of resistance, and the stage of exhaustion.

In the initial alarm stage, the pituitary gland secretes adrenocortico-trophic hormone, or ACTH. This hormone stimulates the adrenal glands, which immediately start pumping further powerful hormones called corticoids into the blood stream. At first these corticoids help the body to resist attack. For example, they cause inflammation around a wound—the body's way of defending itself against infection. After a period of time this immediate reaction becomes exhausted and a different type of corticoid starts to dominate, acting to suppress the inflammation. This helps the local healing process in the case of a wound, for example, but it also lays the body more open to infection from other sources. This cycle of events helps to explain why people often respond to stress by falling ill in some apparently quite unconnected way. Victims of stress may go to their physicians to be treated for disorders that do not always appear to have any physical origin. These illnesses are called *psychosomatic disorders*. Medical treatment can alleviate the symptoms for a time, but they are likely to return when the patient is again confronted with a stress situation.

# 16. The Development of Psychosomatic Problems

PSYCHOSOMATIC illnesses occur frequently in school-going children and are amongst the commonest causes of repeated absence from school. Perhaps the most interesting (certainly the most common) of childhood psychosomatic disorders is bronchial asthma. Asthma is estimated to be responsible for nearly one-quarter of the days reported lost from school on account of chronic illness (Schiffer and Hunt, 1963). As many as 2% of children suffer from this illness (Graham *et al.*, 1967). The figure has been put as high as 5% (Purcell and Weiss, 1970). A discussion of asthmatic problems is relevant to a consideration of developmental problems because of the common belief among practitioners and theorists that life-history events (especially early developmental factors) influence the condition and the conviction that most asthmatic children are neurotic (Kelly and Zeller, 1969). The research into this problem also illustrates the pitfalls and difficulties of the sort of clinical research in which psychology, physiology and medicine meet.

The term "asthma" is derived from the Greek word meaning "panting". Asthma is a recurrent disorder of respiration characterized by severe paroxysms of difficult breathing, usually followed by a period of complete relief. The dyspnoea is a result of partial obstruction of the smaller bronchi due to contraction of the plain muscle, excessive secretion of mucous, and turgescence of the mucous lining. The bronchiolar constriction usually results from foreign antigens, such as foods or serums, which enter the bloodstream and act directly on the sensitized bronchiolar musculature to produce spasm (Ratner, 1960). In the immediate allergic reaction the union of antigen with reaginic antibody leads to the release of spasmogens and other mediators of the anaphylactic reaction. The bronchial plugging is usually due to an inhalent which enters the air passages directly and produces its chief reaction in the lumen of the bronchi, with oedema, excess mucous secretion, inflammation and resultant obstruction.

The respiratory apparatus works in such a fashion that the narrowing of the bronchioles is a greater obstruction to expiration than to inspiration; in consequence, the lungs become distended with air, the patient's chest becomes more and more expanded and he labours with increasing difficulty to rid his chest of air in order to breathe. The recurrence of attacks over many years can lead in time to permanent changes in the lung, the bony and muscular components of the chest, and the heart, which may, in the end, cause the death of the patient.

Among other predisposing or contributory precipitating causes of asthma are bronchial infections, and also stress conditions such as cold, over-exertion and fatigue. These are, of course, physical factors. So it is necessary to ask what justification there is for a psychological investigation of asthma—a disease involving organic factors, and belonging traditionally to the field of somatic medicine. There is, in fact, considerable empirical evidence for the contribution of psychological factors to the precipitation of asthma attacks (Leigh, 1953; Kelly and Zeller, 1969).

## The Role of Emotion in the Asthma Attack

From the earliest commentaries on the subject, beginning with Hippocrates' aphorism advising all asthmatics to abstain from anger and shouting, numerous examples have been cited to demonstrate that attacks may be precipitated by situations that provoke violent emotions, particularly acute fear and anger. A survey of the literature shows that almost any sudden, intense, emotional stimulus can trigger the attack. Jealousy, guilt, sexual excitement, anxiety, grief and disgust have also been frequently quoted.

The evidence, based mainly upon clinical observations, falls into the following categories:

(1) Emotional upsets may result in the precipiation or exacerbation of asthmatic attacks. This is the most common type of report (French and Alexander, 1941; Leigh, 1953; Dunbar, 1954; Herbert, 1965). Rees (1956) on the basis of a large, well-controlled study, has enumerated the commoner precipitants of asthmatic attacks: anxiety with tension; anticipatory pleasurable excitement; tension due to frustration of any need; anger; humiliation; depression; laughter; guilt feelings; joy and elation.

(2) Acute emotions may abort an asthma attack (McDermott and Cobb, 1939; Groen, 1951). McDermott and Cobb (1939) state that it seems reasonable to suppose that the mechanism involved in such patients is dual; first there is caused by emotional stress a heightened irritability of the Autonomic Nervous System which (combined with the allergen or the allergic tendency) precipitates an asthma attack. Then, later, if the emotion reaches the intensity of passionate anger, hate or eroticism, adrenalin is secreted by the

patient himself in large enough amounts to stop the asthma—he gives himself his own "hypodermic" injection.

(3) The asthma attack is said to be associated very often with the suppression or inhibition of acute emotions, particularly anger and hostility. Many asthmatics tend to "bottle up" their feelings (Van Helmont, 1648; Groen, 1953; Waal, 1951). The suppression or inadequate expression of emotions appears to give rise to mounting or prolonged states or tension which are conducive to the precipitation of asthmatic attacks. Alexander (1935) postulates the following sequence of events to account for the effects of inhibited aggression and other emotions. (a) Emotions are always associated with active patterns expressed through a portion of the autonomic nervous system and its innervated organs. (b) For specific emotions there are appropriate vegetative patterns. (c) Emotions suppressed from overt expression lead to chronic tension, thus intensifying in degree and prolonging in time the concomitant vegetative innervation. (d) The resulting excessive organ innervation leads to disturbance of function ending eventually in morphological changes in the tissues.

(4) Attacks of asthma seem to be associated with a considerable variety of emotional conflicts. These are discussed in the context of:

## (a) Precipitating factors

Dekker and Groen (1956) conducted a number of experiments in which it was possible to register a decrease in vital capacity, associated in some cases with attacks of typical asthmatic dyspnoea, after the exposure of asthmatic subjects to certain emotive environmental stimuli which were chosen from their case histories. Faulkner (1941) thinks there is some evidence that emotion can produce bronchospasm. He observed constriction and dilation of bronchi under bronchoscopic examinations in response to psychological stimuli. An interesting find was reported by Stevenson and Wolff (1943) who observed increased mucous secretion (sometimes as much as eight-fold) in an asthmatic subject, associated with feelings of anxiety and resentment evoked by discussion of stressful life situations. The mucous secretions diminished when the stress was over.

## (b) Predisposing factors

French and Alexander (1941) maintain that asthma is associated with a specific emotional constellation (in the sense of there being what psychoanalysts call a nuclear conflict at work); they postulate the specific "psychic predisposition" in the following terms: "Throughout the lives of patients who suffer from psychogenic asthma attacks, there seems to run a continuous undercurrent, more or less deeply repressed, a fear of estrangement from the mother upon whom the patient is usually very dependent in an infantile way. The cause of this fear of estrangement is usually the patient's own forbidden impulses which he thinks will offend the mother." (French and Alexander, op. cit.)

Whatever the aetiological role of emotion in asthma, the emotional *effects* of the attacks are undeniable. The subjective distress caused by the inability to breathe easily, the choking sensation and sheer exhaustion, often going hand in hand with a very real fear of death, must have important psychological consequences for the asthmatic child and his parents. This is an important consideration in an evaluation of the contribution of psychological factors to the aetiology of the disease.

The different innervations of the respiratory tract, including nasal mucosa, larynx, trachea, bronchi, and bronchioles, comprise both sympathetic and parasympathetic nerves. The smooth muscle of the respiratory tract is innervated by both sympathetic and parasympathetic fibres. The glands in the mucous membranes are innervated directly only through the parasympathetic system. The effect of vagal action in the bronchi is to cause contraction of the bronchial muscle with decrease in size of the lumen, and also increased secretion and swelling of the bronchial mucous membrane. The mechanisms whereby emotional or psychological stimuli are translated into the physiological response (e.g., spasm of the bronchioles) of the asthma attack are not precisely understood.

Graham *et al.* (1967) speculate that disease can occur as a learned response without prior manifestation as an unlearned response. They postulate physiological activities of the same type as in disease, but of lesser duration or intensities; these may become associated by learning mechanisms with stimuli previously ineffectual in eliciting them. Subsequently, it becomes possible for these physiological responses to be elicited with sufficient duration and intensity to be labelled as illness. Some theorists believe that emotional factors become superimposed on an already existing asthmatic diathesis, so that they become capable (along with organic substances such as allergens) of triggering individual attacks. The processes postulated to form the link in this psychosomatic equation include mediated learning (Purcell *et al.*, 1962a, 1962b) and classical conditioning (French and Alexander, 1941; Herxheimer, 1951; Dekker *et al.*, 1957; Turnbull, 1962). Knapp (1963) however, obtained negative results in attempts to condition attacks, and Dekker *et al.* (1961) have reported that they could not replicate the original classical conditioning of attacks of asthma in human subjects. Experiments on the instrumental conditioning of vegetative functions (Miller and Di Cara, 1967) while not focusing directly on respiration, suggests interesting possibilities for further research. Whatever the mechanisms involved, the finding that asthma can be precipitated by emotional stimuli has important implications if it can be demonstrated that asthmatics share certain chronic emotional tensions (viz. a personality type), or characteristic ways of reacting to stress situation (viz. ANS specificity) which result in a disordered respiratory pattern—namely asthma.

## Patterning of ANS Responses

The preoccupation with relationships between personality and illness has led to a search for patterning in the responses of the ANS (autonomic nervous system). A search for such underlying ANS mechanisms is essential. It is often assumed in psychosomatic medicine that differences in personality (where there appears to be a correlation between personality and disease) are part of the aetiological process leading to the illness. But, of course, correlations do not necessarily imply causal relationships.

Graham *et al.* (1962) and Grace and Graham (1952) produce evidence which points to the *possibility* (and it cannot be put more strongly) that the attitudes typical of different personality types may be associated with particular patterns of ANS response. It is postulated that these in turn may predispose individuals to particular physiological disturbances. Interviews with patients suffering from particular psychosomatic illnesses tend to reveal an association between the type of disease and a particular predominating attitude to life.

Ax (1953) found differing patterns of physiological change depending on whether he induced fear or anger in his experimental subjects. The changes in fear resembled those produced by the injection of adrenaline while the responses which were concomitants of anger were like those produced by the combined action of adrenaline and noradrenaline. Funkenstein *et al.* (1954) distinguished between anger directed outwards (viz. rage), and anger directed inwards (viz. depression). The physiological changes accompanying the former emotional response consisted, in the main, of an increase in the secretion of noradrenaline. Anger directed against the self produced physiological changes in which the predominant factor was the secretion of adrenaline.

Studies of the patterning of autonomic nervous system responses have undermined simplistic models of arousal. The general concept of "response specificity" was introduced to take account of the fact that individuals manifest idiosyncratic patterns of autonomic response, some showing their greatest reactivity in terms of blood pressure, others in terms of skin conductance and so on. Several terms were introduced to describe the stimulus and subject patterning that were discovered.

Malmo and Shagass (1949) were the first research workers to examine such autonomic response patterning. They investigated the reaction of psychiatric patients to pain. They found that heart rate measures were all reliably higher for a group of cardiovascular patients, while muscle potential scores were higher for patients complaining of neck- and headaches. This study and other findings led Malmo and his colleagues (1950a, b) to formulate the principle of "symptom specificity". According to this principle, psychiatric patients with a somatic symptom will show maximal activation to a stressor in the physiological mechanism underlying the symptom.

Malmo's study of "symptom specificity" prompted other investigators to study the patterning of autonomic responses to varied stimulus situations. Lacey (1967) has summarized a large body of evidence from the resulting work (primarily from the psychosomatic literature) to support his view that arousal (activation) processes are multidimensional. Lacey argues that the evidence suggests that autonomic arousal, electrocortical arousal, and behavioural arousal are different forms of arousal. He states that they are imperfectly coupled, and complexly interacting systems.

In reviewing such work on autonomic response patterning, Lacey and his colleagues (Lacey, 1950, 1956; Lacey et al., 1953, 1963) have stressed that the ANS, far from being a homogeneous system responding simply or in a balanced way to various stimuli (as arousal theorists have tended to assume), shows fractionations and specificities which relate to both stimulus and subject variables. He contends (a) that neither inter-individual nor intra-individual correlations among autonomic measures are large enough to justify their use as criteria for gauging the arousal level; (b) that different stimulus situations reliably produce different patterns of somatic response, or what is called "situational stereotypy"; (c) that there are experimental demonstrations of dissociation of behavioural and electrophysiological indices of arousal; and (d) that the neurophysiological evidence shows that cardiovascular changes can have inhibitory rather than excitatory effects on cortical functioning. The ANS is not always a passive index of CNS functioning; on occasions the CNS and other arousal mechanisms interact cybernetically thus producing "homeostatic brakes" upon one another.

Lacey lists the following forms of autonomic response stereotype:

(1) Intra-stressor stereotypy—which refers to idiosyncratic response patterns which are reliably reproduced by a single form of stressor.
(2) Inter-stressor stereotypy—which refers to patterns of responding which are reproduced to a similar extent by different types of stressor.
(3) Symptom stereotypy—which refers to the constancy of the physiological measure in which maximum activation is induced by stressful experience in patients with psychosomatic disorders—the area of maximal activation being consistent with the somatic complaint.
(4) Situational stereotypy—which refers to changes in average response pattern which are produced by changes in stressors or which accompany different affective experience.

Autonomic response specificity is itself a complicated matter. An individual's response hierarchy itself may vary. Some subjects may exhibit an almost random pattern of responding, showing one response hierarchy to one stimulus, another to another stimulus and so on (Lacey and Lacey, 1958). At the other extreme are individuals who seem not to be flexible, as can be observed in their production of the same response hierarchy in the same measures in situation after situation.

What one is left with is a highly complex and somewhat contradictory picture; certainly a simple model of a generalized arousal level causing *uniform* changes is inappropriate. There does seem to be a degree of generality and specificity in autonomic responding.

## Personality Structure of Asthmatics

The fact that certain people react to emotional situations as well as specific organic substances with asthma attacks, has led to the view that the various precipitating causes find some constitutional and/or acquired predisposition, which might conceivably be psychological, viz.: a specific personality structure.

The literature dealing with bronchial asthma contains numerous studies of the contribution of personality factors to the aetiology and course of the illness. Several authors (Groen, 1951; Dunbar, 1943; Halliday, 1948) claim to have identified a distinctive asthmatic personality type, or profile of traits. The profiles of the "typical" asthmatic tend to vary from study to study. A survey (Herbert, 1965) of 65 studies in which personality attributes are described, shows that a multiplicity of terms are applied, in various combinations, to the asthmatic. The descriptive terms often lack precise and meaningful definition. It is not surprising that the profiles sometimes appear to be ambiguous and contradictory, as they are frequently formulated on the basis of subjective, uncontrolled observations or methodologically unsound investigations.

In order to test this and other criticisms concerning asthmatic personality typologies, the author investigated (op. cit.) a group of 75 South African Indian children (asthmatics, "normals" and stammerers) by means of personality and intelligence tests, interviews and case-history records. The analysis failed to identify clear-cut differences between the asthmatic and stammering groups; a majority of the stammerers would be misclassified as asthmatics if the sole criteria were these allegedly crucial personality factors. An examination of the patterns of personality traits presented by each subject, revealed an absence of the homogeneity required to support the concept of a type *peculiar* to asthma. However, symptoms of maladjustment and dependency traits were prominent attributes of the asthmatic children. They were also characteristic of the stammerers.

It is of interest that Rees (1963), while finding a high frequency of meekness, sensitivity, anxiety, meticulousness, perfectionism and obsession in 388 asthmatic children admitted to an outpatient clinic, discovered no evidence for specificity of personality-type. Franks and Leigh (1959) administered the Maudsley Personality Inventory (M.P.I.) to asthmatics, neurotics and normal subjects, and found no specific asthmatic personality type although there was a common core of neuroticism which they thought might be reactive to the illness itself. This is an important observation. There is evidence that at least some of the observed emotional conflicts and problems are a *response* to a chronic form of illness. A carefully matched series of asthmatic and cardiac-disease children did not show significant personality differences on psychological testing (Neuhaus, 1958).

The available evidence does not confirm the existence of personality types specific to asthmatic or other illnesses (see: Hamilton, 1955). It is not possible to claim that theories like that of Groen's are satisfactorily refuted by investigations such as those mentioned above. As Eysenck (1957) has stated, it is almost impossible to prove a null hypothesis.

An epidemiological study was carried out by Graham *et al.* (1967) in which the population of 9, 10 and 11-year-old children living on the Isle of Wight was analysed. They asked the question:

Is asthma a psychiatric disorder in its own right? The difficulty inherent in this view is that it gives rise to no unambiguous testable predictions, and certainly our findings cannot provide an answer to this question. If asthma is a type of neurosis, it might be predicted that the rate of psychiatric disorder, judged by independent criteria, would be less in asthmatics than in the general population, because such children were able to deal with their conflicts by developing asthmatic attacks. Alternatively, because neurotic attempts to deal with conflict are usually partially unsuccessful and other modes of emotional discharge are called into play, asthmatic children might be expected to show a higher rate of psychiatric disorder.

Graham and his colleagues found that concomitant psychiatric disorder was more common in the asthmatic group (10·5%) than in the general population (6·3%). However, a similar rate to that occurring amongst the asthmatic children was found amongst children suffering from a miscellaneous group of other physical disorders. The authors commented: "The present study, by virtue of the fact that the children with psychiatric disorder had little in common except their asthma, suggests either that the asthma itself was responsible for the psychiatric disorder or that, in general, factors quite unrelated to the asthma played the major part in causation". The authors concluded that it may be that in a small proportion of asthmatic children emotional factors outweigh all others in importance and psychological methods of treatment offer the best hope of therapeutic success. However, the finding that asthmatic children who show behaviour disturbances come as frequently from those with heavy allergic or genetic loading as from those without such adverse elements in their constitution does argue against the presence of an important dichotomy between asthma of psychogenetic origin and asthma of organic origin. They feel that it is almost as probable, perhaps just as probable, to find important psychological mechanisms at work where organic factors are obvious as where they are apparently absent.

Aitken *et al.*, (1972) questioned whether the high incidence of psychopathology reported in asthmatics was based on samples of patients truly representative of the disease. In their own investigation of 68 patients selected at random from registers of diagnosed cases they found virtually no evidence that the distribution of psychopathology differed from that found in the general population. Some of the patients had extensive neurotic disorders while others were remarkably stable. The present author in a study of (*inter alia*) 44 asthmatics from a general allergy clinic at Kings College Hospital, London (Herbert, 1967), found the multiplicity of aetiological factors which is usual in cases of asthma, ranging along a continuum from the mainly organic to the mainly psychogenic.

# 17. Problems of Under-achievement

PROBLEMS OF "under-achievement" refer to situations in which the child's academic performance is significantly below that predicted on some measure of intellectual level or scholastic aptitude. Perhaps one of the most serious consequences of emotional maladjustment, is its deleterious effect on the child's learning in the classroom and hence, his achievement (Chazan, 1959). The concept of achievement is frequently used as a criterion of performance for cognitive and intellectual development. The concept (like so many other criterion and predictor variables used in developmental and clinical studies) is not a unitary one. It has been used to refer to a form of motivation (a need to be successful or to achieve a standard of excellence), and a measure of and opinion about, proficiency. There are many determinants of under-achievement in children.

The National Survey of Health and Development reports (Douglas, 1964; Douglas *et al.*, 1968) make it clear that children from economically or culturally deprived homes are burdened with a cumulative series of hindrances to achievement and educational handicaps. A sample of 5,362 young people was selected from all those born in Great Britain in the first week of March 1946 (see: Douglas, 1964) in order to study, *inter alia*, the progress of the children through primary schools. It was found that not only did the children from deprived backgrounds suffer because education was little valued in their homes, but they were disadvantaged at school itself. The "streaming" or selection procedures (attainment and intelligence tests) which are conducted in many primary schools when children turn seven or eight, tend to be unreliable at this tender age and they are likely to underestimate the ability of children from poor homes. Misclassifications or errors of placement can theoretically be corrected by subsequent transfers between streams or classes. However, as Douglas and his colleagues point out:

... such transfers were rare and, when they did take place, reinforced the original social bias against the boys and girls from the poorer homes. As they grew older, pupils in each stream increasingly conformed to the earlier assessments of their ability; those in the top stream improved in tests of ability and attainment and those in the lower stream fell behind. It is probable that these changes were a result of streaming rather than an indication of the soundness of the original assessments. The earlier predictions were constantly being reinforced in the classrooms and probably also in the home, and so were self-fulfilling. The pupils came to set their sights and to assess their own ability according to the expectations of parents and teachers (Douglas *et al.*, 1968).

We return shortly to a further experimental consideration of the self-fulfilling prophecy; there is, however, another important determinant of under-achievement—the existence of emotional problems in the child.

The National Survey of Health and Development demonstrated (Douglas, 1964; Douglas *et al.*, 1968) a close relationship at 8, 11 and 15 years of age between adjustment on the one hand and ability and attainment on the other. Children who were divided at 15 years of age into the categories "well adjusted" (27%) and "least well adjusted" (28%) showed marked differences in school performance: the least well adjusted (i.e., maladjusted) children had the poorest results in terms of non-verbal ability, verbal ability, reading and mathematics.

Chazan (1959) found that even highly intelligent maladjusted pupils tend to have real difficulties in school performance. He observes that although not all maladjusted children have learning difficulties, the available evidence suggests that a considerable number are seriously handicapped. It is not only grossly maladjusted pupils whose achievements at school are blocked. Douglas and his colleagues (1964, 1968) conclude that there is a continuous gradient in ability and attainment, running from those who have no adverse teacher's comments, no symptoms reported, and low neuroticism, to those who are picked out by all three indices. See Table VIIIa and b below.

The greater the number of problems reported, the poorer, on the whole, is school performance. There is evidence (Chazan, 1959) that the source of most of the educational difficulties described above can be traced to the pre- or early school years.

## Self-esteem, "Good Adjustment" and Achievement

A reasonable agreement between the self-concept ("myself as I am") and the concept of the ideal self ("myself as I would like to be") is one of the most important conditions for a favourable psychological adjustment—at school and in other aspects of the child's life (Ausubel *et al.*, 1954; Crandall and Bellugi, 1954). Marked discrepancies (i.e., negative self-concepts) arouse anxiety, unhappiness and general dissatisfaction with life. (Lipsitt, 1958; Crandall and Bellugi, 1954; McCandless *et al.*, 1956; Hanlon, Hofstaetter and O'Connor, 1954). Under-achievers at school

TABLE VIII. (a) Aggregate test* scores related to a combination of neuroticism, behaviour ratings and symptoms at 15. (Based on population estimates.) (b) Test scores† at 15 related to a combination of neuroticism, behaviour ratings and symptoms at 15. (Based on population estimates.) Douglas, J. W. B. *et al.* (1968) "All Our Future," Peter Davies, London.

(a)

| | Neuroticism Scores | | | | | |
| | High Behaviour Ratings and Symptoms | | | Other Behaviour Ratings and Symptoms | | |
| | High | Average | Low | High | Average | Low |
|---|---|---|---|---|---|---|
| Test score at age:  8 | 46·2 | 49·4 | 51·2 | 48·6 | 50·6 | 52·1 |
| 11 | 45·9 | 49·2 | 51·8 | 48·4 | 50·8 | 52·9 |
| 15 | 45·2 | 49·9 | 51·6 | 48·1 | 51·1 | 53·3 |
| Percentage of sample (percentaged across) | 6 | 14 | 13 | 18 | 33 | 16 |

(b)

| Test Scores at age 15 | Neuroticism Scores | | | | | |
| | High Behaviour Ratings and Symptoms | | | Other Behaviour Ratings and Symptoms | | |
| | High | Average | Low | High | Average | Low |
|---|---|---|---|---|---|---|
| Non-verbal | 47·8 | 50·8 | 51·2 | 49·1 | 51·5 | 53·1 |
| Verbal | 45·7 | 50·3 | 51·9 | 48·4 | 51·1 | 52·6 |
| Reading | 46·3 | 49·7 | 52·2 | 48·3 | 50·9 | 53·7 |
| Mathematics | 45·6 | 50·6 | 51·7 | 49·3 | 51·8 | 53·3 |

* The aggregate test scores were obtained by summing the four standardized scores at each age and re-standardizing these on the population that sat all three test batteries to a mean of 50 and a S.D. of 9·5.

† Each test was standardized on the population taking the test to a mean of 50 and a S.D. of 10.

have poorer self-concepts than normal achievers and reflect feelings of defensiveness, loneliness and undue restriction on their freedom (Ausubel *et al.*, 1954).

Coopersmith (1967) conducted a series of studies of self-esteem with a representative sample of 102 normal boys aged 10 to 12; they were followed up from this pre-adolescent stage to early adulthood. Various indices of self-esteem were used. After determining the individual boys' levels of self-esteem and rating them according to three categories—high, medium or low in self-esteem—the investigations proceeded along three lines. These were:

(1) Laboratory tests of the subjects' memory, perception, level of aspiration, conformity and responses to stress;

(2) Clinical tests and interviews designed to reveal level of ability, personality attributes, attitudes, insights and styles of response;

(3) Studies, including interviews with their parents, that looked into factors of upbringing or experience that might be related to each boy's self-esteem.

Coopersmith found that children with a high degree of self-esteem were active, expressive individuals who tended to be successful both academically and socially. They initiated rather than merely listened passively in discussions, were eager to express opinions, and not evade disagreement, were not particularly sensitive to criticism, were very interested in public affairs, showed little destructiveness in early childhood and were little troubled by feelings of anxiety. They seemed to trust their own perceptions and reactions, and were confident in the likelihood of success in their endeavours. Their approach to other persons was based upon the expectation that they would be well received. Their general optimism was not misplaced, but founded upon accurate assessments of their own abilities, social skills and personal qualities. They were not self-conscious or obsessively preoccupied with personal problems. They were much less frequently affected with psychosomatic disorders (insomnia, headaches, fatigue, intestinal upset) than were youngsters of no self-esteem.

The boys with low self-esteem presented a picture of discouragement and depression. They tended to feel isolated, unlovable, incapable of expressing or defending themselves and too weak to confront or overcome their deficiencies. They were anxious about angering others and shrank from exposing themselves to the limelight in any way. In the presence of a social group, be it school or elsewhere, they remained in the shadows as audience rather than participants, sensitive to criticism, self-conscious, preoccupied with inner problems. This dwelling on their own problems not only exacerbated their feelings of malaise but also isolated them from opportunities for the friendly relationships such persons need for emotional support.

The boys tended to gauge their individual worth primarily by their achievement and treatment in their own interpersonal environment, rather than by more general and abstract norms of success. A correlation of 0·36 was found between positive self-concept and school achievement. Self-esteem and popularity correlated 0·37. The teachers, in the main, judged these youngsters very much as they judged themselves.

The parents of the high self-esteem children proved to be less permissive than those of children with lower self-esteem. They demanded high standards of behaviour and were strict and consistent in enforcement of the rules. Yet their discipline was by no means harsh; indeed, these parents were less punitive than the parents of the boys who were found to be lacking in self-esteem. They used rewards rather than corporal punishment or withdrawal of love as disciplinary techniques, and their sons praised their fairness. The parents of the low self-esteem boys tended to be extremely permissive but inflicted harsh punishment when their offspring gave them trouble. These boys considered their parents unfair and they interpreted the absence of clearly defined rules and limits to their behaviour as a sign of lack of parental interest in them.

## Environmental Influences on Achievement

McClelland (1961) has reached certain conclusions based on two decades of research on achievement motivation, about the influences enhancing its development. He claims that an emphasis on the child meeting certain achievement standards between the ages of 6 and 8 is desirable; he should also receive a training in independence and mastery. He is likely to be highly motivated if, in addition, he is held in warm regard by both parents who are ambitious for him but not too dominating, and who have a strong, positive attitude towards his achievements. There seems to be general agreement in the literature that the home environment is a most potent factor in determining the child's attainment at school.

The mother's early encouragement of independence promotes concern in the child for intellectual competence (see: Crandall, 1967). The educational aspirations of the parents for the child, the literacy of the home, the interest of the parents in the child's work, the physical amenities of the home, the father's occupation, and the parents' own educational level— all have a bearing on the level of the child's achievement.

Crandall (1967) has studied the personality attributes of American pupils who achieve well. In contrast to other children who perform less well, the achievers are not dependent upon adults, although they do accept their demands and the importance which they attach to achievement. As Crandall puts it:

They are also able to work without being immediately rewarded for their efforts, show initiative, self-reliance, and emotional control. While achieving children of preschool and early elementary age are somewhat aggressive and competitive, their social relationships are generally good. Achievement, however, seems to be exacting in its toll. By later elementary school or junior high age, aggression and competition have become accentuated, relationships with siblings, peers, and adults show some disruption, and the children are less creative, more anxious, and less able to resist the temptation to cheat. Research on high school students . . . indicates that these attributes become increasingly pronounced at later ages. Does this mean that the effort to achieve "produces" the less desirable personality attributes? Or does it mean that only if children have acquired such a personality constellation will they then be able to achieve in our highly competitive, post-Sputnik educational system? Cause and effect relations cannot be determined ... but it is obvious that our "education for excellence" is accompanied by certain psychological costs.

A series of studies conducted at the Fels Institute (Crandall, 1963; Katkovsky *et al.*, 1964) show that parents' attitudes concerning their own achievements and interest in their children's achievements are the basic necessities for achievement behaviours and hard work in children.

If parents are not encouraging, if they take little interest or are always negative and destructive in their criticism, the child is likely to be demoralized and will give up. The reinforcement given by parents to their offspring, and by teachers to their pupils, is vitally important (Douglas, 1964). It isn't so much what has happened to the child that is important, but what he chooses to tell himself *about* what has happened. What he believes (and a child is influenced by his parents valuation of himself) may be a more potent determinant of his behaviour than the "facts" that he does not believe. The so-called "self-fulfilling prophesy" (as we saw earlier) can also be a potent influence on outcomes. For example, the mere assumption by teachers that they are working with "superior" children has a beneficial influence on their performance. Rosenthal and Jacobson (1968) conclude from their experiments that people, more often than not, do what is expected of them. They describe findings from an investigation in which 20% of the children in a classroom were "identified" to their teachers as having unusually high abilities. Teachers were told which of the children in their class would demonstrate intellectual "spurting" and "blooming". Intelligence tests were administered at the beginning of the experiment and also one and two years later. The group of allegedly superior children when re-assessed was found to have made considerable gains in IQ and achieved much more than the others in the classroom. It didn't matter that the children assigned to the experimental and control groups were selected at random, and in fact, enjoyed no real advantage at the beginning. What was crucial was the matter of being so identified. After that everyone concerned—teachers, children and proud parents—set about to fulfil the prophesy of the "tests". As the authors suggest: "One person's expectation for another person's behaviour can quite unwittingly become a more accurate prediction simply for its having been made."

The child, as we have seen, learns what expectations to have. These are based on previous experiences and also on the information he has, or imagines he has, about a given situation. Rotter *et al.* (1972) have explored these important components of the self-concept, and their relationship to social learning theory. It is proposed that the effectiveness of a reward depends in part on the expectancy of success in a particular undertaking. Each child has his own subjective expectation of his future achievements, his likelihood of success in different situations. The main factor which determines how he rates himself is his past performance—the ability he has previously shown in trying to achieve certain objectives. If he has done well in the past, he will expect to do well in the future. A series of achievements will set up in his mind what are called "subjective hypotheses"—theories about his accomplishments and potentialities—which he will use to predict his own performance. Each subsequent performance will add to what he already knows about a particular activity and may modify his ideas about the probability of success at it. If the child has been repeatedly successful in a particular endeavour, it is likely that he will acquire a generalized expectation of success, and each performance of the activity will be accompanied by rising expectations. Success may also result in an increased liking for the activity and in increased motivation to succeed.

If the child has a low expectancy of success for mastering a mathematical problem, yet succeeds, the value of the reinforcement through success is likely to be great. Rewards such as praise and success tend to motivate the unsuccessful child highly but probably do not do all that much extra for the consistently successful youngster. The effects of feelings of failure are far more variable than those of success and thus more difficult to predict. If a child does not achieve what he had expected to achieve but accepts his failure in a realistic manner, he will lower his expectation for the next performance. Sometimes, however, a child will react to failure by raising his expectations. He may simply blame his failure on some external obstacle. The expectations of people important to the child also play a part in the way he reacts to failure. If there is pressure on him he may continue to base his expectations at a level far above what is realistic. Success, as we have seen, in the case of a child who has a low expection of passing and yet does so, has great reinforcement value. Failure may have similar consequences depending on the individual child's expectations. As McCandless (1969) puts it:

> Criticism or failure may serve as an excellent motivating device for the bright and able child yet discourage and handicap the child who is already doing poorly; whereas reward does not do very much "extra" for the bright and successful but motivates the unsuccessful child highly ... The bright child expects to succeed, hence success and praise do not surprise him or raise him to new levels of performance. He does not expect to fail or be criticised; hence, when such things happen to him, the effect is great. The punishment, as it were, is so severe that he redoubles his efforts to avoid encountering it again. The failing child expects failure and criticism, hence it has little effect on him except to confirm his beliefs.

The under-achieving child usually grows up in the sort of home which does not value education, independence, or individual achievement. He tends to have poor relationships with his parents. The parents, especially the father, either show limited interest in academic matters or try to put undue pressure on their children to succeed. Being unable to obtain satisfaction from his parents, the under-achiever is liable to turn to his peer group in his search for satisfying human relationships. He will often find himself allied with other rebellious and angry children. Under-achievers generally find school unsatisfying, and develop negative attitudes toward teachers.

Most under-achievers fail to find academic work rewarding, and when they do work, they exert little effort. They tend to be distractible, seldom complete their work, and set themselves low standards of academic achievement. Birney and his colleagues point out on the basis of their research (Birney *et al.*, 1969) that there are children who are unable to attain their own goals or the goals of their parents because they are dominated by a fear of failure and therefore avoid, at all costs, achievement situations. They also note the unfortunate paradox which arises when a society presses for achievement; the rewards and situations which are presented as being worth the struggle can usually be attained by only a fraction of those who are in the "rat race". As Birney *et al.* say:

The measure of success is essentially determined by who and how many others have accomplished the same thing. The successful person needs those who have failed, and those who have failed need hope that some day the tables will be reversed. There is no total escape from the achievement race, although an alarming number are trying.

## Language and Retarded Performance at School

Many potentially bright children are blocked from realizing their creative potential because "normal experiences" of learning are denied to them by their restricted verbal skills. Language lies at the heart of our thinking, our understanding and perception of the world, and our self-expression. Unfortunately, the more complex and phylogenetically late the acquisition of bio-social skills, the more vulnerable they are to insults of a biological and/or social nature. As man's latest phylogenetic acquisition, language is most vulnerable of all. Rees (1973) observes that:

A normal child's thinking is initially talking instructions to himself, and a fundamental task of early childhood is to learn to integrate such increasingly internalized talking and doing. Thinking and reasoning depend on being able to code internal and external realities, past, present and future, in the manageable symbols of language, which may not necessarily be verbal. Thus the individual is free from bondage to current environmental stimuli, and so can solve problems one at a time by the process of the internal dialogue we call thought. The clarifying of both internal and external environments is mediated through language schemata, by means of which order is imposed on a child's view of the world and of himself. Only thus can cognitive experience be communicated to others. The fabric of human intercourse, whether in social exchanges, or in the conveyance of emotions by the arousal of feelings of any kind, depends upon the possession of language. Through language persons and things are anchored to reality by being given a word-label. Thus a child can acquire the knowledge that people and things in the environment, such as parents and home, have a permanence even when temporarily absent.

Bernstein (1960, 1964), on the basis of research carried out in England, points out that when humans speak, their speech—vocabulary and structure—is patterned in different ways according to the pattern of their background social relations. He likens the control of speech by social factors to a coding system. Different social systems throw up different forms of communication which are related to different ways of experiencing the world. In one type of social group the children are controlled in the family by references to positions in a pattern. They must do what they are told because they are children, because they are older or younger, or boy or girl. No other reason than the pattern they belong to is offered as explanation. In another type of family the logical and emotional possibilities are explored verbally, so that the child gets an idea of his unique self but no prescribed pattern into which he fits. Use is made continually of an elaborated code as opposed to a restricted one.

The elaborated code differs from the other in both syntax and function. It is explicit and signifies the individuality of both speaker and listener. People are assumed to have various viewpoints. As a result, speech tends to be complex, using complicated sentences which include a wide variety of adjectives and adverbs and qualifying phrases. Bernstein, like Hess and Shipman (1965) in the USA, found that working-class families use words mainly to denote objects and action. Middle-class families use them more often to indicate relationships. What is so vital is the fact that differences in speech patterns and thinking processes arise from these differences. Language is a major factor in adapting to life and many children are starting off at a disadvantage.

Elaborate language tends to be associated with middle-class usage, where, as Ravenette (1968) explains, it is considered important to recognize individuality and where verbal techniques involving explanation are used for social training. The language to be found in books, certainly at more advanced levels than the first early readers, tends to be "elaborate" rather than "restricted". Thus the child of working-class families is confronted at school with a linguistic code with which he is unfamiliar at home, and which in many ways fails to convey the sorts of meaning with which he is acquainted. The child of a middle-class family, in other words, is introduced to a set of roles and speech forms which is geared to success in school and the outside world, where verbal explicitness counts.

For a working-class child school is not simply a place where he goes to learn facts; he has to learn a new language. And it is not just a matter of the child being handicapped in acquiring new concepts because of the limitations of his restricted code. It goes deeper than that. We are, to a large extent, what we say. In other words, language—the way we express ourselves—is at the centre of our being. It is part of the child, and part of his family and community. When the teacher "puts down" and devalues the child's language in an insensitive and sudden manner, he is devaluing the child himself and his background—whether or not that was the intention.

There are those who would go so far as to say that, irrespective of innate ability or intelligence, a child by the time he is five may be in-educable because, through his communication code, he has come to be a member of a world different to the world of formal education. Such theoreticians believe it is the culturally determined communication code which determines a child's educability.

In America, Hess and Shipman (1965) have studied "culturally dis-advantaged" children and their mothers. The children from deprived backgrounds score well below middle-class children on standard tests of intelligence, a gap that increases with age. They arrive at school without the skills necessary for coping with the first year curriculum, their language development is relatively poor and their auditory and visual skills are not well developed. Hess and Shipman tried to find out how the mothers teach simple problems to their four-year-old offspring. From this and other investigations they produced evidence that:

(1) The behaviour that leads to social, educational and economic poverty is socialized in early childhood.
(2) The central quality involved in the effects of cultural deprivation is a lack of *cognitive meaning* in the communications between mother and child. The lower-class mothers lacked the basic vocabulary to explain simple tasks and thus required non-verbal cues for communication.
(3) The growth of cognitive (thinking and intellectual) processes is fostered in family systems of control. Cognitive growth is restricted by a system which offers predetermined solutions and few alternatives to the child for consideration and choice. Behaviour is controlled by status rules. Something is right because "mother says so!" The child is not en-couraged to be reflective and to attend to the characteristics of the particular problem.

## Family Structure and Achievement

Research workers have explored the ways in which variations in the structure of the family may make a difference to the child's personality and other characteristics. The size of the family appears to make a difference to the way children are reared and the attributes they develop, but the effects are small and depend upon a variety of circumstances (see: Clausen, 1964). The large family is usually less effective at producing striving, success-seeking individuals than the small family, whose children tend to gain higher scores on intelligence tests and do better at school. Children in the National Survey in Britain (Douglas *et al.*, 1968) who had many brothers and sisters made, on average, lower test scores than those who had few. The children from small families gained more places at grammar schools than those from large ones. These differences cannot be explained in terms of poorer environmental conditions, and remain a puzzle.

Ordinal position also has an effect (see: Sutton Smith and Rosenberg, 1970; Douglas *et al.*, 1968). The evidence indicates that only children, like first-borns with siblings, are strongly achievement-orientated and in general successful in performance. As first children tend to be slightly more at risk than others in developing emotional problems (they tend to appear proportionately more often on the files of child guidance clinics than later children) it would appear to be a case of "what you lose on the swings, you gain on the roundabouts".

## Intellect and Achievement

Among the most vital aspects of the child's adjustive equipment for mastering his environment is his ability. Nowhere is the importance of intellectual level more marked than in his coping with the school environment. Of all the disabilities that get in the way of the child achieving success at school, probably none is more handicapping than mental subnormality—a state of arrested development of the mind existing from birth or from an early age. Mental subnormality is not a diagnostic entity; it is an administrative term. The conventional assumption that just under three per cent of the population is retarded—meaning, very roughly, the arbitrary IQ 70 and below—gives us a mass of individuals very different in nature.

According to the World Health Organization Report (1954) on the problem of subnormality, it is possible to distinguish (within broad limits) those mentally subnormal individuals whose disability is attributable primarily to a demonstrable defect of brain structure or chemistry from those whose malfunction is the result of learning deficiencies, which in their turn result from many aetiological influences. Unfavourable environmental influences early on—inadequate opportunities for learning and insufficient stimulation—have been blamed for the handicap of this large group of apparently non-brain-damaged subnormals.

The evidence concerning poor early environments and their adverse effects on learning ability in children, and on their IQ scores ("cumulative deficit") has been reviewed by Bayley (1955), Anastasi (1958), and Bloom (1964). There is substantial support for the theory giving great weight to the child's early environment in shaping his later cognitive abilities (see: Bruner, 1959). As we saw earlier, Bloom's review (1964) of longitudinal studies leads him to conclude that in terms of intelligence measured at 17 years of age, approximately 50% of the variances can be accounted for by age four. In other words, as much intellectual growth is achieved between birth and four years of age as is achieved for the remaining 13 years.

Such a hypothesis of differential growth rates for human intellectual ability also makes plausible the notion of intellectual development in early life being highly sensitive. Hebb (1949) believed that experience is an essential mediator of neural connections and a requirement for the formation of what he called "cell assemblies". Subsequently these neural assemblies become relatively fixed functional units—"autonomous central processes"—whose sequence and phasing in the associative cortex can only be formed by sensory experience.

Hunt (1964) incorporates Hebb's neurophysiological concepts of intellectual growth in his own conception of learning and intelligence as a form of dynamic information-processing dependent upon infantile experience. This earliest experience or "primary" learning, forms much of the pattern for later information-processing capability in the system and serves as the "programmer of the human brain-computer".

The extent to which adverse environmental effects can be mitigated, and retardation of higher level mental skills reversed, remains to be clarified. There appear to be extremes of social and cultural deprivation beyond which compensatory training provides only limited benefit (Zingg, 1940). There have been reports of dramatic improvements when the child is transferred to a more favourable environment. Skeels (1966) followed up 25 institutionalized babies after a lapse of 21 years. Thirteen children had been judged to be mentally retarded as infants while the babies in the control group had IQ's which were higher. Bearing in mind the difficulty of assessing the cognitive level of infants, dramatic shifts in intelligence followed the transfer of the children in the experimental group to an improved environment at ages ranging from six to fifty-two months. They showed a marked improvement in their mental ability. The control group, who did not get such treatment, showed a corresponding decline. The change in each group was so dramatic that their mental status (on average) was reversed. These differences persisted into their adulthood. The close social interaction with an interested adult during these early years had produced enough of a difference to ensure that the experimental subjects were living relatively normal lives.

## Educational Subnormality

The term "educational subnormality" is applied to children who have an IQ somewhere in the range of 55 to about 75. Like the broader concept of "mental subnormality" the term does not necessarily imply a uniform degree of handicap. What it does imply from an official point of view is that, although slow to learn and restricted in potential, the child can make use of many of the intellectual aspects of formal schooling. These broad categories never do justice to the individuals within them. This is not the place to go into the complex subject of mental subnormality. Excellent reviews of the topic are provided by Clarke and Clarke (1958).

ESN children who are socially well-adjusted often cease to be regarded as subnormal when they become adult. It is possible that some youngsters are assessed as ESN in childhood partly because their language is not adequate for the demands made by the school (and intelligence test) situation. They may never have been thought of as "slow" or "dull" in their own environment and the labelling may only occur because of their difficulties with formal education.

# 18. Resistance to Temptation

A SENSE OF guilt, although crucial in the development of the child as a social and moral being, is only a second line of defence in his compliance with the rules. When a child has developed a conscience it generally means that he is able to restrain himself from doing wrong much of the time even when no one else will ever know about his misdemeanour. If he does give way to temptation he feels guilty afterwards. Parents can encourage their children to feel guilt when they have transgressed and yet be relatively feeble in controlling their impulses. Wright (1971) puts the choice open to parents in this way:

They can try to bring up their children able to resist temptation reasonably well while experiencing relatively mild guilt (as far as most ordinary misdeeds are concerned) and, as important, able to relieve feelings of guilt by taking constructive steps to rectify the wrong. Alternatively, they can fail to stimulate in their child an ability to resist temptation well while encouraging acute guilt after misbehaviour.

There is a substantial body of research on the conditions under which children develop a resistance to temptation, conscience and related attributes such as moral aspirations (see: Wright, 1971). It throws some light on the often used (and misused) word, "morality".

There are as many as four components which make up moral behaviour. First, there is the braking mechanism against misbehaviour even when unobserved. This component is known as *resistance to temptation*. Next there is the acute emotional discomfort that follows transgression of the rules and leads to confession, reparation or blaming oneself. This is called *guilt*. *Altruism* is yet another facet and represents acts of kindness, generosity, sympathy and service to others. Lastly we use the terms *moral insight and belief* to cover all the things which people think and say about morality, including their willingness to blame others who do wrong. Each of these facets of morality is complex, and they are not related to each other in any simple manner. A question of great interest is whether the child who can resist temptation in one situation is likely to do so in another. Is honesty a general trait, or is it specific to particular situations?

Hartshorne and May (1928) studied some 12,000 subjects between the ages of 11 and 16 years. The children performed on a variety of tests of deceitful behaviour such as stealing, lying and cheating. The subjects could act in a dishonest manner without the apparent likelihood of being caught at it. In reality, their behaviour was closely observed, and was at all times under rigorous experimental control. Ingenious techniques for measuring such "character" qualities as persistence, charitability, and self-control, were also included in the test situation. When the scores from these various tests were submitted to statistical analysis, it was found that the correlations between them, although positive, were low. They concluded from their findings that:

(1) It is not possible to divide the world into honest and dishonest people. Almost everyone cheats some of the time. Only about 6% of school children *never* cheat. Cheating is distributed in a normal distribution around a level of moderate cheating.

(2) If a child cheats in one situation, it does not necessarily mean he will or will not do so in another situation. See Fig. 7.

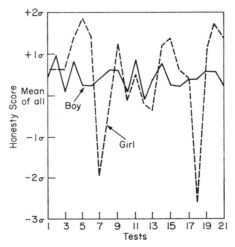

FIG. 7. Honesty profiles, showing consistency of one boy and inconsistency of one girl. (Adapted from Hartshorne and May 1930.)

A child who cheats in the classroom may not do so at games and vice versa. There is very little correlation between situational cheating tests. In other words, it is not a general character trait that makes a child cheat in a given situation. If it were, one could predict he would cheat in other situations.

(3) Children's verbal moral values about honesty have little to do with how they act. Those who cheat express as much or more moral disapproval of cheating as those who do not cheat.

(4) The decision to cheat or not is largely determined by expediency. The tendency to cheat depended upon the degree of risk of detection and the effort required to cheat. Children who cheated in more risky situations also tended to cheat in less risky situations. Thus, noncheaters appeared to be primarily more cautious, not more honest, than cheaters.

(5) Even when honest behaviour is not dictated by concern about punishment or detection, it is largely determined by immediate situational factors of group approval and example (as opposed to being determined by internal moral values). Some classrooms showed a high tendency to cheat, while other classrooms in the same school (seemingly identically composed) showed little tendency to cheat.

The correlations obtained by Hartshorne and May (1928) were, as was stated, nearly all positive. In a re-analysis of some of their data, Burton (1963) was able to show that there was a significant (if small) tendency for children who were honest on one test, to be so on others. Brogden (1940) analysed a large battery of character tests, and found that measures of honesty tended to form a single dimension. Sears *et al.* (1965) obtained six measures of resistance to temptation from five-year-old children, and found them to be positively associated with each other. It seems fair to conclude, therefore, that existing evidence does support the assumption that the capacity to resist temptation in private is a personality trait of some generality; but it is also clear that situational factors exert a powerful influence upon it. In other words, the truth of the matter probably lies somewhere in between the "specific trait" and "general trait" points of view. While there is probably a general disposition of moral restraint, in any situation in which the child is tempted this trait is only one of a number of personality and situational factors which determine whether he will succumb or not. According to Wright (1971), the evidence suggests that moral self-restraint is one aspect of a more general control factor—a generalized capacity to check or suppress one's impulses in situations which do not raise moral issues. This is the factor called "ego control".

Most studies have been unable to find any stable difference between the sexes on measures of resistance to temptation in private (Grinder, 1962; 1964; Rebelsky *et al.*, 1963; Burton *et al.*, 1966). Hartshorne and May (1928) found no overall difference, but on some measures girls cheated more. Sears *et al.* (1965) found a slight tendency for girls to resist temptation more, but since the subjects in this study were very young, this could be attributed to the tendency for girls to develop more quickly than boys. Girls are much less often delinquent than boys, but there are many possible explanations of this fact which do not depend upon differences in resistance to temptation.

We stated earlier that moral behaviour has several dimensions. There are individuals who, as Wright (1971) observes, are highly moral in all respects, and others who are scarcely, if at all, moral in any. Many people seem to concentrate their development in one or other of the dimensions. Again, some people are relaxed and easy-going about their personal moral temptations, while generous in giving of themselves and their possessions in the service of others. There are others who spend much of their time in an unremitting conflict with temptation, a continual battle to resist and avoid committing sins. Yet others lack sympathy and altruism; although their own conduct may not be particularly praiseworthy, they condemn others for moral lapses and meannesses. Contrary to what one might expect, the ability to resist temptation is not highly correlated with proneness to guilt. Those who resist temptation well are not always those who experience the most intense guilt when they err.

No relationship has been found between age and resistance to temptation in private, at least between the ages of eleven and sixteen years (Hartshorne and May, 1928) and seven and eleven years (Grinder, 1964). There is evidence that delinquents first show serious antisocial behaviour at an early age, in fact by the age of eight (Glueck and Glueck, 1950), though it also appears that a large number of delinquents have "grown out" of their delinquency by the middle twenties.

Parents may have, in a sense, a choice as to whether they bring out to less or greater degree one or other of the attributes of guilt and resistance to temptation in their children. This will depend primarily on two things: the timing of the sanctions they administer for misconduct, and the nature of the explanation they provide when they do so. There is evidence that suggests that punishment which immediately *precedes* a forbidden act maximizes resistance to temptation and minimises guilt (Aronfreed, 1964; Aronfreed and Reber, 1965). The experimental work which produces this evidence (see: Aronfreed, 1968) is worth examining in detail, as it illustrates some of the complexities of using punishment in the shaping of behaviour (Solomon, 1964; Marshall, 1965).

Each child in the initial experimental situation (N=88 boys; ages nine and ten) was required to choose between two toys on each of nine trials. In each case, one toy was highly attractive, the other relatively unattractive. The child was told that certain toys were meant for older boys, and that he was not supposed to choose these toys. The choice for the child involved picking up the toy that he "wished to tell about" and describing its function to the experimenter. When a child chose the attractive toy he was punished with verbal disapproval: "No!—that's for the older boys". Children quickly learned to discriminate, consistently choosing the unattractive toy after only two or three trials. It was found that children who were punished as they reached for the toy (i.e., at the initiation of transgression) learned to inhibit the prohibited behaviour significantly more quickly than children who were punished two or three seconds after they had lifted the toy.

In a test of internalization in which the child was left without surveillance with yet another pair of toys, a smaller incidence of transgression (touching the attractive toy) was found among the children who received punishment at the point of initiation of transgression. Twenty-five out of thirty-four of these children resisted the temptation to touch the forbidden toy, compared with ten out of thirty-four of the children who were punished after their transgression.

Aronfreed continued the investigation, intensifying the punishment by adding deprivation of candy to verbal disapproval and giving no cognitive structure ("toys for older children") to aid discrimination. Four variations in the timing of punishment were used. Timing of punishment did not have a significant effect on speed of learning although there was a tendency for inhibition to appear more slowly as the delay of punishment was increased. However, timing directly influenced strength of internalization in the post-training test, in the expected direction. This suggests as Aronfreed puts it, that "suppression of the initiation of transgression is controlled by the anxiety that becomes attached to the intrinsic correlates of the incipient act" (Aronfreed, 1968). The typical post-training test behaviour of the children was picking up the unattractive toy. This also points to the role of non-punished behavioural alternatives in inducing stable inhibition. Where non-punished behavioural choices are available (in situations where strong motivation to transgress conflicts with strong internalized inhibition) these alternatives may have anxiety-reducing functions.*

Aronfreed (1966) extended his investigations in order to demonstrate the power of "cognitive structure" in internalizing inhibition. The role played by the child's ability to recall behaviour in representational and symbolic form is something that needed to be clarified. The temporal locus of punishment, as we know, is of crucial importance, and yet, under natural conditions, punishment is frequently far removed in time from the transgression. In the next phase of the analysis it was found that when the child was told he would be punished for choosing toys which were "hard to tell about" and therefore only appropriate for older children, this markedly facilitated suppression in the post-training test. A reliable difference appeared between the situation in which the child received the

---

* In real-life situations, acceptable behavioural alternatives to prohibited actions are frequently directly rewarded. Such interactions between punishment and reward in temptation situations may account for the ambiguity of some research findings (Sears, Rau and Alpert, 1965, ch. 6).

verbal cognitive structure at the same time as the punishment and the situation in which the cognitive structure was presented between trials. The latter produced less stable internalization. It would seem that punishment results in anxiety attaching to cognitive representations according to the same temporal gradient observed in regard to the behaviour itself.

Finally an experimental situation was designed which focused on the child's intentions. He was informed that he would be punished for *wanting* to pick up a toy appropriate only for older children. A verbalized cognitive structure focusing on the child's intention produced even stronger suppression than that which made no reference to intention. Even when the cognitive structure was changed to emphasize wanting to *tell* about the toy (so that the child actually picked up the prohibited toy before punishment) this was found to be equivalent (in strength of internalization produced) to the original condition—in which the child was punished immediately on reaching for the toy. But the effect disappeared when punishment occurred after both picking up and telling—thus underlining once more the importance of timing of punishment. Sanctions must be closely and distinctly linked to the intention itself as it forms.

Aronfreed and Leff (1963) have demonstrated that punishment that is above a certain optimal level of intensity produces a state of "emotionality" in the child which appears to interfere with learning. If discrimination of the punished choice is difficult, intense punishment is actually more likely, subsequently, to lead to transgression. This finding has clear implications for disciplinary practices. A child who is unable to distinguish what aspect of his behaviour is being punished will be unable to exercise control over the outcomes of his behaviour. He is therefore subject to periods of prolonged anxiety and frustration, and will also fail to experience the anxiety reduction associated with non-punished behavioural alternatives and so will not learn them.

There seems to be a subtle interaction between the child's cognitive structuring of situations, his ability to represent to himself punishment contingencies, and the extent of emotional arousal which is associated with his cognitions, during the socialization process. The child's intellectual level, his verbal ability, and his ability to make a cognitive structure of the learning situation, are important sources of control. They facilitate control by representing the potential outcomes of his behaviour and by enhancing the internalization of the social rules.

## Juvenile Delinquency

As children grow older those problems which involve disobedience of rules and inability to resist temptations are labelled "conduct" disorders if they have antisocial connotations. And they are called "delinquency" if they infringe the law. The trouble with a term like "juvenile delinquency" is that it is not possible to draw a clearcut line of demarcation between delinquents and non-delinquents. Recent surveys have shown that it is not only, or even usually, children known to the police who have committed acts contrary to the law. A large number of English grammar-school boys were asked (Gibson, 1967) about their delinquencies. About one-half of them admitted committing some sort of antisocial act. A large proportion of them, moreover, said that they had committed an act which could have landed them in a Juvenile Court had they been found out. Over half of the boys had stolen money, two-thirds had shop-lifted and nine out of ten had stolen something from school. In a survey (Elmhorn, 1965) of 1,000 school children aged nine to fourteen carried out in Norway and Sweden, 89% confessed to petty illegal offences, 39% ordinary theft, 17% breaking in and 14% wilful damage to property. In a Polish study (Malewska and Muszynski, 1970) of children aged twelve to thirteen, over 63% admitted that they had taken other people's property.

The term "juvenile delinquent" is a very flexible one, being in part a function of a particular set of laws and law enforcement policies. Although many children commit "delinquent" acts at one time or another, certain children are more likely than others to avoid detection. Children who attend a school which is conscious of its good name are, if caught stealing, more likely to have the incident dealt with privately between headmaster and parents. A boy who is caught shop-lifting is more likely to be dealt with leniently if he is known to come from a "respectable" middle-class home.

The point is that the term "juvenile delinquent" is basically an administrative one; the range of delinquent acts is enormous. Juvenile delinquents, too, are extremely diverse in their attributes. So unsuccessful have been the attempts to differentiate *sharply* between those who commit "delinquent" acts and non-offenders, in terms of intelligence, physique, personality, social background, and the like, that some theorists reject the concept of "delinquent behaviour" as a viable topic for scientific study. They have abandoned the search for general hypotheses to explain "delinquency" as such; they deny the possibility of accommodating this heterogeneous phenomenon within one explanatory model. Some researchers have concentrated on particular categories of crime and law-breaker. A distinction has been drawn between "social" and "psychological" offenders. In the former case it is suggested that delinquent activity may be a rational strategy, an adaptation to a delinquent subculture, to privation, or some other social reality. The psychological offender is thought to manifest delinquent behaviour as a consequence of some innate defect or as an expression of some underlying emotional disturbance. These categories will be considered shortly.

Despite the difficulties of formulating general theories of delinquency, and the paucity of hard facts concerning the problem, theorists have not been deterred from making the attempt. Sadly, none of the brave efforts at a major synthesis are entirely convincing, and our understanding of the nature of juvenile delinquency remains at an elementary level.

Among the more plausible attempts at a general theory—and one which puts the origins of criminal behaviour within a developmental context— is that of Trasler. His striving after an all-embracing theory is made explicit in the title of his monograph "The Explanation of Criminality" (Trasler, 1962). Trasler's ideas link up strongly with the social learning theories of Mowrer (1960), and the personality theories of Eysenck (1964). Trasler begins with the observation made by Walker (1965) that most crimes take the form of acquisitive, violent or sexually-aggressive behaviour which may, with reason, be attributed to basic and universal human motives. The delinquent range of acts is separated from non-criminal behaviours by the fact that they are prohibited by the criminal law and often (but not necessarily) by the mores or norms of society. Most crimes do not depend upon special skills or techniques. It follows, Trasler argues, that the fundamental problem in explaining delinquency or criminality is not to discover the manner in which criminal habits are acquired, but to explain why certain individuals fail to inhibit those activities that society formally proscribes, and which the majority of the population has learned to avoid.

On reflection, the behaviour of small children is often anti-social and judged by adult criteria, "delinquent". Toddlers lash out at each other, inflicting pain; they "steal" each other's possessions, and what is more, show no remorse after transgressing the rules. They do not need to learn "delinquent" behaviours or attitudes. These tendencies occur quite spontaneously and to the child they have a logic of their own. What happens, as the child matures, is that he must learn to avoid certain behaviours; that is to say he must be trained to check certain impulses and to regulate his behaviour in terms of certain informal and formal rules of conduct (including the law). The basic question to be answered by a theory of delinquency is not therefore "Why are some children delin-quent?" but "Why are most children eventually law-abiding, given that in early childhood they were so anti-social?"

Ryall (1968) states that

one possible answer is that as we grow up we learn the nature of the law, that if we perform certain acts we may be punished. This answer suggests that we balance the benefit from doing the forbidden act against the risk of being caught and the probable punishment that would follow. If we do not fancy the penalty, even at the small risk of being caught, we do not commit the offence. This calculation almost certainly occurs in the minds of many motorists before they park in a no-parking zone or before they drive having had too much to drink.

However, where acts of dishonesty are concerned for most people this calculating process does not take place. Even if the circumstances are such that the chance of detection is nil, they still do not steal. Most people have an aversion to stealing which cannot simply be explained as being caused by a fear of the consequences.

This strong aversion to dishonest acts is sometimes explained in terms of our conscience or "super-ego". However, these concepts do not bring us closer to answering the basic question of *how* most people come to develop this strong aversion, or conscience, or super-ego. When that question is answered, an explanation can be sought as to why some people do not develop this aversion and so are likely to become criminal. The answer put forward by theorists like Eysenck and Trasler is that children *learn* not to be anti-social. We have already seen (pages 197–199) the role of conditioning in training the child to avoid certain acts. When a child is conditioned *not* to do something the process is known as "passive avoidance conditioning"; responses of fear and anxiety are elicited automatically in the youngster when he contemplates transgressing the rules. These emotions persist throughout his life if the early conditioning processes have been effective. Learning theorists suggest that delinquents are youngsters whose early social conditioning has been ineffective, and who consequently have failed to develop an adequate conscience—in other words, a strong aversion to acts of dishonesty, a capacity to resist temptation and a feeling of remorse when this breaks down. These are among the bastions which support the law-abiding inclinations of society.

The question of why there should be such dramatic individual differences in social conditioning usually finds an answer in terms of personality factors (in part inherited) and different constellations of environmental factors (e.g., particular patterns of child-rearing). Specific defects in avoidance learning due to an inability to form anticipatory fear responses have been postulated (see page 207). The effectiveness of social conditioning, after all, depends upon the strength of the unconditioned response (anxiety) with which it is associated. Another constitutional factor—"conditionability"—is also suggested. Eysenck (1964) postulates the existence of stable individual differences in conditionability, i.e., in speed of acquisition and resistance to extinction of conditioned responses of all kinds. These differences are thought to be a function of personality (extraversion–introversion). As we saw on page 204, extraverts are thought to be resistant to conditioning and therefore less readily socialized than introverts. Franks (1956) states that there are two categories of recidivists: "the introverted ones, who condition well and who readily learn the rules of their (undesirable) environment and the extraverted—possibly psychopathic—ones, who condition poorly and who find great difficulty in learning the rules of their environment (desirable or otherwise)". It has always seemed a problem to the author, that the relatively simple conditioning of small scale reflexes (as in eye-blink conditioning) has to bear an enormously heavy burden in its extrapolation to such complex processes as are implied in social training. It is not self-evident that the personality factors relevant to eye-blink experiments are also pivotal to the many-sided story of socialization. While it may prove to be an important theme, its centrality is questionable. In any event, several investigators have failed to demonstrate differences between psychopaths (individuals who manifest a dramatic failure to be socialized) and others, in terms of eye-blink conditioning (e.g., Miller, 1966). The generality of conditionability as a personality variable is also in dispute (see: Trasler, 1973). Another problem arises from the observation that although learning theory predicts quite well the over-representation of delinquent behaviour in the lower social classes, it does not predict the *relatively* late entry of children into the delinquent ranks. If delinquency is caused by the failure of early social conditioning, it might be predicted that a delinquent's acts would be predominantly antisocial from earliest childhood. This is so in some cases; but many boys in approved schools do not make their first court appearance until after they have turned twelve and their previous history is unremarkable for deviant acts. Antecedent events other than faulty conditioning are necessary to account for the relatively late onset of some delinquent or criminal careers.

On the environmental side, where there is a strong dependent relationship between a child and his parents, the sanction of withdrawal or the threat of withdrawal of love or approval evoke intense anxiety. We shall return to a detailed discussion of these parent–child factors shortly. Suffice it to say that social conditioning is most effective where sanctions are applied reliably and consistently. If many forbidden acts go unnoticed the training process will take longer, and might possibly go uncompleted. If misbehaviour is ever rewarded by giving it parental approval it may become difficult if not impossible subsequently to condition feelings of anxiety to that particular undesirable act. Socialization is particularly effective when training is presented in terms of a few well-defined principles. When a mother gives explanations and reasons as to *why* the child is punished and why she disapproves of a particular act she is providing the child with a cognitive structure or mental representation of the act (or category of acts) to which the anxiety becomes attached (see page 285). It is thought to be desirable that explanations are given in general terms as he gets older and can understand general principles. If a child steals from his friend's money box his mother may simply say "don't ever do that again" in which case he associates the punishment with stealing from his friend's money box. What the child needs to understand is that he is being punished for stealing, that all acts of theft are wrong. Some theorists (e.g., Trasler, op. cit.) argue that middle-class parents go to greater lengths in explaining and defining general principles in training their offspring than do working-class parents, which may contribute to the allegedly more effective social training (and lesser incidence of delinquent acts) of middle-class children.

Although a large number of young people commit crimes, few develop into adult offenders. After a steady increase in the frequency of delinquent acts during childhood, reaching a peak in later adolescence, there is a fairly sharp decline in the delinquency rates in the early twenties (see: Wright, 1971; and Chapter 4). The large majority of delinquents gradually merge with the law-abiding population—settled down perhaps by the responsibilities of a job, marriage and family life—and do not appear before the courts again.

Those who resort to crime in adult life tend in most cases to have a history of delinquency in their youth. The earlier they started to commit offences, the more gloomy is the outlook. Robins' study (Robins, 1966) of 524 children seen at the St. Louis Municipal Children's Guidance Clinic in the 1920's and re-examined when they were (on average) 43 years of age revealed that antisocial behaviour in childhood was a very powerful predictor of poor adult outcomes, superior predictively than any other symptoms. Social class was a poor predictor. In the case of a youngster who was only mildly antisocial, the fact of having an antisocial father greatly increased the risk of the child's antisocial behaviour as an adult.

A study of reform school (Borstal) boys (Gibbens, 1963), demonstrated that there is some truth in the theory that those convicted quite early in life are more likely to relapse into crime than those who are convicted later. Borstal boys who were convicted before the age of eleven had a 55% relapse rate while the figure was 46% for those who had their first conviction between the ages of sixteen and twenty-one. Glueck and Glueck (1968) also concluded from their findings that those who offend at a young age are likely to continue in this way and go on to commit the more serious crimes. Some of the family characteristics found as a background to juvenile delinquency are listed in Table IX below.

Delinquency is mainly a male phenomenon throughout the age range. Although it is usually thought of as a problem of adolescence, the fact is that the police do apprehend children under the age of thirteen on a large number and variety of offences, ranging from absconding from home to murder.

## Types of Delinquency

Hewitt and Jenkins (1946) formulated a theory in which individual differences in inhibitory controls are made to account for three patterns

TABLE IX. Contrasts between 500 delinquents and 500 nondelinquents with respect to percentage evidencing certain family characteristics and relationships (From S. and Eleanor Glueck, "Unravelling Juvenile Delinquency," Commonwealth Fund, New York, 1950.)

| Characteristic | Delinquents | Nondelinquents |
| --- | --- | --- |
| Mother mentally retarded | 33 | 9 |
| Father mentally retarded | 18 | 6 |
| Mother emotionally disturbed | 40 | 18 |
| Father emotionally disturbed | 44 | 18 |
| Drunkenness in mother | 23 | 7 |
| Drunkenness in father | 63 | 39 |
| Criminality in mother | 45 | 15 |
| Criminality in father | 66 | 32 |
| Haphazard routine of household | 30 | 16 |
| No family self-respect | 43 | 10 |
| Poor conduct standards in home | 90 | 54 |
| Unsuitable supervision of children by mother | 64 | 13 |
| No family group recreation | 67 | 38 |
| No cohesiveness in family | 25 | 1 |
| Indifferent, hostile or rejective attitudes of father toward boy | 60 | 19 |
| Indifferent, hostile or rejective attitudes of mother toward boy | 28 | 4 |
| Boy attached to mother | 65 | 90 |
| Boy attached to father | 32 | 65 |
| Father unacceptable for emulation by boy | 31 | 7 |
| Number of family moves (8 or more) | 53 | 18 |
| Boy has left home at some time | 71 | 9 |

of delinquency found among children. They distinguish between the following types of disorder:

(1) Over-inhibited neurotic behaviour with delinquent overtones;
(2) Unsocialized aggressive behaviour where the child is openly at odds with others;
(3) Socialized (pseudosocial) delinquency, where the child is on good terms with his peers but offends against the adult code, so that he may truant and steal.

These three categories of problem appear to be related in large part to parental attitudes. The nature of this relationship is illustrated in terms of the Figure we discussed on page 153, which is reproduced again below. (The severity of the child's behaviour problems will depend on how extreme the parental attitudes are plus other factors such as the child's inherited constitution and his life experiences.)

Hewitt and Jenkins (op. cit.) conceive of the personality as having a

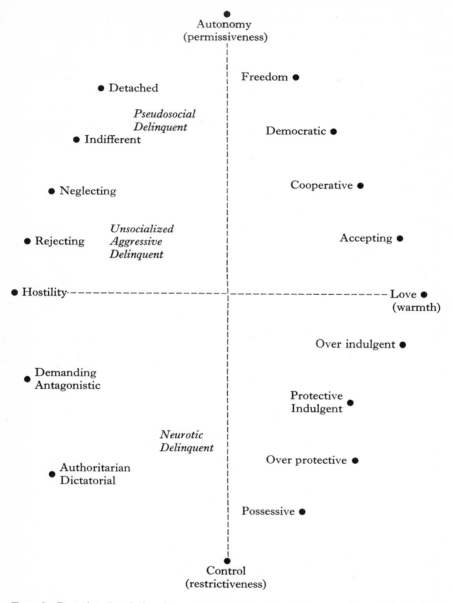

FIG. 8. Postulated relationship between type of delinquent (see: Hewitt and Jenkins, 1946) and parent-child relations.*
(* Plotted in terms of Schaefer's circumplex model of maternal behaviour; see: Schaefer, 1959).

central core of atavistic impulses on the lines of the Freudian notion of "id". In the normal individual there is a surrounding shell of inhibition, corresponding to the concept of the superego. Their studies suggest that some individuals develop an excessively rigid shell of inhibition. They become overinhibited and react to intense intrapsychic superego-id conflicts by developing neurotic symptoms. The *neurotic* delinquent is described as sensitive, over-inhibited, lonely and anxious. He suffers from strong feelings of inadequacy and inferiority, tends to be submissive, apathetic and dreamy. His delinquencies take the form of compulsive and solitary stealing, furtive sadism and sexual problems such as exhibitionism and voyeurism. He does feel guilt for the wrongs he commits. He is usually well-behaved at school and reasonably obedient and truthful at home. Wright (1971) gives a thumb-nail sketch of his home background:

The neurotic delinquent tends to come from a small, middle-class and intact family, where attachments to parents are strong, where the mother is over-protective and over-anxious, where there is some emotional instability in either or both of the parents, and where the parents set austere and uncompromising standards for their children. Sanctions against the child are predominantly psychological, in the sense that they threaten rejection or withdrawal of love. These are the conditions which in psychoanalytic theory are said to lead to strong identification with the parents and the development of a harsh, rigid and irrational superego. When they do not result in neurosis or compulsive delinquency, they produce the highly conscientious and tense character, who leads an impeccably respectable life, but whose own instinctual satisfactions are severely curtailed, and who cannot tolerate "immorality" in others.

For another type of child brought up in a run-down overcrowded slum area, delinquency may almost be a way of life. Take the so-called *pseudosocial* delinquent; he is a loyal gang member and has a normal shell of inhibition. But he shows it only towards members of his own group. There is little inhibition of antisocial tendencies in relation to the out-group. Though he is suspicious, defiant and hostile to those in authority (for example, parents, teachers and the police) he is not a victim of violent uncontrollable impulses, but adjusts well to other members of his peer group and feels a sense of obligation toward them. In many ways the gang is a substitute family for the child and an emotional crutch.

In the case of the families of *pseudosocial delinquents* it is not the actively rejecting and punitive attitudes which are rampant, but rather parental neglect, coldness and distance. Parent–child relationships have the quality of mutual indifference about them. These boys are environmental offenders in the sense that they conform to the life-style of the gang and the neighbourhood because the gang is their only source of emotional sustenance.

Other individuals have another sort of problem; they (and society) are the victims of their inadequate shell of inhibition. The under-development of inhibitory processes produces severe problems: those of the unsocial-ized aggressive individual who gives free run to his primitive impulses. The *unsocialized, aggressive* delinquent is defiant of authority, malicious, sullen and characteristically hostile and coercive to the people around him. He is always putting the blame on others, and feels hard-done-by and persecuted. He is relatively unmoved by praise or punishment and he shows little guilt or remorse. He is usually unpopular because of his cruelty and malice, but at the same time he is feared for his aggression and vengefulness, and respected as a leader. He needs his gang around him, not because of the friendship it provides, but the self-esteem its subservience gives him.

The *unsocialized aggressive delinquent* most often comes from a lower-class family in which the parent–child interactions are marked by mutual suspicion, hostility and rejection. The parents punish severely and are inconsistent and unjust. It is difficult for the child to identify with such parents and thus the aggression they provoke is not intropunitive as it is in the case of a child with a conscience. It is turned outwards and vented on society.

Whatever the overall constellation of factors in the home, there seem to be three main influences on delinquent patterns of behaviour which are related to the discipline used in that home. There is firstly the type of home where the policy seems to be "anything goes!" The discipline is lax or non-existent because of "don't-care" or hostile attitudes toward the child. Most likely the attitudes of such parents are inconsistent. The child's real parents may or may not be living together. The parents' control, tenuous at the best of times, may have been so undermined that even young children come and go as they please, and at all hours of the night. The absence of a father, or the presence of a father with whom there is a disturbed relationship, is commonly a factor related to the incidence of delinquent behaviour (see: Rutter, 1972). But why should inconsistent discipline play such a part in delinquent patterns of behaviour? Wright (1971) explains this as follows:

Not only will the delinquent be confused over what is right and wrong, but he will be angered by injustice and he will learn that whether or not he is rewarded or punished is not predictably related to his own behaviour. This last point is of great importance. In a home where parents are consistent, the child learns that his own behaviour to a large extent determines how others respond to him and this is a crucial element in his general feeling that he can exercise some control over how others behave towards him. If, on the other hand, the child learns to dissociate his own behaviour from the rewards and punishments that come from others, he will feel that bit more powerless to influence his social environment. This in turn will contribute to that general alienation from society which sociologists have noted to be a feature of delinquents. Many students of delinquency have observed the prevalence of fatalistic attitudes among delinquents. To them it seems that the only way they can elicit a predictable response in others is through provoking their angry indignation by acts of theft and vandalism.

Secondly, there is a type of home which is almost the opposite of the one we have just looked at. The child is given no freedom whatsoever; all signs of independence are stamped on. The parents lay down hundreds of cast iron rules which are enforced by punishment. Outsiders introduced by the child are discouraged by the parents. This repressive regime invites rebellion.

Thirdly, there is the association we observed in Chapter 11, between the excessive use of physical punishment by parents and delinquent (in particular, antisocial aggressive) behaviour. Physical assaults carried out persistently against a background of no affection, tend to provoke retaliatory aggression in the child which in turn is the beginning of a slippery slope toward delinquent behaviour.

## The Child's Peer Group

In urban environments, the pre-adolescent children (and especially the adolescent youngsters) tend to acquire their values more and more from outside the family; their peers tend to replace to some extent the parents as interpreters and enforcers of the moral code. This is especially so now that we live in a period of rapid social change and rapid communication. Changes in attitudes and values are so quick to occur and so radical in nature that we get a hiatus between one generation and the next, the so-called generation gap. Such an alienation between parent–child generations adds to the role of age mates in the socialization process.

Wright (1971) provides a guide to the different types of character suggested by the available research evidence. The typology, which (as he admits) is somewhat speculative is set out in Fig. 9. It describes six main types of character, arranged like a two-dimensional map.

The horizontal line indicates the relative importance during upbringing of the two major socializing influences: the child's parents and other adults in authority, and his peer group. The mid-point represents a hypothetical point of balance between these two influences. The mid-point of this horizontal dimension also represents a predominance of relationships of mutual respect in upbringing, that is a rich experience of individual friendships and democratic moments with adults. The vertical dimension has four related meanings. It indicates the degree of effectiveness of the socializing agent and therefore also the degree of internalization of that influence. It is also an index of the extent to which the child's character is *currently* under the control of that influence. We can see from

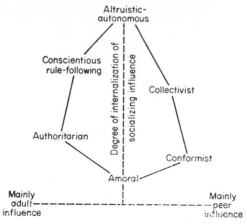

Fɪɢ. 9. The character typology. (Adapted from Wright 1971.)

this diagram that both the *amoral* and the *altruistic-autonomous* types of character are relatively free of the influences of both authority and the social group, the former because they have never come under their influence, and the latter because they have grown beyond it. As a consequence, this vertical line also represents the degree of developmental maturity of the character. Two of the typologies are relevant to our discussion of delinquency.

The distinctive features of the *conformist* character, as we saw on page 201, arise from the fact that attachment to group norms takes precedence over parental norms. If the norms involve antisocial acts he will be delinquent (something which happens in the case of the "pseudosocial" delinquent). He experiences shame rather than guilt. He feels anger on behalf of his group, either against outsiders or against insiders who fail to conform.

In the case of the *amoral* character, temptation is never resisted out of obligation to a moral rule or out of concern for others; it is only resisted, if at all, out of self-interest. For example, the fear of the immediate and certain consequences of an act may be sufficient to inhibit it. Guilt feeling and self-blame are not in his repertoire, though misdeeds may be followed by action intended to avert punishment. Altruistic action, if it occurs at all, takes the form of advance payment for some future benefit—never for past benefits received nor out of sympathy for others. Though he may be able to explain what the moral value of his society is, they have no real significance for him, and his reasoning on moral issues is dominated by the pursuit of pleasure and the avoidance of pain.

Wright has this to say about the amoral character:

. . . it includes the *premoral infant*, the *psychopath*, and the *unsocialized aggressive delinquent*. But we must also suppose that there is the *normally amoral* person, who may have learned the art of simulating moral sentiment and who may be adept at exploiting the self-restraint of others, but who feels no moral compunctions himself. If intelligent, and captured by the desire for power, fame or wealth, he may well be numbered among the successful in society. Such a person is likely to have had an upbringing devoid of close, affectionate relationship and filled with the amoral example of others (Wright, 1971).

Children with long histories of delinquent behaviour have been treated by means of behaviour therapy. Wetzel (1966) describes the treatment of a problem of compulsive stealing—the case of a ten-year-old boy named Mike who had a long history of uncontrollability and stealing (Wetzel, 1966). After he had been placed in a Home for mildly disturbed children, his behaviour improved somewhat, with the exception of his stealing and bedwetting. Because it was thought that he might be stealing to obtain affection, Mike was then placed in a foster family described as "exceptionally warm". An attempt was made to provide him with a loving maternal figure. Unfortunately his behaviour deteriorated, and after several months he was readmitted to the Children's Home. The stealing appeared to get worse; it occurred almost every day in the Home, school or shops, and had a disruptive effect on the boy's relationships with the other children and the staff. A programme called "response cost" was applied to his problem. A good relationship between Mike and Maria, a cook in the Home, was made use of in the treatment—one which involves the temporary deprivation of customary rewards or privileges. Maria agreed to cooperate in creating opportunities for this relationship to form the basis of social reinforcement for appropriate behaviour by the boy. It was arranged that Maria would be told whenever Mike was found to have stolen something; as soon as possible she would then say to him, "I'm sorry you took so-and-so's . . . because now I can't let you come home with me tonight". She would not enter into any further discussion of the matter with him. This constituted the "cost" of stealing. In the later stages of the programme, a positive reinforcement programme for non-stealing was added. According to the records kept, after three and a half months on the regime, stealing had stopped completely, and this continued during another two months of systematic follow-up.

These principles have also been used in treatment to modify aggressive problems. Burchard and Tyler (1965) report how a very difficult boy named Donny (aged 13) responded to such treatment. This youngster had been in an institution for delinquents since he was nine. The problems that had brought him there included behaviours that were criminal, disruptive, destructive and cruel. Donny was so uncontrollable that in the year before treatment was initiated, he had spent two hundred days off and on and recently on a continuous basis, in an isolation room. His intractable behaviour tended to attract considerable staff attention and this would lead to punishment. Later on the staff often felt guilty and visited the boy in isolation, where he was also given snacks. The other boys tended to reinforce Donny's misbehaviour with attention, praise and sympathy. In contrast, good behaviour brought little attention or praise because the over-extended staff had to focus their efforts on the troublesome boys. A new treatment programme was instituted in which any unacceptable behaviour requiring punishment was followed immediately by placement in isolation ("time out") for three hours, during which communication with staff and peers was reduced to bare essentials. The boy was given tokens (positive reinforcement) for certain periods of time spent out of isolation, with which he could pay for such things as cigarettes, trips to town, and cinema visits. Otherwise these privileges were not available to him. Over six months Donny became easier to control, he spent a third less time in isolation, and there was a decline in the seriousness of his transgressions.

# Epilogue
# What Happens to Children with Emotional Problems?

WE HAVE DEALT with a wide variety of problem children in the preceding chapters. The obvious question that comes to mind is: "What happens to problem children—in the short and long-term?" The "continuity hypothesis" suggests that the untreated, emotionally disturbed child is expected to become, eventually, an emotionally disturbed adult. The "intervention hypothesis" tells us that effective therapeutic intervention during childhood should not only improve the child's adjustment "here and now", but also ought to result in a noticeable reduction in the future incidence of adult mental disorders. Kagan and Moss (1962) find evidence for suggesting that the early years of school-going appear to be a sensitive period in personality development. The more enduring traits—those that continue into adulthood—become manifest from about 6 years of age to 10. Predictions before 6 for most personality variables are poor. Kagan and Moss (1960) found that the degree of continuity of behaviours depended upon whether the behaviours were in accord with society's norms. If they were, they tended to persist; if not, they slowly changed.

In the case of emotional problems, most are age-specific, i.e. the "symptoms" change from one phase of development to another. The exceptions include destructiveness, sombreness, jealousy, excessive reserve and attention-demanding (MacFarlane et al., 1954). When these were manifested at 6 or 7 years of age they were also likely to be present at 13 or 14. Children with *many* symptoms at one age tend to have many symptoms later on, but this prediction cannot be made until the child has reached the age of six or seven (Robins, 1972). Very early behaviours and problems have poor predictive value (see: Kohlberg et al., 1972). Most children with emotional problems seen in clinics, whether treated or untreated, are considered as well or improved a year or two later. It is the neurotic type of problem which is much more liable to disappear or improve in the short term than are psychotic symptoms or antisocial behaviour. Robins (op. cit.) believes that there are fairly firm criteria for predicting *which* children will develop a behaviour problem, however we define the disorder. To quote the guide lines:

We know that psychiatric illness in the parents is reflected in an elevated rate of behaviour problems in their children, and that antisocial parents have antisocial children. When the parents' antisocial behaviour takes the form of physical abuse of the child, the child shows very severe disability. We also know that childhood behaviour problems are more common in the lower classes, and that this relationship may be largely accounted for by the higher prevalence of antisocial and psychiatrically ill parents in the lower classes. To what extent the influence of the parent's disturbance on the child's behaviour is genetic and to what extent it is environmental is still an unanswered question.

We can also predict certain behaviour disorders of later childhood from behaviour first observable around the age of starting school. A combination of poor relationships with schoolmates, working below intellectual capacity, and failing to accept the teacher's authority predict delinquency. A high level of neurotic symptoms predict poor school success. Early behaviour predictors of other kinds of childhood disorders are not yet clearly identified (Robins, 1972).

There is some evidence about the adult prognosis for disturbed children. Reports by Robins (1966) on the follow-up of some 500 child guidance clinic attenders, revealed that, for the most part, neurotic children become fairly well adjusted adults. The outcome for anti-social aggressive children was generally poor. Many in adult life were diagnosed as psychopaths, but the most striking finding was the very wide range of disturbances they showed when grown up. They exhibited very substantially increased rates of divorce, unemployment, financial dependency, social isolation, alcoholism, and psychiatric problems. In addition, they had a high rate of neurotic and somatic symptoms and poor physical health. Other childhood problems which are relatively permanent include infantile autism and childhood schizophrenia (see: Rutter, 1965). Robins (op. cit.) observes that psychotic children do tend to have an "illness" that continues into adulthood, but it accounts for only a small proportion of hospitalized adults. The evidence suggests that children with psychoses appearing before puberty are never or almost never, presenting an early form of adult schizophrenia. Many, however, will spend a large part of their lives in institutions.

What might be called "normal" problems—the type which occur in connection with development—have a high probability of diminishing and disappearing as the child gets older. It is possible to list the following problems as being relatively short-lived in duration: school phobia, tics, shyness, nervousness, tantrums, reading problems, seclusiveness, fears, hypersensitivity and speech problems. Even the more worrying so-called "neurotic" problems of childhood are not very good predictors of adult psychopathology. In other words, a large number of problem children grow up to attain a reasonably adequate adult adjustment. It is almost impossible to postulate any clear-cut causal relationship between the emotional problems of childhood and later psychiatric disabilities.

Furthermore, the evidence (Levitt, 1971) suggests that about two in every three children improve whether or not they receive systematic psychotherapy. Theorists like Eysenck (1969a) conclude that the evidence fails to prove that psychotherapy facilitates the recovery of neurotic patients because the results are no better than the spontaneous recovery rates. (An exception is often made to this generalization in the case of behaviour therapy (see: Paul, 1966; Rachman, 1962).) Of course, statistics and criteria of recovery are debatable issues and these criticisms of psychotherapy have not gone unchallenged (see: Malan, 1959). Apart from questioning the criticisms in general terms, it is suggested that the statistics mask the success rates of skilled therapists who may do better than the spontaneous remission rates and the effects of psychonoxious therapists who may do worse. Whatever the facts may be about the usefulness of psychotherapy, the worried mother with a disturbed child needs help at a particular moment in time and this cannot be denied her.

# Appendix

J. D. AND H. B. KRUMBOLTZ * have described thirteen principles which concern the modification of the important controlling variables involving the treatment of children's problems; these are described below. Practical examples in the text which illustrate these principles are referred to in parentheses.

## Strengthening New Behaviour Patterns

(1) *Positive Reinforcement:* In order to improve or increase a youngster's performance of certain acts, matters are arranged so that an immediate reward follows the correct performance of the desired behaviour (see page 161).

## Developing New Behaviour Patterns

(2) *Successive Approximations:* In order to encourage a child to act in a way in which he has seldom or never before behaved, approximations to the correct act are rewarded. The successive steps to the final behaviour require an increasingly rigorous criterion of the approximation to be reinforced (page 111).

(3) *Modelling:* In order to teach a child a new pattern of behaviour the child is given the opportunity to observe a person who is significant to him, performing the desired behaviour (page 256).

(4) *Cueing:* In order to train a child to act at a specific time, it is arranged for him to receive a cue for the correct performance just before the action is expected, rather than after he has performed incorrectly (page 164).

(5) *Discrimination:* In order to teach a child to act in a particular manner under one set of circumstances but not another, he is trained to identify the cues that differentiate between the appropriate and inappropriate circumstances. He is rewarded only when his action is appropriate to the cue (page 298).

* "Changing Children's Behaviour", Prentice-Hall, N.Y., 1972.

## Maintaining New Behaviour

(6) *Substitution:* In order to reinforce a child with a reward which was previously ineffectual, it is presented just before (or as close in time to) the moment in which a more effective reward is presented.

(7) *Intermittent Reinforcement:* In order to encourage a child to continue performing an established pattern of behaviour with few or no rewards, the frequency with which the correct behaviour is reinforced is gradually and intermittently decreased (page 164).

## Stopping Inappropriate Behaviour

(8) *Satiation:* To get a child to desist from acting in a particular way, he may be allowed or made to continue performing the undesired act until he tires of it (page 211).

(9) *Extinction:* To stop a child from acting in a particular way, conditions are arranged so that he receives no rewards following the undesired act (page 148).

(10) *Incompatible Alternative:* To stop a child from acting in a particular way, an alternative action that is inconsistent with, or cannot be performed at the same time as, the undesired act, is rewarded (page 177).

(11) *Negative Reinforcement:* To stop a child from acting in a particular way, it is arranged for him to terminate a mild aversive situation immediately by changing his behaviour in the desired direction (page 211).

## Modifying Emotional Behaviour

(12) *Avoidance:* To teach a child to avoid a certain type of situation, the situation to be avoided (or some representation of it) and some aversive condition (or its representation) are simultaneously presented to the child (page 164).

(13) *Fear Reduction:* To help a child overcome his fear of a particular situation, his exposure to the feared situation is gradually increased while he is otherwise comfortable, relaxed, secure or rewarded (page 246).

*Differential Reinforcement:* is a combination of (1) and (9). The stimulus with which reinforcement is to be connected is called the discriminative stimulus ($S^D$) while the stimulus with which reinforcement is not associated is referred to as S delta ($S^\Delta$). When a desired response is more likely to occur in the presence of the $S^D$ than in the presence of the $S^\Delta$ it is said that stimulus control has been established (page 172).

# Bibliography

ADORNO, T. W., FRENKEL-BRUNSWIK, E., LEVINSON, D. J., and LEVINSON, R. N (1950) "The Authoritarian Personality." Harper and Row, New York.

AGRAS, W. S. (1972) The behavioral therapies: Underlying principles and procedures. *In:* Agras, W. S. (Ed.) "Behaviour Modification: Principles and Clinical Applications." Little Brown, Boston.

AINSWORTH, M. D. (1963) The development of infant–mother interaction among the Ganda. *In:* Foss, B. M. (Ed.) "Determinants of Infant Behaviour II." 67–112. Methuen, London.

AINSWORTH, M. D., *et al.* (1962) "Deprivation of Maternal Care: A Reassessment of its Effects." World Health Organization, Geneva.

AINSWORTH, M. D. S. (1967) "Infancy in Uganda: Infant care and the growth of Love." Johns Hopkins University Press, Baltimore.

AINSWORTH, M. D. S. (1969) Object relations, dependency and attachment: A theoretical review of the infant–mother relationship. *Child Development,* **40** 969–1025.

AINSWORTH, M. D. S. (1970) Attachment and Dependency: A comparison. *In:* Gewirtz, J. L. (Ed.) "Attachment and Dependence: The utility of the concepts and of the distinctions between them." Academic Press, London and New York.

AINSWORTH, M. D., and BELL, S. M. (1970) Attachment, exploration and separation: illustrated by the behaviour of one-year-olds in a strange situation. *Child Develop.,* **41**, 49–67.

AINSWORTH, M. D. S., and WITTIG, B. A. (1969) Attachment and exploratory behavior of one-year-olds in a strange situation. *In:* Foss, B. F. (Ed.) "Determinants of Infant Behaviour IV", 111–136. Methuen, London.

AITKEN, R. C. B., ZEALLEY, A. K., and BARROW, C. G. (1972) The treatment of psychopathology in bronchial asthmatics. *In:* Physiology, Emotion and Psychosomatic Illness. Ciba Foundation Symposium 8, 375–380. Elsevier, Excerpta Medica, London.

ALBERTI, R. E., and EMMONS, M. L. (1971) "Your Perfect Right: A Guide to Assertive Behaviour." Impact, San Luis Odsipo, California.

ALEXANDER, F. (1935) The logic of emotions and its dynamic background. *Internat. J. Psychoanal,* **16**, 339–413.

ALEXANDER, F., and FRENCH, T. M. (1948) "Studies in Psychosomatic Medicine." Ronald Press, New York.

ALLPORT, G. W. (1937) "Personality: A Psychological Interpretation." Constable, London.

ALLPORT, G. S. (1960) "Personality and Social Encounter." Beacon Press, Boston.

ANASTASI, A. (1958) Heredity, environment and the question "How". *Psychol. Rev.*, **65**, 197–208.

ANDREWS, G. and HARRIS, M. (1964) "The Syndrome of Stuttering." *Clinics in Developmental Medicine*, **17**. Heinemann Medical Books.

ANNELL, A. L. (1953) "Pertussis in Infancy as a Cause of Behaviour Disorders in Children." *Boktryckeri A.B.*, **3**, 49. Almquist and Wiksells, Uppsala.

ANNETT, M., LEE, D. and OUNSTED, C. (1961) Intellectual disabilities in relation to lateralized features in the E.E.G. *Proc. Second National Spastics Society Study Group*, Heinemann, Bristol, London.

ANTHONY, E. J. (1957) An experimental approach to the psychopathology of childhood: Encopresis. *Brit. J. Med. Psychol.*, **30**, 146–175.

ANTHONY, E. J. (1958) An experimental approach to psychopathology of childhood: autism. *Brit. J. Med. Psychol.*, **31**, (3 and 4) 211–225.

ANTHONY, E. J. (1959) An experimental approach to the psychopathology of childhood: sleep. *Brit. J. Med. Psychol.*, **32**, 19–37.

ANTONOVSKY, H. F. (1959) A contribution to research in the area of the mother–child relationship. *Child Develop.*, **30**, 37–51.

ARGYLE, M. (1964) Introjection: a form of social learning. *Brit. J. Psychol.*, **55**, 391–402.

ARONFREED, J. (1969) The concept of internalization. *In:* Goslin, D. A. (Ed.) "Handbook of Socialization Theory and Research," 263–324. Rand McNally, Chicago.

ARONFREED, J. (1961) The nature, variety and social patterning of moral response to transgression. *J. Abnormal Soc. Psychol.*, **63**, 223–240.

ARONFREED, J. (1964) The origins of self-criticism. *Psychol. Rev.*, **71**, 193–218.

ARONFREED, J. (1966) The internalization of social control through punishment. *Proc. of 18th International Congress of Psychology*, Moscow.

ARONFREED, J. (1968) "Conduct and Conscience." Academic Press, New York and London.

ARONFREED, J. (1969) The Problem of Imitation. *In:* Lipsitt, L. P. and Reese, H. W. (Eds.) "Advances in Child Development and Behaviour," Vol. IV, Academic Press, New York and London.

ARONFREED, J., and LEFF, R. (1963) "The effects of intensity of punishment and complexity of discrimination upon the learning of internalized suppression." Unpubl. manuscript, University of Pennsylvania.

ARONFREED, J., and REBER, A. (1965) Internal behavioural suppression and the timing of social punishment. *J. Pers. and Social Psychol.*, **1**, 3–16.

ARSENIAN, J. M. (1943) "Young children in an insecure situation." *J. Abnorm. Soc. Psychol.*, **38**, 225–249.

ASCH, S. E. (1952) "Social Psychology." Prentice-Hall, New York.

ASCH, S. E. (1956) Studies of independence and conformity: I. A minority of one against a unanimous majority. *Psychol. Mongr.*, **70** (9), No. 416.

ASH, G. (1949) The reliability of psychiatric diagnosis. *J. Abnorm. Soc. Psychol.*, **44**, 272–276.

ASRATIAN, E. A. (1965) "Compensatory Adaptations, Reflex Activity and the Brain." Pergamon Press, Oxford.

AUSUBEL, D. P., BALTHAZAR, E. E., ROSENTHAL, I., BLACKMAN, L. S., SCHPOONT, S. H., and WELKOWITZ, J. (1954) Received parent attitudes as determinants of children's ego structure. *Child Develop.*, **25**, 173–183.

AUSUBEL, D. P., and SULLIVAN, E. V. (1970) "Theory and Problems of Child Development." (2nd ed.) Grune and Stratton, London.

AVAKIAN, S. A. (1961) The applicability of the Hunt-Minnesota Test for Organic Brain Damage to children between the ages of ten and sixteen. *J. Clin. Psychol.*, **17**, 45–49.

AX, A. F. (1953) Physiological differentiation between fear and anger in humans. *Psychosom. Med.*, **5**, 433–442.

BANCROFT, J. H. J. (1970) Homosexuality in the male. *Brit. J. Hosp. Med.*, **3**, 168–181.

BANDURA, A. (1960) Relationship of family patterns to child behaviour disorders. *Progress Report, Stanford Univ. Proj.* No. **M.1734**, US Publ. Health Serv.

BANDURA, A. (1962) Social learning through imitation. *In:* Jones, M. R. (Ed.) 211–269. *Nebraska Symposium on Motivation*, Univ. Nebraska Press, Nebraska.

BANDURA, A. (1965a) Vicarious processes: A case of no-trial learning. *In:* Berkowitz, L. (Ed.) "Advances in Experimental Social Psychology," Vol. 2. Academic Press, London and New York.

BANDURA, A. (1965b) Influence of models' reinforcement contingencies on the acquisition of imitative responses. *J. Pers. Soc. Psychol.*, **1**, 589–595.

BANDURA, A. (1969a) "Principles of Behaviour Modification." Holt, Rinehart and Winston, New York.

BANDURA, A. (1969b) Social-learning theory of identificatory processes. *In:* Goslin, D. A. (Ed.) "Handbook of Socialization Theory and Research." Rand McNally, New York.

BANDURA, A., and WALTERS, R. H. (1959) "Adolescent Aggression." Ronald Press, New York.

BANDURA, A., and WALTERS, R. H. (1963) "Social Learning and Personality Development." Holt, Rinehart and Winston, New York.

BANDURA, A. (1973) "Aggression; A Social Learning Analysis." Prentice-Hall, Englewood Cliffs, N.J.

BANNISTER, D. (1960) Conceptual structure in thought-disordered schizophrenics. *J. Ment. Sci.*, **106**, 1230–1249.

BANNISTER, D. (1963) The genesis of schizophrenic thought disorder: A serial invalidation hypothesis. *Brit. J. Psychiat.*, **109**, 680–686.

BANNISTER, D. (1966) A new theory of personality. *In:* Foss, B. M. (Ed.) "New Horizons in Psychology." Penguin Books, Harmondsworth.

BAR-ADON, A. and LEOPOLD, W. F. (1971) "Child Language: A Book of Readings." Prentice-Hall, Englewood-Cliffs, NJ.

BARON, R. M. (1966) Social reinforcement effects as a function of social reinforcement. *Psychol. Rev.*, **73**, 527–539.

BARRON, F. (1953) An ego-strength scale which predicts response to psychotherapy. *J. Consult. Psychol.*, **17**, 327–333.

BATESON, G., JACKSON, D. D., HALEY, J. and WEAKLAND, J. H. (1956) Toward a theory of schizophrenia. *Behav. Sci.*, **1**, 251–264.

BAUMRIND, D. (1966) Effects of authoritative parental control on child behaviour. *Child Develop.*, **37** (4), 887–907.

BAUMRIND, D. (1971) Current patterns of parental authority. *Develop. Psychol. Monogr.*, **4**, (1), Pt. 2. 1–103.

BAUMRIND, D. and BLACK, A. E. (1967) Socialization practices associated with dimensions of competence in pre-school boys and girls. *Child Develop.*, **38**, 291–327.

BAYLEY, N. (1955) On the growth of intelligence. *Amer. Psychol.*, **10**, 805–818.

BEACH, F. A. (1948) "Sexual Behaviour in Animals and Man." The Harvey Lectures, **43**, 259–279.

BEACH, F. A. (Ed.) (1965) "Sex and Behaviour." Wiley, New York.

BECK, H. S. and LAM, R. L. (1955) Use of the W.I.S.C. in predicting organicity. *J. Clin. Psychol.*, **11**, 154–157.

BECKER, W. C. (1964) Consequences of different kinds of parental discipline. *In:* Hoffman, M. L. and Hoffman, L. W. (Eds.) "Review of Child Development Research" (Vol. 1), 169–208. Russell Sage Foundation, New York.

BEECH, H. R. (1963) Some theoretical and technical difficulties in the application of behaviour therapy. *Bull. Brit. Psychol. Soc.*, **16**, 25–33.

BEECH, H. R. (1966) Personality theories of behaviour therapy. *In:* Foss, B. (Ed.) "New Horizons in Psychology." Penguin Books, Harmondsworth.

BEECH, H. R. (1969) "Changing Man's Behaviour." Penguin Books, Harmondsworth.

BEECH, R. and FRANSELLA, F. (1968) "Research and Experiment in Stuttering." Pergamon Press, Oxford.

BEHRENS, M. L. (1954) Child rearing and the character structure of the mother. *Child Develop.*, **25**, 225–238.

BEILIN, H. (1959) "Teachers' and clinicians' attitudes towards the behaviour problems of children: a reappraisal." *Child Develop.*, **30**, 9–25.

BELL, S. M. (1970) The development of the concept of the object and its relationship to infant–mother attachment. *Child Develop.*, **41**, 291–312.

BELLER, E. K. (1955) Dependency and independence in young children. *J. Genet. Psychol.*, **87**, 25–35.

BELLER, E. K. (1959) Exploratory studies of dependency. *Trans. N.Y. Acad. Sci.*, **20**, 414–426.

BELOFF, H. (1957) The structure and origin of the anal character. *Genet. Psychol. Monogr.*, **55**, 141–172.

BENDER, L. (1938) A Visual Motor Gestalt Test and its clinical uses. *Res. Monogr.*, No. **3**, New York.

BENDER, L. (1947) Childhood schizophrenia: a clinical study of 100 schizophrenic children. *Amer. J. Orthopsychiat.*, **17**, 40.

BENDER, L. (1966) The concept of plasticity in childhood schizophrenia. *In:* Hoch, P. and Zubin, J. (Eds.) "Psychopathology of Schizophrenia." Grune and Stratton, New York.

BENDER, L. (1969) The nature of childhood psychoses. *In:* Howells, J. G. (Ed.) "Modern Perspectives in International Child Psychiatry." Oliver and Boyd, Edinburgh.

BENDER, L. and GRUGETT, A. E. (1956) A study of certain epidemiological factors in a group of children with childhood schizophrenia. *Amer. J. Orthopsychiat.*, **26**, 131–143.

BENEDICT, R. (1934) Anthropology and the abnormal. *J. Gen. Psychol.*, **10**, 59–82.

BENSBERG, G. J. (1952) Performance of brain-injured and familial mental defectives on the Bender-Gestalt Test. *J. Consult. Psychol.*, **16**, 61–64.

BENTON, A. L. (1955) "The Revised Visual Retention Test: Clinical and Experimental Applications." University of Iowa, Iowa City.

BERECZ, J. M. (1968) Phobias of childhood. *Psychol. Bull.*, **70**, 694–720.

BERENDA, R. W. (1950) "The Influence of the Group on Judgments of Children." King's Crown Press, New York.

BERG, E. (1948) A simple objective technique for measuring flexibility in thinking. *J. Gen. Psychol.*, **39**, 15–22.

BERG, I. A. and BASS, B. M. (Eds.) (1961) "Conformity and Deviation." Harper, New York.

BERGER, A. (1965) A test of the double-bind hypothesis of schizophrenia. *Fam. Process.*, **4**, 198–205.

BERKOWITZ, L. (1962) "Aggression: A Social Psychological Analysis." McGraw-Hill, New York.

BERLYNE, D. E. (1960)"Conflict, Arousal and Curiosity." McGraw-Hill, New York.

BERNSTEIN, B. (1960) Language and social class. *Brit. J. Sociol.*, **11**, 271–276.

BERNSTEIN, B. (1964) Elaborated and restricted codes: their social origins and some consequences. *Amer. Anthropol.*, **66**, (6), 55–69.

BIJOU, S. W. (1968) Child behavior and development: A behavioral analysis. *Int. J. Psychol.*, **3**, (4), 221–238.

BIJOU, S. W. (1970) Reinforcement history and socialization. *In:* Hoppe, R. A., Milton, G. A. and Simmel, E. C. (Eds.) "Early Experiences and the Processes of Socialization." Academic Press, New York and London.

BIJOU, S. W. (1965) Experimental studies of child behaviour, normal and deviant. *In:* Krasner, L. and Ullmann, L. P. (Eds.) "Research in Behaviour Modification." 56–81. Holt, Rinehart and Winston, London.

BIJOU, S. W. and PETERSON, R. F. (1971) The psychological assessment of children: a functional analysis. *In:* McReynolds, P. (Ed.) "Advances in Psychological Assessment." Vol. 2, Science and Behaviour Books, Palo Alto.

BIRNEY, R. C., BURDICK, H. and TEEVAN, R. C. (1969) "Fear of Failure." Van Nostrand-Reinhold, New York.

BLOM, G. E. (1972) A psychoanalytic viewpoint of behavior modification in clinical and educational settings. *J. Amer. Acad. of Child Psychiat.*, **11**, (4), 675–693.

BLOMFIELD, J. M. and DOUGLAS, J. W. B. (1956) Bedwetting—prevalence among children aged 4–7. *Lancet*, **i**, 850–852.

BLOOM, B. S. (1964) "Stability and Change in Human Characteristics." Wiley, New York.

BOBBITT, R. A. (1958) The repression hypothesis studied in a situation of hypnotically induced conflict. *J. Abnorm. Soc. Psychol.*, **56**, 204–212.

BOWER, E. M. (1960) "The Early Identification of Emotionally Handicapped Children in School." Thomas, Springfield, Illinois.

BOWLBY, J. (1944) Forty-four juvenile thieves. *Int. J. Psychoanal.*, **25**.

BOWLBY, J. (1951) "Maternal Care and Mental Health." (2nd ed.) *Geneva World Health Organization: Monograph Series*, No. **2**.

BOWLBY, J. (1958) The nature of the child's tie to his mother. *Int. J. Psychoanal.*, **39**, 350.

BOWLBY, J. (1961) Childhood mourning and its implications for psychiatry. *Amer. J. Psychiat.*, **118**, 481.

BOWLBY, J. (1969) "Attachment and Loss: Vol. 1. Attachment." Hogarth Press, London.

BRACKBILL, Y. (1958) Extinction of the smiling response in infants as a function of reinforcement. *Child Develop.*, **29**, 115–124.

BRAINE, M. D. S., HEIMER, C. B., WORTIS, H. and FREEDMAN, M. (1966) Factors associated with impairment of the early development of prematures. *Monogr. Soc. Res. Child Develop.*, **30**, (4), Serial No. 106.

BRANDON, S. (1960) An Epidemiological Study of Maladjustment in Childhood. M. D. Thesis, Univ. of Durham.

BREGER, L. and McGAUGH, J. L. (1965) A critique and reformulation of "learning theory" approaches to psychotherapy and neurosis. *Psychol. Bull.*, **63**, 338–358.

BROGDEN, H. E. (1940) A factor analysis of 40 character traits. *Psychol. Monogr.*, **25**, No. 3 (Whole No. 234)

BRONFENBRENNER, U. (1958) Socialization and social class through time and space. *In:* Maccoby, E. E., Newcomb, T. M. and Hartley, E. L. (Eds.) "Readings in Social Psychology." 400–425. Holt, Rinehart and Winston, New York.

BRONFENBRENNER, U. (1960) Freudian theories of identification and their derivatives. *Child Develop.*, **31**, 15–40.

BROSSARD, M. and De CARIE, T. G. (1971) "The effects of three kinds of perceptual–social stimulation on the development of institutionalized infants: Preliminary report of a longitudinal study." *Early Child Develop. Care.*, **1**, 211–230.

BROWN, F. (1961) Depression and childhood bereavement. *J. Ment. Scie.*, **107**, 754–777.

BROWN, R. (1965) "Social Psychology." Collier-Macmillan, New York.

BROWN, P., and ELLIOT, R. (1965) Control of aggression in a nursery school class. *J. Exp. Child Psychol.*, **2**, (2) 103–107.

BROWN, J. S., MARTIN, R. C. and MORROW, M. W. (1964) Self-punitive behaviour in the rat: Facilitative effects of punishment on resistance to temptation. *J. Compar. Physiol. Psychol.*, **57**, 127–133.

BROWNING, R. M. and STOVER, D. O. (1971) "Behaviour Modification in Child Treatment." Aldine Atherton, Chicago.

BRUCH, H. (1954) Parent education or the illusion of omnipotence. *Amer. J. Orthopsychiat.*, **24**, 723.

BRUNER, J. S. (1959) The cognitive consequences of early sensory deprivation. *Psychosom. Med.*, **21**, 89–95.

BRUTTEN, E. J. and SHOEMAKER, D. J. (1968) "The Modification of Stuttering." Prentice-Hall, Englewood Cliffs.

BURCHARD, J. and TYLER, V. (1965) The modification of delinquent behaviour through operant conditioning. *Behav. Res., Ther.*, **2**, 245–250.

BURT, C. and HOWARD, M. (1952) The nature and causes of maladjustment among children of school age. *Brit. J. Stat. Psychol.*, **5**, 39–60.

BURTON, R. V. (1963) The generality of honesty reconsidered. *Psychol. Rev.*, **70**, 481–499.

BURTON, R. V., ALLINSMITH, W. and MACCOBY, E. E. (1966) Resistance to temptation in relation to sex of child, sex of experimenter, and withdrawal of attention. *J. Pers. Soc. Psychol.*, **3**, 253–258.

BUSS, A. H. and DURKEE, A. (1957) An inventory for assessing different kinds of hostility. *J. Consult. Psychol.*, **21**, 343–349.

BUTLER, N. R. and BONHAM, D. G. (1963) "Perinatal Mortality." Livingstone, Edinburgh.

CAIRNS, R. B. (1962) Antecedents of social reinforcer effectiveness. *Progress Report USPHS Research Grant M-4373.*

CALDWELL, B. M. (1964) The effects of infant care. *In:* Hoffman M. L. and Hoffman, L. W. (Eds.) "Review of Child Development Research." Russell Sage Foundation, New York.

CALDWELL, B. M. (1967) What is the optimal learning environment for the young child? *Amer. J. Orthopsychiat.*, **37**, 8-21.

CAMERON, K. (1955) Diagnostic categories in child psychiatry. *Brit. J. Med. Psychol.*, **28**, 67–71.

CAMPBELL, J. D. (1964) Peer relations in early childhood. *In:* Hoffman, M. L.

and Hoffman, L. W. (Eds.) "Review of Child Development Research," Vol. 1. Russell Sage Foundation, New York.

CAMPBELL, D., SANDERSON, R. E. and LAVERTY, S. G. (1964) Characteristic of a conditioned response in human subjects during extinction trials following a simple traumatic conditioning trial. *J. Abnorm. Soc. Psychol.*, **68**, 627–639.

CAPUTO, D. V., EDMONSTON, W. E., L'ABATE, L. and RONDBERG, S. R. (1962) Extended report: Type of brain-damage and intellectual functioning in children (Paper read at Midwestern Psychol. Assoc. meeting in Chicago, May 5). University School of Medicine Publ., Washington.

CAREERA, F. and ADAMS, P. L. (1970) An ethical perspective on operant conditioning. *J. Amer. Acad. of Child Psychiat.*, **8**, (4), 607-623.

CASE, H. W. (1960) Therapeutic methods in stuttering and speech blocking. *In:* Eysenck, H. J. (Ed.) "Behaviour Therapy and Neuroses." 207–220. Pergamon, Oxford.

CASLER, L. (1968) Perceptual deprivation in institutional settings. *In:* Newton, G. and Levine, S. (Eds.) "Early Experience and Behaviour." Thomas, Springfield, Illinois.

CASTANEDA, A., McCANDLESS, B. R. and PALERMO, D. S. (1956) The children's form of the Manifest Anxiety Scale. *Child Develop.*, **17**, 317–326.

CHAZAN, M. (1959) Maladjusted children in grammar schools. *Brit. J. Educ. Psychol.*, **29**, 198–206.

CHAZAN, M. (1962) School phobia. *Brit. J. Educ. Psychol.*, **32**, 209–217.

CHERRY, C. and SAYERS, B. Mc. A. (1956) Experiments upon the total inhibition of stammering by external control and some clinical results. *J. Psychosom. Res.*, **1**, 233–246.

CHEYNE, J. A. and WALTERS, R. H. (1969) Timing of punishment, intensity of punishment and cognitive structure in resistance to temptation. *J. Exper. Child Psychol.*, **8**, 127–138.

CHEYNE, J. A. and WALTERS, R. H. (1970) Punishment and prohibition. *In:* Craik, K. (Ed.) "New Directions in Psychology." Vol. 4. Holt, Rinehart and Winston, London.

CLARIDGE, G. S. (1967) "Personality and Arousal." Pergamon Press, Oxford.

CLARKE, A. D. B. (1968) Problems in assessing the later effects of early experience. *In:* Miller, E. (Ed.) "Foundations of Child Psychiatry." Pergamon Press, Oxford.

CLARKE, A. D. B. (1962) Problems in the role of early human learning. Unpubl. paper Symposium on Early Learning. Ann. Conf. of Br. Psychol. Soc.

CLARKE, A. M. and CLARKE, A. D. B. (1958) "Mental Deficiency: The Changing Outlook." (2nd ed. 1965). Methuen, London.

CLARKE, A. M. and CLARKE, A. D. B. (1959) 'Recovery from the effects of deprivation'. *Acta Psychologica*, **16**, 133–144.

CLARKE, A. M. and CLARKE, A. D. B. (1960) Some recent advances in the study of early deprivation. *J. Child. Psychol. and Psychiat.*, **1**, 26–30.

CLARKE, A. M., CLARKE, A. D. B. and REIMAN, S. (1958) Cognitive and social changes in the feeble-minded—three further studies. *Brit. J. Psychol.*, **49**, 144–157.

CLAUSEN, J. A. (1964) Family structure, socialization and personality. *In:* Hoffman, L. W. and Hoffman, M. L. (Eds.) *Review of Child Development Research.* (Vol. 2.) Russell Sage Foundation, New York.

CLAWSON, A. (1962) Relationship of psychological tests to cerebral disorders in children: a pilot study. *Psychol. Rep.*, **10**, 187–190.

CLYNE, M. B. (1966) "Absent." Tavistock Publications, London.
COATES, B., ANDERSON, E. P. and HARTUP, W. W. (1971) Inter-relations in the attachment behaviour of human infants. *Develop. Psychol.*, **6** (2) 218–230.
COLLINS, L. F., MAXWELL, A. E. and CAMERON, K. (1962) A factor analysis of some child psychiatric clinic data. *J. Ment. Sci.*, **108**, 274–285.
COOLIDGE, J. C., MILLER, M. L., TESSMAN, E. and WALDFOGEL, S. (1960) School phobia in adolescence: a manifestation of severe character disturbance. *Amer. J. Orthopsychiat.*, **30**, 599–607.
COOPER, J. B. and BLAIR, H. A. (1959) Parent evaluation as a determiner of ideology. *J. Gen. Psychol.*, **94**, 93–100.
COOPERSMITH, S. (1967) "The Antecedents of Self-Esteem." W. H. Freeman, London.
CORAH, A. E. J., PAINTER, P., STERN, J. A. and THURSTON, D. (1965) Effect of prenatal anoxia after seven years. *Psychol. Monogr. Gen. Appl.*, **79**, (3) Whole No. 596.
CORCORAN, D. W. J. (1961) Individual Differences in Performance after Loss of Sleep. Unpubl. Ph.D. Thesis., Univ. of Cambridge.
CORNER, G. W. (1944) "Ourselves Unborn." Yale Univ. Press, New Haven.
CORNER, G. W. (1961) Congenital malformations: the problem and the task. 7–17. *In:* "Congenital Malformations." Lippincott, Philadelphia.
COSTELLO, C. G. (Ed.) (1970) "Symptoms of Psychopathology." John Wiley, London.
COSTELLO, C. G. (1963) Behaviour therapy: criticisms and confusions. *Behav. Res. Ther.*, **1**, 159–161.
COSTELLO, C. G. (1967) Behaviour modification procedures with children. *Canad. Psychol.*, **8**, 73–75.
COTTON, C. B. (1941) A study of the reactions of spastic children to certain test situations. *J. Gen. Psychol.*, **58**, 27–44.
CRANDALL, V. J. (1963) Achievement. *In:* Stevenson, H. W. (Ed.) "Child psychology: The sixty-second year book of the National Society for the Study of Education." Part 1. 416–459. Univ. of Chicago Press, Chicago, Illinois.
CRANDALL, V. (1967) Achievement behaviour in young children. *In:* Hartup, W. W. and Smothergill, N. L. (Eds.) "The Young Child." 165–185. Washington D. C. Nat. Assoc. Educ. of Young Children.
CRANDALL, V. J. and BELLUGI, U. (1954) Some relationships of interpersonal and intrapersonal conceptualizations to personal-social adjustment. *J. Pers.*, **23**, 224–232.
CREAK, E. M. (1961) Schizophrenic Syndrome in Childhood: progress report of a working party (April 1961). *Cerebral Palsy Bull.*, **3**, 501–504.
CROSBY, N. D. (1950) Essential enuresis: successful treatment based on physiological concepts. *Med. J. Austr.*, **2**, 533–543.
CRUICKSHANK, W. M., BENTZEN, F. A., RATZEBURG, F. H. and TANNHAUSER, M. T. (1961) "A Teaching Method for Brain-Injured and Hyperactive Children." Syracuse Univ. Press, Syracuse.
CRUCHFIELD, R. S. (1955) Conformity and character. *Amer. Psychol.*, **10**, 191–198.
CUTLER, R., HEIMER, C. B., WORTIS, H. and FREEDMAN, M. (1965) The effects of prenatal and neonatal complications on the development of premature children at age 2½ years. *J. Gen. Psychol.*, **107**, (2) 261–276.
DANZIGER, K. (1971) "Socialization." Penguin Books, Harmondsworth.
DARWIN, C. (1859) "Origin of Species." John Murray, (Dent Ed.), London.
DAVIE, R., BUTLER, N. and GOLDSTEIN, H. (1972) "From Birth to Seven." (National Children's Bureau.) Longman, London.

DAWE, H. C. (1934) An analysis of two hundred quarrels of preschool children. *Child Develop.*, **5**, (2), 139–157.

DEKKER, E., BARENDREGT, J. T. and DE VRIES, K. (1961) "Allergy and neurosis in asthma. *In:* Jores, A. and Freyburger, H. (Eds.) "Advances in Psychosomatic Medicine." 235–240. R. Brunner Inc., New York.

DEKKER, E. and GROEN, J. (1956) Reproducible psychogenic attacks of asthma: A laboratory study. *J. Psychosom. Res.*, **1**, 58.

DEKKER, E., PELSER, H. E. and GROEN, J. (1957) Conditioning as a cause of asthmatic attacks. *J. Psychosom. Res.*, **2**, 97–108.

DE JONGE, G. A. (1971) Epidemiology of enuresis: a study of 10,000 children in Eindhoven and surroundings. *Paper presented at the Colloquium on Recent Advances in Knowledge of Bladder Control.*, Newcastle-upon-Tyne.

DIXON, J. J., DE MONCHAUX, C. and SANDLER, J. (1957) Patterns of anxiety: the phobias. *Brit. J. Med. Psychol.*, **30**, 34–40.

DOLLARD, J., DOOB, L., MILLER, N., MOWRER, O., SEARS, R., FORD, C. S., HOVLAND, C. I. and SOLLENBERGER, R. T. (1939) "Frustration and Aggression." Yale Univ. Press, New Haven.

DOLLARD, J. and MILLER, N. E. (1950) "Personality and Psychotherapy." McGraw-Hill, New York.

DOLPHIN, J. E. and CRUICKSHANK, W. M. (1951) The figure-background relationship in children with cerebral palsy. *J. Clin. Psychol.*, **7**, 228–231.

DOUGLAS, J. W. B. (1948) "Maternity in Great Britain." Oxford Univ. Press, London.

DOUGLAS, J. W. B. (1964) "The Home and the School." MacGibbon and Kee, London.

DOUGLAS, J. W. B. and BLOMFIELD, J. M. (1958) "Children Under Five." Allen and Unwin, London.

DOUGLAS, J. W. B., ROSS, J. M. and SIMPSON, H. R. (1968) "All Our Future." Peter Davies, London.

DRILLIEN, C. M. (1964a) "The Growth and Development of the Prematurely Born Infant." Williams and Wilkins, Baltimore.

DRILLIEN, C. M. (1964b) The effect of obstetrical hazard on the later development of the child. *In:* Gardner, D. (Ed.) "Recent Advances in Paediatrics." Churchill, London.

DUBIN, R. and DUBIN, E. R. (1965) Children's social perceptions: A review of research. *Child Develop.*, **36**, (3).

DUDLEY, D. L., MARTIN, C. J. and HOLMES, T. H. (1964) Psychophysiologic studies of pulmonary ventilation. *Psychosom. Med.*, **26**, 645–660.

DUFFY, E. (1962) "Activation and Behaviour." Wiley, New York.

DUNBAR, H. F. (1943) "Psychosomatic Diagnosis." Hoeber, New York.

DUNBAR, H. F. (1954) "Emotions and Bodily Changes." Columbia Univ. Press, New York.

DURFEE, R. A. (1969) Another look at conditioning therapy. *J. Rehabilitation*, **35**, (4), 16–18.

EBBS, J. H., TISDALL, F. H. and SCOTT, W. A. (1941/2) The influence of prenatal diet on the mother and child. *J. Nutrition.*, **22**, 515–526.

EISENBERG, L. (1957) Psychiatric implications of brain damage in Children. *Psychiat. Quart.*, **31**, 72–92.

EISENBERG, L. and KANNER, L. (1956) Early infantile autism. *Amer. J. Orthopsychiat.*, **26**, 556–566.

ELMHORN, K. (1965) Study in self-reported delinquency among schoolchildren. *In:* "Scandanavian Studies in Criminology." Tavistock Publications, London.

EPSTEIN, L. J. (1941) An analysis of teachers' judgements of problem children. *J. Gen. Psychol.*, **59**, 101–107.

ERIKSON, E. (1960) The problem of ego-identity. *In:* Stein, M. R. (Ed.) "Identity and Anxiety." Free Press of Glencoe, Illinois.

ERIKSON, E. (1965) "Childhood and Society." (Rev. Ed.) Penguin Books, Harmondsworth.

ERNHART, C. B., GRAHAM, F. K., EICHMAN, P. L., MARSHALL, J. M. and THURSTON, D. (1963) Brain-injury in the preschool child: some developmental considerations: (2) Comparison of brain-injured and normal children. *Psychol. Monographs. General and Applied.*, **77**, Whole No. 574.

ERON, L. D., WALDER, L. O., TOIGO, R. and LEFKOWITZ, M. M. (1963) Social class, parental punishment for aggression, and child aggression. *Child Develop.*, **34**, 849–867.

ERRERA, P. (1962) Some historical aspects of the concept, phobia. *Psychiat. Quart.*, **36**, 325–336.

ESCALONA, S. and HEIDER, G. M. (1959) "Prediction and Outcome: A Study in Child Development." Basic Books, New York.

EVANS, D. R. and HEARN, M. T. (1973) Anger and desensitization: A follow-up. *School Rep.*, **32**, 569–570.

EYSENCK, H. J. (1957) "The Dynamics of Anxiety and Hysteria." Routledge, Kegan Paul, London.

EYSENCK, H. J. (1960) The development of moral values in children. *Brit. J. Educ. Psychol.*, **30**, 11–21.

EYSENCK, H. J. (1960a) "Behaviour Therapy and the Neuroses." Pergamon Press, Oxford.

EYSENCK, H. J. (1960b) (Ed.) "Handbook of Abnormal Psychology." Pitman, London.

EYSENCK, H. J. (1964) "Crime and Personality." Routledge, Kegan Paul, London.

EYSENCK, H. J. (1967) "The Biological Basis of Personality." Thomas, Springfield, Illinois.

EYSENCK, H. J. (1968) A theory of the incubation of anxiety/fear responses. *Behav. Res. Ther.*, **6**, 309–321.

EYSENCK, H. J. (1969) "The Effects of Psychotherapy." Science House Inc., New York.

EYSENCK, H. J. (1970) Behaviour therapy and its critics. *J. Behav. Ther. and Exp. Psychiat.*, **1**, 5–15.

EYSENCK, H. J. and PRELL, D. B. (1951) The inheritance of neuroticism. *J. Ment. Sci.*, **97**, 441–465.

EYSENCK, H. J. and RACHMAN, S. (1965) "The Causes and Cures of Neurosis." Routledge, Kegan Paul, London.

FARETRA, G. and BENDER, L. (1962) Pregnancy and birth histories of children with psychiatric problems. *Proc. III World Cong. Psychiat.*, **2**, 1329.

FAULKNER, W. B. (1941) Bronchoscopic observations of changes due to psychic factors. *Pacific Coast Med.*, **8**, 22.

FELDMAN, I. S. (1953) Psychological differences among moron and borderline mental defectives as a function of etiology. Visual motor functioning. *Amer. J. Ment. Defic.*, **57**, 484–494.

FENICHEL, O. (1945) "The Psychoanalytic Theory of the Neuroses." Norton, New York.

FERREIRA, A. J. (1960) The pregnant mother's emotional attitude and its reflection upon the newborn. *Amer. J. Orthopsych.*, **30**, 553–561.

FERREIRA, A. J. (1965) Emotional factors in the prenatal environment. *Rev. Med. Psychosom.*, **4**, 16–17.

FERSTER, C. B. (1961) Positive reinforcement and behavioural deficits of autistic children. *Child Develop.*, **32**, 437–456.

FERSTER, C. B. and SKINNER, B. F. (1957) "Schedules of Reinforcement." Appleton-Century-Crofts, New York.

FERSTER, C. B. and DE MYER, M. K. (1961) The development of performance in autistic children in an automatically controlled environment. *J. Chronic Dis.*, **13**, 312–345.

FESHBACH, S. (1970) Aggression. *In:* Feshbach, S. and Mussen, P. H. (Eds.) "Carmichael's Manual of Child Psychology." 159–260. Wiley, London.

FESSEL, W. J. (1962) Mental stress, blood proteins and the hypothalamus. *Arch. Gen. Psychiat.*, **7**, 427–435.

FIELD, J. C. (1960) Two types of tables for use with Wechsler's intelligence scales. *J. Clin. Psychol.*, **16**, 3–7.

FINNEY, J. C. (1961) Some maternal influences on children's personality and character. *Genet. Psychol. Monogr.*, **63**, 199–278.

FLANAGAN, B., GOLDIAMOND, I. and AZRIN, N. (1958) Operant stuttering: The control of stuttering behaviour through response-contingent consequences. *J. Exp. Anal. Behav.*, **1**, 173–178.

FOXWELL, H. R. (1966) The development of social responsiveness to other children through experimental use of social reinforcement. An unpublished MA Thesis, University of Kansas.

FRANK, G. H. (1965) The role of the family in the development of psychopathology. *Psychol. Bull.*, **64**, 191–203.

FRANKS, C. M. (1956) Recidivism, psychopathy and personality. *Brit. J. Delinq.*, **6**, 192–201.

FRANKS, C. M. (1960) Conditioning and abnormal behaviour. *In:* Eysenck, H. J. "Handbook of Abnormal Psychology." Pitman, London.

FRANKS, C. M. and LEIGH, D. (1959) The theoretical and experimental application of a conditioning model to a consideration of bronchial asthma in man. *J. Psychosom. Res.*, **4**, 88.

FRASER, M. S. and WILKS, J. (1959) The residual effects of neonatal asphyxia. *J. Obstet. Gynaec.*, **66**, 748–752.

FREED, E. X. (1964) Frequencies of rotations on group and individual administration of the Bender-Gestalt test. *J. Clin. Psychol.*, **20**, 120–121.

FREEMAN, G. L. (1948) "The Energetics of Human Behaviour." Cornell Univ. Press, New York.

FRENCH, L. A. (1948) Psychometric testing of patients who had brain tumours removed during childhood. *J. Neurosurg.*, **5**, 173–177.

FRENCH, T. M. and ALEXANDER, F. (1941) Psychogenic factors in bronchial asthma. *Psychosomatic Medicine, Parts 1 and 2. Monogr. IV.* Nat. Res. Council, Washington.

FREUD, A. (1937) "Ego and the Mechanisms of Defence." Hogarth Press, London.

FREUD, S. (1966) "The Standard Edition of Sigmund Freud's Works." (S.E.) (Strachey, J., Ed.) Hogarth Press and the Institute of Psychoanalysis, London.
(1939) "Outline of Psychoanalysis." S.E. Vol. XXIII.
(1901–1905) "Three Essays on Sexuality." S.E. Vol. VII.
(1917) "Mourning and Melancholia." S.E. Vol. XIV.
(1923–1925) "The Ego and the Id." S.E. Vol. XIX.
(1900) "The Interpretation of Dreams." S.E. Vol. IV.

(1916–1917) "Introductory Lectures on Psychoanalysis." S.E. Vol. XVI.

FRIEDMAN, P. H. (1970) Limitations in the conceptualizations of behaviour therapists: Toward a cognitive-behavioural model of behaviour therapy. *Psychol. Reports.*, **27**, (1) 175–178.

FRIES, M. E. (1935) The formation of character observed in the well-baby Clinic. *Amer. J. Dis. Childhood.*, **49**, 28–42.

FROMM, E. (1956) "The Sane Society." Routledge, Kegan Paul, London.

FROST, B. P. (1960) An application of the method of extreme deviations to the W.I.S.C. *J. Clin. Psychol.*, **16**, 420.

FULLER, G. B. (1963) Perceptual considerations in children with a reading disability. (Paper read at) *American Psychological Association*, August 31.

FULLER, G. B. and LAIRD, J. T. (1963) "The Minnesota Percepto-Diagnostic Test." *J. Clin. Psychol. Monogr. Suppl.* **16**, 1–33.

FUNKENSTEIN, D. H., KING, S. H. and DROLETTE, M. (1954) The direction of anger during a laboratory stress-inducing situation. *Psychosom. Med.*, **16**, (5), 404–413.

FURNEAUX, W. D. (1965) "Manual of Nufferno Speed Tests." University of London Press, London.

GALLAGHER, J. J., BENOIT, E. P. and BOYD, H. F. (1956) Measures of intelligence of brain-damaged children. *J. Clin. Psychol.*, **12**, 69–71.

GALLAGHER, J. J. (1957) "A comparison of brain-injured and non-brain-injured mentally retarded children on several psychological variables." *Child Develop. Mongr.*, **22**, No. 2, Ser. 65, 1–79.

GARVEY, W. P. and HEGRENES, J. R. (1966) Desensitization techniques in the treatment of school phobia. *Amer. J. Orthopsychiat.*, **36**, 147–152.

GAY, M. J. and TONGE, W. L. (1967) The late effects of loss of parents in childhood. *Brit. J. Psychiat.*, **113**, 753–759.

GEBHARD, P. H., POMEROY, W. B., MARTIN, C. E., and CHRISTENSON, C. V. (1958) "Pregnancy, Birth and Abortion." Harper and Row, New York.

GELBER, H. and MEYER, V. (1965) Behaviour therapy and encopresis: The complexities involved in treatment. *Behav. Res. Ther.*, **2**, 227–231.

GELFAND, D. M. (Ed.) (1969) "Social Learning in Childhood." Brooks-Cole, Belmont.

GELFAND, D. M. and HARTMANN, D. P. (1968) Behaviour therapy with children: A review of and evaluation of research methodology. *Psychol. Bull.*, **69**, 204–215.

GESELL, A., HALVERSON, H. M., THOMPSON, H., ILG, F. L., CASTNER, B. M., AMES, L. B., and AMATRUDA, C. S. (1940) "The First Five Years of Life." Harper and Row, New York.

GESELL, A. and ILG, F. L. (1943) "Infant and Child in the Culture of Today." Harper and Row, New York.

GIBBENS, T. C. N. (1963) "Psychiatric Studies of Borstal Lads." Oxford University Press.

GIBSON, H. B. (1967) Self-reported delinquency among schoolboys and their attitudes to the police. *Brit. J. Soc. and Clin. Psychol.*, **6**, 168–173.

GIBSON, H. B. (1968) The measurement of parental attitudes and their relationship to boys' behaviour. *Brit. J. Ed. Psychol.*, **38**, 233–239.

GILES, D. K. and WOLF, M. M. (1966) Toilet training institutionalized severe retardates: An application of operant behaviour modification techniques. *J. Ment. Defic.*, **70**, 766–780.

GITTELMAN, M. (1965) Behaviour research as a technique in child treatment. *J. Child Psychol., and Psychiat.*, **6**, 251–255.

GLIDEWELL, J. C., GILDEA, M. C. L., DOMKE, H. R. and KANTOR, M. B. (1959) Behaviour symptoms in children and adjustment in public schools. *Human Organisation*, **18**, 123–130.

GLIDEWELL, J. and SWALLOW, C. (1968) "The Prevalence of Maladjustment in Elementary Schools." Univ. of Chicago Press, Chicago.

GLUECK, S. and GLUECK, E. (1950) "Unraveling Juvenile Delinquency." Harvard Univ. Press, Cambridge, Mass.

GLUECK, S. and GLUECK, E. (1968) "Delinquents and Nondelinquents in Perspective." Harvard Univ. Press, Cambridge, Mass.

GOLDBERG, S. and LEWIS, M. (1969) Play behaviour in the year-old infant: Early sex differences. *Child Develop.*, **40**, 22–31.

GOLDFARB, W. (1943) The effects of early institutional care on adolescent personality. *J. Exp. Educ.*, **12**, 106–129.

GOLDFARB, W. (1945) Psychological deprivation in infancy and subsequent adjustment. *Amer. J. Orthopsychiat.*, **15**, 247–255.

GOLDFARB, W. (1947) Variations in adolescent adjustment of institutionally reared children. *Amer. J. Orthopsychiat.*, **17**, 449–457.

GOLDSTEIN, K. and SCHEERER, M. (1941) Abstract and concrete behaviour, an experimental study with special tests. *Psychol. Monogr.*, **53**, No. 2.

GOODENOUGH, F. L. (1931) "Anger in Young Children." (Institute Child Welfare Monograph Series, No. 9.) Univ. Minnesota Press, Minneapolis.

GORER, G. (1955) *Exploring English Character*. Cresset Press, London.

GRACE, W. J. and GRAHAM, D. T. (1952) Relationship of specific attitudes and emotions to certain bodily diseases. *Psychosom. Med.*, **14**, 243–251.

GRAHAM, D. T., LUNDY, R. M., BENJAMIN, L. S., KABLER, J. D., LEWIS, W. C., KUNISH, N. O. and GRAHAM, F. K. (1962) Specific attitudes in initial interviews with patients having different "psychosomatic" diseases. *Psychosom. Med.*, **24**, 257.

GRAHAM, F. K., ERNHART, C. B. and BERMAN, P. (1960) Development in preschool children of the ability to copy forms. *Child Develop.*, **31**, 339–359.

GRAHAM, F. K. and KENDALL, B. S. (1960) Memory-for-Designs: Revised General Manual. *Percept. Motor Skills*, **11**, 147–188.

GRAHAM, P. J. (1967) Perceiving disturbed children. *Special Education*, **56**, 29–33.

GRAHAM, P. J. and RUTTER, M. L. (1968) The reliability and validity of the psychiatric assessment of the child, II. Interview with the parent. *Brit. J. Psychiat.*, **114**, 581–592.

GRAHAM, P. J., RUTTER, M. L., YULE, W. and PLESS, I. B. (1967) Childhood asthma: a psychosomatic disorder? Some epidemiological considerations. *Brit. J. Prevent. Soc. Med.*, **21**, (2), 78–85.

GRAHAM, P., RUTTER, M. and GEORGE, S. (1973) Temperamental characteristics as predictors of behaviour disorders in children. *Amer. J. Orthopsychiat.*, **43**, (3), 328–339.

GRAY, J. (1964) "Pavlov's Typology." Pergamon Press, Oxford.

GRAY, J. (1967) Strength of the nervous system, introversion–extraversion, conditionability and arousal. *Behav. Res. and Ther.*, **5**, 151–169.

GRAZIANO, A. M. (1971) (Ed.) "Behaviour Therapy with Children." pp. 1–29. Aldine Atherton, New York.

GREENACRE, P. (1945) The biological economy of birth. *In:* "The Psychoanalytic Study of the Child." 31–51. Internat. Univ. Press, New York.

GREGORY, I. (1965) Anterospective data following childhood loss of a parent. *Arch. Gen. Psychiat.*, **13**, 110–120.

GRIFFITH, W. (1952) "Behaviour Difficulties of Children as Perceived and Judged by Parents, Teachers and Children themselves." Univ. of Minnesota Press, Minneapolis.

GRINDER, R. E. (1962) Parental child rearing practices conscience and resistance to temptation of sixth-grade children. *Child Develop.*, **33**, 803–820.

GRINDER, R. E. (1964) Relations between behavioural and cognitive dimensions of conscience in middle childhood. *Child Develop.*, **35**, 881–891.

GROEN, J. (1951) Emotional factors in the aetiology of internal diseases. *J. of the Mount Sinai Hospital*, NY., **18**, (2).

GROEN, J. (1953) Psychosomatic aspects of bronchial asthma. *Nederl. Fydschr. Geniesk.*, **97**, 1946–1955.

HAGMAN, E. (1932) A study of fears of children of preschool age. *J. Exper. Educ.*, **1**, 110–130.

HAHN, E. (Ed.) (1956) "Stuttering: Significant Theories and Therapies." Stanford Univ. Press, Stanford.

HALLGREN, B. (1957) Enuresis: A clinical and genetic study. *Acta Psych. et Neurol. Scand.* Supp. **112**.

HALLIDAY, J. L. (1948) "Psychosocial Medicine." Norton, New York.

HAMILTON, M. (1955) "Psychosomatics." Chapman and Hall, London.

HAMPSON, J. L. and Hampson, J. G. (1961) The ontogenesis of sexual behaviour in man. *In:* Young, W. C. and Corner, G. W. (Eds.) "Sex and Internal Secretions," Vol. II. (3rd Ed.). Williams and Wilkins, Baltimore.

HAMPSON, J. L. (1965) Determinants and psychosexual orientation. *In:* Beach, F. A. (Ed.) "Sex and Behaviour." Wiley, New York.

HANAWALT, H. G. (1959) Review in "The Fifth Mental Measurements Yearbook." Buros, O. K. (Ed.) The Gryphen Press, New Jersey.

HANLON, T. E., HOFSTAETTER, P. R. and O'CONNOR, J. P. (1954) Congruence of self and ideal self in relation to personality adjustment. *J. Consult Psychol.*, **18**, 215–218.

HARE, R. D. (1960) "Psychopathy: Theory and Research." Wiley, London.

HARE, R. D. (1965) Temporal gradient of fear arousal in psychopaths. *J. Abnorm. Psychol.*, **70**, 442–445.

HARLOW, H. F. (1958) The nature of love. *Amer. Psychol.*, **13**, 673–685.

HARTSHORNE, H. and MAY, M. A. (1928–1930) "Studies in the Nature of Character." Macmillan Co., New York.

HARTUP, W. W. (1963) Dependence and independence. *In:* Stevenson, H. W. (Ed.) "Child Psychology." Nat. Soc. for Study of Educ. Yearbook. Pt. 1. 333–363. Chicago Univ. Press, Chicago.

HARTUP, W. W. and ZOOK, E. A. (1960) Sex role preferences in three- and four-year-old children. *J. Consult. Psychol.*, **24**, 420–426.

HATFIELD, J. S., FERGUSON, P. E., RAU, L. and ALPERT, R. (1967) Mother–child interaction and the socialization process. *Child Develop.*, **38**, 365–414.

HAVIGHURST, R. J. (1953) "Human Development and Education." Longmans Green, New York.

HAWKINS, R. P., PETERSON, R. F., SCHWEID, E. and BIJOU, S. W. (1966) Behaviour therapy in the home: amelioration of problem parent–child relations with the parent in a therapeutic role. *J. Exp. Child Psychol.*, **4**, (1), 99–107.

HEALY, W., BRONNER, A. F. and BOWERS, A. M. (1930) "The Structure and Meaning of Psychoanalysis." A. A. Knopf, New York.

HEATHERS, G. (1953) Emotional dependence and independence in a physical threat situation. *Child Develop.*, **24**, 169–179.

HEATHERS, G. (1955) Emotional dependence and independence in nursery school play. *Child Develop.*, **28**, 37–57.

HEBB, D. O. (1949) "The Organization of Behavior." Wiley, New York.

HEILBRUN, A. B. (1965) The measurement of identification. *Child Develop.*, **36**, 111–127.

HEINICKE, C. and WESTHEIMER, I. (1966) "Brief Separations." Longmans Green, London.

HEINSTEIN, M. (1966) "Child rearing in California." Bureau of Maternal and Child Health. State of Calif. Dept. of Pub. Health, Berkeley, Calif.

HELLER, M. D. A. (1963) A study of psychiatric patients tested on the Wechsler Intelligence Scales; with particular reference to children with wide discrepancies between verbal and performance IQs. Unpublished D.P.M. Dissertation. Institute of Psychiatry, University of London.

HELLMAN, I. (1962) Sudden separation and its effect followed over twenty years: Hampstead Nursery follow-up studies. *Psychoanal. Stud. Child.*, **17**, 159–174.

HEPNER, R. (1958) Maternal nutrition and the fetus. *J. Amer. Assn.*, **168**, 1774–1777.

HERBERT, M. (1964) The concept and testing of brain-damage in children: A review. *J. Child Psychol. and Psychiat.*, **5**, 197–216.

HERBERT, M. (1965) Personality factors and bronchial asthma: A study of South African Indian Children. *J. Psychosom. Res.*, **8**, 353.

HERBERT, M. (1967) Olfactory precipitants of bronchial asthma. *J. Psychosom. Res.*, **11**, 195–202.

HERBERT, M. (1970) "'Strength of the Nervous System' and its Relationship to other Personality Variables and Indices of Arousal." Unpublished Ph.D. Thesis. Univ. of London.

HERBERT, M. and KEMP, M. (1969) The reliability of the brain. *Science Journal*, **5**, (5), 47–52.

HERBERT, M. and SLUCKIN, W. (1969) Acquisition of colour preferences by chicks at different temperatures. *Anim. Behav.*, **17**, 213–216.

HERMELIN, B. (1963) Response behaviour of autistic children and subnormal controls. *Paper to the XVII International Congress of Psychology*, Washington.

HERMELIN, B. (1966) Psychological Research. *In:* Wing, J. K. (Ed.) "Childhood Autism: Clinical, Educational and Social Aspects." Pergamon Press, Oxford.

HERMELIN, B. and O'CONNOR, N. (1964) Crossmodal transfer in normal, subnormal and autistic children. *Neuropsychologia*, **2**, 229.

HERSOV, L. A. (1960) Persistent nonattendance at school/Refusal to go to School. *J. Child Psychol. and Psychiat.*, **1**, 130–136.

HERXHEIMER, H. G. (1951) Induced asthma in man. *Lancet*, **1**, 1337–1341.

HESS, R. D. and SHIPMAN, V. (1965) Early experience and the socialization of cognitive modes in children. *Child Develop.*, **36**, 869–886.

HESS, R. D. and SHIPMAN, V. (1965) Early blocks to children's learning., *Children*, **12**, 189–194.

HETHERINGTON, E. M. (1965) A developmental study of the effects of the dominant parent on sex-role preference, identification and imitation in children. *J. Person. Soc. Psychol.*, **2**, 188–194.

HETHERINGTON, E. M. (1967) The effects of familial variables on sex typing, on parent–child similarity and on imitation in children. *In:* Hill, J. P. (Ed.) *Minnesota Symposia on Child Psychology.* Vol. 1, Univ. of Minnesota Press.

HETHERINGTON, E. and BRACKBILL, Y. (1963) Etiology and covariation of obstinacy orderliness, and parsimony in young children. *Child Develop.*, **10**, 919–943.

HEWITT, L. E. and JENKINS, R. L. (1946) "Fundamental Patterns of Maladjustment: The Dynamics of their Origin." Thomas, Springfield, Illinois.

HILL, H. (1944) Stuttering I and II. *J. Speech Dis.*, **9**, 245–261; 289–324.

HILL, O. W. and PRICE, J. S. (1967) Childhood bereavement and adult depression. *Brit. J. Psychiat.*, **113**, 743–751.

HIRSCHI, D., LEVY, H. and LITVAK, A. M. (1948) The physical and mental development of premature infants: A statistical survey with a five-year follow-up. *Arch. Pediat.*, **65**, 648–653.

HOAKLEY, Z. P. and FRAZEUR, H. A. (1945) A comparison of the results of the Stanford and Terman-Merrill revisions of the Binet. *Amer. J. Ment. Defic.*, **50**, 263–267.

HOFFMAN, M. L. (1970) Moral development. *In:* Mussen, P. H. (Ed.) "Carmichael's Manual of Child Psychology." 261–359. Wiley, London.

HOFFMAN, M. L. and HOFFMAN, L. W (Eds) (1964) "Review of Child Development Research. (2 Vols.) Russell Sage Foundation, New York.

HOFFMAN, M. L. and SALTZSTEIN, H. D. (1967) Parent discipline and the child's moral development. *J. Pers. Soc. Psychol.*, **5**, 45–57.

HOLMES, F. (1935) An experimental study of fear in young children. *In:* Jersild. A. and Holmes, F. "Children's Fear." Child Develop. Monogr. No. 20.

HONZIK, M. P., HUTCHINGS, J. J. and BURNIP, S. R. (1965) Birth record assessments and test performance at eight months. *Amer. J. Dis. Children*, **109**, 416–426.

HORNEY, K. (1945) "Our Inner Conflicts." Norton, New York.

HUNT, H. F. (1943) "The Hunt-Minnesota Test for Organic Brain Damage." (Test manual.) Univ. Minnesota Press.

HUNT, J. McV. (1964) The psychological basis for using pre-school enrichment as an antidote for cultural deprivation. *Merrill-Palmer Quart. Behav. Develop.*, **10**, 209–248.

HUTT, C. (1972) "Males and Females." Penguin Books, Harmondsworth.

HUTT, C., HUTT, S. J. and OUNSTED, C. (1963) A method for the study of children's behaviour. *Develop. Med. Chil. Neurol.*, **5**, 233–245.

HUTT, M. L. and GIBBY, R. G. (1959) "The Child: Development and Adjustment." Allyn and Bacon, Boston.

INHELDER, B. and PIAGET, J. (1958) "The Growth of Logical Thinking from Childhood to Adolescence." Basic Books, New York.

INHELDER, B. and PIAGET, J. (1964) "The Early Growth of Logic in the Child. Routledge, Kegan Paul, London.

IRWIN, O. C. (1960) Language and communication. *In:* Mussen, P. J. (Ed.) "Review of Research Methods in Child Development." 487–516. Wiley, London.

IRWIN, O. C. (1949) Infant speech. *Scientific American*, **417**, 1–7.

ISRAEL, S. L. (1962) Hypothalamus function and reproduction. *Obstet. Gynec.*, **20**, 826–835.

JACKSON, D. D. (Ed.) (1960) "The Aetiology of Schizophrenia." Basic Books, London.

JAHODA, M. (1958) "Current Concepts of Positive Mental Health." Basic Books, New York.

JEHU, D. (1970) The role of social workers in behaviour therapy. *J. Behav. Ther. and Exper. Psychiatry*, **1**, 17–28.

JEHU, D. (1974) Proposal on the treatment of hyper-aggressive behaviour. Research Proposal to Dept. Health and Social Security. (University of Leicester.)

JENSEN, A. R. (1957) Authoritarian attitudes and personality maladjustment. *J. Abnorm. Soc. Psychol.*, **54**, 303–311.

JERSILD, A. T., MARKETY, F. V. and JERSILD, C. L. (1933) "Children's Fears, Dreams, Wishes, Daydreams, Likes, Dislikes, Pleasant and Unpleasant Memories." Columbia University Press, New York.

JERSILD, A. T. (1960) "Child Psychology." (Original publication date 1933.) Prentice-Hall, Englewood Cliffs.

JERSILD, A. T. and HOLMES, F. B. (1935) Methods of overcoming children's fears. *J. Psychol.*, 1, 75–104.

JOFFE, J. M. (1968) "Prenatal Determinants of Behaviour." Pergamon, Oxford.

JOHNSON, W. (1956) Stuttering. *In:* Johnson, W., Brown, S. J., Curtis, J. J., Edney, C. W., and Keaster, J. (Eds) "Speech Handicapped Schoolchildren." Harper, New York.

JOHNSON, A. M., FALSTEIN, E. I., SZUREK, S. A. and SVENDSEN, W. (1941) School phobia. *Amer. J. Orthopsychiat.*, 11, 702–711.

JOHNSON, R. C. and MEDINNUS, G. R. (1965) "Child Psychology: Behaviour and Development." Wiley, New York.

JONES, M. C. (1924a) A laboratory study of fear: The case of Peter. *Pedagog. Sem.*, 31, 308–315.

JONES, M. C. (1924b) The elimination of children's fears. *J. exp. Psychol.*, 7, 383–390.

JONES, E. (1948) Anal-erotic character traits. Ch. 24. *In:* "Papers on Psychoanalysis." (5 Ed.) Wood, New York.

JONES, H. G. (1968) Behaviour therapy and conditioning techniques. *In:* Miller, E. (Ed.) "Foundations of Child Psychiatry. Pergamon Press, Oxford.

KAGAN, J. (1958a) Acquisition and significance of sex-typing and sex-role identity. *In:* Hoffman, M. L. and Hoffman, L. W. (Eds). "Review of Child Development Research." Vol. 1. Russell Sage Foundation, New York.

KAGAN, J. (1958b) The concept of identification. *Psychol. Rev.*, 65, 296–305.

KAGAN, J. and MOSS, H. A. (1960) "The stability of passive and dependent behaviour from childhood through adulthood." *Child Develop.*, 31, 577–591.

KAGAN, J. and MOSS, H. A. (1962) "Birth to Maturity: A Study in Psychological Development." Wiley, New York.

KAHN, J. H. and NURSTEN, J. P. (1964) "Unwillingly to School." Pergamon Press, Oxford.

KALLMANN, F. J. (1952) A comparative twin study on the genetic aspects of male homosexuality. *J. Nerv.*, 115, 283–298.

KANFER, F. H. (1961) Comments on learning in psychotherapy. *Psychol. Rep.*, 9, 681–699.

KANFER, F. H. (1965) Issues and ethics in behaviour manipulation. *Psychol. Rep.*, 16, 187–196.

KANFER, F. H. and SASLOW, G. (1969) Behavioural diagnosis. *In:* Franks, C. M. (Ed.) "Behaviour Therapy: Appraisal and Status." McGraw-Hill, New York.

KANNER, L. (1943) Autistic disturbances of affective contact. *Nervous Child.*, 2, 217–250.

KANNER, L. (1944) Early infantile autism. *J. Pediatrics*, 25, 211–217.

KANNER, L. (1953) "Child Psychiatry." Thomas, Springfield, Illinois.

KANNER, L. (1960) Do behaviour symptoms always indicate psychopathology? *J. Child Psychol. and Psychiat.*, 1, 17–25.

KATAHN, M. and KOPLIN, J. H. (1968) Paradigm clash: comment on "Some recent criticisms of behaviourism and learning theory with special reference to Breger and McGaugh and to Chomsky." *Psychol. Bull.*, 69, 147–148.

KATKOVSKY, W., PRESTON, A. and CRANDALL, V. J. (1964) Parents' attitudes towards their personal achievements and toward the achievement behaviours of their children. *J. Gen. Psychol.*, **104**, 67–82.

KAUFMANN, L. M. and WAGNER, B. R. (1972) Barb: A systematic treatment technology for temper control disorders. *Behav. Ther.*, **3**, 84–90.

KAY, D. W. K. (1963) Late paraphrenia and its bearing on the aetiology of schizophrenia. *Acta Psychiat. Scand.*, **39**, 159–169.

KELLY, G. (1961) The abstraction of human processes. *Proc. 14th Int. Congr. Psychol., Copenhagen.*, 220–229.

KELLY, E. and ZELLER, B. (1969) Asthma and the psychiatrist. *J. Psychosom. Res.*, **13**, 377–395.

KENDLER, T. S. and KENDLER, H. H. (1959) Reversal and non-reversal shifts in kindergarten children. *J. Exp. Psychol.*, **58**, 56–60.

KENDLER, T., KENDLER, H. H. and WELLS, D. (1960) Reversal and non-reversal shifts in nursery school children. *J. Compar. Physiol. Psychol.*, **53**, 83–88.

KENYON, F. E. (1970) Homosexuality in the female. *Brit. J. Hosp. Med.*, **3**, 183–206.

KIESLER, D. J. (1966) Some myths of psychotherapy research and the search for a paradigm. *Psychol. Bull.*, **65**, 110–136.

KIMBLE, G. A. (1961) "Hilgard and Marquis' Conditioning and Learning." Appleton-Century-Crofts, New York.

KIMMINS, C. W. (1920) "Children's Dreams." Longmans Green, London.

KINSEY, A. C., POMEROY, W. B. and MARTIN, C. E. (1948) "Sexual Behaviour in the Human Male." W. B. Saunders, Philadelphia.

KINSEY, A. C., POMEROY, W. B., MARTIN, C. E. and GEBHARD, P. H. (1953) "Sexual Behaviour in the Human Female." W. B. Saunders, Philadelphia.

KIRK, S. A. and McCARTHY, J. J. (1962) The Illinois Test of Psycholinguistic Abilities—An approach to differential diagnosis. *Amer. J. Ment. Defic.*, **66**, 399–412.

KLINE, P. (1972) Fact and Fantasy in Freudian Theory. Methuen, London.

KLINEBERG, O. (1963) Negro–white differences in intelligence test performance: A new look at an old problem. *Amer. Psychol.*, **18**, 198–203.

KNAPP, P. H. (1963) Emotional expression—past and present. *In:* Knapp, P. H. (Ed.) "Expression of the Emotions in Man." Internat. Univ. Press, New York.

KNOBLOCK, H. and PASAMANICK, B. (1962) Etiologic factors in "early infantile autism" and "childhood schizophrenia". *Unpubl. paper 10th Int. Congr. Pediat.*, Sept. 9–15th. Lisbon, Portugal.

KNOBLOCK, H. and PASAMANICK, B. (1966) Prospective studies on the epidemiology of reproductive casualty: Methods, finding and some implications. *Merrill Palmer Quart. of Behav. and Develop.*, **12**, 27–43.

KNOBLOCK, H. and GRANT, D. K. (1961) Etiologic factors in "early infantile autism" and "childhood schizophrenia". *Amer. J. Dis. Childhood*, **66**, 399–412.

KNOBLOCK, H., RIDER, R., HARPER, P. and PASAMANICK, B. (1959) Effect of prematurity on health and growth. *Amer. J. Publ. Hlth.*, **49**, 1164–1173.

KOHLBERG, L. (1963) Moral development and identification. *In:* Stevenson, H. W. (Ed.) "Child Psychology." Univ. of Chicago Press, Chicago.

KOHLBERG, L. (1967) A cognitive-developmental analysis of children's sex-role concepts and attitudes. *In:* Maccoby, E. (Ed.) "The Development of Sex Differences." Tavistock Publications, London.

KOHLBERG, L. (1970) "Moral Development." Holt, Rinehart and Winston, New York.

KOHLBERG, L. and TURIEL, E. (1971) "Research in Moral Development: The Cognitive-Developmental Approach." Holt, Rinehart and Winston, London.

KOHLBERG, L., LA CROSSE, J. and RICKS, D. (1972) The predictability of adult mental health from childhood behaviour. *In:* Wolman, B. B. (Ed.) "Manual of Child Psychopathology". 1217–1284. McGraw-Hill, London.

KOPPITZ, E. M. (1962) Diagnosing brain damage in young children with the Bender-Gestalt Test. *J. Consult. Psychol.*, **26**, 541–546.

KRALOVICH, A. M. (1959) A study of performance differences on the Cattell Infant Intelligence Scale between matched groups of organic and mongoloid subjects. *J. Clin. Psychol.*, **15**, 198–199.

KRASNOGORSKI, N. I. (1925) The conditioned reflexes and children's neuroses. *Amer. J. Dis. Child.*, **30**, 753–768.

KUSHLICK, A. (1968) Social problems of mental subnormality. *In:* Miller, E. (Ed.) "Foundations of Child Psychiatry." Pergamon Press, Oxford.

LACEY, J. I. (1950) Individual differences in somatic response patterns. *J. Comp. Physiol. Psychol.*, **43**, 338–350.

LACEY, J. I. (1956) The evaluation of autonomic responses: toward a general solution. *Ann. N.Y. Acad. Sci.*, **67**, 123–164.

LACEY, J. I. (1967) Chapter in Appley, M. and Trumbull, R. (Eds) "Psychological Stress." 14–31. Appleton-Century-Crofts, New York.

LACEY, J. I., KAGAN, J., LACEY, B. C. and MOSS, H. A. (1963) The visceral level: situational determinants and behavioural correlates of autonomic response patterns. *In:* Knapp, P. N. (Ed.) "Expression of the Emotions in Man." Internat. Univ. Press, New York.

LACEY, J. I. and LACEY, B. C. (1958) Verification and extension of the principle of autonomic response-stereotopy. *Amer. J. Psychol.*, **71**, 50–73.

LACEY, J. I., BATEMAN, D. E. and VAN LEHN, R. (1953) Autonomic response specificity. *Psychosom. Med.*, **15**, 10–21.

LAING, R. D. (1961) "The Self and Others." Tavistock Publications, London.

LAING, R. D. and ESTERSON, A. (1970) "Sanity, Madness and the Family." Penguin Books, Harmondsworth.

LANGNER, T. S. and MICHAEL, S. T. (1962) "Life Stress and Mental Health." The Free Press, Illinois.

LAPOUSE, R. and MONK, M. A. (1958) An epidemiologic study of behaviour characteristics in children. *Amer. J. Publ. Health*, **48**, (9).

LAPOUSE, R. and MONK, M. A. (1959) Fears and worries in a representative sample of children. *Amer. J. Orthopsychi.*, **29**, 803–818.

LAYCOCK, S. R. (1934) Teachers' reactions to maladjustments of school children. *Brit. J. Educ. Psychol.*, **4**, 11–29.

LAYMAN, C. (1959) Personal communication to McCandless (1969) p. 15.

LAZERSON, A. (Ed.) (1971) "Developmental Psychology Today." C. R. M. Books, Del Mar, California.

LEE, S. G. M. and HERBERT, M. (Eds) (1970) "Freud and Psychology." Penguin Books, Harmondsworth.

LEE, S. G. M., WRIGHT, D. S. and HERBERT, M. (1972) Aspects of the Development of Social Responsiveness in Young Children. *Rep. to Social Science Research Council, UK.*

LEFF, R. (1968) Behavior modification and the psychoses of childhood: A review. *Psychol. Bull.*, **69**, (6) 396–409.

LEIGH, D. (1953) Asthma and the psychiatrist: a critical review. *Int. Arch. Allergy*, **4**, 227.

LENNARD, H., BEAULIEU, M. R. and EMBREY, N. G. (1965) Interaction in families with a schizophrenic child. *Arch. gen. Psychiat.*, **12**, 166–183.

LEVITT, E. E. (1957) A follow-up study of cases treated at the Illness Institute for Juvenile Research: An evaluation of psychotherapy with children. *Report of the Mental Health Project No. 5503.* Dept. of Pub. Welfare, State of Illinois.

LEVITT, E. E. (1971) Research on Psychotherapy with Children. *In:* Bergin, A. E. and Garfield, S. L. (Eds) "Handbook of Psychotherapy and Behaviour Change." Wiley, London.

LEVY, D. M. (1943) "Maternal Overprotection." Columbia Univ. Press, New York.

LEWIS, M. M. (1951) "Infant Speech: A Study of Beginning of Language." (2nd Ed.) Routledge, Kegan Paul, London.

LEWIS, H. (1954) "Deprived Children." Oxford Univ. Press, London.

LIBERMAN, R. P. (1972) "A Guide to Behavioural Analysis and Therapy." Pergamon Press, Oxford.

LIDDELL, H. S. (1944) Conditioned reflex method and experimental neurosis. *In:* Hunt, J. McV. (Ed.) "Personality and the Behaviour Disorders." Ch. 12. Ronald, New York.

LIDZ, T., CORNELISON, A. R., FLECK, S. and TERRY, D. (1957) The intrafamilial environment of schizophrenic patients II. Marital schism and marital skew. *Amer. J. of Psychiat.*, **114**, 241–248.

LIDZ, T., FLECK, S. and CORNELISON, A. R. (1965) "Schizophrenia and the Family." Internat. Univ. Press, New York.

LIDZ, T. (1968) "The Person." Basic Books, New York.

LIPPITT, R. and GOLD, M. (1959) Classroom social structure as a mental health problem. *J. Soc. Issues.*, **15**, (1) 40–49.

LIPSITT, L. P. (1958) A self-concept for children and its relationship to the Children's Form of the Manifest Anxiety Scale. *Child Develop.*, **29**, 463–472.

LIPSITT, L. P. (1963) Learning in the first year of life. *In:* Lipsitt, L. P. and Spiker, C. C. (Eds) "Advances in Child Development and Behaviour." 147–195. Academic Press, New York and London.

LOEVINGER, J. (1966) The meaning and measurement of ego development. *Amer. Psychol.*, **21**, 195–206.

LORENZ, K. Z. (1935) Imprinting. *In:* Birney, R. C. and Teevan, R. C. (Ed.) 1961. "Instinct." Van Nostrand, London.

LORENZ, K. Z. (1966) "On Aggression." Harcourt, Brace and World, New York.

LOVAAS, O. I. (1966) Learning theory approach to the treatment of childhood schizophrenia. Paper to Symposium on Childhood Schizophrenia, *Amer. Orthopsychiat. Assoc.*, San Francisco.

LOVIBOND, S. H. (1964) "Conditioning and Enuresis." Pergamon, Oxford.

LOVIBOND, S. H. (1965) Personality and Conditioning. *In:* Maher, B. A. (Ed.) "Progress in Experimental Personality Research", Vol. 1. 115–163. Academic Press, New York and London.

LOVIBOND, S. H. (1966) The current status of behaviour therapy. *Canad. Psychol.*, **7**, 93–101.

LOWE, G. R. (1972) "The Growth of Personality: from Infancy to Old Age." Penguin Books, Harmondsworth.

LURIA, A. R. (1960) Verbal regulation of behaviour. *In:* Brazier, M. (Ed.) "The Central Nervous System and Behaviour." 359–423. Princetown, New Jersey.

LURIA, A. R. (1961) "The Role of Speech in the Regulation of Normal and Abnormal Behaviour." Pergamon, Oxford.

LYKKEN, D. T. (1957) A study of anxiety in the sociopathic personality. *J. Abnorm. Soc. Psychol.*, **55**, 6–10.

MACFARLANE, J. W., ALLEN, L. and HONZIK, M. (1954) "A Developmental Study of the Behaviour Problems of Normal Children." Univ. of California Press, Berkeley.

McCANDLESS, B. (1969) "Children: Behaviour and Development." (2nd Ed.) Holt, Rinehart and Winston, London.

McCANDLESS, B. R., CASTANEDA, A. and PALERMO, D. S. (1956) Anxiety in children and social status. *Child Develop.*, **27**, 385–392.

McCLELLAND, D. (1961) "The Achieving Society." Van Nostrand, Princeton.

McCORD, W. and McCORD, J. (1959) "The Origins of Crime: A New Evaluation of the Cambridge-Somerville Youth Study." Columbia Univ. Press, Columbia.

McCORD, W. and McCORD, J. (1964) "The Psychopath." Van Nostrand, London.

McCORD, W., McCORD, J. and HOWARD, A. (1961) Familial correlates of aggression in nondelinquent male children. *J. Abnorm. Soc. Psychol.*, **62**, 79–93.

McCORD, W., McCORD, J. and VERDEN, P. (1962) Familial and behavioural correlates of dependency in male children. *Child Develop.*, **33**, 313–326.

McCORD, J. and McCORD, W. (1958) The effects of parental role models on criminality. *J. Soc. Issues*, **14**, 66–75.

McDERMOTT, M. and COBB, S. (1939) A psychiatric survey of 50 cases of bronchial asthma. *Psychosom. Med.*, **1**, 203.

McFIE, J. (1960) Psychological testing in clinical neurology. *J. Nerv. and Ment. Dis.*, **131**, 383–393.

McFIE, J. (1961) Intellectual impairment in children with localized post-infantile cerebral lesions. *J. Neurol. Neurosurg. Psychiat.*, **24**, 361–365.

McMURRAY, J. C. (1954a) Rigidity in conceptual thinking in exogenous and endogenous mentally retarded children. *J. Consult. Psychol.*, **18**, 366–370.

McMURRAY, J. C. (1954b) Visual perception in exogenous and endogenous mentally retarded children. *Amer. J. Mentl. Defic.*, **58**, 659–663.

MACCOBY, E. E. (1961) The taking of adult roles in middle childhood. *J. Abnorm. Soc. Psychol.*, **63**, 493–503.

MACCOBY, E. E. (1971) Stability of attachment behaviour: a transformational analysis. *Paper presented at Soc. Res. in Child Develop. Meetings.* Symposium on Attachment: Studies in Stability and Change; April, 1971, Minneapolis.

MACCOBY, E. E. and MASTERS, J. (1970) Attachment and Dependency. *In:* Mussen, P. H. (Ed.) "Carmichael's Manual of Child Psychology." Vol. 2. 73–158. Wiley, New York.

MACLEAN, I. C. (1966) "Child Guidance and the School." Methuen, London.

MAGOUN, H. W. (1963) "Waking Brain." Thomas, Springfield, Illinois.

MAHER, B. A. (1964) The application of the approach-avoidance conflict model to social behaviour. *J. Conflict Resol.*, **8**, 287–291.

MAHER, B. A. (1970) "Principles of Psychopathology." McGraw-Hill, New York.

MAHLER, M. S. (1952) On childhood psychoses and schizophrenia: autistic and symbiotic infantile psychoses. *Psychoan. Study Child*, **7**, 286–305.

MAIER, N. R. F. (1939) "Studies of Abnormal Behaviour in the Rat." Harper and Row, New York.

MAIER, N. R. F. (1956) Frustration theory: Restatement and extension. *Psychol. Rev.*, **63**, 370–388.

MALAN, D. H. (1959) On assessing the results of psychotherapy. *Brit. J. Med. Psychol.*, **32**, 86.

MALEWSKA, H. E. and MUSZYNSKI, H. (1970) Children's attitudes to theft. *In:* Danziger, K. (Ed.) "Readings in Child Socialization." Pergamon Press, Oxford.

MALMO, R. B. and SHAGASS, C. (1949) Physiologic study of symptom mechanisms in psychiatric patients under stress. *Psychosom. Med.,* **11,** 25–29.

MALMO, R. B., SHAGASS, C. and DAVIS, F. H. (1950a) Specificity of bodily reactions under stress. *Proc. Ass. Res. Nerv. Ment. Dis.,* **29,** 231–261.

MALMO, R. B., SHAGASS, C. and DAVIS, F. H. (1950b) Symptom specificity and bodily reactions during psychiatric interviews. *Psychosom. Med.,* **12,** 362–376.

MANN, C. (1959) Habitual abortion. *Amer. J. Obstet. Gynec.,* **77,** 706–718.

MARKS, I. M. and GELDER, M. G. (1965) A controlled retrospective study of behaviour therapy in phobic patients. *Brit. J. Psychiat.,* **111,** 561–573.

MARKS, I. M. and GELDER, M. G. (1966) Common ground between behaviour therapy and psychodynamic methods. *Brit. J. Med. Psychol.,* **39,** 11–23.

MARSHALL, H. H. (1965) The effects of punishment on children: a review of the literature and a suggested hypothesis. *J. Gen. Psychol.,* **106,** 23–33.

MARSHALL, H. R. (1961) Relations between home experiences and children's use of language in play interactions with peers. *Psychol. Monogr.,* **75,** No. 5.

MARSHALL, H. R. and McCANDLESS, B. R. (1957) Relationships between dependence on adults and social acceptance. *Child Develop.,* **28,** 413.

MASSERMAN, J. (1946) "Principles of Dynamic Psychiatry." Saunders, Philadelphia.

MAXWELL, A. E. (1959) A factor analysis of the Wechsler Intelligence Scale for Children. *Brit. J. Educ. Psychol.,* **29,** 237–241.

MAXWELL, A. E. (1961) Discrepancies between the pattern of abilities for normal and neurotic children. *J. Ment. Sci.,* **107,** 300–307.

MAY, R. (1950) "The Meaning of Anxiety." Ronald, New York.

MEAD, M. (1935) "Sex and Temperament in Three Primitive Societies." Routledge, Kegan Paul, London.

MEHLMAN, B. (1952) The reliability of psychiatric diagnosis. *J. Abnorm. Soc. Psychol.,* **47,** 577–578.

MESSER, S. B. and LEWIS, M. (1970) Social class and sex differences in the attachment and play behaviour of the year-old infant. *Research Bulletin Educational Testing Service, Princeton.*

MEYER, V. (1957) Critique of psychological approaches to brain damage. *J. Ment. Sci.,* **103,** 80–109.

MEYER, V. and CRISP, A. H. (1966) Some problems in behaviour therapy. *Brit. J. Psychiat.,* **112,** 367–381.

MEYER, E. and SIMMEL, N. (1947) Psychological appraisal of children with neurological defects. *J. Abnorm. Soc. Psychol.,* **42,** 193–205.

MICHAELS, J. (1955) "Disorders of Character." Thomas, Springfield, Illinois.

MILLER, J. G. (1966) Eyeblink conditioning of primary and neurotic psychopaths. *Diss. Abstr.,* **27b,** III.

MILLER, N. E. (1941) The frustration-aggression hypothesis. *Psychol. Rev.,* **48,** 337–342.

MILLER, N. E. (1944) Experimental studies of conflict. *In:* Hunt, J. McV. (Ed.) "Personality and the Behaviour Disorders." Ronald Press, New York.

MILLER, N. E. (1959) Liberalization of basic S-R concepts: Extension to conflict behaviour, motivation and social learning. *In:* Koch, S. (Ed.) "Psychology: A Study of a Science." 196–292. McGraw-Hill, New York.

MILLER, N. E. (1969) Learning of visceral and glandular responses. *Science*, **163**, 434–445.

MILLER, N. E. and DICARA, L. (1967) Instrumental learning of heart rate changes in curarized rats: Shaping, and specificity to discriminative stimulus. *J. Compar. and Physiol. Psychol.*, **63**, 12–19.

MISCHEL, W. (1967) A social-learning view of sex differences in behaviour. *In:* Maccoby, E. (Ed.) "The Development of Sex Differences." Tavistock Publications, London.

MISCHEL, W. (1970) Sex-typing and socialization. *In:* Mussen, P. H. (Ed.) "Carmichael's Manual of Child Psychology." 2, 3–72. Wiley, New York.

MISHLER, E. G. and WAXLER, N. E. (1965) Family interaction processes and schizophrenia: A review of current theories. *Merrill-Palmer Quart. of Behav. and Develop.*, **11**, 269–315.

MISHLER, E. G. and WAXLER, N. E. (1968) "Interaction in Families." Wiley, New York.

MITCHELL, S. and SHEPHERD, M. (1966) A comparative study of children's behaviour at home and at school. *Brit. J. Educ. Psychol.*, **36**, 248–254.

MONEY, J. (1965) Psychosexual differentiation. *In:* Money, J. (Ed.) "Sex Research: New Developments." Holt, Rinehart and Winston, London.

MONTAGU, M. F. A. (1962) "Prenatal Influences." Thomas, Springfield, Illinois.

MONTAGU, M. F. A. (1963) "Human Heredity." Signet Science Libr., New York.

MONTAGU, M. F. A. (1964) "Life Before Birth." A Four Square Book. The New English Library.

MOORE, N. (1966) Behaviour therapy in bronchial asthma: a controlled study. *J. Psychosom. Res.*, **9**, 257.

MOORE, T. W. (1966) Difficulties of the ordinary child in adjusting to primary school. *J. Child. Psychol. and Psychiat.*, **7**, 299.

MORGAN, R. T. T. and YOUNG, G. C. (1972) The conditioning treatment of childhood enuresis. *Br. J. Social Wk.*, **2**, 503–509.

MOSS, H. A. (1967) Sex, age and state as determinants of mother–infant interaction. *Merrill-Palmer Quart.*, **13**, 19–36.

MOWRER, O. H. (1960) "Learning Theory and Behaviour." Wiley, New York.

MOWRER, O. H. (1960) "Learning Theory and Symbolic Processes." Wiley, New York.

MOWRER, O. H. (1954) Learning theory and identification, I. Introduction. *J. Gen. Psych.*, **84**, 197–199.

MOWRER, O. H. and MOWRER, W. (1938) Enuresis: A method for its study and treatment. *Amer. J. Orthopsychiat.*, **8**, 436–447.

MOYES, F. A. (1969) A Validational Study of a Test of Motor Impairment. Unpubl. M.Ed. Thesis, Univ. of Leicester.

MURPHY, D. P. (1947) "Congenital Malformation." Lippincott, Philadelphia.

MUSSEN, P. H. (Ed.) (1960) "Handbook of Research Methods in Child Development." Wiley, New York.

MUSSEN, P. H. (1963) "The Psychological Development of the Child." Prentice-Hall, New Jersey.

MUSSEN, P. H. (Ed.) (1970) "Carmichael's Manual of Child Psychology." (2 Vols.) Wiley, London.

MUSSEN, P. and DISTLER, L. (1959) Masculinity, identification, and father–son relationships. *J. Abnorm. Soc. Psychol.*, **59**, 350–356.

MUSSEN, P. and DISTLER, L. (1960) Child rearing antecedents of masculine identification in kindergarten boys. *Child Develop.*, **31**, 89–100.

MUSSEN, P. H., CONGER, J. J. and KAGAN, J. (1969) Child Development and Personality. (3rd Ed.) Harper, Row, New York.

MUSSEN, P. and RUTHERFORD, E. (1963) Parent–child relations and parental personality in relation to young children's sex role preferences. *Child Develop.*, **34**, 581–607.

NEALE, D. H. (1963) Behaviour therapy and encopresis in children. *Behav. Res. Ther.*, **1**, 139–149.

NEBYLITSYN, V. D. (1960) Typological features of higher nervous activity. *Quart. J. Exp. Psychol.*, **2**, 17–25.

NEUHAUS, E. C. (1958) A personality study of asthmatics and cardiac children. *Psychosom. Med.*, **20**, 181.

NEWSON, J. and NEWSON, E. (1965) "Infant Care in an Urban Community." Penguin Books, Harmondsworth. (London: Allen and Unwin, 1963).

NEWSON, J. and NEWSON, E. (1970) "Four Years Old in an Urban Community." Penguin Books, Harmondsworth.

NIJHAWAN, H. K. (1972) "Anxiety in School Children." Wiley Eastern Private Ltd, New Delhi.

NORRIS, H. (1960) The W.I.S.C. and diagnosis of brain damage. Unpublished dissertation; for the University of London Diploma in Abnormal Psychology.

NUNNALLY, J. C. (1961) "Popular Conceptions of Mental Health: Their Development and Change." Holt, Rinehart and Winston, New York.

NURSTEN, J. P. (1963) "Projection in the later adjustment of school phobic children." *Smith College Studies in Social Work*, **33**, 210–217.

NYSWANDER, M. (1956) "The Drug Addict as a Patient." Grune and Stratton, New York.

O'CONNOR, N. (1958) Ch. 9: Brain Damage and Mental Defect. *In:* Clarke, A. M. and Clarke, A. D. B. (Ed.) "Mental Deficiency—the Changing Outlook." Methuen, London.

O'LEARY, K. D. (1972) The assessment of psychopathology in children. *In:* Quay, H. C. and Werry, J. S. (Eds) "Psychopathological Disorders of Childhood." 234–272. Wiley, London.

O'NEALE, P. and ROBINS, L. N. (1958) The relation of childhood behaviour problems to adult psychiatric status: A 30-year follow-up study of 150 subjects. *Amer. J. Psychiat.*, **114**, 961–969.

ORLANSKY, H. (1949) Infant care and personality. *Psychol. Bull.*, **46**, 1–48.

OWEN, D. R. (1972) The 47, XYY Male: A review. *Psychol. Bull.*, **78**, 209–233.

PARKE, R. D. (1969) The modification of the effectiveness of punishment training by a cognitive-structuring procedure. *Child Develop.*, **40**, 213–235.

PARKE, R. D. and WALTERS, R. H. (1967) Some factors influencing the efficacy of punishment training for inducing response inhibition. *Soc. Res. Child Develop. Monogr.*, No. **109**.

PASAMANICK, B. and KNOBLOCH, H. (1959) Complications of pregnancy and neuropsychiatric disorder. *J. Obstet. Gynaec.*, **66**, 753–755.

PASAMANICK, B. and KNOBLOCH, H. (1960) Brain damage and reproductive casualty. *Amer. J. Orthopsychiat.*, **30**, 298–305.

PASAMANICK, B. and KNOBLOCH, H. (1961) Epidemiologic studies on the complications of pregnancy and the birth process. *In:* Caplan, G. (Ed.) "Prevention of Mental Disorders in Childhood." Basic Books, New York.

PASAMANICK, B., ROGERS, M. E. and LILIENFELD, A. M. (1956) Pregnancy experience and the development of behaviour disorders in children. *Amer. J. Psychiat.*, **112**, 613–618.

PASAMANICK, B., ROGERS, M. E. and LILIENFELD, A. M. (1966) Retrospective studies on the epidemiology of reproductive casualty: old and new. *Merrill-Palmer Quart.*, **12**, 7–26.

PATTERSON, G. R. (1971) "Families: Application of Social Learning to Family Life." Research Press Co., Champaign, Illinois.

PATTERSON, G. R. (1973) Reprogramming and families of aggressive boys. *In:* Thorensen, C. (Ed.) "Behaviour Modification in Education." 154–192. 72nd Yearbook, Nat. Soc. Study of Educ. Univ. of Chicago Press, Chicago.

PAUL, G. (1966) "Insight Versus Desensitization in Psychotherapy." Stanford Univ. Press, Stanford.

PAVLOV, I. P. (1927) "Conditioned Reflexes." (Transl. G. V. Anrep). Clarendon Press, Oxford.

PAVLOV, I. P. (1941) "Conditioned Reflexes and Psychiatry." (Transl. W. H. Gantt.) Internat. Publ., New York.

PAVLOV, I. P. (1957) "Experimental Psychology and Other Essays." Philosophical Library, New York.

PAWLICKI, R. (1970) Behaviour-therapy research with children: a critical review. *Canad. J. Behav. Sci.*, **2**, (3) 163–173.

PAYNE, D. E. and MUSSEN, P. H. (1956) Parent–child relations and father identification among adolescent boys. *J. Abnorm. Soc. Psychol.*, **52**, 358–362.

PENFIELD, W. and ROBERTS, L. (1959) "Speech and Brain Mechanisms." Princeton Univ. Press, New Jersey.

PETERSON, D. R. (1968) Behaviour problems of middle childhood *In:* Quay, H. C. (Ed.) "Children's Behaviour Disorders." 32–40. Van Nostrand, Princeton.

PETERSON, D. R. and LONDON, P. (1964) Neobehaviouristic psychotherapy. *Psychol. Record*, **14**, 469–474.

PETRIE, A. (1967) "Individuality in Pain and Suffering: The Reducer and Augmenter." Univ. of Chicago Press, Chicago, Illinois.

PIAGET, J. (1926) "Language and Thought of the Child." Routledge, Kegan Paul, London.

PIAGET, J. (1929) "The Child's Conceptions of the World." Routledge, Kegan Paul, London.

PIAGET, J. (1932) "The Moral Judgement of the Child." Harcourt, Brace, New York.

PIAGET, J. (1950) "The Psychology of Intelligence." Routledge, Kegan Paul, London.

PIAGET, J. (1951) "Play, Dreams and Imitation in Children." Routledge, Kegan Paul, London.

PIAGET, J. (1952a) "The Origins of Intelligence in Children." Internat. Univ. Press, New York.

PIAGET, J. (1952b) "The Child's Concept of Number." Routledge, Kegan Paul, London.

PIAGET, J. (1954) "The Construction of Reality in the Child." Basic Books, New York.

PIERCY, M. (1964) The effects of cerebral lesions on intellectual function: A review of current research trends. *Brit. J. Psychiat.*, **110**, (466), 310–352.

PINNEAU, S. R. (1955) The infantile disorders of hospitalism and anaclitic depression. *Psychol. Bull.*, **52**, 429–459.

PLOWDEN REPORT (1966) "Children and Their Primary Schools." Report of the Central Advisory Council for Education.

POND, D. A. (1961) Psychiatric aspects of epileptic and brain-damaged children. *Brit. Med. J.*, **2**, 1377–1382; 1454–1459.

PRATT, K. C. (1954) The Neonate. *In:* Carmichael, L. (Ed.) "Manual of Child Psychology." 215–291. (2nd Ed.) Wiley, New York.

PRINCE, G. S. (1968) School phobia. *In:* Miller, E. (Ed.) Foundations of Child Psychiatry." 413–436. Pergamon Press, Oxford.

PRINGLE, M. L. K., BUTLER, N. and DAVIE, R. (1966) "11,000 Seven-Year-Olds." Longmans Green, London.

PROVENCE, S. A. and LIPTON, R. C. (1962) "Infants in Institutions: A Comparison of Their Development with Family-reared Infants During the First Year of Life." Internat. Univ. Press, New York.

PURCELL, K. and WEISS, J. (1970) *In:* Costello, C. G. (Ed.) Symptoms of Psychopathology. 597–623. Wiley, New York.

PURCELL, K. and METZ, J. R. (1962) Distinctions between subgroups of asthmatic children: Some parent attitude variables related to age of onset of asthma. *J. Psychosom. Res.*, **6**, 251–258.

PURCELL, K., TURNBULL, J. W. and BERNSTEIN, L. (1962) Distinctions between subgroups of asthmatic children: Psychological test and behaviour rating comparisons. *J. Psychosom. Res.*, **6**, 283–291.

QUAY, H. C. (Ed.) (1968) "Children's Behaviour Disorders." Van Nostrand, London.

RACHMAN, S. (1962) Learning theory and child psychology: therapeutic possibilities. *J. Child Psychol., Psychiat.*, **3**, 149–163.

RACHMAN, S. (1971) "The Effects of Psychotherapy." Pergamon Press, Oxford.

RAINER, J. D. (1966a) Genetic aspects of depression. *Canad. Psychiat. Ass. J. Suppl.*, **11**, 29–33.

RAINER, J. D. (1966b) The contributions of Franz Josef Kallmann to the genetics of schizophrenia. *Behav. Sci.*, **11**, 413–437.

RAMSEY, C. V. (1943) The sexual development of boys. *Amer. J. Psychiat.*, **56**, 217–233.

RANDALL, J. (1970) Transvestism and transsexualism. *Brit. J. Hosp. Med.*, **3**, **3**, 211–213.

RANK, O. (1929) "The Trauma of Birth." Harcourt, Brace, New York.

RATNER, B. (1960) Asthma in children. *J. Amer. Med. Assoc.*, **142**, (8) 538.

RAVENETTE, A. T. (1968) "Dimensions of Reading Difficulties." Pergamon Press, Oxford.

REASON, J. T. (1968) Relationships between motion after-effects, motion sickness, susceptibility and "receptivity". Unpubl. Ph.D. thesis, Univ. of Leicester.

REBELSKY, F. G., ALLINSMITH, W. and GRINDER, R. E. (1963) Sex differences in children's use of fantasy confession and their relation to temptation. *Child Develop.*, **34**, 955–962.

REES, H. (1974) "Assessment and Treatment of Language Disordered Children.' In Press.

REES, L. (1956) Physical and emotional factors in bronchial asthma. *J. Psychosom. Res.*, **1**, 98.

REES, L. (1963) The significance of parental attitudes in childhood asthma. *J. Psychosom. Res.*, **7**, 181.

RHEINGOLD, H. L. (1956) The modification of social responsiveness in institutional babies. *Monogr. Soc. Res. Child Develop.*, **21**, (63), 1–48.

RHEINGOLD, H. L. (1968) "Infancy." International Encycl. Soc. Sci. Macmillan, New York.

RHEINGOLD, H. L. (1969) The effect of a strange environment on the behaviour of infants. *In:* Foss, B. M. (Ed.) "Determinants of Infant Behaviour" (IV). Methuen, London.

RHEINGOLD, H. L. and ECKERMAN, C. O. (1970) The infant separates himself from his mother. *Science,* **168**, 78–83.

RICHIE, J. and BUTLER, A. J. (1964) Performance of retardates on the Memory for Designs Test. *J. Clin. Psychol.,* **20**, 108–110.

RIMLAND, B. (1964) "Infantile Autism." Appleton-Century-Crofts, New York.

RIMM, D. C., DE GROOT, J. C. and BOARD, P. (1971) Systematic desensitization of anger response. *Behav. Res. and Ther.,* **9**, 273–280.

ROBBINS, L. C. (1963) The accuracy of parental recall of aspects of child development and of child rearing practices. *J. Abnorm. Soc. Psychol.,* **66**, 261–270.

ROBINS, L. N. (1966) "Deviant Children Grown Up." Williams and Wilkins, Baltimore.

ROBINS, L. N. (1970) Antecedents of character disorder. *In:* Roff, M. and Ricks, D. F. (Eds) "Life History Research in Psychopathology." Univ. of Minnesota Press, Minneapolis.

ROBINS, L. N. (1972) Chapter *In:* Quay, H. C. and Werry, J. S. (Eds.) "Psychopathological Disorders of Childhood." Wiley, London.

ROBERTSON, J. and BOWLBY, J. (1952) Responses of young children to separation from their mothers. *Courr. Cent. Int. Enf.,* **2**, 131–142.

ROGERS, M. E., LILIENFELD, A. M. and PASAMANICK, B. (1955) Prenatal and paranatal factors in the development of childhood behaviour disorders. *Acta Psychiat. et Neurol Scand.,* Suppl. **102**.

ROSEN, E. and GREGORY, I. (1965) "Abnormal Psychology." W. B. Saunders, Philadelphia. 2nd Ed. with R. Fox. 1972

ROSENTHAL, R. and JACOBSON, L. (1968) "Pygmalion in the Classroom: Teacher Expectation and Pupils' Intellectual Development." Holt, Rinehart and Winston, New York.

ROSENZWEIG, S. (1944) An outline of frustration theory. *In:* Hunt, J. McV. (Ed.) "Personality and the Behaviour Disorders." Ronald, New York.

ROSENZWEIG, S. (1948) The Children's Form of the Rosenzweig Picture-Frustration Study. *J. Psychol.,* **26**, 141–191.

ROTTER, J. B., CHANCE, J. E. and PHARES, E. J. (Eds) (1972) "Application of a Social Learning Theory of Personality." Holt, Rinehart and Winston, London.

ROWLEY, V. N. (1961) Analysis of the W.I.S.C. performance of brain-damaged and emotionally disturbed children. *J. Consult. Psychol.,* **20**, 343–350.

ROWLEY, V. N. and BAER, P. E. (1961) Visual Retention Test performance in emotionally disturbed and brain-damaged children. *Amer. J. Orthopsychiat.,* **31**, 579–583.

RUTTER, M. (1965) The influence of organic and emotional factors on the origin, nature and outcome of childhood psychoses. *Dev. Med. Child Neurol.,* **17**, 518.

RUTTER, M. (1965a) Speech disorders in a series of autistic children. *In:* Franklin, A. W. (Ed.) "Children with Communication Problems." Pitman, London.

RUTTER, M. (1966) "Children of Sick Parents." Oxford Univ. Press, London.

RUTTER, M. (1967) Brain-damaged children. *New Education,* **3**, (1) 10–12.

RUTTER, M. (1968) Concepts of autism: A review of research. *J. Child Psychol. and Psychiat.,* **9**, 1–25.

RUTTER, M. (1970) Psychological development—predictions from infancy. *J. Child Psychol. and Psychiat.,* **10**, 49–62.

RUTTER, M. (1971) Normal psychosexual development. *J. Child Psychol. and Psychiat.*, **11**, 259–283.

RUTTER, M. (1972) Parent–child separation: Psychological effects on the children. *J. Child Psychol. and Psychiat.*, **12**, 233–260.

RUTTER, M. (1972a) "Maternal Deprivation Reassessed." Penguin Books, Harmondsworth.

RUTTER, M., YULE, W., TIZARD, J. and GRAHAM, P. (1966) Severe reading retardation: Its relationship to maladjustment, epilepsy and neurological disorders. Report to the Proc. Int. Conf. Assoc. for Special Education, London.

RUTTER, M., TIZARD, J. and WHITMORE, K. (Eds) (1970) "Education, Health and Behaviour." Longmans Green, London.

RUTTER, M. L. and GRAHAM, P. J. (1966) Psychiatric disorder in 10 and 11 year old children. *Proc. Roy. Soc. Med.*, **59**, 382–387.

RYALL, D. (1968) From theory to treatment: The contribution of learning theory. *Approved Schools Gazette.* August, 250–254.

SANTOSTEFANO, S. (1960) Anxiety and hostility in stuttering. *J. Speech Hear. Res.*, **3**, 337–347.

SCHAEFER, E. S. (1959) A circumplex model for maternal behaviour. *J. Abnorm. Soc. Psychol.*, **59**, 226–235.

SCHAFFER, H. R. (1958) Objective observations of personality development in early infancy. *Brit. J. Med. Psychol.*, **31**, 174–183.

SCHAFFER, H. R. (1966) The onset of fear of strangers and the incongruity hypothesis. *J. Child Psychol., Psychiat.*, **7**, 95–106.

SCHAFFER, H. R. and EMERSON, P. E. (1964a) Patterns of response to physical contact in early human development. *J. Child Psychol. Psychiat.*, **5**, 1–13.

SCHAFFER, H. R. and EMERSON, P. E. (1964b) "The development of social attachments in infancy." *Monogr. Soc. Res. Child Develop.*, **29**, 5–77, No. 94.

SCHAFFER, H. R. and CALLENDER, W. M. (1959) Psychological effects of hospitalization in infancy. *Pediatrics*, **24**, 528–539.

SCHEINFELD, A. (1967) "The Basic Facts of Human Heredity." Pan Books (Rev. Ed.), London.

SCHIFFER, C. G. and HUNT, E. P. (1963) "Illness among Children." Children's Bureau, US. Dept. of Hlth and Welf.

SCHOFIELD, M. (1966a) "The Sexual Behaviour of Young People." Longmans Green, London.

SCHOFIELD, M. (1965b) "Aspects of Homosexuality." Longmans Green, London.

SCHOFIELD, W. and BALIAN, L. (1959) A comparative study of the personal histories of schizophrenic and nonpsychiatric patients. *J. Abnorm. Soc. Psychol.*, **59**, 216–225.

SCHRUPP, M. H. and GJERDE, C. M. (1953) Teacher growth in attitudes toward behaviour problems. *J. Educ. Psychol.*, **44**, 203–214.

SCHUHAM, A. I. (1967) The double-bind hypothesis a decade later. *Psychol. Bull.*, **68**, 409–416.

SCHULMAN, J. L., KASPAR, J. C. and THRONE, F. M. (1965) "Brain Damage and Behaviour." Thomas, Springfield, Illinois.

SCOTT, J. P. (1958a) "Aggression." Cambridge Univ. Press, London.

SCOTT, W. A. (1958b) Social psychological correlates of mental illness and mental health. *Psychol. Bull.*, **55**, (2) 65–86.

SCOTT, W. A. (1958c) Research definitions of mental health and mental illness. *Psychol. Bull.*, **55**, 29–45.

SEARS, R. R., MACCOBY, E. E. and LEVIN, H. (1957) "Patterns of Child Rearing." Row, Peterson, Evanston, Illinois.

SEARS, R. R., RAU, L. and ALPERT, R. (1965) "Identification and Child Rearing." Stanford Univ. Press, Stanford.

SEARS, R. R., WHITING, J. W. M., NOWLIS, V. and SEARS, P. S. (1953) Some child-rearing antecedents of aggression and dependency in young children. *Genet. Psychol. Monogr.*, **47**, 137–234.

SECHREST, L. and WALLACE, J. (1967) "Psychology and Human Problems." Charles E. Merrill, Columbus, Ohio.

SECORD, P. F. and BACKMAN, C. W. (1964) "Social Psychology." McGraw-Hill, New York.

SELYE, H. (1952) The general adaptation syndrome. *In:* "The Biology of Mental Health and Disease." Hoeber-Harper, New York.

SELYE, H. (1957) "The Stress of Life." Longmans Green, London.

SHAPIRO, M. B., BRIERLY, J., SLATER, P. and BEECH, H. R. (1962) Experimental studies of a perceptual anomaly. VII. A new explanation. *J. Ment. Sci.*, **108**, 655–668.

SHAW, M. C. and CRUICKSHANK, W. M. (1956) The use of the Marble Board Test to measure psychopathology in epileptics. *Amer. J. Ment. Defic.*, **40**, 813–817.

SHEEHAN, J. G. (1953) Theory and treatment of stuttering as an approach-avoidance conflict. *J. Psychol.*, **36**, 27–49.

SHEEHAN, J. G. (1951) The modification of stuttering through nonreinforcement. *J. Abnorm. Soc. Psychol.*, **46**, 51–63.

SHEEHAN, J. G. (1958) Projective studies of stuttering. *J. Speech Dis.*, **23**, 18–25.

SHEPHERD, M., OPPENHEIM, B. and MITCHELL, S. (1966) Childhood behaviour disorders and the child-guidance clinic. *J. Child Psychol. and Psychiat.*, **7**, 39–52.

SHEPHERD, M., OPPENHEIM, B. and MITCHELL, S. (1971) "Childhood Behaviour and Mental Health." Univ. of London Press, London.

SHIRLEY, M. M. (1938) Development of immature babies during their first two years. *Child Develop.*, **9**, 347–360.

SHIRLEY, M. M. (1939) A behaviour syndrome characterizing prematurely born children. *Child Develop.*, **10**, 115–124.

SIEGELMAN, M. (1966) Loving and punishing parental behaviour and introversion tendencies in sons. *Child Develop.*, **37**, 985–992.

SIEVERS, D. J. (1959) A study to compare the performance of brain-injured mentally retarded children on the Differential Language Facility Test. *Amer. J. Ment. Defic.*, **63**, 839–847.

SIEVERS, D. J. and ROSENBERG, C. M. (1961) The Differential Language Facility Test and electroencephalograms of brain-injured mentally retarded children. *Amer. J. Ment. Defic.*, **65**, 46–50.

SILVERSTEIN, A. B. and MOHAN, P. J. (1962) Bender-Gestalt figure rotations in the mentally retarded. *J. Consult. Psychol.*, **26**, 386–388.

SKEELS, H. M. (1966) Adult status of children with contrasting early life experiences. *Monogr. Soc. Res. Child Develop.*, **31**, (3).

SKEELS, H. M. and DYE, H. A. (1939) A study of the effects of differential stimulation on mentally retarded children. *Proc. Amer. Assn. Ment. Defic.*, **44**, 114–136.

SKEELS, H. M. and HARMS, I. (1948) Children with inferior social histories: their mental development in adoptive homes. *J. Gen. Psychol.*, **72**, 283–294.

SKODAK, M. and SKEELS, H. M. (1949) A final follow-up study of one hundred adopted children. *J. Gen. Psychol.*, **75**, 85–125.

SLATER, E. and COWIE, V. (1971) "The Genetics of Mental Disorders." Oxford Univ. Press, London.
SLUCKIN, A. (1973) Social work intervention in cases of encopresis: a behavioural and cognitive approach. (Personal Communication.)
SLUCKIN, A. and JEHU, D. (1969) A behavioural approach in the treatment of elective mutism. *Brit. J. Psychiat. Soc. Wk.*, **10**, (2) 70–73.
SLUCKIN, W. (1964) "Imprinting and Early Learning." Methuen, London.
SLUCKIN, W. (1967) "The Impressionable Age." An Inaugural Lecture, Leicester Univ. Press, Leicester.
SLUCKIN, W. (1970) "Early Learning in Man and Animal." George Allen and Unwin, London.
SMITH, H. T. A. (1958) A comparison of interview and observation measures of mother behaviour. *J. Abnorm. Soc. Psychol.*, **57**, 278–282.
SMITH, K. U., ZWERG, C. and SMITH, N. J. (1963) Sensory feedback analysis of infant control of the behavioural environment. *Percept. Mot. Skills.*, **16**, 725–732.
SOLOMON, R. L. (1964) Punishment. *Amer. Psychol.*, **19**, 239–253.
SOLOMON, R. L., KAMIN, L. J. and WYNNE, L. C. (1953) Traumatic avoidance learning: the outcome of several extinction procedures with dogs. *J. Abnorm. Soc. Psychol.*, **48**, 291–302.
SOLOMON, R. L. and WYNNE, L. (1954) Traumatic avoidance learning: the principles of anxiety conservation and partial irreversibility. *Psychol. Rev.*, **61**, 353–385.
SOLOMON, R. L., TURNER, L. H. and LESSAC, M. S. (1968) Some effects of punishment on resistance to temptation in dogs. *J. Pers. and Soc. Psychol.*, **8**, 233–238.
SONTAG, L. W. (1941) The significance of fetal environmental differences. *Amer. J. Obstet. Gynec.*, **42**, 996–1003.
SONTAG, L. W. (1944) Differences in modifiability of fetal behaviour and physiology. *Psychosom. Med.*, **6**, 151–154.
SONTAG, L. W. (1950) The genetics of differences in psychosomatic patterns in childhood. *Amer. J. Orthopsychiat.*, **20**, 479–489.
SONTAG, L. W. (1960) The possible relationship of prenatal environment to schizophrenia. *In:* "The Etiology of Schizophrenia." Basic Books, New York.
SONTAG, L. W. (1962) Psychosomatics and somatopsychics from birth to three years. *Mod. Probl. Paediat.*, **7**, 139–156.
SONTAG, L. W. (1966) Implications of fetal behaviour and environment for adult personalities. *Ann. N.Y. Acad. Sci.*, **134**, 782–786.
SPENCE, K. W. (1958) A theory of emotionally based drive (D) and its relation to performance in simple learning situations. *Amer. Psychol.*, **13**, 131–141.
SPIELBERGER, C. D. (1966) Theory and research on anxiety. *In:* Spielberger, C. D. (Ed.) "Anxiety and Behaviour." Academic Press, New York and London.
SPITZ, R. A. (1945) Hospitalism: An enquiry into the genesis of psychiatric conditions in early childhood. *Psychoanal. Study. Child.*, **1**, 53–74.
SPITZ, R. A. (1946) Hospitalism: A follow-up report. *Psychoanal. Study Child.*, **2**, 113–117.
SROLE, L., LANGNER, T. S., MICHAEL, S. T., OPLER, M. K. and RENNIE, T. A. C. (1962) "Mental Health in the Metropolis." McGraw-Hill, New York.
STAATS, A. W. and BUTTERFIELD, W. H. (1965) Treatment of nonreading in a culturally-deprived juvenile delinquent: An application of reinforcement principles. *Child Develop.*, **36**, 925–942.

STACEY, M., DEARDEN, R., RILL, R. and ROBINSON, D. (1970) "Hospitals, Children and their Families: The Report of a Pilot Study." Routledge, Kegan Paul, London.

STARR, R. H. (1971) Cognitive development in infancy: assessment, acceleration and actualization. Merrill-Palmer. *Quart.*, **17**, 153–186.

STAYTON, D. J., HOGAN, R. and AINSWORTH, M. (1971) Infant obedience and maternal behaviour: The origin of socialization reconsidered. *Child Develop.*, **42**, 1057–1069.

STECHLER, G. (1964) A longitudinal follow-up of neonatal apnea. *Child Develop.*, **35**, 333–348.

STEIN, L. and MASON, S. E. (1968) Psychogenic and allied disorders of communication in childhood. *In:* Miller, E. "Foundations of Child Psychiatry." Pergamon Press, Oxford.

STEIN, Z. A. and SUSSER, M. (1960) Families of dull children. *J. Ment. Sci.*, **106**, 1296–1319.

STEIN, Z. A. and SUSSER, M. (1967) The social dimension of a symptom: a sociomedical study of enuresis. *Soc. Science and Medicine*, **1**, 183–201.

STENDLER, C. B. (1952) Critical periods in socialization and over-dependency. *Child Develop.*, **23**, 3–12.

STEVENSON, H. (1962) The effectiveness of social reinforcement after brief and extensive institutionalization. *Am. J. Ment. Defic.*, **66**, 589–594.

STEVENSON, H. W. (1961) Social reinforcement with children as a function of CA, sex of E and sex of S. *J. Abnorm. Soc. Psychol.*, **63**, 147–154.

STEVENSON, H. W. (1965) Social reinforcement of children's behaviour. *In:* Lipsitt, L. P. and Spiker, C. C. (Eds) "Advances in Child Development and Behaviour." Vol. 2. 97–126. Academic Press, London and New York.

STEVENSON, I. (1950) Variations in the secretion of bronchial mucous during periods of life stress. *In:* Wolff, H. G. (Ed.) "Life Stress and Bodily Disease." *Proc. Ass. Res. in Nerv. and Ment. Dis.* Waverley Press, Baltimore.

STEVENSON, I. and RIPLEY, H. S. (1952) Variations in respiration and in respiratory symptoms during changes in emotion. *Psychosom. Med.*, **14**, 476–490.

STEVENSON, I. and WOLFF, H. G. (1943) Life situations, emotions and bronchial asthma. *J. Nerv. and Ment. Dis.*, **108**, 380.

STEWART, N. (1949) Teacher's concept of "behaviour problems". *In:* "Growing Points in Educational Research." American Educational Research Assoc. Rep., Washington.

STORR, A. (1968) "Human Aggression." The Penguin Press, Allen Lane.

STOTT, D. H. (1957) Physical and mental handicaps following disturbed pregnancy. *Lancet*, **1**, 1006–1012.

STOTT, D. H. (1959) Evidence for prenatal impairment of temperament in mentally retarded children. *Vita Humana*, **2**, 125.

STOTT, D. H. (1962) Evidence for a congenital factor in maladjustment and delinquency. *Amer. J. Psychiat.*, **118**, (9), 781–794.

STOTT, D. H. (1965) Congenital indications in delinquency. *Proc. R. Soc. Med.*, **58**, 703–706.

STOTT, D. H. (1966) "Studies of Troublesome Children." Tavistock Publications, London.

STOTT, D. H., MOYES, F. A. and HEADRIDGE, S. E. (1966a) Three years to study the ham-fisted. *Times Educ. Suppl.* Apr. 8.

STOTT, D. H., MOYES, F. A. and HEADRIDGE, S. E. (1966b) "Test of Motor Impairment." Dept. of Psychology. Univ. of Glasgow.

STRAUS, M. A. (1969) "Family Measurement Techniques." Univ. of Minnesota, Minneapolis.

STRAUSS, A. A. and LEHTINEN, L. E. (1947) "Psychopathology and Education of the Brain-Injured Child." Grune and Stratton, New York.

STRECKER, E. A. (1946) "Their Mothers' Sons: The Psychiatrist Examines an American Problem." Lippincott, Philadelphia.

STROH, G. and BUICK, D. (1964) Perceptual development in childhood psychosis. *Brit. J. Med. Psychol.*, **37**, 291–299.

SULLIVAN, H. S. (1953) "The Interpersonal Theory of Psychiatry." Norton.

SUTTIE, I. D. (1935) "The Origins of Love and Hate." Routledge, Kegan Paul, London.

SUTTON SMITH, B. and ROSENBERG, B. (1970) "The Sibling." Holt, Rinehart and Winston, London.

SYMONDS, P. M. (1939) "The Dynamics of Parent–Child Relationships." Bureau of Public, Teachers College, Columbia Univ., New York.

TANNER, J. M. (1970) Physical growth. *In:* Mussen, P. H. (Ed.) "Carmichael's Manual of Child Psychology." Vol. 1, 77–156. Wiley, London.

TAUSSIG, H. B. (1962) The thalidomide syndrome. *Sci. Ameri.*, **207**, 29–35.

TAYLOR, J. A. (1956) Drive theory and manifest anxiety. *Psychol. Bull.*, **53**, 303–320.

TAYLOR, A. and SLUCKIN, W. (1968) Shifts of colour preference in day-old chicks after training and delay. *Percept. Mot. Skills.*, **27**, 955–958.

TEPLOV, B. M. (1956) Typological Features of Higher Nervous Activity in Man (2 Vols). *Moscow: Acad. Ped. Sci.*, **33**. (See: Gray, 1964, for a full translation and interpretation.)

THARP, R. G. and WETZEL, R. J. (1969) "Behaviour Modification in the Natural Environment." Academic Press, London and New York.

THOMAS, A., BIRCH, H. G., CHESS, S., HERTZIG, M. E. and KORN, S. (1963) "Behavioural Individuality in Early Childhood." Internat. Univ. Press, New York.

THOMAS, A., CHESS, S. and BIRCH, H. G. (1968) "Temperament and Behaviour Disorders in Children." University of London Press, London.

TOLOR, A., SCARPETTI, W. L. and LANE, P. A. (1967) Teachers' attitudes towards children's behaviour revisited. *J. Educat. Psychol.*, **58**, 175–180.

TRASLER, G. (1962) "The Explanation of Criminality." Routledge, Kegan Paul, London.

TRASLER, G. (1973) Criminal Behaviour. *In:* Eysenck, H. J. (Ed.) "Handbook of Abnormal Psychology." Pitman Medical, London.

TREUTING, T. F. and RIPLEY, H. S. (1948) Life situations, emotions and bronchial asthma. *J. Nerv. Ment. Dis.*, **108**, 380–396.

TURNBULL, J. W. (1962) Asthma conceived as a learned response. *J. Psychosom. Res.*, **6**, 59.

TURNER, E. K. (1956) The syndrome in the infant resulting from maternal tension during pregnancy. *Med. J. Australia.*, **1**, 221–222.

TURNER, R. K. (1974) Conditioning treatment of nocturnal enuresis: present status. *In:* Kolvin, I., MacKeith, R. C. and Meadow, S. R. (Eds) "Recent Advances in the Knowledge of Bladder Control in Children. (In press.) London S.I.M.P. with Heinemann Medical Books.

TURNER, C. H., DAVENPORT, R. K. and ROGERS, C. M. (1969) The effect of early deprivation on the social behaviour of adolescent chimpanzees. *Amer. J. Psychiat.*, **125**, 1531–1536.

TYERMAN, M. J. (1968) "Truancy." University of London Press, London.

UCKO, L. E. (1965) A comparative study of asphyxiated and non-asphyxiated boys from birth to 5 years. *Develop. Med. and Child Neurol.*, **7**, (6), 643–657.

ULLMANN, L. P. and KRASNER, L. (1965) "Case Studies in Behaviour Modification." Holt, Rinehart and Winston, New York.

ULLMANN, L. P. and KRASNER, L. (1969) "A Psychological Approach to Abnormal Behaviour." Prentice-Hall, Englewood Cliffs, New Jersey.

VALENTINE, C. (1956) "The Normal Child and Some of His Abnormalities." Penguin Books, Harmondsworth.

VAN HELMONT, J. B. (1648) "Ortus Medicinae." Amsterdam. Reported in French and Alexander (1941).

VAN KREVELEN, D. A. (1962) The psychopathology of autistic psychopathy. *Acta Paedopsychiat.*, **29**, 22.

VAN KREVELEN, D. A. (1963) On the relationship between early infantile autism and autistic psychopathy. *Acta Paedopsychiat.*, **30**, 303.

VERNON, D. T. A., FOLEY, J. M., SIPOWICZ, R. R. and SCHULMAN, J. L. (1965) The Psychological Responses of Children to Hospitalization and Illness. Thomas, Springfield, Illinois.

VERNON, P. E. (1964) "Personality Assessment: A Critical Survey." Methuen, London.

WAAL, N. (1951) The correlation between chronic muscular tension, breathing disturbances and psychiatric diagnosis of mental disorders in adults and children, especially with regard to children with behaviour disorders and bronchial asthma. Savvegarde de l'Enfance, Paris.

WAHLER, H. J. (1956) A comparison of reproduction errors made by brain-damaged and control patients on a Memory-for-Designs Test. *J. Abnorm. Soc. Psychol.*, **52**, 251–255.

WALKER, N. D. (1965) "Crime and Punishment in Britain." University Press, Edinburgh.

WALLIN, P. and RILEY, R. P. (1950) Reactions of mothers to pregnancy and adjustment of offspring in infancy. *Americ. J. Orthopsych.*, **20**, 616–622.

WALTERS, R. H. and PARKE, R. D. (1964a) Influence of response consequences to a social model on resistance to deviation. *J. Exper. Child Psychol.*, **1**, 269–280.

WALTERS, R. H. and PARKE, R. D. (1964b) Social motivation, dependency, and susceptibility to social influence. *In:* Berkowitz, L. (Ed.) "Advances in Experimental Social Psychology." 231–276. Vol. 1. Academic Press, New York and London.

WALTERS, R. H. and PARKE, R. D. (1965) The role of the distance receptors in the development of social responsiveness. *In:* Lipsitt, L. P. and Spiker, C. C. (Eds) "Advances in Child Development and Behaviour." Vol. 2. Rev. ed. Academic Press, New York and London.

WALTERS, R. H. and PARKE, R. D. (1967) The influence of punishment and related disciplinary techniques on the social behaviour of children. *In:* Maher, B. A. (Ed.) "Progress in Experimental Personality Research," **3**, 179–228.

WALTERS, R. H., PARKE, R. D. and CANE, V. A. (1965) Timing of punishment and the observation of consequences to others as determinants of response inhibition. *J. Exp. Child Psychol.*, **2**, 10–30.

WALTERS, R. H., CHEYNE, J. A. and BANKS, R. D. (Eds) (1972) "Punishment." Penguin Books, Harmondsworth.

WALTON, D. and MATHER, M. D. (1964) The application of learning principles to the treatment of obsessive-compulsive states in the acute and chronic phases of illness. *In:* Eysenck, H. J. (Ed.) "Experiments in Behaviour Therapy." 117–151. Pergamon Press, London.

WARD, N. (1968) Born Criminals? *New Society*, **19**, Dec.

WARREN, W. (1960) Some relationships between the psychiatry of children and of adults. *J. Ment. Sci.*, **106**, 815–826.

WATSON, U. D. and CRICK, F. H. C. (1953) A structure for deoxyribose nucleic acids. *Nature*, **171**, 737–738.

WATSON, J. B. and RAYNER, R. (1920) Conditioned emotional reactions. *J. Exper. Psychol.*, **3**, 1–14.

WEATHERWAX, J. and BENOIT, E. P. (1958) Concrete and abstract thinking in organic and non-organic mentally retarded children. *Amer. J. Ment. Defic.*, **62**, 548–553.

WEDELL, K. (1960) Variations in perceptual ability among types of cerebral palsy. *Cerebral Palsy Bull.*, **2**, 149–157.

WEINBERG, M. S. and BELL, A. P. (1972) "Homosexuality: An Annotated Bibliography." Harper and Row, London.

WEISS, A. A. (1964) The Weighl-Goldstein-Scheerer Color-Form Sorting Test: Classification of performance. *J. Clin. Psychol.*, **20**, 103–107.

WERNER, H. (1946) Abnormal and sub-normal rigidity. *J. Abnorm. Soc. Psychol.*, **41**, 223–225.

WERNER, H. and STRAUSS, A. A. (1941) Pathology of figure-background relation in the child. *J. Abnorm. Soc. Psychol.*, **36**, 236–248.

WERRY, J. S. (Ed.) (1972) "Psychopathological Disorders of Childhood." Wiley, New York.

WEST, D. J. (1968) "Homosexuality." (3rd Ed.) Duckworth, London.

WETZEL, R. (1966) Use of behavioural techniques in a case of compulsive stealing. *J. Consult. Psychol.*, **30**, 367–374.

WHITE, J. C. (1959) Walton's Modified Word-Learning Test with Children. *Brit. J. Med. Psychol.*, **32**, 221–225.

WHITING, B. B. (Ed.) (1963) "Six Cultures: Studies of Child Rearing." Wiley, New York.

WHITING, J. W. M. and CHILD, I. L. (1953) "Child Training and Personality." Yale Univ. Press, New Haven, Conn.

WICKMAN, E. K. (1928) "Children's Behaviour and Teachers' Attitudes." Commonwealth Fund, New York.

WIESEL, T. N. and HUBEL, D. H. (1963) Single cell responses in striate cortex of kittens deprived of vision in one eye. *J. Neurophysiol.*, **26**, 1003–1017.

WIGGINS, J. S. (1973) "Personality and Prediction: Principles of Personality Assessment." Addison-Wesley, London.

WILLIAMS, R. J. (1956) "Biochemical Individuality." Wiley, New York.

WING, J. K. (Ed.) (1966) "Childhood Autism: Clinical, Educational and Social Aspects." Pergamon Press, Oxford.

WITTENBORN, J. R. (1956a) "The Placement of Adoptive Children." Thomas, Springfield, Illinois.

WITTENBORN, J. R. (1956b) A study of adoptive children: III Relationship between some aspects of development and some aspects of environment. *Psychol. Monogr.*, LXX (410).

WOLBERG, L. R. (1967) "The Technique of Psychotherapy." Heinemann, London.

WOLFF, S. (1967a) Behavioural characteristics of primary school-children referred to a psychiatric department. *Brit. J. Psychiat.*, **113**, 885–893.

WOLFF, S. (1967b) The contribution of obstetric complications to the etiology of behaviour disorders in children. *J. Child Psychol. and Psychiat.*, **8**, (1), 57–66.

WOLFF, S. and CHESS, S. (1965a) A behavioural study of schizophrenic children. *Acta Psychiat. Scand.*, **40**, 438–466.

WOLFF, S. and CHESS, S. (1965b) An analysis of the language of 14 schizophrenic children. *J. Child Psychol. and Psychiat.*, **6**, 29.

WOLPE, J. (1958) "Psychotherapy by Reciprocal Inhibition." Stanford Univ. Press, Stanford.

WORLD HEALTH ORGANISATION (1954) "The Mentally Subnormal Child." WHO Technical Report Series, No. **75**.

WRIGHT, D. S. (1970a) Sexual Behaviour. *The Listener*, **84**, 2156, 101–103.

WRIGHT, D. S. (1970b) Moral Development. *In:* Wright, D. S. and Taylor, A., Davies, D. R., Sluckin, W., Lee, S. G. M. and Reason, J. T. (co-authors). "Introducing Psychology: An Experimental Approach." Penguin Books, Harmondsworth.

WRIGHT, D. S. (1971) "The Psychology of Moral Behaviour." Penguin Books, Harmondsworth.

WYNNE, L. C. and SINGER, M. T. (1963) Thought disorder and family relations of schizophrenics: II Classification of forms of thinking. *Arch. Gen. Psychiat.*, **9**, 199.

WYNNE, L. C., RYCOFF, I. M., DAY, J. and HIRSCH, S. I. (1958) Pseudomutuality in the family relations of schizophrenia. *Psychiatry*, **21**, 205.

YACORZYNSKI, J. K. and TUCKER, B. E. (1960) What price intelligence? *Amer. Psychol.*, **15**, 201–203.

YARROW, L. J. (1961) Maternal deprivation: toward an empirical and conceptual revaluation. *Psychol. Bull.*, **58**, 459–490.

YARROW, L. J. (1963) Research in dimensions of early maternal care. *Merrill-Palmer Quart.*, **9**, 101–114.

YARROW, L. J. (1967) Exceptional Infant (I). *Special Child Publications*, 428–442. Seattle, Washington.

YARROW, M. R., CAMPBELL, J. D. and BURTON, R. V. (1968) "Child Rearing: An Inquiry into Research and Methods. Jossey-Bass, San Francisco.

YATES, A. J. (1954) The validity of some psychological tests of brain damage. *Psychol. Bull.*, **51**, 359–379.

YATES, A. J. (1962) "Frustration and Conflict." Wiley, New York.

YATES, A. J. (1970) "Behaviour Therapy." Wiley, London.

ZIGLER, E. and CHILD, I. L. (1969) Socialization. *In:* Lindzey, G. and Aronson, E. (Eds) "Handbook of Social Psychology." Vol. 3. Addison-Wesley, New York.

ZINGG, R. M. (1940) Feral man and extreme cases of isolation. *Amer. J. Psychol.*, **53**, 487–517.

ZUBIN, J. (1967) Classification and the behaviour disorders. *In:* Farnsworth, P. R., McNemar, O., and McNemar, Q. (Eds). "Annual Review of Psychology." California Annual Reviews, Inc., Palo Alto.

# Author Index

# Subject Index